The Banking Jungle

WILEY PROFESSIONAL BANKING AND FINANCE SERIES

EDWARD I. ALTMAN, Editor

THE STOCK MARKET, 4TH EDITION

Richard J. Teweles and Edward S. Bradley

TAX SHELTERED FINANCING THROUGH THE R & D LIMITED PARTNERSHIP

James K. La Fleur

CORPORATE FINANCIAL DISTRESS: A COMPLETE GUIDE TO PREDICTING, AVOIDING, AND DEALING WITH BANKRUPTCY

Edward I. Altman

CREDIT ANALYSIS: A COMPLETE GUIDE

Roger H. Hale

CURRENT ASSET MANAGEMENT: CASH, CREDIT, AND INVENTORY

Jarl G. Kallberg and Kenneth Parkinson

HANDBOOK FOR BANKING STRATEGY

Richard C. Aspinwall and Robert A. Eisenbeis

THE BANKING JUNGLE: HOW TO SURVIVE AND PROSPER IN A BUSINESS TURNED TOPSY TURVY

Paul S. Nadler and Richard B. Miller

The Banking Jungle

HOW TO SURVIVE AND PROSPER IN A BUSINESS TURNED TOPSY TURVY

PAUL S. NADLER
RICHARD B. MILLER

JOHN WILEY & SONS
New York • Chichester • Brisbane • Toronto • Singapore

ISBN 0-471-87290-3

Printed in the United States of America

10 9 8 7 6 5 4 3 2 1

We dedicate this book to
the following people whom we love
and without whose help the
work would have been completed
at least a year earlier:

Saul,
David,
Margaret, and
Julie Nadler
Ruth,
Brad,
Katherine,
Vance, and
Margaret Miller

SERIES PREFACE

The worlds of banking and finance have changed dramatically during the past few years, and no doubt this turbulence will continue through the 1980s. We have established the Wiley Professional Banking and Finance Series to aid in characterizing this dynamic environment and to further the understanding of the emerging structures, issues, and content for the professional financial community.

We envision three types of books in this series. First, we are commissioning distinguished experts in a broad range of fields to assemble a number of authorities to write specific primers on related topics. For example, some of the early handbook-type volumes in the series concentrate on the Stock Market, Investment Banking, and Financial Depository Institutions. A second type of book attempts to combine text material with appropriate empirical and case studies written by practitioners in relevant fields. An early example is a forthcoming volume on The Management of Cash and Other Short-Term Assets. Finally, we are encouraging definitive, authoritative works on specialized subjects for practitioners and theorists.

It is a distinct pleasure and honor for me to assist John Wiley & Sons, Inc. in this important endeavor. In addition to banking and financial practitioners, we think business students and faculty will benefit from this series. Most of all, though, we hope this series will become a primary source in the 1980s for the members of the professional financial community to refer to theories and data and to integrate important aspects of the central changes in our financial world.

EDWARD I. ALTMAN

Professor of Finance
New York University,
Schools of Business

PREFACE

This book is for America's bankers—members of an industry that has seen its ground rules change drastically over an extremely short period of time. As the title indicates, banking has become a jungle, with the pitfalls and dangerous predators a jungle environment harbors. Through practical ideas and pragmatic commentary, we wish to present a means of survival to the professional banker, thrift executive, and those others whose lives and work are subject to the impact of banking.

Some of the material presented here has appeared earlier in *Bankers Monthly*, *The Bankers Magazine*, and the *American Banker*. For permission to reproduce our articles in this book, we thank Alvin Youngquist, Theodore Cross, and William Zimmerman of those respective publications.

It goes without saying that all material included here has been revised and further developed to reflect current conditions. Still, with the dynamics of banking, some of our material almost surely will have been made obsolete through changing practice and legislation by the time this book appears.

Today, banking is as much a jungle for the outside observer as it is for the participant. But it certainly can be fun tracking the changes taking place and trying to envision what lies beyond the jungle's borders.

PAUL S. NADLER
RICHARD B. MILLER

Summit, New Jersey
Cresskill, New Jersey
September 1984

CONTENTS

PART 3. THE HUMAN SIDE OF BANKING

PART 4. THE FINANCIAL SIDE OF BANKING

PART 5. THE BUSINESS OF BANKING

PART 1 What Has Happened

Tarzan and Jane were sitting in their tree house. Tarzan got up, went to the table, and poured himself another martini—his third.

JANE: What's wrong, Tarzan?

TARZAN: You don't understand, my dear. It's a bloody jungle out there.

1 Goodbye to Traditional Banking

As a 90-year-old semi-retired bank president relaxed contentedly after a meeting he had attended, the speaker of the evening was introduced to him. The speaker said, "You must have seen a lot of changes in banking in your day." "Yes, and I fought every one of them," the old man replied.

This response was typical of traditional commercial bankers just a short time ago. Banking was an industry whose motto could well have been, "Never do something the first time," and whose more progressive members probably would have responded, "You have to do everything a first time, but not now."

This was the industry that allowed savings banks to develop because it would not accept the savings of small depositors; that allowed savings and loans to develop because it would not make mortgage loans; and that allowed finance companies to flourish because most banks hesitated to make personal loans. It was the industry with the reputation that bankers would lend you an umbrella when it wasn't raining—and demand it be returned as soon as the precipitation started. It was the industry that was associated with business in general and big business in particular, to the exclusion of the needs of the small businessman and people in general. It was an industry that offered potential employees low salaries but with the chance to wear a white shirt, have prestige in the community, and hold a lifetime job.

This, then, was traditional banking. By its very nature, banking was an industry whose operations and goals made the banker a person apart from his community, someone generally looked upon by the public as a special, isolated, privileged person.

THE BIG CHANGE

How different is the image the banker tries to project today! The concept often presented is that of a friendly banker offering the public a full spectrum of financial services. In many communities, the banker is now an innovator offering new, previously unavailable services, encroaching on areas formerly the exclusive province of other institutions, and striving to have everyone in the community feel that the services match his every need and desire.

To be sure, the United States still has many commercial banks that operate under the old traditions, oppose changes, and feel they are doing the public a favor by opening their doors from 10 to 2, five days a week. But, in a nation that allows approximately 14,000 banking institutions to flourish (as opposed to Canada's ability to meet basic banking needs with fewer than half a dozen major banks), there is bound to be great variety among banks, bankers, and banking services.

Yet no one can doubt that banking in general has been changing drastically in the United States. The institutions that are setting the pace in stature, profit, and growth today are certainly worlds apart from the traditional banking image.

What has happened? What has brought about such a change in banking in the United States over the past few years? Some might answer that nothing has really happened. They might reply that all the new emphasis on such things as service and public relations is a cover-up, putting a streamlined facade on a banking industry that basically operates just as it always has—plodding along, impervious to the true changing needs of the communities the banks are supposed to serve.

A deeper examination of the motives for banking's changes indicates that this view is not correct. In reality, the conditions and environment within which banking operates have been so altered during the past decade that the industry has been forced to make drastic changes in its goals, whether its managers really wanted these changes or not. It is these fundamental new forces in the banking environment that must be examined in order to clearly determine what has happened to traditional banking.

The Competition

The changes in banking have, basically, been due to competition. Without the cold light of competition forcing individuals and institutions to face reality and adjust to new conditions, inertia usually rules. In banking, the new competition has been from both within the industry and outside of it.

A key to the new competition that each commercial bank faces is the fact that the United States has switched from being a capital surplus to a capital short nation. This has vast implications for interest rate levels and the competition for funds. It is hard to remember from the vantage point of this decade, which began with the highest interest rates ever, that as recently as the late 1950s, United States Treasury Bills sold at a yield of a low of .56%. In fact, for many years the major problem of financial institutions was finding profitable uses for the funds that were so abundantly available rather than the gathering of funds.

The Capital Shortage Impact on Banking

Undoubtedly, the greatest impact on the banks of this lessened availability of capital was a decline in the growth rate of demand deposits. In the past, customers had left idle funds in demand deposit balances for lack of good alternative uses. As interest notes rose, however, the banks saw their large depositors utilizing their excess funds more effectively by placing them into Treasury bills, commercial paper, and other money market instruments. At the same time, individuals were moving their surplus funds from demand deposits to interest-bearing accounts at savings banks and savings and loan associations.

The depositors' motives were clear.

The commercial banks still assumed they could get all the funds they needed through the acceptance of demand deposits, on which no interest payment was allowed. Therefore, they did not compete for the funds their depositors wanted to place into time and savings deposits. By the time the bankers woke up to the fact that the growth rate of these thrift institutions and the popularity of the money market instruments were seriously eroding the commercial banks' role in the financial structure, the competition was well entrenched. The banks had to counterattack with heavy and expensive promotion of their own time and savings deposit forms just to gain back their traditional share of the nation's monetary growth.

The development of the computer and its popularization has also had an impact on demand deposit growth at commercial banks. The improvements in cash management techniques made feasible by the computer gave bank depositors a series of new procedures to help in this demand deposit paring process. As a result, the growth of lockbox collection systems, accounts reconciliation programs, and other techniques of cash management all combined to help the customer better understand exactly how much he had to keep in demand deposit form—and how much of his cash balances could be removed and placed into interest-bearing deposits or instruments.

Finally, as if this were not enough, the new bank programs of check credit, daily interest payment, and the credit card began to backfire by giving the public a way of tapping emergency fund sources as required, instead of having to leave excess balances hanging around in demand deposit form just in case they should be needed.

Buying Growth

Finally, bankers realized that the industry could no longer rely on interest-free demand deposits as the basic source of funds. If banks were to grow, they would have to buy their growth via the time and savings deposit route. If they were unwilling to do so, they would have no alternative but to watch the growth in deposits—and the growth in loans and investments—move to the other banks that did buy growth and to the other institutions and instruments that now competed so heavily for the nation's liquid funds.

Ironically, just as the banks found themselves forced to compete and buy the growth they formerly obtained without cost, they found the competition in lending also intensified. One would think that those institutions making loans would find it ever easier to place funds to work profitably in a nation moving from capital glut to capital shortage. But, this has not been the case.

The apparent paradox was caused by the profit squeeze faced by the banks when they had to buy funds. With the banks forced to pay for deposit growth, their immediate challenge was to improve earnings on the use of their funds. This involved (1) developing imaginative lending forms that could command higher yields and (2) the invasion of lending areas formerly considered the exclusive province of competitors. When banks saw that opportunities existed for making longer-term loans and loans to institutions located outside of their immediate trading areas, the entire loan picture exploded with new competition. As a result, the individual banker's role expanded to include aggressive loan solicitation.

On top of this, the banks found new loan competition arising from the most unexpected corners. As interest rates rose, bank customers found that they could improve profits by using their surplus funds to finance their own customers. To get the interest income their customers formerly paid to the banks, some companies developed captive finance subsidiaries to finance their products. Other companies provided their customers the funds without cost—through more generous credit terms—using money as a basic weapon in the competition for sales volume. In other cases, companies that developed captive finance subsidiaries, and those that gave more generous credit terms, as well as other firms that formerly had relied on bank credit, developed new and cheaper fund sources—primarily through the sale of commercial paper on the open market to the very companies that had reevaluated their need for deposit balances and were now placing their excess funds to work in the open market.

The rise in interest rates, then, placed the commercial banking industry in a classic squeeze play. In the years when money was plentiful, companies placed excess funds in bank demand deposits, and those in need of funds came to the banks to borrow. Today, those with surplus funds frequently place them into the money market instruments, such as commercial paper, while those in need of funds turned away from banks, with their high cost loans and compensating balance requirements, and moved over to the sale of commercial paper themselves. In effect, the borrowers and lenders met directly, developing the so-called "second banking system" and short-circuiting banking growth.

This is a normal response when a commodity becomes scarce—for both borrowers and lenders try to economize on the cost of money in a period of developing capital shortage. And if the process of economization involves cutting off the profits of the banking industry, so much the worse for the banks.

As credit conditions tightened, then, the banks were prime among those companies feeling the pinch as business tried to get around the impact of tight money. Tight money, new techniques of money mobilization, and attempts to lessen the cost of borrowing through development of techniques to circumvent banks all combined to make a competitive financial environment in which banking had to operate.

The sharp banker read the handwriting on the wall and concluded that his operations also had to change to match the new times; otherwise, his institution and the industry would erode and become ever less of a force in the financial community. This was certainly no time to stick to the tenets of traditional banking and the motto "Never do something the first time."

The Coming of the Computer

While the switch from capital glut to capital shortage was the basic cause of banking's change, the computer is considered the second major motivator of banking innovation. As already mentioned, the computer played a role both in speeding the turnover of demand deposits and in lessening the willingness of depositors to leave funds in demand deposit balances. In addition, the very availability of the computer served as a motivator of more change, as banks tried to get their money's worth out of this radical innovation in data processing.

Today, with computers, mini-computers, and timesharing over phone wires available to companies too small for even modest computer systems, it is difficult to remember how rare computers were just a few short years ago. Because of the quantity and complexity of the data processing chores banks face, banks were the first major private industry to tap the computer in volume. In fact, the commercial bank was often the only company in the community to own a computer system. To be sure, the computers bought by some banks were not actually needed; many banks could have handled their data processing needs by cooperative ownership of one computer, had the bankers been willing to work together. Be this as it may, the fact that many banks did have computers at a time when few were available, and that the banks were trying to justify their cost, was a significant factor in bank innovation.

Bankers quickly recognized that the computer would not pay for itself if the bank used it "just to do faster what grandpa had done with the rack and the Boston Ledger." They started utilizing the computer's spare time to provide data processing services for their customers, to broaden the bank's service base, and to gain better introspective knowledge of the bank's cost and the value of each of its varied customers. The bank had one advantage in this area: customers were used to having the bank handle financial data for them, and most customers had no objection to banker knowledge of their personal and corporate financial information. After all, the banker usually knew more about a man's finances than his wife did even before the computer came along.

Still, it was more than the availability of the computer and the presence of spare computer time that motivated banks to change. The computer altered the face of commercial banking in these additional ways:

1 Banks found a need for the presence of bank officers on the decision-making level who understood the computer and its potential. These skilled people, brought in or trained by the bank, serve as catalysts for change in other areas of the bank as well: A computer person is first a computer person and second a banker. Thus, the banks learned that some banking talents were interchangeable with those of other industries.

2 Banks also found that to keep good data processing people, bank salaries would have to be on a par with those paid elsewhere. The salary ranges necessary to keep good programmers and officers thus served as a wedge to force changes in the entire banking salary structure. Bank wages were brought in line with those in other areas of government and business.

3 The computer also made money more mobile than ever before. With the guts of the bank now consisting of a magnetic memory core or tape reels of information that could be transferred over telephone lines, money became a concept of a stream of information rather than a tangible good. The result was that computers could be tapped from distant locations by money machines and magnetically encoded credit cards plus point-of-sale computer terminal in stores, gas stations, and other locations where customers trade. While the development of this mobility of money in a checkless society has been slow to date, bankers realize that the computer can rob each individual bank of the geographical uniqueness it formerly had based on the convenience of location. Just as airlines now handle customer inquiries throughout the nation from centralized locations, banks, too, can handle the information called "money" from distant central locations. This can be used as a means of intense geographic competition within the industry.

THE CHANGING SOCIETY

Beyond the changing financial environment and the development of the computer, another major force affecting banking has been American society itself. As our society has changed, so have the demands placed on the nation's banking system.

American society has changed in a number of ways—all of which have had their influence on the nation's banks—but perhaps foremost among these has been the change in what people expect and demand from the society. The passage of years since the Great Depression has eradicated the store of liquidity in the nation and brought us to conditions of capital shortage, as well as making us more confident and demanding of our economy. Though President Kennedy said: "Ask not what your country can do for you, ask what you can do for your country," Americans have turned this around, expecting economic security and counting upon it in decision-making.

How has this feeling of economic security affected the banks? For one thing, it has robbed the industry of what once was its chief attribute: safety. Gone is the big sign in the window advertising the protection of the bank's capital and surplus. Today, the public counts on the Federal Deposit Insurance Corporation to provide safety for deposits, while looking to the bank for services, a reasonable return on its money, and a relatively low cost of credit. Denied this basic selling point of a bank deposit, the banking industry has been forced to become more innovative as it strives to develop other attractions. In the eyes of the public, commercial banks, savings banks, savings and loans, finance companies, credit unions, and other personal financial institutions are all "banks" and all are assumed to be government protected.

The growth of the American economy has also brought a prosperity that has intensified the sophistication of the demands placed by the public on financial institutions. When the bulk of American workers wore blue collars in factories, most never entered a bank. They preferred to be paid in cash, and their family budget was worked to stretch out that cash until the next payday. By the end of the 1970s, however, over one-half of American jobs had become white collar. We have moved from a production-oriented "Smokestack America" to a service-oriented economy. A service economy, with a high preponderance of white collar workers, is an economy that demands financial sophistication. It relies far more heavily on financial institutions than does a production society. The financial institutions that prosper in such an environment, therefore, are those that provide both wholesale services to business and full retail services of greater sophistication to the general public.

The rise in America's educational attainments has also affected the banking industry. Since 1940, the proportion of young adults with college degrees has almost tripled, moving from 6 to 16%, and the percentage with a high school diploma has advanced from 38 to 75%. Such advances in education are bound to be felt in the kinds of demands placed on financial institutions by their customers. People are becoming more sophisticated about their money; they want more services and better utilization of funds.

Connected with this educational growth has been a far more critical attitude toward institutions that do not meet new demands—a critical attitude that has been intensified by the current trend toward consumerism and social activism. More recently, the United States has switched from its emphasis on Gross National Product to greater concern for quality of environment and so-called "Gross National Byproduct." This, too, has had a great impact on the financial institutions of the nation, and has begun to turn the public away from those ignoring the new emphasis and just practicing business as usual. The financial institutions must serve their economic and psychological needs. If they do not, people simply will go elsewhere.

Banks as Employers

As society has changed no shift in public perception has affected banking more than the change in attitude of those who enter banking as employees. By and large, banking now recognizes what the new data processing employees began to tell it over a decade ago: bank employment is no privilege that serves as a reward by itself. Rather, banking must make its jobs as lucrative and challenging as any other job if it is to get the kind of talent needed for the future.

Not too many years ago, however, the chance to be a bank teller—to wear a white shirt and serve the public from behind a cage—was so exalting that a bank felt it had to offer prospective employees little else in the way of remuneration. The Great Depression added considerably to this sense of worthiness of bank employment. Although one-half of America's banks failed in the late 1920s and early 1930s, the many that remained open generally provided the rare feature of job security during the Depression.

Yet it was this very job security that served as a curse to the industry in the years following World War II. The people with bank jobs before the depression were, for the most part, kept on the payroll, but no new people were added. The industry and its employees faced the crises of the 1930s in an atmosphere of intense conservatism. The prime goal of most banks was the maintenance of solvency, rather than the development of services or the improvement of profit through acceptance of normal risk.

By the end of World War II, many banks were being run by the men and a few women who held tightly to their jobs during the Depression and who valued safety above all else. Since no hiring had gone on for fifteen or more years, there was no echelon of younger employees behind the top officers to prod them out of this conservatism.

While the gap in employment may have made banking conservative through the 1950s, it served as a blessing in disguise. As the top officers remaining from the depression era retired, the banks had no place to turn for successors but to those far younger, who had been hired right out of the armed services in the late 1940s. These new officers brought with them a desire and will for change that had been lacking in the industry for so long. The proof of this is a quick look at the ages of chief executives in banking today. In no other industry does one find as many top executives in their forties and early fifties.

The New Breed of Employee

The trend toward innovation has quickly filtered down to the lower management levels, as banks try to win and keep bright college graduates.

The college graduates who make up this new generation of bank employees are highly-educated people who want instant success, challenge, and a feeling that their work has meaning. There is far more truth than humor to the comment made by a bank president that he could not get college students with the Master of Business Administration degree to come to work for him until he changed the name of his training program from "Executive Training Group" to "Pre-presidential Orientation."

In many cases, banks have had to innovate and diversify simply to give its highly-educated young people new responsibility. They feared that if these employees were asked to hang around for years waiting for a challenge, they would leave. Similarly, some banks now have started to look at social action goals, as part of the price they must pay to retain young employees who feel that an institution must have more complex motives than merely remaining solvent.

BANK PROFITS

An additional motive for change in banking that has developed in the last decade or so has been the striving for profit. Why are bank profits only a recent goal of the industry, rather than the prime motivator since banks first opened their doors? Ironically, many banks have stressed other goals, such as growth, public service, and pleasant employment opportunities. Typically, the top officer of a bank could have told you his "footings," or the total assets on hand, almost to the penny for the close of the previous day. Yet, when asked what the bank's profit was, he would answer something like, "Ask the accountant, he comes in next March."

Except in a period of heavy economic recession, such as the late 1920s in agricultural areas and the 1930s everywhere, banks generally have been able to survive, at least until recently. This was true no matter how little emphasis they placed on profit, provided they did not suffer a major defalcation.

How did banks survive? Largely, it was by underpaying staff. The owners, too, were underpaid. The vast bulk of banks were family banks, owned and managed by the same family, and passed down as an inheritance from father to son. In many such banks, the owners would have been far better paid by closing the bank and going to work for someone else. But pride and optimism often replaced this alternative with the decision to continue the bank as it was.

This was especially true in many of the small community banks. For the most part, these small country banks are not setting the pace and tone of American banking today, even though they vastly outnumber the larger, more varied institutions. In terms of total bank assets, the large branch banks, and the holding companies, under which a number of banks are allowed by law in some states to come together under common ownership, far outweigh the community banks. Additionally, in the main, the larger institutions have been the ones that were innovative enough to have changed banking's image.

Banks must now compete for investors' capital against other potential investment outlets, just as other large corporations must compete for the investor's funds. In addition, as bank stock ownership becomes more institutionalized—held more by insurance companies, mutual funds, and other institutional investors—the large banks whose stock these investors purchase are under far greater pressure to keep earnings up than is the case when the stocks are mainly owned by individuals who hold them for safety, pride, and sentiment, and even out of inertia once they have bought them.

Even in the family banks, when it becomes time to sell out because of the lack of successor management or to meet inheritance tax liabilities, the owners realize the value of a marketable stock whose price reflects the worth of the bank. After all, obtaining a decent stock price involves profitable operation.

Thus, profit has finally become a far more basic motivation. Many bankers now look at the impact a decision has on the price of the stock before setting policy. The profit goal is, therefore, a change in banking that has helped cause the new innovations and changed the attitudes of so many of the nation's banks.

To the public, the changes mean that banking service today is far more innovative and available than in the past. The competition among banks and their nonbank financial competitors has given the public the benefit of higher returns on deposited funds and more imaginative forms of credit.

However, the banker himself has felt the most drastic changes. The death of traditional banking, coupled with the changing and more varied goals of the industry, have made the inside of the bank a far more exciting place to work than ever before.

2 Changes in the Bathtub of Credit

The Federal Reserve used to be the keeper of the bathtub of credit. It decided how much water would be in the tub. Then the bankers would jump in and push the soap from side to side. This is no longer true. Now the Fed, the regulatory agencies, and Congress have all jumped into the tub with the bankers; the decision as to who gets the soap is far from an independent, banker-determined function.

PROTECTING AGAINST MARKET FORCES

Why has this happened? Why have we switched from an environment in which the Federal Reserve determined overall credit availability and allowed the bankers to determine whose credit demands would be satisfied and whose would be denied to today's different environment? It seems that now every decision on credit has to be made while thinking about whether it will be in compliance with regulations and laws and whether some legislative or regulatory body will take exception to a policy that was formerly routinely determined.

Part of the answer involves the basic changes in our American society. We have grown accustomed to following the precept: "I believe in free enterprise, just keep out the lousy competition.

All of us, from the banker desiring to keep the thrifts out of consumer credit to the thrift executive trying to keep the interest rate differential, to the worker asking for a closed shop, to the farmer asking for subsidies, to the business manager asking for import restraints, down to the present writer—a college professor with tenure—all of us are hypocrites in this regard.

In this desire to gain protection against free market decisionmaking, the American people have asked their bankers as well as the government to make decisions that are politically popular, instead of continuing to rely on free market forces and the banker's own judgment as to what provides the best combination of risk-free income and liquidity in a loan or investment decision. In trying to protect people from the harshness of reality in the marketplace, programs have been developed to keep rates below what the free market would dictate. And bank funds have been allocated not on the basis of who is the best borrower from this standpoint of risk, income, and liquidity but on what is going to most help those sectors of the economy that are less powerful in the free market.

Much of this pressure for governmental intervention to help determine who gets the soap in the bathtub of credit also stems from poor policies that bankers and other lenders have initiated in the past. These policies have brought about the governmental efforts to help moderate bank decisonmaking. As some wise observer once remarked, "The Government never comes in unless the private sector has done a poor job; but once it is in, it never leaves." That is a sad but true comment on the role of regulators in our economy.

Compliance Laws

The whole gamut of compliance laws—Truth-in-Lending, the Equal Credit Opportunity Act, Electronic Funds Transfer controls under Regulation E, the Fair Housing Act, the Community Reinvestment Act (CRA), the various state usury ceilings—all stem from behavior by banks and other lenders that made lawmakers and regulators decide that intervention in the bathtub of credit was necessary.

Are bankers unhappy about CRA? Well, there was a time when many banks and other lenders did "redline" areas of town—that is, they determined that no loan should be made in a certain area, because it was an area with a high nonperformance history on loans—no matter how good an individual borrower who lived in that area might be as a credit risk.

Are bankers unhappy about the Truth-in-Lending laws? Sure. But bankers must remember the days when many would hide discount rates and advertise in such a manner that the public would think it paid to borrow money on consumer loans (at only 4% discount) and place them in a bank savings account at 4.5%!

Are there electronic funds transfer regulations? Sure. But bankers have to think of the cases in which banks left the customer feeling helpless in a complaint situation because there was no paper documentation available to determine if the customer was correct in his complaint or not.

To put it another way, where there is smoke there is fire. The bankers who are concerned about government intervention in the bathtub of credit have to take a portion of the blame for the fact that these new companions have joined them in the tub.

Liability Management

Undoubtedly the most significant example of a banker decision that has led to governmental intervention has been the development of liability management by the banking industry.

At first, bankers kept loans and investments extremely short because they feared liquidity problems. Then, a process of asset allocation was developed. This involved matching assets to liabilities based on the character of deposits that happened to come on board.

If a bank received short-term money (deposits that were hot to trot), it would place the funds into short-term loans. If the money being deposited were of a more stable and long-term nature (money in heat to retreat), the bank would place it in longer-term loans.

But, as New York City's Mayor LaGuardia used to say when he addressed the reporters: "Be sure you have your facts straight before you distort them." Liability management developed because bankers had a similar need to distort. What would happen when a customer came in for a long-term loan and all the bank had available were short-term deposit funds?

"Good morning Mr. Banker, I'd like a ten-year loan to build a factory," the customer would state.

"I'm sorry, we utilize asset allocation. All we have available are short-term funds," the banker would respond. "How would you like a 90-day loan to build a small factory?"

The customer's response to this, of course, would be to change banks.

Bankers eventually decided that they would have to turn the procedure around if they wanted to keep customers. First they would have to make the loans, and then they would have to find funds of the nature that would fill these loan demands that had been accommodated. Thus, liability management developed—make the loans, then go out and sell Certificates of Deposits (CDs), borrow Eurodollars, buy Fed funds, do whatever else necessary to obtain the needed funds.

This, however, became the tail that wagged the dog. As bankers developed liability management, they realized that they could get all the money they wanted to fill the complete credit demands of good customers by buying funds as needed and paying whatever the funds might cost. Moreover, they could do this no matter how hard the Fed was trying to contain credit growth and limit economic activity.

There was no way the bankers could create more money through their policies; the Fed did and still does control the amount of water in the bathtub of credit. What happened is that the major banks that practiced liability management were able to draw in funds from other banks around the nation and make themselves immune to credit restraints. However, that left the burden of restraint to be borne by banks that could not buy funds. Those banks found themselves losing deposits to banks paying more attractive rates for money.

The regulatory authorities feared this development. After all, the customers having good relationships with major banks that could practice liability management could get all the credit they needed. Other customers—notably small business, state and local governments, and individuals—dependent upon the banks that were losing deposits to the majors, ended up with less credit than they otherwise would have obtained because of the flow of funds into the banks of aggressive liability managers.

It was to offset this strength of the majors and to make sure that credit was more evenly spread among the various potential leaders that the various aspects of regulation and legislation, summed up under the terms "credit allocation" and "compliance," were first developed. And the fact that there had been some notable abuses by banks and other lenders in allocating credit has intensified this pressure for governmental intervention into the bathtub of credit through compliance laws and regulations.

COPING WITH COMPLIANCE

Meeting the compliance regulations under the six areas mentioned—Truth-in-Lending, Reg B: the Equal Credit Opportunity Act, Reg E on Electronic Funds Transfer, the Fair Housing Act, the Community Reinvestment Act and the various state usury ceilings—sometimes seems to take more of bankers' time than running the bank. Yet other bankers have admitted that meeting compliance requirements is more a case of using common sense and not making any exceptions than of anything else.

However, five of these six areas subject the bank to civil liability. This means that failure to meet the requirements of the legislation can lead to class action suits instituted by those who feel they have been discriminated against. In such suits, there is no limit to the settlement claims that the courts can require.

In the sixth area, Community Reinvestment Act compliance, there is no civil liability requirement. There is a different problem. The CRA is a so-called hot button to regulators; they find this to be one of the areas of greatest concern to the public. Thus, they dig deeper into the question of whether the banks are serving their communities adequately under this law than they do in most other areas of bank operations subject to their review.

CLASS ACTION

Class actions by themselves can be a tremendous problem, whether justified or not. The bank's defense against such suits can be so expensive that many banks and other defendants settle regardless of the merits of the case.

The best defense against class action suits, however, is ensuring that the bank is in compliance with the law in the first place. This, in turn, involves developing a program that covers the bases the lawmakers and regulators are concerned about. A compliance program contains several features:

- The bank should have a written program of compliance, indicating that it understands the law and intends to follow it.
- There should be written procedures for meeting policy standards.
- There should be a control program to ensure that policies and procedures are carried out.

If these recommendations are followed, then the onus is on the regulator to prove the bank is in violation. And that is a lot easier for the bank than proving it is meeting the law.

Compliance Complications

Why do so many banks get into trouble on compliance? Inconsistency is the problem. A bank can have as harsh a set of requirements for lending and as stiff a set of service charge fees as it wants, but it must not make an exception to these rate and quality standards for anyone. If the bank relaxes its standards for one or two customers and the news gets out to others, the bank risks a suit.

This does not mean that all loans must be treated identically or all accounts must be assessed the same service charge. The customer with a large balance, or the account that controls a substantial amount of corollary business in other accounts, naturally can—and should—be treated differentially. But such preference must be spelled out and applied to all who meet the same requirements.

What should be done when examiners feel there has been a compliance violation? Sitting down with the examiner and talking things out is far superior to waiting until matters have hardened into a written report. Moreover, talks with correspondent banks and others who have handled similar problems are generally felt to be superior to calling a lawyer who may well "reinvent the wheel" at your expense.

The CRA, however, has to be handled differently from the other five areas of compliance that generally go under this new policy of government jumping into the bathtub of credit with the bankers. Remember, there is no civil liability, so regulators have little power to enforce correction of what they feel to be CRA violations—unless and until the bank wants something from the regulators.

But beware what happens then. What might otherwise be a routine approval of a request for a branch, capital changes, or the like may well be rejected because of a bank's previous intransigence on a CRA complaint. Regulators have long memories.

Thus, CRA compliance should involve the same approach of written policies and procedures, an effective program of control and review, and a policy of no favoritism as is needed in the five areas of civil liability.

Cooperation

Compliance can be costly, both in time and money. So why must each bank have someone to review the new regulations and make sure the bank is in compliance? Cannot state associations or other cooperative groups develop checklists so that a banker more easily can review what his bank is doing to ensure compliance?

An "old-boy network" through the state bankers association—letting the other banks know how a bank has handled an unusual problem—could be useful. There also should be frequent dialogue on compliance issues between regulators and bankers long before matters become formal issues. This tactic will ensure that banks are meeting the intents of the laws and that the public interest is served. (This is a far cry from what is frequently seen in CRA issues—with one bank that wants another denied a branch making a complaint that the other bank is in violation of the Act. Such a procedure may win the complaining bank a delay or rejection of its competition's desire. But it also helps the regulators set precedents that can later be used against the first complainant and against all other banks, as the CRA network of regulations, precedents, and procedures grows.)

Basically the keys are communication and consistency. If bankers show that they are honestly trying to meet compliance requirements, the adversary attitude of many regulators should be lessened substantially. Moreover, it should take the steam out of the complaints of class action lawyers.

CONCLUSION

Consumer protection is part of our economic environment today. But the additional steps of protecting many weaker borrowers from the free market is, in the feeling of many (including this writer), carrying consumer protection too far.

Yet we have seen compliance, credit allocation programs, government moral suasion, and other procedures develop that involve the government joining the bankers in the bathtub of credit to help allocate the soap. Bankers may dislike the change and yearn for the good old days when they were the only ones in the tub, but these changes can be made livable—and the bathtub guests more acceptable—with a healthy dose of common sense, proper procedures, and a good communication system with the regulators.

As bankers reflect on the role they played in bringing about the intervention of guests into the bathtub of credit by their own poor choices in policies of the past, they should also reflect on the future. The best approach a banker can take is to examine the policies and procedures of today to ensure that their banks are being as fair as possible to each of their three publics—the community, the employees, and the shareholders. Otherwise, bank policies of today may be paving the way for more governmental intervention in the bathtub of credit in the future.

PART 2 Organization and Structure

The organization and structure of banking as we have known it, are being buffeted by the winds of change.

Mergers and acquisitions are altering bank sizes, market areas, and the lives of people who make banking a career. Yet it is apparent that the frenzy of acquisitions and sales of banking organizations will continue to impact on how business is done generally at many, if not all, institutions for some time to come.

Technology, of course, is also causing great changes in just about every phase of banking—in the way transactions are processed, in the services available, and in the cost of doing business.

Together, these forces are having a profound effect on community banks, which is why they are included in this section. While community banks are undergoing change, and some are merging with larger organizations, new banks are starting up almost every day. The community bank has been a strong part of the banking scene in this country since the beginning, and it seems increasingly certain that it will remain so in the years ahead.

3 Mergers and Acquisitions

3-1 HOW SHOULD A BANK EXPAND?

This is an era of unprecedented financial institution mergers—banks with banks, thrifts with thrifts, banks with thrifts, and all of the above with nonbanking organizations. Yet a merger may not always be the best way to move into new territory. It makes sense to analyze all of the options before taking action.

When a holding company or branch bank looks at a new community, there are several things it hopes to gain from the acquisition of an established bank:

- It certainly wants deposits and outstanding loans. In other words, it wants to take over a going concern that is accepted in the community and has a good base of customers for future growth and profitability.
- It is buying a knowledge of the community and its surroundings, and the good will that the local bank has developed through its years of service to the community. Good will cannot be built overnight, and it is worth a fair price.
- A bank buys what it hopes will be loyal and capable employees and managers. Contrary to popular opinion, a bank holding company does not come in and remove the people from the local office. Generally, it is just the opposite, the larger unit needs all the talent it can get both at home and for its own expansion.

WHY A NEW BANK?

Thus, if a major bank decides to go de novo (brand new) into a community instead of acquiring a going organization, it must be because something was wrong with one or all of these three features of the local banks in town.

What are some of these drawbacks?

1 The price asked for the local bank might be so high that the profits for many years ahead would be absorbed in the acquisition price. A larger bank has an obligation to its stockholders not to pay so high a price for an acquisition that the new bank will not pay for itself for a number of years. Size alone is of no consequence to a bank holding company or branch network if it is not accompanied by profit potential.

   However, a high price may be warranted when the smaller bank is so inefficiently run that the larger bank can gain added profitability through changed methods, tax-swapping the bond account, and other tactics. In such a case, the high price-to-earnings multiple may be offset by future earnings potential.

2 The knowledge of the community and the good will factor can also be often offset. Just because a bank serves a community does not mean that the community loves the bank. If the local bank has not done its job, it may be harder for a larger bank to build business by buying it, with all its enemies and its bad reputation, than it would be to start a new bank with a clean slate.

3 Problems and benefits can occur with regard to the people as well. Banks and nonbank companies have frequently bought a going concern because that concern had good management that owned and operated the business, and nurtured it lovingly. Sometimes, however, after the takeover is completed this very management decides that it is time to relax—and the talent that made the concern go is denied the people who bought it. Certainly, people sign management contracts, but one cannot gain a contract that promises enthusiasm. And when larger companies that have been burned in the past look to smaller banks and other companies whose major shareholders have also been the vital moving force, they are concerned that they are buying a retirement home, not a going concern. If the smaller bank does not have a good array of aggressive middle managers, and the bank has really been a one-man shop, the larger banks are certainly practicing sound judgment when they weigh de novo banking as an alternative to a takeover.

4 Similarly, employee loyalty cannot be purchased along with the bank. Some heads of major bank holding companies complain bitterly of having bought a smaller bank only to find that the management of the smaller bank now looks upon the larger group as the "enemy." The result is they give loans to friends, try to boost salaries without truly earning them, and generally feel that they are in an adversary relationship—such as that of labor and management—instead of recognizing that when they sold their bank they also were assumed to have sold their loyalty to the holding company and its profit goals. The thought of this happening may make the de novo route a less distasteful alternative than it otherwise would.

5 Another problem can be too much loyalty. Should you buy a bank with a 75-year-old president who has no intention of ever retiring and who hopes to manage the bank from the grave later on? Of course, the holding company can always depose him once it has taken over. But with holding companies trying to maintain a good reputation among executives of acquired banks so

that future holding company acquisitions by that group look attractive to other independent banks, a disruptive removal of a bank president or chairman is not a good idea. It is usually preferable to go around that bank and take another or go the de novo route.

When it comes to commercial bank acquisition versus de novo start-up of a new operation, it appears that the smaller banks themselves really have the control over whether they will face new competition from de novo offices of larger banking units. Other things being equal, it is by far the easier path to buy a going bank and gain that bank's deposit and loan base, credit files, good will, and location.

Starting a new bank is never easy in a nation such as the United States, where banking habits are conservative and people seldom move their account unless they physically move their residences, are insulted or otherwise ill-treated by the existing bank, or are enticed away by some major new gimmick, such as a free checking account, forever. Thus, when a major bank decides to go de novo into a territory, it is either because it is a growing area that will support additional banks, or because the existing banks make it so unattractive for the larger institution to acquire them that it really had no choice.

3-2 ACQUISITION CANDIDATES—BRIDES OR BRIDESMAIDS?

Holding companies and branch units have paid high prices for the banks they have wooed and won. In fact, one study, sponsored by the Federal Reserve Bank of Boston, showed that the smaller banks have done very well when they have sold out to holding companies, but that the holding companies themselves have gained little so far, except for possibly better management of the capital position of the smaller bank. This is because they paid so much for the banks they acquired.

Thus, it is now becoming quite clear that holding companies undertaking the expense of courting and trying to win smaller banks for their systems must be sure they are getting something with potential. If the potential for added earnings is not there, then there is no reason for the acquisition.

With the expense of applying to the Federal Reserve for approval so great, holding companies are also limiting themselves to applications that have a reasonable chance of being approved.

Thus, many banks that looked upon the opening up of their states to holding companies as a real opportunity to sell out at a large paper profit and to gain a marketable stock of a major holding company to boot, are finding that they are destined to be the bridesmaid, not the bride.

CHOOSING WHO TO WOO

How does a holding company go about deciding which banks it wants to woo?

In the first place, many holding company executives feel that the decision is not based on the simple approach of courting those that come to them in the hopes of joining. With the specific goals of a well-run holding company, the chances are not great that a bank that comes in and offers itself for sale will possess just the right criteria that the holding company is looking for.

In fact, some holding company executives report that while they look into every suggested acquisition, virtually all of the cases in which acquisition has resulted have been initiated by the holding company and not by the independent bank.

In this regard, the smaller bank may be lucky. For if a holding company haphazardly accepts any candidate for membership, the fabric of the company can be weakened. And after each bank has joined and its shareholders have been given holding company stock for their old stock, then its shareholders would be among those hurt by the earnings dilution in the next haphazard acquisition made by the holding company.

Thus banks joining holding companies that have actively sought them out because they fit into the structure can rest assured that future acquisitions will also be carefully tailored; with the result that expansion will augment rather than reduce holding company profitability and the value of the shareholders' investment.

The most important criteria considered by the holding company are discussed below.

Economic Potential of the Market

No holding company wants a bank office just because it is an office. If the territory is static and offers little opportunity for development of profitable new business, then holding companies generally turn elsewhere.

To the individual bank, this attitude of the holding company makes more poignant than ever the old dictum that the future of the bank is dependent upon the future of the community. If the bank has not been involved in industrial development, if the bank has not made loans to keep the community strong but rather has placed its funds in the municipal bond market or lent it out as federal funds, then the bank has played a major role in making its territory unattractive for holding company acquisition.

Management's Record

How has the management done with the potential for bank profits the community offers? What has been the historic trend of the bank's share of market in the community? How has the bank done in earnings on resources?

These are important points, because the management is bought along with the bank. The people who run the bank as an independent will basically be the people who run the bank as part of a holding company. And, if they cannot do the job, it is extremely difficult for the holding company to remove them and put in better people without creating bad blood in the bank and in the local community. Thus, the holding company usually avoids the problem from the start by making sure that it is getting people with a performance record.

In this regard, some holding company managers now admit that they are stressing autonomy less in their discussions with the independent banks, so that they have more freedom to rotate people. But you can't keep the buildings and change all the personnel, so the track record still remains important.

Quality of the Assets

A holding company has to live with what it acquires. An independent bank that does not have top quality assets is far less attractive as a marriage partner than one whose assets are of prime quality. Given a choice, the bank that has built a profitable loan and investment portfolio of top rating will get the nod from the holding company.

Indirect Benefits

Can the independent bank provide other potential profits for the holding company? Does it have insurance that can be handled by the holding company? Can the holding company save money by taking over its data processing and eliminating a cost here? Are there opportunities for profit from tax swapping of the bond portfolio that can offset part of the premium paid for the bank in terms of earnings commanded by its former shareholders relative to earnings provided by their bank?

Geographic Fit

Does the new bank fit into the geographic structure of the holding company? It is highly unlikely that the Federal Reserve and the Justice Department will allow a holding company to acquire a bank that is in a location already served by another affiliate of the same company. End-to-end acquisitions that open up new territories have a much better chance of gaining approval than ones that lead to concentration in a community.

THE COST OF ACQUISITION

One cannot blame good holding companies for being fussy. As indicated above, an acquisition is costly in terms of earnings commanded relative to earnings supplied by the shareholders of the acquired bank.

Book value means little or nothing to a bank, except in liquidation, and banks do not expect to liquidate their assets.

Market price is a poor indication of cost because the smaller banks usually have stock whose market price is an unrealistic quote—not truly determined by supply and demand. Therefore, a high premium over market offered in an acquisition may still be cheap to the holding company in terms of what the stock of the acquired bank would be worth in a true auction market.

Thus, the only real test of price paid is how much the new bank contributed to total earnings of the holding company, and how much the new shareholders gained as their proportion of the total company's earnings that their shares command.

A holding company must find ways to offset any premium above market paid to new shareholders for their bank by improving the earnings of the bank that has been acquired. Generally, holding company officials feel that if the criteria set out above are not met, then the chance to recoup this premium paid on earnings becomes slim indeed.

ALTERNATIVES FOR SMALLER BANKS

What can a smaller bank do to insure that if it wants to be acquired it will become the bride and not be left waiting at the church (or more realistically, not be asked to the church in the first place)? It can try to improve (1) its management record, (2) the quality of its assets, (3) the economic potential of its community.

These are three of the areas in which the independent bank can have a direct impact on its chances for being courted by a holding company.

If a bank is too important in its community to be courted by a major holding company without a good chance of regulatory disapproval, then it must decide either to join a smaller holding company, establish its own holding company, or remain independent.

Similarly, if holding company banks already operate throughout its territory and no holding company could acquire it without intensifying its market share in that community, the bank must establish a new holding company or go it alone.

These situations are still rare in most states. A careful examination of what holding companies are looking for should leave most independent banks with the feeling that if they do want to join a holding company, they will have a large say in determining whether they can become attractive candidates.

3-3 SELLING THE BANK

In spite of all that has been said so far, banks *will* be bought and sold. Therefore, if a bank wants to sell, it should do everything possible to get the highest price. Fortunately, for banks that do wish to be acquired, there are a number of steps that can be taken to insure that they receive the best possible offer:

Prepare market forecasts that indicate (1) just how profitable the bank is likely to be in the years ahead and (2) what growth is anticipated. It is up to the bank to put its own best foot forward. No potential buyer will undertake that.

Plan how long top executives will stay in office after the acquisition of the bank by a larger company. This has a twofold effect. First, the company can plan on how long it can keep people who are known in the community and who can help in the transition. Second, it can help a buyer determine how much talent will be necessary to put into the bank and when this infusion of talent will be required. An equally important point here is that a potential buyer will be scared off if present management is aging but has no intention of letting younger people take over the reins.

Plan the bank's portfolio to get rid of sweetheart loans, to work on a realistic charge-off policy, to clean up technical exceptions filed by examiners, and to take other measures that will help get the bank in top shape. A buying bank will raise or lower its offer based on how satisfactory it finds the asset base.

Review the bank's accounting to ensure that the bank's income is not understated. This review involves accreting bond discounts, placing consumer loans on as favorable an accounting basis as possible (including the benefits from prepaid items like insurance policies), and taking all other steps that can improve the income picture of the bank.

Have the bank audited. Every holding company is required to have a five-year audit for all of its components. It is far easier to do this now than it is to recreate it later. Holding companies look upon this as an important factor in evaluating a bank's worth.

Inventory strengths that may not be readily apparent—wills on file, successor trusteeships on file with the trust department, and other items that can place the bank in the best possible light.

Develop an understanding of hidden or indirect benefits the bank may offer a larger unit. These include knowing how much a bank might improve earnings by tax swapping the bond portfolio, how much a holding company or branch might cut costs of the bank through the takeover of data processing operations, and the elimination of other costs that are duplicated in both the acquirer and the acquiree.

There are a couple of other areas that should be mentioned. Does the smaller bank have insurance that can be handled by the larger bank or holding company? Does it offer the potential for other business like receivables financing that is presently handled by outside institutions? These are advantages for an acquiring bank that the smaller bank should understand and stress in any negotiations.

IMPROVING THE STOCK PRICE

In addition to primping, the bank should improve the price of the stock as much as possible in preparation for acquisition bids. Bank acquisition is done on the basis of book value and earnings potential, as indicated later in this chapter. However, it should be understood that to the shareholders, the factor that has immediate meaning is what the new shares received will be worth on the market relative to the shares of the old bank. Holding companies and branch systems recognize that they cannot make an offer that gives the shareholders of the acquired bank a piece of paper worth less than the old shares were worth on the market. Thus, if the smaller bank can boost its own share price, then the offers made by acquiring companies and banks will also have to be higher.

Just what can a bank do to raise its share price? First, the bank must honestly want to do so. In some banks, top management has not cared about stock price and has been happy when the local press did not quote the bank's shares. This lack of communication effectively eliminated the possibility of calls from shareholders unhappy about a recent movement in the stock.

Other banks like to keep the price low so that insiders can have the opportunity to buy up more of the bank at cheap prices from unsuspecting shareholders and then become the main beneficiaries when a sale of the bank does take place. Still other chief executive officers help cause the problem by making the market at their own desks.

There is the all too typical case of the person interested in selling his shares, asking the president what they are worth, and being told, "Well, the last sale was at 40, so that should be fair." This kind of reasoning means that every sale is at the same price as the last sale—and the stock never leaves 40.

IMPROVING THE MARKET

Bankers who do want to improve the market for their stock have several routes available to them. For one thing, they can work more closely with the bank stock dealers in their regions. This involves two steps:

- The bank must be fair in providing the dealers with the opportunity to make a market in all available shares that are bought and sold. A bank stock dealer will be turned off quickly if the bank tells him to make a market and quote the stock, and then, whenever a good-sized block becomes available, turns around and places it themselves. Some banks do not inform the dealer either at all or until the deal has been completed.

  Bank stock dealers want to be given the opportunity to bid on all available shares that come to market. They cannot make a market if they are called upon for the bits and pieces while the profitable blocks go elsewhere. And they cannot afford to make a market and take the risk of pricing if they are not given an opportunity to learn of all available stock for sale and all the interest in stock purchase.
- Bank stock dealers want decent information about the bank. This does not mean illegal insider information. Rather, it means that the dealers who make markets in bank shares want everyone informed on earnings trends,

significant growth developments, and changes in personnel, policies, and pricing important to the bank's prosperity. Once a dealer has recommended a stock, only to find later that unavailable information would have altered his opinion, he will never go out on a limb for that stock again. Conversely, if he recommends a sale, only to learn later that favorable information which later boosted the stock's price had been postponed in its release, that too will be remembered.

One good rule is that a bank should toot its horn on good material, but also release the bad news. If a bank is not willing to tell its full story to the public, there is no reason why a bank stock dealer should take upon himself the responsibility to serve as the bank's proxy in this regard—especially since he lacks the information the bank's own staff has.

There are other actions a bank can take to make sure its stock gets the most favorable market action and the highest possible price-to-earnings multiple.

- A bank can initiate a dividend reinvestment program for shareholders. This is because (1) there is a regular demand for shares from the dividend reinvestment pool, which helps bid up share price, and (2) since dealers know there will be periodic share purchases by the dividend reinvestment pool, they will be willing to be more aggressive in making a market in the stock.
- A bank can survey shareholders to determine what they want. In some banks, management has found that shareholders prefer high-dividend payout. In others, the tax bracket of the shareholders has led to preference for dividends that are smaller and for more reinvestment of earnings. Knowing what shareholders and community people want can help make the shares more attractive in the marketplace.
- The bank can utilize stock splits and stock dividends to adjust the price to a more attractive price range. Studies have shown that most investors like stocks that sell in a moderate price range of from $10 to $20 per share on the low side, to $70 to $80 per share on the high side. Investors seem to feel the stock is too cheap and not representative of quality if it is priced below $10 per share. On the other hand, if the stock is priced above $80 per share it appears to be unreachable.

  Bankers have found that if a stock is too high in price, a split can actually improve market value. For example, a stock selling at $100 a share and split three for one will frequently sell after the split at a price in the $40s, rather than around the $33 level.

- Rights offerings can be utilized to set a price for an infrequently traded stock. Not only do rights offerings raise needed equity capital, they indicate to the shareholder what management feels the stock is worth.

  While no rights offering can be a success if the bank places too high a multiple on its earnings relative to that on other similar bank shares in the region, if the stock has traded below the multiples in the territory, the rights offering can serve to boost the price back up to the norm.

  Actually, banks can use periodic rights offerings, with each at a slightly higher price than the last, to raise the market price of a stock that otherwise would remain fairly static in market price. As long as earnings rise steadily to validate this price rise, the bank's management can offset the vagaries of a thin market for the stock that could otherwise bring flip flops in market price unrelated to developments in earnings.
- Stock dividends can help improve the stock of a bank. Frequent 4-5% dividends may look on the surface to be merely passing out more and more pieces of paper representing the same value and giving work to the bank in handling distribution and fractional shares. Yet this is not always the case. In many banks, frequent stock dividends have been issued while the stock price remains static. This, in essence, involves boosting the share price by 4-5% a year simply by passing out more paper. The informal answer sometimes given by management when people ask about dividend policy is "we give 9% a year—5% in stock and 4% in cash!" While a corporate finance teacher would have a heart attack on hearing this, the shareholders apparently like it. In fact, frequent stock dividends are high on the list of preferences of those shareholders who have been asked their likes and dislikes regarding bank stockholder policy.
- Several banks have even found an auction to be of value as a way of setting a price for a thinly traded stock. In some cases, one bank announces an auction of its stock. In others, all the banks in the community do it co-operatively once a year. But in every case, people who want to buy shares are invited in and shareholders are given the opportunity of selling in an auction setting. The result has often been a pleasant surprise to shareholders in many banks—and a higher price on the stock than could have been established in any other manner.

The bank, then, can do much to cultivate bank stock dealers and the securities analysts who work for these dealer firms. The bank can try to make its stock as attractive as possible. The bank can also do much to emphasize its strengths and minimize its weaknesses as an investment vehicle. The next step becomes one of analyzing the offers that come in from those institutions interested in buying.

ANALYZING THE OFFERS

As independent banks make it known they might be interested in receiving offers from larger institutions and as they analyze the offers received, several basic points must be kept in mind. Most of these involve a realistic view of what the bank is and what it is not. Points to be considered include:

- Making sure the potential merger or acquisition is likely to be consummated. For example, if the bank to be acquired is the biggest in its region and the offer comes from the largest bank in the state, the likelihood is that the deal will ultimately be turned down by the regulatory authorities. Make sure your proposal is not in violation of present statutes and regulatory opinions on concentration of power.
- Making sure the acquisition can be justified on the basis of public interest. Just because it is a good deal for shareholders is no reason for regulators to approve the deal if the public does not benefit.
- Making sure the new banking organization has a reputation of serving the local communities it has entered. Otherwise, the bank will have hurt its community through the deal. Similarly, make sure it has a reputation for treating employees fairly.
- Being honest. Do not try to get too high a multiple or price for the stock if the bank is in a territory where such multiples are not usually paid. If the bank does get a high multiple, the likelihood is that the organization will be just as generous with future acquisitions—but in the future it will be the bank's shares that will be diluted, rather than the shares of outsiders.
- Weighing the factors fairly and ensuring that the personal benefits to the banks top management are not the deciding factor in accepting a particular bid. In other words, a lower bid from one institution should not be accepted over a higher bid from another organization simply because the lower bidding organization intends to treat top management better than the higher bidder did. Bank analysts report that some bankers have been willing to sell out at a much lower price to holding companies that allow them to

keep their titles and their boards of directors (i.e., their power) than a branch network would pay.

- Making sure not too many members of the board get involved in the early stages of the negotiation. This can result in an excess number of demands, and possibly disrupting or even destroying negotiations. The whole board should only be brought in when the general framework of agreement has been carved out.
- Making sure that the bank is not threatening the entire negotiation by hidden factors that eventually come out—long-term lucrative employment contracts to officers, relatives on the payroll, and other deals that the acquiring bank will have to absorb.

After all this, the bank is ready to analyze the specifics.

Book Value

Deciding which offer is most attractive is not as easy as it might appear. If all offers were in cash, there would be no question. But, because of capital gains tax consequences, most shareholders do not want cash payment upon acquisition, and most banks do not want to pay out cash as they acquire other banks. The question becomes one of determining what the stock received in an acquisition is really worth.

For example, bank executives may brag that they were able to get a price of triple book for their bank. Were this in cash, it would be quite a coup. But when payment is made in stock, the matter is less clear. If questioned as to the selling price of the stock paid out in the acquisition, the president has to reply that this, too, is selling at triple book.

It is a little like the boy who told his father he was going to sell his dog for $1 million. When questioned later, he told his father he had been able to sell his dog and had gotten the price he wanted. "Did you get cash?" his father questioned. "No, I took two $500,000 cats," the son responded.

What is wrong with book value as a basis for judgement on an offer? For that matter, what really is book value? One widely used formula is the total of capital, surplus, undivided profits, and one-half of the reserve for loan losses. But different banks take differing views in determining factors such as the value of securities not carried at market, the evaluation of the worth of problem loans, the real worth of property and equipment, and the tax consequences of any differences from stated book. Thus, adjusted book value may mean one figure to one acquiring bank and a different figure to another.

More important, since the acquisition is paid for in stock most of the time, is the price paid really redeemable in terms of bank book value? A bank may have a book value of $50 a share and be offered stock selling at $150 a share—an offer of triple book. But unless the shareholders intend to sell that day, they must consider what the shares they are receiving will be worth later. Since the high price paid for the bank will be likely to dilute the equity of the acquiring bank, the price may fall sharply as soon as the shareholders are on board.

On top of this, there is the question of the thinness of the market. If shareholders want to sell their stock in the acquiring institution as soon as they receive it, what will this do to market price? Is there a deep enough market to absorb a good number of sales without depressing the stock sharply, or will the first sales by the new holders bring the price down sharply and make the offer far less attractive than it had appeared at first?

Sure, the stock price may have appeared in *The Wall Street Journal*, and the deal seemed great on the basis of what the new stock was worth. But there is no trading with *The Wall Street Journal*. As soon as trades start appearing, the price may fall and the shareholders may find they did not get as good a deal as they had thought.

Since most holders will not be anxious to sell as soon as the acquisition is completed and since those that do may depress the market price sharply, the real question that bank management must address is the potential earning power of the organization they are joining and how it compares with the earning power of the bank the management is selling and of other suitors. This should turn out to be the best test of what a bank is getting and what it is giving up.

Earning Power

Earning power is simply a comparison of the percentage of the earnings of the combined bank (that will be supplied by the bank being acquired) with the percent of shares in the combined organization that the shareholders of the acquired bank will command.

As Table 1 indicates, Big Footings Trust Company has made an offer of two shares of Big Footings Trust Company for each share of Schmidlap National Bank. Since Schmidlap people will hold 20% of the total shares outstanding after merger, but only provided 13.04% of the earnings of the combined bank, the shareholders of Schmidlap National now control 20% of combined earnings, or $460,000 of total earnings of $2,300,000, although they contributed a bank providing only $300,000 in earnings to the new organization.

TABLE 1 Analysis of Premium on Earnings*

Terms: For one (1) share of Schmidlap National Bank you receive two shares of Big Footings Trust Company.
Shares outstanding prior to merger: Schmidlap—100,000; Big Footings—800,000.

Earnings December 31, 1984			
	Schmidlap	Big Footings	Total
Income before security transactions	$300,000	$2,000,000	$2,300,000
As % of total	13.04%	86.96%	100%
After Exchange (2 Big Footings for each Schmidlap)			
Number of shares	200,000	800,00	1,000,000
As % of total	20%	80%	100%
Earnings controlled	$460,000	$1,840,000	$2,300,000
As % of total	20%	80%	100%
Earnings received	$460,000		
Less earnings contributed	$300,000		
Premium	$160,000		
Percentage premium paid	53.3%		

* Form Courtesy of Ryan, Beck & Co., West Orange, N.J.

The premium on earnings received by Schmidlap's shareholders is thus $160,000 on a contribution of $200,000, or 53.3%. Because shareholders are joining a going concern and future earnings are what should concern them, this premium on earnings is of great interest. It appears to be the most valid test of whether an offer is worth taking, or whether some other offer is better for the long-range interests of the bank's shareholders.

Yet even this comparison of earnings is not enough. Management of the selling bank has to consider not only today's earnings, but what earnings of the combined bank are likely to be in the future. This involves analyzing both today's earning's statement and what is thought about the larger bank's management, territory, style, and prospects. It should be remembered that except for those few shareholders who plan to sell out immediately, the joining of a holding company or a branch system is not truly a sale by the shareholders. Rather, it is a marriage into a larger organization. And, as with every other marriage, the true test must involve looking beyond the honeymoon and the immediate prospects to what is likely to be in store in the future.

Such an analysis should include the management styles, growth rates, talent, and marketing expertise of the holding company, as well as how it handles acquisitions. Too many banks have grown spectacularly through acquisitions, only to have their earnings per share steadily decline as a result of the continual dilution caused by the acquisitions. Yet in other cases, banks have been able to pay premiums in earnings because they saw potential for earnings growth in the acquired bank that could quickly compensate for the premiun on earnings paid, bringing the entire operation up to a higher level of performance.

An analysis of various bank and holding company histories and styles can lead to a choice that is not as good on the day of closing as another offer might be, but it may be far more favorable to the shareholders over the long run. While a banker owes it to his shareholders, employees, and community to pick the most viable acquisition partner based on long-run potential and not just immediate gain, he also owes it to the acquiring organization to be loyal once he comes on board.

Looking Ahead

The most obvious indication of how a holding company or branch network will treat its new shareholders once the acquisition is concluded is the way it treated the bank before the deal was consummated. If the acquiring company was extremely generous in its treatment—at the expense of its present shareholders' position—then it is likely that it will treat future acquirees just as generously—at the bank's expense.

One might hope that once a holding company or branch network has given the bank a particularly generous offer, it would then become much tougher in evaluating future acquisitions, much like the person who now wants to close a mountain or lake region to further settlement because he bought his cabin retreat last year. But this is not apt to happen. The company that was acquisition-minded at the expense of diluting its earning power is likely to remain that way. Only in the next acquisition it is the bank's earning power that will be diluted.

Thus, some bankers concentrate their attention in the so-called second kicker: what earnings growth the acquirer will show through the years and what the bank's investment will be worth years ahead.

If, as indicated earlier, once a smaller bank has been purchased and an attractive price has been paid, the smaller bank may occasionally look at the parent as an adversary rather than a partner. Why can't a holding company or branch network control dissention and avoid the type of disloyalty described? The answer is that the officers and employees of the bank being acquired hold the trump card in making an acquisition work. They represent the bank in the local community and if they are relieved of their positions, even for cause, the new owners could be blamed for changing the bank and removing local control. People in the local community might well take their business elsewhere without asking questions first.

Other Risks to Consider

Are there risks in the entire acquisition process? Of course. Fortunately, they are usually less serious in bank than in nonbank acquisitions.

A bank may join a holding company or branch network only to find the price of the stock it accepted in the exchange declining sharply later on. The companies that sold out to National Student Marketing, Penn Central, and other conglomerates learned that sad lesson. Still, with bank stock, price-to-earnings multiples are likely to be considerably lower than those of most nonbank operations, unless earnings of the bank fall sharply—which also is unlikely. The stock price is not apt to fall radically below the market price at the time the deal was closed.

There are two exceptions. First, some banks have actively tried to raise their price-to-earnings multiples by aggressive publicity, promotion, and information programs aimed especially at securities analysts. In some of these cases, the claims hold water because the holding companies appear likely to maintain their earnings growth rates at present rates for the years ahead. In other instances, however, banks have been able to puff up earnings temporarily. A bank should do enough analysis when it sells out to insure that the earnings contributed to the venture by the acquiror are earnings that can be counted on in future years. Otherwise it may learn that the earnings involved tremendous effort and a one-time achievement.

Second, a bank holding company can sometimes obtain a higher price-to-earnings multiple than a bank can because of the volatility of earnings that the nonbank operations can achieve. However, this very volatility means that the multiple could fall sharply in poorer earning years. This was the case with nonbank conglomerates that made acquisitions in the halycon days of the late 1960s when their multiples were high, only to have the multiples plummet once the acquired companies were on board.

Another risk a bank must consider before attracting and talking to potential acquiring organizations is: What happens to morale if the deal is disapproved by shareholders or by regulatory authorities? Many a happy bank has become unhappy when the management has planned to join a larger organization and then been rebuffed. A good management should have contingency plans available, detailing new steps to be taken, either to find another merger partner or remain independent. These plans should include a complete explanation of what happened to the proposal and why.

3-4 PUTTING THE DEAL IN PERSPECTIVE

There is nothing worse than selling the bank to a holding company system, only to find that similar banks in equivalent type and size sold out for a lot more. Conversely, as far as management is concerned, acceptance of an attractive offer could please the shareholders, but might make the staff of the bank unhappy and lead to poorer service to the community than had been provided before.

When it is remembered that a bank has to serve its shareholders, its employees, and its community the conflicts that are possible in selling the bank become much more complex than might appear on the surface. While there are no simple, definitive answers to the basic question, having some understanding of the various alternatives and problems can serve as a first step to getting the deal that best serves these three groups and makes all of them look back on whatever decision is made as a move well-taken.

WHAT TO CONSIDER

A banker must be realistic, He must understand what is possible to get and what is not possible. This is important in two ways. One, the job of bargaining is easier when a banker has realistic goals for what the bank is worth. Two, if a banker finds that he can get an unrealistically high price for his bank in holding company stock, he will have to recognize that other banks will be likely to get the same deal. Thus, the new stock he is getting may be diluted in value time and again as a result of future high-priced acquisitions. A branch network or holding company that is a tough bargainer when you are on the opposite side of the table should be equally acute when you have joined the system and they are representing your stock interests in their bargaining.

In addition, a banker must know what his territory is worth. A bank seving an agricultural area in which automation is reducing the number of jobs available in the community cannot expect the same deal for his bank as would be offered to a bank in a growth area where population is burgeoning and new industry is coming in.

Finally, the banker must be honest with himself. He must recognize that if his goal is to keep a going organization intact, with the sale involving as few changes as possible, this will probably result in a smaller offer than would be available if he were willing to have the acquiring company make changes that might improve the profitability of the whole organization.

For example, studies in New Jersey have shown that in that state, in which banks have a choice of joining holding companies, or joining branch systems, the price paid has been about 50 per cent higher when the acquired bank has joined a branch system than when it has entered a holding company organization. In other words, the bank being acquired was willing to accept offers of about double book, if the bank could remain an independent unit in the holding company, with its own structure and board. But if it was willing to join a branch system, give up its independent status and its titles of president and chairman, and switch its board to an advisory capacity, the bank frequently was able to obtain triple book.

Similarly, a banker must understand the holding company or branch system well enough to know what its attitude toward the community will be once it takes over the bank. Some holding companies and branch networks will have the resources to provide more aid to the new community than will others. And while it is seldom that a holding company or branch system will look upon an acquisition as a source of funds from that community to meet loan demands elsewhere, the banker must make sure that is not the case in the particular deal into which he is entering. Unlikely though it may be, if it does turn out that the larger system wants to milk the local community's deposits for its lending needs elsewhere, and the community suffers, it will be difficult for that bank's top officers and board to face their fellow townsmen in later years after the bank is sold.

The result of all this should be a decent deal for the bank, for the employees who are switched to holding company or branch bank employment, and for the community the bank serves.

3-5 CORE DEPOSITS—NEW TEST OF A BANK'S WORTH

As bankers evaluate other banks and branches for acquisition prospects, a new technique has come to the front—pricing based on the amount of core deposits that would be acquired.

To many banking observers, this may appear strange indeed. Book value has traditionally served as the test of a bank's worth. When book value ceased to be held in top esteem, evaluators switched to earning power as the basic test of worth.

Now, many banks trying to decide how much to pay for a bank or branch have replaced these two criteria with an analysis of the quantity of core deposits that would be acquired.

MORE ON THE VALUE OF BOOK

Book value has always been held in greater esteem by bankers than by nonbankers— and for good reason. Book value of a manufacturing or transportation operation means little, for the book value of the assets of these types of firms cannot necessarily be translated into earning power.

During the Depression of the 1930s, for example, a majority position in some major railroads could have been purchased for less than the scrap value of the rails. Yet this meant little, because the Interstate Commerce Commission forced the owners to keep running trains rather than let new owners stop service and sell the rails. Book value might have been there, but to buy book value and end up with operating deficits is no investor's dream.

Earning power means far more than book in most industries. Value is not determined by what it would cost to replace the capital facilities but what a company can earn from utilizing them.

Banking, however, has been different. A bank's book value truly reflects the worth of cash and marketable securities. In banks, the percentage of total funds devoted to building and equipment is small, so a bank's value is largely determined by investments, loans, and vault cash. These assets certainly can be totaled up in dollar-and-cents terms with meaningful results.

Many banks with stock that sells below book are worth more dead than alive. If the buyers of control liquidated a bank, they would realize more than it cost to purchase the institution.

When a bank does sell out, the quote given for the price paid generally is in terms of book—such as "we sold out for double book."

CONSIDER CORE DEPOSITS

In today's high interest-rate environment, however, book means much less than it did in the past. Most long-term, fixed-yield mortgage loans and investments are worth far less on the market than they are valued on the books, due to the below-market coupon yields that most issues have.

A bank that sells out for double book may be selling out for a very high multiple in depreciated book value. Conversely, a buyer of a bank or branch who is trying to strike a fair deal for his own investor interests will be hesitant about accepting book value as being indicative of the assets being purchased.

This is why banks buying other banks and their offices have started to look at core deposits. They are willing to bid a premium for core deposits as a way of dealing with the problems of deposit size. They understand that any bank that wants to grow can simply pay going rates for money market funds and C.D.s, and it does not have to pay a premium to another organization to get 14% or 16% deposits.

Territory has value, and a premium is paid for it. But what is it about a territory that makes it valuable? It appears to be the core deposits that the territory can generate.

In essence, the banking industry is looking to its demand deposits and passbook savings as the backbone of profitability. Not only will investors pay a premium for these deposits, they also will go on the assumption that these deposits are the most valuable properties a bank has to sell.

It is ironic, buying liabilities rather than assets, but this is the way it is.

There are some problems that must be kept in mind. Demand and savings deposits are now subject to intense competitive pressures. A core deposit today may disappear tomorrow. This is especially true if the core deposits are business balances or state and local government balances maintained because of an unusually close relationship with one bank that will be ended if the bank or branch is sold.

Bankers must be wary about paying a premium for core deposits that could well involve buying "whipped up air."

Problems involved in evaluating a bank's worth based on core-deposit totals show how little we can truly tell about the future worth of a bank or office in this era of deregulation and freedom from interest rate ceilings. But, for lack of a decent alternative, core deposits appear to be one best test.

3-6 THE CONSEQUENCES OF BEING ACQUIRED

A banker, who had sold his bank to a large holding company, died a couple of years later. He was met by God, who asked, "Do you want to go to Heaven or Hell?"

"May I look at them?" the banker asked.

"Certainly."

He looked at Heaven and saw people reading the Bible, drinking tea, discussing religion and ethics, and taking sedate walks. In Hell, there was singing, dancing, golf, tennis, and fancy food.

"I'll take Hell," he said. And so God left the banker there.

Immediately Hell changed. It became fire, sweat, and work, with only bread and water for sustenance.

"Why was it so nice before and now it is so terrible?" the banker asked.

"Ah," God replied. "Then you were a tourist. Now you are an immigrant."

In the same vein, executives of smaller banks wonder what will it be like if they become immigrants in branch networks or holding companies.

Any bank that buys another bank must do so with the intention of making the latter more profitable than is now the case. Otherwise, there is no reason for the purchase. If an acquisition does not help the acquiring bank improve earnings per share, then the acquirer would have been far better off simply buying tax-exempt bonds with its money and leaving the smaller bank alone.

There are a few instances in which a bank can be bought for so low a price that the acquirer can make money on its purchase without doing anything to change operations. But these occurrences are rare. It is mote likely to be a situation in which the smaller bank demands a price that reflects the bank's potential rather than present earning levels. If the acquirer does not make enough changes to realize that profit potential, then it is merely going to dilute its own earnings by taking over the other institution.

This is where the question of tourist versus immigrant comes in. When a larger bank talks to a smaller bank about what will happen after the merger or acquisition, the discussion generally centers around the idea that there will be few changes. Frequently, an acquiring institution will leave things as they are for a considerable period of time. After all, if it changes operations in one bank that has been acquired, and the holding company or branch network gets the reputation as being one that does make drastic changes, few other banks will want to join this group.

Thus, until a holding company or branch network has acquired the basic core of banks it wants for statewide or territory-wide operations, it will tread gently. Eventually, however, after the acquirer has built up its basic network and further acquisitions are not needed to complete the desired system, then changes have to take place if the holding company or branch is to make money on the acquisition. That is the day of reckoning—the acquired become immigrants instead of tourists.

BECOME A BRANCH?

If a bank has joined a branch network, it has to expect radical changes. After all, a branch of a bank is quite a different animal from an independent bank.

An independent bank has a board of directors, a chairman, and a president. It has (and needs) a staff to handle all functions. In addition, it makes all decisions on loans, investments, operations, marketing, and the like.

A branch bank is something else. It can be staffed with far fewer people, and it has no board. If he stays around, the president of the independent bank becomes a regional vice-president. Some branch banks try to keep decision-making local while others take it to headquarters. This is especially true on lending policies, rates, charges, and services offered. The community sees a different name, a different style of operation, and, usually, different rates and service charges. People generally forget quickly that the bank once was a locally owned and operated organization.

The changes may be good or bad for the local community, depending on individual operating styles of the former independent and the present branch network. No economic studies have been able to prove that independent banking is superior to branching or branching superior to independent banking.

The real key is: What type of managerial style does the bigger bank have and how much does it need the talent of the people coming on board from the community bank? All too often, one hears the complaint of an officer from the acquired bank: "I'll never make it to the top here. I come from the Schmidlap Bank side and all the decision-makers come from the Frubisher Bank people."

Patterns can be determined. Some banks have promoted people from acquired banks right up to the top rather quickly. Such institutions have looked upon the acquisition of other banks as a source of new blood in their ranks. Others have taken the attitude that the original management knows what it wants. The acquired people are merely part of the operation that is bought along with the tellers' counters, vaults, and mortgages.

This is the key point that bank leaders must consider before they join a branch network. What they learn may make them and their staffs happy or it may not. But it certainly is a matter that must be addressed as bank management asks itself what life will be like when they become immigrants.

JOIN A BHC?

Bank holding companies (BHCs) are usually quite different from branch banks. Interestingly, this is a fairly recent development. There was a time, a little over a decade ago, when most holding company managements looked upon the holding company form as merely an intermediate step between independence and branch operations. The facts bore this out: In no state that allowed statewide branching did any holding company exist, unless it was an interstate holding company. In other words, whenever an organization could combine all its banks into a branch organization, it did so. It only used the holding company either to combine banks when state laws did not allow statewide branching or to combine banks across the state lines. (Interstate holding companies that had been formed before prohibitive laws were passed were allowed to continue in existence, though no interstate branch networks were allowed with a couple of minor exceptions of grandfathered bank offices).

The feeling was that there was no reason to have the complex structure of a holding company, with its various boards, segregated investment portfolios, separate operations departments, and individual CEOs and policies if a group of banks could be consolidated into one unit. This has all changed.

Bankers recognize that the holding company form has decided advantages. The very independence of the board and the CEO give these people more stature and more willingness to achieve because of their independence and authority. It is a great motivator. The public likes the feeling that there is still an independent bank. The board of directors serves as a splendid marketing arm in the community, showing that there is still independence of authority.

Most important, BHC officers can, in most instances, still follow that most important policy of making decisions on the spot without checking with headquarters. This is what holding companies affiliates usually do. It is the reason why so many banks that could combine their holding companies into branch networks are not doing so, but are maintaining this intermediate structure between independence and branching.

Even though the bank remains a locally operated entity, the holding company offers the added flexibility that people can be switched from one bank to another. Also, talent can be hired that works for all banks from the holding company level, such as specialists in complex loans and advisors on investment and trust problems.

However, any banker who feels that joining a holding company will leave life unchanged will almost always end up disillusioned. What are the changes likely to take place when a bank joins a holding company?

First, there is the name. Some banks have tried to keep the local names and use a common logo or words like "A Schmidlap Bank" under the local name to keep local identity while still indicating that the bank is part of a holding company. However, with the high cost of television and print advertising, and the consequent need to gain maximum efficiency from the media, holding companies have been forcing their affiliates to switch to common names so that an entire region can be served by one advertising campaign.

Second, policies with regard to service charges, lending standards, and types of accounts are frequently determined at the holding company level, with affiliate banks "strongly suggested" to accept these.

Third, technical operations usually are centralized to take advantage of efficiencies by avoiding duplication of talent and procedures.

The key decision as to who gets a loan and how fast, however, generally remains on the local level. As one holding company CEO stated, "Anything to do with the customer we leave at the local level. Anything to do with operations and internal decisions, we centralize for efficiency."

It also must be noted that even though holding company operations look like a beautiful compromise, there is still the possibility that after a period of time allowing an affiliate to remain independent, a holding company may decide to combine several affiliates into one larger unit in the region. This may be done where the BHC thinks that efficiencies developed will be profitable enough to make the sacrifice of local autonomy worthwhile.

THE LONGER VIEW

There is another factor to consider before deciding whether to join a holding company or a branch, or to remain independent. Which acquirer will be the better lifetime partner in the years ahead from an investment point of view?

There is the situation of a bank in a northeastern state that had offers from two holding companies. One was a bid that was in the range of what banks are generally offered these days (about 1.6 times book for cash, and 1.2 times book for stock). The other looked far more generous—in fact, too generous. The bank took the second offer. It sold out for stock that was worth about 50% more than the stock it would have received in the first bank's offer would have sold for.

What quickly happened was that the market realized that the second bank was paying too much for its acquisitions, and the price of the second bank holding company's stock started to plummet. It fell to such a degree that it soon was worth one-half what it sold for when the independent bank was acquired. Meanwhile, the bank that made the less generous offer saw its stock rise by about 25% in value.

The stockholders would have been far better off by questioning the decision of trading local stock for the stock of a holding company that was too generous in passing out paper for acquisitions. Even though this bank was at first the beneficiary of the generosity, in all subsequent acquisitions it would be one of the losers through the further dilution that the holding company accepted to gain more territory.

The bank that joins a larger unit is making a nonreversible decision. From the viewpoint of stockholders, employees, board members, and top management, the decision has to be made realistically. And this, it must be concluded, requires a lot deeper analysis than one needs for initial evaluation.

3-7 WHAT PRICE INDEPENDENCE?

Many bankers throughout the country are afraid that their banks—and, indeed, their very jobs—will disappear. Yet, in truth, unfriendly takeovers are rare, though this situation may be changing. In most cases where a bank has been swallowed up by a holding company or a branch network, it has been because the board and top officers wanted to join, not because someone came in and did the job over their strong resistance.

The proof is in the performance. Achievement of a return of 1% or more on assets is not unusual in smaller banks. Some have even exceeded 3% on assets! In the large money center bank, such a goal is almost impossible to contemplate. There just is virtually no way in which the large bank has an advantage over the smaller institution—*if the smaller bank wants to survive.*

In a big bank, labor and administrative costs are higher. The community bank is likely to have a larger base of cheaper core deposits. In addition, computer costs have shrunk to the point where there are no economies of size in using them.

At a meeting of the Independent Bankers of Georgia, a prize was offered to the first banker to name an area in which a large bank has an advantage over a smaller one. The eventual winner dug up the fact that a larger bank can get better rates on buying bankers' acceptances because it buys them in bigger blocks. But that one-eighth of 1% on acceptances is hardly a reason for smaller banks to merge into larger organizations.

UNWANTED SUITORS

What about unfriendly takeovers? Will a large bank bid so much for a community bank that the stockholders will sell out against the recommendation of the board and top officers? What does a large bank stand to gain by undertaking an unfriendly takeover?

Certainly the acquiring bank gets the buildings and facilities of the acquired bank. In many cases, however, these are obsolete facilities, often poorly located, that the bank would be glad to change for a new fuel-efficient plant located where the town is moving. The acquiring bank also gets the assets of the other bank. However, a great percentage of these assets may be mortgages and other fixed-rate credits that yield well below market rates. This, too, is no bargain.

On the liability side, the acquiring bank obtains the deposits. The most valuable of these are the core deposits that cost far less than going rates for money today. Yet these deposits may be shrinking in size. Also, the liability base of banks is more often being purchased at the going rate for funds—making them no bargain at all.

What the bigger bank basically gets, then, is the existing good will in the community, that is, the stature that comes from acquiring the services of local officers and board members. But in an unfriendly takeover, these benefits are often forfeited.

Thus, an unfriendly takeover will take place only if a bank has been doing so poorly relative to its potential in the local marketplace that the acquirer thinks it can overcome the good will issue and make a real bundle on the acquisition anyway. This matter of doing poorly involves either the bank earning so little or the stock selling so much below book (or both) that the prospective buyer feels it can quickly turn the institution around and make a substantial profit based on the price that has to be offered the shareholders to acquire it.

Because of all these factors, banks that want to remain independent have remained independent. The banks that want to form their own holding companies are beginning to structure them. But nothing else has changed.

THE THREAT TO INDEPENDENCE

What, then, is the threat to independent banking in the United States? Ironically, it comes from inside the industry rather than outside: Some of the most vehement banking voices against holding companies and branches in years past have been the first to sell out when state laws on bank structure were relaxed. Despite all the protests of the value of independent banking, the boards and CEOs of some banks have rushed to solicit offers from larger institutions as soon as they saw the handwriting on the wall for holding companies and branch networks. Why?

There is the story of the judge in a movie industry case who was told by one side: "If you decide in our favor, you get $50,000 and a night with any starlet in our studio."

"Arrest that man," the judge told his bailiff.

"Why, your honor? For trying to bribe you?"

"No, for coming too close to my price."

What is the price of staying independent? In many instances, it is substantial. Banks that want to get into territories and want the good will that comes from having a friendly takeover, under which the board and the staff become loyal to the new institution, are willing to pay double book and even triple book for the acquisition. The payment of double and triple book is becoming less frequent, however, as bankers recognize that electronic banking has made the geographical advantages of a local franchise less significant. Even so, no bank will be able to buy another bank unless it offers a price that is well above the market price of the acquired bank's stock today. So, turning down an acquisition has a dollar and cents cost to present board members, top officers and other shareholders.

There has been a relationship between price paid and amount of control tendered. A few years back, for example, when state banking laws were first being relaxed, some banks found that they were offered double book by holding company networks and triple book by branch organizations. In effect, the bank's board had to decide whether it would sacrifice a 50% higher return to shareholders for the advantages of having (1) the board remain the bank's board and not become an advisory board and (2) the CEO remain the CEO instead of becoming senior vice president and head regional officer of the merged bank.

This is a price that many stockholders have been forced to pay so that board members and officers could keep their positions of importance and power. Will shareholders continue to be willing to pay? In many instances, the answer is "no." The leading board members and top shareholders often feel that they could sell the bank and earn far more investing the proceeds in tax-exempt bonds.

However, there are those who are willing to pay the price for independence:

Smaller Stockholders Small shareholders generally do not compare holding stock in the local bank with holding other types of investments. Therefore, they are willing to accept lower yields on their local bank stock. Sometimes they are fooling themselves, since banks often pay a low dividend of, say, 4% on market plus a 5% stock dividend. Shareholders feel they are getting 9%—4% in cash and 5% in stock. Remaining independent robs these shareholders of the chance to gain a much higher yield and, often, a much more marketable stock.

Employees One reason community banks can perform so well is that they frequently pay lower salaries than larger institutions do. These lower salaries are often accompanied by lower levels of aggravation, greater job satisfaction, more personal appreciation, and other noncash benefits. Be this as it may, employees often do far better in holding companies and branch networks than in community banks on a strict cash and benefits comparison.

Officers Officers of community banks often find they are paid in interesting work, appreciation, challenges, and other noncash benefits, rather than with high salaries. They also frequently find the path to advancement more difficult than at small banks. In a larger bank structure, an individual can take advantage of opportunites to grow at an affiliate bank or branch. Many community bank officers feel that the opportunity of challenging work in the home community is worth the price.

The Community In some communities, the local bank does not offer either going rates on savings, the most attractive certificates of deposits, or the most creative loans. These communities suffer from being served by a community bank. In far more instances, however, the reverse is true. The community gains the benefit of lower cost loans, lower service charges, and personal service. The price is paid by the community bank's employees and shareholders.

How is it possible to reconcile the lower cost loans and lower service charges with the higher return on assets small banks generally earn? Some of this comes from more efficient operations and lower salaries, and some from the greater availability of core low-cost deposits. In more and more high performance banks, however, the answer to this apparent paradox is that the smaller bank can no longer afford to offer low service charges or below standard rates on loans. For that matter, the community is not being as well served at the expense of shareholders or employees in the way it has been in the past.

THE OPPORTUNITY FOR PRICE OF INDEPENDENCE

Some banks will receive attractive offers and turn them down because they prefer independence to an attractive buyout, and in these cases the shareholders will have paid the price. Many others will find, however, that the offers they are waiting for just won't appear. The major banks are no longer so interested in buying out community banks when they can get more deposit money with one phone call from the money market desk than they can from operating 10 or even 100 branches for a full week.

If bank officers and the board are willing to pay the price of remaining independent, and shareholders are willing to continue to look at a bank stock investment as almost an emotional decision rather than a financial one, there is nothing that larger institutions can do to shake the viability of the independent bank. This is true no matter what happens to the laws that govern bank structure and no matter how many legal and practical chinks are put in the armor that has up to now protected bank market areas.

4 Community Banks

4-1 STRENGTHS OF COMMUNITY BANKS

Despite all the talk in recent years about the imminent demise of the community bank, the independent banking institution appears to be alive and well—in fact, it may be in better health than ever before.

A decade or so ago, when there were 13,800 banks, people speculated about a decline to 5,000 banks by the mid-1970s or at least by 1980. Yet now, in the mid-1980s, a new decade is upon us, the number of banks has risen to about 14,500.

To be sure, a great many small banks have disappeared. They have blended into holding companies and branch networks. But it has almost always been on their own volition, with the shareholders and directors feeling that in their particular situation they had something to gain by joining a larger organization. And, as the growing number of banks in the nation testifies, we have had enough new banks chartered to more than replace the banks that have joined together.

The reason for this hardiness of the community bank can be stated simply: community banking is a people business. There is nothing in the efficiency of large organizations or in new machines and techniques that can replace the genuine smile of a banker-neighbor who knows his customer.

The community banker knows his customer. He will go out of his way for him even though the requests often require unorthodox banking. Moreover, the community banker generally knows enough about his costs and pricing to make his institution profitable too.

When one looks at the lists of high performance banks, the independent bank is represented to a far greater extent than its numbers would justify because of its ability to generate core deposits and operate a tight ship. The coexistence of community banks and giant institutions is one of the basic strengths of the American financial structure.

It is interesting to note that in California, the state with the longest history of statewide banking, there have been more new banks chartered every year than in any other part of the country. Obviously, there must be something that these independent banks have going for them that lets them compete and thrive against the banking giants that have developed in this nation.

Why can community banks do so well and be among the high performance organizations in today's banking climate? Several forces come immediately to mind:

Public Loyalty One of the major strengths that community banks have is public loyalty to the local institution. People like to bank at the local bank.

They feel they are supporting the home town organization and home town people. We have seen how difficult it is for a distant bank coming into a community to win the deposits of local people and business firms. And it has been almost impossible for these new entrants into the community to win public deposits, except when public deposits are placed on a basis of competitive bidding and on no other determinant.

The local bank knows the people of the community. The local bank officers sit on the dais at almost every local function and are leaders in just about every community cause. Although the larger organizations try to develop a feeling of closeness by having their people work just as hard in the community, the community generally views them as outsiders.

People A second factor that should never be underestimated is that the bank's employees know the people in the community. Nothing pleases an individual more than to walk into the bank, be recognized as a friend, and have his request approved without question. Being known by the bank is a major desire of American people, and community banks excel in providing this recognition.

People strength also refers to members of the bank's board of directors. A good board always is thinking of the community and the bank and is serving as one of the latter's best marketing arms. There is no way in which an advisory board can be as effective in a community as a local board.

There was a director of a major bank holding company who had formerly been a director of a community bank. When his bank had been sold, he was placed on the holding company board, so he could compare the way things were with the way they had changed. His comment was this:

"When we had an independent bank, a person could come in and he would be known immediately. He could cash a check without any question, and he could borrow up to his limit in a matter of seconds. Now with the holding company, we are spending millions to put in a computer system that lets us recognize people as soon as their account number is entered into the machine. Through this system we will be able to cash checks for them immediately, and we will know how much credit we can give them in a matter of seconds. Just how far have we really come?"

For more on the value of the bank board to its bank, see Chapter 21, "What Directors Can Do for the Bank."

Efficiency One of the forces that helps the community bank in its fight against the industry giants of today is that we have few so-called economies of scale in banking beyond a certain minimum level.

In automobiles, for example, it takes a giant firm to be able to provide the heavy capital investment necessary for efficient production of cars. Thus we have seen the number of U.S. automakers shrink from a score or more to less than a handful today. Similarly, economies on a large scale are important in steel and in some forms of retail marketing. But not in banking.

Once a bank reaches a size at which it can afford to use the computer of a distant bank or of a service bureau, it can have the same efficiency as any larger bank. In fact, many of the highest performance banks in terms of earnings are smaller institutions, because they are able to keep employee costs down by sometimes having employees perform several functions.

Yet another efficiency is accomplished by the low rate of employee turnover. Because the overall job is often more challenging, many independent banks report they can get and keep better people than would otherwise be the case.

Many individuals who were trained in large organizations and have now gone to smaller ones would never go back. They explain that the diversity and challenges of being in a smaller bank that does not place people into slots and keep them there is the reason why they are so much happier in the community organizations.

Costs of Funds Another advantage many community banks have going for them is that they often have more stable, lower cost funds than the larger banks can obtain. One of the most difficult parts of banking is having to buy funds and compete against the open market for money at whatever rate commercial paper, Treasury bills, and other money market instruments are offering at the time.

Community banks, as a general rule, are not as dependent upon money market sources and the sale of CDs for their available funds because they have a harder core base of demand deposits and regular savings deposits financing their operations. This, in turn, not only keeps fund costs down but also makes it easier to insure that money will always be available to fund longer term credit demands. Of course, this does not mean that community banks are immune to the problems of securing funds. For more on this, see Section 4-2, "Options Open to Community Banks."

Between lower cost funds and an efficient operation, many community banks are able to keep their cost of credit below that of the larger institutions. This can be a real plus for borrowers at community banks, particularly when the national prime rate is rising at times of credit restraint.

NO TIME FOR COMPLACENCY

The one real fear that outside observers have as they look at community banks is that of a complacency that some of the smaller banks have developed. They have liked their major role in the community and have developed a feeling that no one can ever replace them in this role. Many have found to their sorrow that this is just not the case. Savings and loans and savings banks have come in and taken over much of their savings market. Finance companies have come into the community and captured the consumer loan market. Other independents have been established and taken over business from existing banks.

The public wants to be loyal. It likes the convenience and friendliness of the local bank. And the banker who has opened his bank on a Sunday to sell travelers checks to a vacationing customer who forgot to get them during banking hours—the kind of thing a great many community banks have done at one time or another—is not likely to lose that customer to any competitor that moves into town.

It should be remembered that the public expects good rates, good service, and a bank that does not take its business for granted. It is only when a community banker starts to think his position will always remain secure, no matter what he does or does not do for his customers, that the economic, financial, and psychological strengths the community bank has going for it begin to erode.

4-2 OPTIONS OPEN TO COMMUNITY BANKS

Community banks have been doing rather well for almost all of our banking history. However, there seem to be forces afoot—moves toward interstate banking, deregulation allowing banks to offer an expanding array of services—that could diminish the number of such banks in the years ahead. At the same time, there are indications that community banks will survive (see Section 4-1). The following options are do-able—without the assistance of government legislation and regulation.

OPTION NO. 1—MAKING A PROFIT

Profit has become the key to banking survival for both large and small banks. In the past, a bank's size was the sign that the public wanted it. There was no point in worrying about profits . . . somehow the profits would always be there. In many cases, this was the result of underpaying shareholders and employees.

This is changing. Size is going to be dependent upon profitability in the years ahead. Regulation Q is essentially gone, and soon banks will be allowed to pay whatever they want for money. Convenience alone will not attract customers anymore.

People are now demonstrating that they will move their money to get a higher return. Money market funds—handled by mail, involving applications forms, available only in lump sums of $500 or more—are certainly not convenient. Yet the public says "if interest rates are higher there, I am going." In other words, bank efficiency, anything that can build income, is important. Without the ability to pay going rates for money, there simply will not be growth.

This also means that banks have to be careful with cost control. Offices are a key—the bank that spends too much money on brick and mortar may lose out in two ways: (1) in terms of having too much money tied up in the physical building; and (2) in terms of the fact that brick and mortar are becoming so expensive and use up so much money that the bank may not be able to pay the going rates for money.

The community bank must be concerned with its profitability. The customer certainly is.

OPTION NO. 2—SPREAD MANAGEMENT

Banking has existed to a great extent on guessing, and even on gambling. Some highly respected banks have gotten into trouble because the managements thought that they knew what was going to happen with interest rates and they were in the market. Those banks thought rates would go down, but rates went up and they were stuck with a long-term portfolio. Instead of giving them a spectacular profit, their guesses gave them a spectacular loss.

The community banker answers this by declaring that he doesn't gamble. But in many ways he does. He gambles every time he makes a fixed rate loan and every time he takes a certificate of deposit and locks in the cost of funds for a certain period of time.

Many banks are victims of the cycle. If interest rates rise and a bank is stuck with fixed rate assets, its income goes down; if interest rates fall and the bank has fixed rate assets and people keep them on the books, the income goes up. If a bank is locked into a long-term supply of certificate money and interest rates rise, it is in good shape. If a bank has locked itself into the same supply and interest rates fall, it is in bad shape.

Because of this kind of situation, the banking industry is increasingly turning toward flexibility. Bankers want to have flexible assets and flexible liabilities in terms of yields and will manage the spread in the middle. They want to manage that spread; they want to be in a position where their assets and liabilities go up as interest rates rise, while they both go down in yield as the cost of interest falls.

For more on this important topic, see Section 4-3, "Spread Management."

OPTION NO. 3—BANK FUNDS

Without money, there is no bank. Demand deposits used to be the basic source of a bank's funds. Today, few banks keep excess demand deposits. The public has learned how to keep its money working. Even time and savings deposits are getting tougher to get, unless a bank pays competitive rates. Moreover, with money market funds a continuing investment vehicle, it is obvious that this trend spells trouble for the community bank.

Money market funds are drawing in money from all over the country. They are advertising in every part of the country. The funds take this money and put it into the negotiable CDs, Eurodollars, and treasury paper. This means that buying funds, both demand and time, is going to be tougher than ever before.

The impact of NOW accounts nationwide has not been the major problem originally feared. As George Bernard Shaw said when asked what it's like being 90 years old, "Considering the alternatives it's pretty good." And considering the alternatives, the money market funds, and outfits like Sears getting the money, the NOW account is not so bad.

Actually, the NOW account has made the small bank the beneficiary—rather than the loser—of cash management. The NOW is turning every individual customer of the bank into his own cash manager: A customer has money in the bank earning 5% until he writes a check to pay the phone bill. In the past he may have paid it as soon as he received it. But now he figures if he holds it for two weeks, he has that money for two weeks earning 5%, so the phone company can wait. And the community bank keeps the money longer. In many instances the NOW account puts some float into the hands of the community bank.

It is important to accept the fact that if the community bank is going to continue to grow, it will have to rely to a greater extent on larger-sized funds—on larger certificates, on tapping areas of the market that many community banks have not had to tap in the past.

Community banks can no longer count on consumers keeping their money in the bank for a long time. Consumers are running their money over faster and faster and the rate of savings is falling correspondingly. This means the smaller banks must get more of the mid-size business. It is interesting to note that when some New York City banks went upstate and took over small and medium-sized banks there, they thought they were going to get IBM- and Eastman Kodak-type business. However, they found that the really neglected areas were Sam's Clothing Store and the farmer who did not know what to do with all his money and needed a trust service. In other words, much of getting sizable balances is simply mobilizing the bank and going out and generating business.

A bank must start planning and looking to see where the community's money really is. It will find that a lot will come in just by paying some attention to the customer. Much can be learned from Billy Rose's answer to the question of why short fat men marry tall statuesque blondes. He replied: "They propose to them."

Getting new deposits is a major job for the community bank. Money does not stay with a bank just because it is there. Electronic banking makes it easier for people to move money elsewhere. In addition, rates are becoming super important in a Regulation Q-less environment. But plain old-fashioned marketing sense—going out and asking—is also tremendously important in getting the deposits that the banks need.

OPTION NO. 4—BANK CAPITAL

There was a time when a bank had a one-to-ten ratio—$1 of capital to $10 of deposit. But capital has become a bargaining game. The bank examiner wants more and the bank wants less so that it has more leverage. Consequently, the minimum capital a bank needs generally turns out to be the minimum it can get away with. If it can show the examiner that it is prepared for the future, more than likely the examiner will go along with the situation. One of the major complaints of community banks is that they feel that the large banks, at least until now, have gotten away with far less capital. Yet the regulators say the reason is simply that the larger banks are prepared for the future: They provide details about what they are going to do, and they have made plans to have enough capital to meet the needs of the years ahead.

The community bank often simply says it will have retained earnings. Some community banks, however, report that when they do sit down and and prepare a capital plan of how much capital they intend to generate from retained earnings, how much they intend to grow, how much they intend to pay out in dividends, and what they intend to get from external sources, the regulators are impressed and let them go with a lower capital ratio.

One solution used by a great many banks is the concept of controlled growth. One idea is to originate loans and then sell and service them. This is an effective way to keep capital needs down because if you've made the loan you've served the customer; then you sell the loan and you still service him but you don't have your capital tied up in that loan.

The sale and leaseback of the bank's building is another way to cut capital needs because the building is the least liquid asset the bank has. If the bank is rid of that building and replaces it with cash through the use of a subsidiary to borrow the money, capital needs are reduced.

If a bank doesn't require a compensating balance but asks for a decent fee instead, then the customer doesn't borrow more money than he needs. If a customer must maintain a balance, he will borrow $120,000 when he only needs $100,000, then leaves $20,000 with the bank as a balance. The bank then has to keep reserves against that deposit. This is why an increasing number of banks are looking at the concept of controlled growth. Why grow if there is no profit in it? All it does is add to capital pressures. Community banks simply must be more acute in managing their capital positions today.

OPTION NO. 5—AUTOMATION

The small bank is not at a disadvantage against a larger competitor in the field of automation, though many experts felt this would be the case when automation first came along. One reason for this is that the banks that have developed programs of EDP and EFTS and all these fancy alphabet-letter systems have been willing to sell their services to their correspondents simply to help share the cost of doing business.

Some of the biggest failures in terms of automatic funds transfers, remote teller stations, and remote collections have been where a bank tried to go it alone without having somebody else share the cost. Now, in some states, it is required by law that if a bank wants to go off-premises with any funds transfer systems it has to be shared. Also, often when inflation was high, one thing that dropped in price was the cost of moving data. Automation has come down in price, computers have come down in price, smaller minicomputers have been developed. The technology is all there for the community bank to have the same opportunities as the larger bank.

Moreover, automation is being accepted. As a result, automation gives the community bank the opportunity to follow its customers wherever they go. People borrow with their credit cards, they have automatic deposit arrangements, and they do not need to visit the bank all the time.

The key to automation remains pricing. Nobody is going to take something just because it's shiny and new. There has to be something in it for him to make it worthwhile. Consequently, banks that have said "If you want to use our automatic teller machines there will be no service charge; if you want a human to help you, that's going to cost money" have found much greater public acceptance of remote banking, of automated banking, of paperless banking.

OPTION NO. 6—TALENT

This is one area in which the community bank really stands out, despite the disadvantage in terms of salaries. Can the small bank keep the talented in a world where the major banks are paying $25,000 or $30,000 for MBAs? The answer is "yes." The graduates that go into community banking do like the feeling that they are involved in every aspect of the bank and know what is going on. Major banks also bring in and train new talent. Often, however, these new employees are dissatisfied because they are locked into specific slots in the organization and are not given the authority they want.

The president of a $2 billion bank in New Jersey once said, "I miss the old days when I ran a $3 million bank. A man would come in and want to put an extra bay in his gas station, and I helped him figure out how we could afford it. Or a widow would come in and we would work out a way for her to put her son through college. That was banking, not sitting here and looking at the computer printout."

Community banks can get the people. Many bankers have moved from major institutions to smaller banks. Many others have never left. This does not mean that a community bank can ignore the need to train. Fortunately, the banking industry has placed more emphasis on training than almost any other industry.

For more on capital for community banks, see Section 4-5 "A Matter of Capital."

A CERTAIN FUTURE

There is little that the community bank has to fear if it is meeting its options. That does not mean that all community banks are going to make it. A number of them are going to be swallowed up by the big banks, sometimes happily. Others are going to find that they are taken over because they are not viable on their own.

Government assistance is not the solution for community banks. Every one of the options discussed is available to community banks as they face their future. Every one of them is controllable by the bankers' own actions. Community banks have tremendous strengths going for them. They simply must utilize those strengths.

4-3 SPREAD MANAGEMENT

In addition to a new emphasis on pricing and costing with profit in mind, the viability and prosperity of community banks depend on the development and implementation of modern techniques of asset and liability management. This means working toward the goal of flexible rate assets and liabilities, so that the sharp swings in monetary policy and financial conditions no longer can play so important a role in determining bank profitability.

In the vast majority of banks that have had difficulties during the last few years, the difficulty has resulted from an imbalance between asset maturities and liability maturities. Consider this classic case: The bank made long-term loans and investments at then-current yields, funding them with short-term liabilities. As interest rates rose, the bank had to refund the liabilities and pay even higher rates for the deposit funds, while the long-term assets remained fixed in yield. The result—a serious squeeze on the spread, where the bank actually operates with negative operating earnings.

In such instances the bankers who faced this situation had no one to blame but themselves. They had gambled and lost.

Most lending officers report that the companies that have gotten into trouble generally have done so not in their own day-to-day operations but because of a gamble taken to augment profits. Maybe the company took on too much inventory, expecting it would go up in value, or maybe it expanded when such growth was uncalled for. But in any event, the borrower unable to repay his debts frequently must accept the fact that greed was the motive for the actions that got him into trouble.

Similarly, some bankers have felt that they could do a better job of guessing what interest rate trends would be than the average individual can. Those who thought rates would rise tried to lock in long-term liabilities. And those who thought rates would fall tried to make long-term fixed yield loans.

When their predictions turn out to be right, profits can be unusually large. But when they are incorrect, the bank is hurt. A banker has no one to blame but himself for his willingness to take risks on interest rate changes.

Most community bankers look at such situations with little sympathy, however. They feel that it is not the banker's job to gamble. What does bother them is when, in the course of normal operations, they are forced to generate an imbalance between asset and liability maturity simply because that is what their customers' needs dictate.

Just a few years ago, most community banks were locked in to long-term mortgage loans and fixed yields. At the same time, the cost of funds kept rising as the public developed an interest in the short term money market certificate. This imbalance cost the banks dearly, but it was beyond the bankers' control. Many astute community bankers have determined that this imbalance will never again be so severe, no matter what happens to the interest rate cycle, because the banks are trying to make both asset and liability yields more flexible, so that no matter what happens to interest rates, they will remain with assets whose yields reflect today's costs of funds and with liabilities of similar flexibility.

It is easier to talk about switching the public from a fixed rate mentality to a flexible-rate mentality than it is to actually do so. But it is something that should be worked at. Consequently, bankers are attempting public acceptance of flexible-rate credits and deposits. The eventual acceptance of this type of loan, something other countries have accepted for years, is inevitable.

Once this is accomplished, the key to bank profitability will be how effectively the bank manages the spread between cost of funds and returns on assets. Assets and liabilities will eventually move up and down in yield simultaneously.

STEPS TO TAKE

Some steps bankers can take to improve spread management so they are ready for the days of true asset/liability flexibility include:

Cost Control Although this is something bankers have always been concerned with, it is more important now than ever before.

Pricing Services on a Realistic Basis Good spread management means making sure that each service pays its own way.

Cash Management A bank that manages its own cash aggressively markedly enhances its profits. This involves making sure that all balances held as reserves are kept to the minimum, with excess funds placed to work. It involves monitoring cash letter fund flow to make sure that unused balances do not pile up at correspondents or in the Fed. It also involves making sure that correspondent balances are no larger than necessary to pay for services needed.

Tax Strategy The bank that does tax planning to reduce its tax liability to a minimum has far more left available for its shareholders. Taxes are part of the cost of doing business that is involved in spread management. If taxes can be held down, for example by selling depreciated bonds, they should be.

Physical Plant With increasing public acceptance of remote banking through point-of-sale terminals and automatic teller machines (ATMs) there is less and less need for branch offices to provide for public convenience. Where offices are provided, they frequently can be storefront offices, instead of far more expensive stand-alone structures. In fact, many banks report that one ATM in a hospital or a factory does more business for the bank than a beautifully decorated branch office that costs far more to construct and operate.

4-4 INCOME THROUGH DISCOUNT BROKERAGE

As deregulation changes the face of banking, one service that more and more banks appear to be offering their customers is a discount brokerage operation. It is also a service that will satisfy a real need, particularly as time goes on.

After 50 years of strict separation between banking and securities operations, the laws that separated the two are being weakened to a considerable degree. Banks that want to provide themselves with an entering wedge into all types of investment activities for their customers are looking at discount brokerage service as a good place to start. Some larger banks have established a separate discount brokerage unit. Others have bought a discount brokerage firm and operate it as a subsidiary. Most banks are utilizing the services of a broker offering discount services.

What does it actually involve? Very little. A bank can assign one or two people to take orders from customers for stocks, bonds, and other investment vehicles. The bank, in turn, simply routes the orders to an investment dealer who is willing to provide this service at a commission well below that demanded by so-called full service investment houses.

In a smaller bank, this service can even be handled on a part-time basis by one person. Yet the public is given the opportunity to have its cake and eat it too—that is, it can get the discount rates that these discount brokerage firms offer, while still doing business with the local bank and not having to route orders by phone to an impersonal order taker in some distant city. These order takers, it may be added, change with every phone call so that the transaction is as impersonal as calling up a major airline for tickets. Moreover, in many communities, this service would not be available to the public except through the bank.

Has discount brokerage been a profitable bank tool up to now?

In most banks, the answer is "no." The number of trades that have been generated by the discount brokerage operation in banks, even in the most prosperous of communities where the public is used to buying and selling stocks and where one would think that the potential for bank profit would be great has been disappointingly small. But many bankers respond that the actual commitment of resources to the operation has been small, so that even if an office only generates four or five trades a day, as some bank discount brokerage operations do, the actual loss to the bank is small. Most important, the bankers who are optimistic about the development of discount brokerage look to its potential for future income and expansion; they feel that it is worth the trouble of providing the service even though there is little income being generated at the present time.

POTENTIAL

What is the potential of discount brokerage for the typical bank? Based on the experience of the major discount brokerage operations in developing this service, the potential can be great.

According to the brokerage firm of Quick and Reilly—an original developer of the discount brokerage approach—there are two facets of importance in a discount brokerage operation that are optimistic for commercial banks: (1) it does not take too many trades to make a discount operation profitable, and (2) the public likes to do its trading near to home.

Take the first factor—the number of trades needed for profitability. Leslie Quick, Chairman of Quick and Reilly, has indicated that an office staffed with two or three people and doing only 35 trades a day can make a profit. If this data can be applied to banks, the number of trades necessary for profitability is even fewer. After all, a bank does not have to rent new space for its discount brokerage operation. It must only put one or two new desks into space already being paid for.

Can 30 or 35 trades a day be achieved? At present, this seems like a high goal when many banks report they are doing only 4 to 6 in many instances. However, most banks have not really pushed their discount brokerage operations.

The bank makes an announcement that it has a discount brokerage operation, but there is generally no effective follow up through cross-selling.

Why, for example, can't a bank try to cross-sell those customers who come and go at the safe deposit vault frequently? These obviously are people who are trading in securities, and they are top prospects for a bank brokerage service. Why can't a bank follow up on customers who have written large checks to brokerage firms, to see if the people who are dealing with these firms realize that they can get the same job done cheaper and more conveniently at home?

Is there not a great pool of retired people who have time and money to engage in securities transactions? The bank can tell which of its customers are likely to be in that category.

On the other side, banks also have an opportunity to cross-sell regular banking service to those who come in to utilize discount brokerage operations. Some banks, for example, report that as much as 45% of the usage of the discount brokerage service is by people who have had no previous relationship with the bank. This means that these are prospects for reverse cross-sell. They can be talked into using other bank services once they have come in through the entering wedge of discount brokerage.

CONVENIENCE

While the ability to develop discount brokerage profitability through acute marketing efforts provides an optimistic potential, the ability to generate business because of convenience is an even more optimistic scenario for banks. Quick and Reilly reports that 90% of the customers live within 25 miles of the office, and that even in New York City 40% of the customers have actually visited an office of the firm!

What the public is saying, then, is that it wants to feel that there can be a physical contact with the broker in case of need. And the bank that offers this opportunity for closeness, coupled with the lower commission rates that a discount brokerage operation provides, appears to offer the best of all possible worlds to the customer for brokerage service of a strict execution nature.

SERVICE

What about service? Banks are known for their service and their willingness to consult with the customer about any and all problems. In fact, many bankers report that they spend more time as therapists for their customers and staff than they spend as bankers.

Compare the typical discount brokerage operation with the typical bank relationship:

In a discount brokerage operation, the customer usually calls an 800 number, waits a long time, and then gets a clerk who says "What do you want?" The customer tells exactly what he or she wants and then hangs up. Later, some other clerk calls and confirms what took place and at what price. Consider this verbatim exchange:

"Buy me 200 General Motors," ordered the buyer.

"What's the symbol for the stock?" the broker responded.

"Isn't that your business?" the buyer replied.

"I'm new here, I won't be a veteran until Thursday," the clerk responded.

Compare this with the full service and hand-holding that a bank is generally known for.

A discount brokerage operation of a bank is, thus, a far cry from the full service counseling a banker generally provides on financial matters. One wonders how long a bank can go on telling its customers that the banker is a friend who is there for them and will help in any way, only to have to tell the customer who calls the discount brokerage section and asks advice on a stock or a trade: "I'm sorry. All I can do is to take your order. I can't give you any opinion or advice on anything."

It appears likely that discount brokerage will be broadened in the near future to include the opportunity to provide consulting service for an extra fee.

Even Quick and Reilly has recognized this void in its service package. It is planning to set up a consulting service that provides financial counseling, investment advice, and the opportunity to discuss securities and financial plans, but for a fee of several hundred dollars a year.

Think of the opportunity this could be for banks. If a bank could sell some of the time of its financial experts for a hard dollar fee, this could help cover the costs of the professionals the bank has on board, while providing the type of noncredit income that banking so needs in today's environment of deregulation.

Bankers can be true financial planners for a public that needs planning advice. Yet, today, such services are provided by a financial planning profession that runs the gamut from truly dedicated professionals to charlatans using the aegis of financial planner to sell tax shelters, tangible assets, such as gold coins, and any other vehicle that provides a generous commission to the planner—no matter its value to the investor.

Banks can provide a synergism of offering brokerage with banking in an environment of trust that truly can be what the public needs.

Discount brokerage is thus an entering wedge. It may not be too profitable today. But it serves as an advance indicator of the type of full financial service that all banks—community and large banks alike—are bound to be providing to their customers as deregulation progresses.

4-5 A MATTER OF CAPITAL

Community bankers have many concerns in today's increasingly competitive financial marketplace. None is higher on the list than the availability of capital. Capital is needed to both cushion deposit growth and provide a solid base for growth.

The capital squeeze affects many banks these days. Community banks are affected more intensely than many larger banks, largely because the bigger banks have a greater ability to tap the capital market. To be sure, when bank stocks are selling at depressed prices and few institutions have market prices that exceed book value, most banks would not be willing to sell new stock even if they could. Offering new stock when a bank's shares are selling well below book value involves penalizing present shareholders by diluting their equity positions to obtain new capital. For community banks, the choice of raising capital by diluting equity positions of present holders is generally not available since sales of new stock are difficult or impossible unless the shares are sold to present owners.

The use of debt capital is another approach to the problem of capital shortage. However, this vehicle is difficult for any bank—and particularly community banks—to use. This is because of the high interest rates that debt capital must offer to find any buyers. In addition, attractive alternative debt instruments, such as high yield bonds and new mortgage passthrough securities, are competing for the same funds that banks want placed in their debentures. On top of this, the public is being wooed into money market accounts, money market mutual funds, and savings certificates.

Thus, sale of debt capital is difficult for all banks And for community banks, with their lower profile and nonexistent or poor secondary market for subsequent resale, it is almost impossible.

The problem is intensified for community banks because they generally must keep more capital relative to deposits than larger banks have to maintain. This may not be a conscious decision on the part of the regulators. However, community bankers often complain that large institutions in major cities need one-half the amount that they do.

CAPITAL SOLUTIONS

As serious as capital problems may be, the situation is by no means hopeless. The simplest solution to the capital dilemma is for the community bank to earn so much on capital and on assets that it solves its problems through generous retention of earnings. But this solution is synonymous to the response given by the president of a prestigious university to the question of how to gain admittance into that college: "Have him choose his grandparents carefully."

Community bankers who have been successful in solving their capital problems have taken the following steps:

- They have concentrated on traditional banking and expense control. "Back to basics" has become their motto.
- They are pricing aggressively, and have determined that they can no longer give local customers below-rate loans and free service just because these people have known the bankers for years. If an account is not profitable, the bank has simply raised the fees and told the customer that this is the way it is going to be. If the customer responds by moving the account across the street, the banker is unhappy. But he is less unhappy than he would be keeping an account that deflates the bank's bottom line and its ability to generate new retained earnings to solve its capital dilemma.
- They are trying to reduce their need for capital by giving the bank the opportunity to provide the same service and earn the same income but with a smaller base of deposits.

The last step requires further clarification. Growth in deposits necessitates growth in capital. Thus, many community banks are turning from requiring payment with balances to full payment with fees for loans and services provided. If the balances simply mean that the bank must generate more capital to back the rising balances, then why generate them? It is far better to be paid in fees and avoid this unnecessary growth in deposits.

REGULATORY REQUIREMENTS

The reason regulatories frequently allow the larger bank to operate with lower capital is because the larger bank has explained to the regulators how liquid the bank is, where new capital is coming from, and how well-positioned the bank is to provide the protection for deposit growth that will be necessary to maintain standards of safety and prudence. The community bank that has plans for internal capital generation, that can show its regulator that its deposits and assets are diversified so it is not subject to risks in poor business cycle conditions, and that has a reasonable, healthy game plan for its balance sheet changes can frequently win the regulator over to a more lenient attitude with regard to the bank's capital needs.

Without question, this is an excellent—and often the best—approach to the capital dilemma. And it is an approach that community banks can utilize just as well as larger banks can.

GENERATING DEPOSITS

In today's banking environment, getting the right type of deposits in the right quantities is essential for a community bank. This situation requires considerable attention because it is a fact of banking life that noninterest bearing demand deposits will be strictly limited in quantity in the years ahead.

There was a time when banks could rely on this free money as the basic source of lendable funds. After all, there was little else the public could do with its resources. Consequently, money was kept in the bank out of lack of alternatives. Now, however, there are extremely attractive alternative outlets both inside and outside the banks. Community banks, as well as every other banking institution, sees that individuals, corporations, municipalities, and every other type of depositor works hard at cash management, that is, they are trying to make their funds work and earn a return instead of sitting idly in a demand deposit.

Most banks now realize that their future depends upon time and savings deposits. While time and savings deposits are less attractive than demand deposits, they are far more attractive than the other possibility—no deposits.

Community banks must follow the same rules the larger banks follow in order to generate needed deposits. They must offer competitive rates on large deposits and on consumer deposits; they must solicit business by going to the corporations and other large depositors who are utilizing major city institutions almost exclusively and explain the value of using the community bank for a portion of their funds. By supporting local institutions, the companies will help the local economy. Most important, they must place the onus for meeting the cost of this aggressive competition for large- and medium-sized certificate funds squarely on the person these funds are attracted for: the borrower. In essence, then, the days when the community bank could afford to be a low cost lender to its community are over if the banks want the funds their customers need.

5 Technology and Banking

5-1 THE HUMAN SIDE OF ELECTRONIC BANKING

The banking industry has widely accepted the use of electronic funds transfer services (EFTS). The high cost of labor—including higher social security requirements, higher minimum wage levels, rising fringe benefits, and just plain higher salaries—has forced the banking industry to trim the labor component of overall costs even further than it already has. The electronic movement of funds, through automatic deposits (e.g. payrolls, dividends, social security checks, and other fund inputs) and automatic movement of funds out of banks without using a paper check, are mandatory for this labor cost-cutting operation.

As bankers look upon the need for greater acceptance of EFTS, with its automatic deposit of funds, debit cards, telephonic money transfer, and automatic payment of bills for the depositor, the industry finds that the basic problems of getting to a more automated state are not technical. They involve the human side of banking instead.

Customer resistance to the newer techniques of banking has been the number one roadblock to greater reliance on more efficient banking techniques. Overcoming this customer resistance is claiming the attention of more and more bankers. Based on recent studies, it would appear that these efforts are paying off.

PRICING

Pricing of bank services can do a great deal to overcome the public's reluctance to change.

People like things the way they were in the past, and they must be given an awfully good reason for changing tradition and moving on to something new.

Banks are finding that gaining public acceptance of change can be given considerable impetus by a pricing approach that rewards depositors willing to accept the new techniques and penalizes those sticking to tradition. For example, with bank costs of as much as 52 cents to clear one check from beginning to end, some leading edge banks are beginning to price their services to encourage the public to turn away from the check. If an individual wants to use the traditional check, there is a rather substantial bank service charge on each item deposited or withdrawn. But if the individual is willing to use automatic deposit and withdrawal mechanisms that do not involve a paper trail and all its inherent costs, the bank is willing to cut the service charge markedly or eliminate it altogether.

Pricing is the best weapon available to banking as it fights to make its delivery services for the customer more efficient than they have been in the past.

HANDLING FEARS

However, pricing is not the total answer to gaining acceptance of EFTS in America today. There are many public fears of the changes that banks are proposing. These fears must be overcome before people will be willing to go along with more efficient banking. No matter how much the bank tries to entice the public over to automatic deposit and withdrawal through its pricing mechanisms, if the public is afraid of what EFTS means, there is no price differential that will do the job.

Psychological studies have shown that when the machine misfunctions or does not work at all, the individual frequently feels it is a personal affront to him or her, and that somehow the bank is doing it only against this individual depositor.

While this may seem far-fetched, banks have found that when they install two automatic teller machines in the same location rather than just one, the public is much happier. The chance of both machines going down at once is far less than the chance of a single machine not working.

Banks have also found that people dislike the feeling that someone is looking over their shoulders as they do their banking business with the machine. This is why a few banks are providing a sliding shield that closes like a voting booth, so that the individual engaged in a transaction with the machine has more privacy.

One of the most serious oppositions to automated banking is the fear that many people have that if they accept automatic deposit of paychecks, social security checks and other deposit items, the money will not be in the bank when they expect it to be. If an individual makes his own deposit, he knows when the money is in the bank. He is sure that when he does write checks against this money, they will not be returned for insufficient funds.

All too often, individuals have heard of others who have had their checks bounced because of a delay in the receipt of the tape or check from the employer making the automatic deposit, or because the social security money did not reach the bank on time.

In answer, banks must be able to guarantee that the funds will be available at a specific time each week or month, whether the check or tape from the depositor has arrived or not. It may cost the bank a small amount from time to time in having checks clear on funds not yet received, but the saving in cost of handling the accounts that automatic deposit of funds allows far more than makes up for any infrequent costs involved.

STOP PAYMENTS

Similarly, the public does not want to lose control over the account.

As banking is now constituted, an individual can stop payment on a check and has the option of paying or not paying a bill that comes to him, depending upon whether he feels the bill is justified.

Under a system of automatic bill paying, the public must still have the op-poortunity to control the account.

Some banks have solved this by the simple technique of allowing a reversal of any transaction for a certain time period after it is recorded. Others have taken the more expensive route of giving advance notification that an item will be debited to the account in a certain amount of time unless objection is announced.

PRIVACY

The privacy issue is another area where banks have had to face problems of gaining public acceptance.

Everyone recognizes the fear of the "big brother" aspect of automated data flow, and many people honestly worry that some giant computer is gathering up all the information on them that flows through the bank, with the ultimate recipient being either the Internal Revenue Service (IRS) or some other equally displeasing authority. Also, a customer who does not want other members of his own family to know too much about his financial affairs may think that is just what will happen if paychecks are deposited automatically, instead of cashing the paycheck himself and allocating the money as he pleases. Bankers must make every effort to insure that privacy will be the same under EFTS as formerly.

In regard to privacy, the banks have one thing going for them. This is the anonymous nature of borrowing transactions done by overdrawing an account. Instead of the potential embarrassment of having to tell a bank employee that the customer wants money, a customer can simply use his credit card, once a line of credit has been established.

EVIDENCE OF PAYMENT

Another factor that inhibits acceptance of electronic banking is the fear of lack of evidence of payment made. To a large extent, this is the banking industry's own fault.

For years, banks have advertised checking accounts by pointing out the benefit of having a check as a receipt of payment. Now, the same banks are trying to tell the public that no receipt is necessary and that automated movement of funds can do the job just as well. Banking will have a lot of reverse selling to do in this area before it can get its new approach across.

Happily, the institutions, largely credit unions, that have given up return of cancelled checks, find that the IRS and others are becoming more accommodative in accepting the carbon of the draft and the bank statement as evidence of payment made instead of demanding a cancelled voucher.

Finally, there is the issue of float time that is eliminated with automatic funds transfer. An individual who is accustomed to playing the float and writing checks several days before he places the money in the bank to cover them is not anxious to switch over to a debit card that moves the money out of his account the very day or minute he spends it.

Again, it is up to the bank to price its services so attractively that the customer finds the loss of float is worth it in terms of either service charges foregone or added interest earned on the funds actually kept in the bank.

5-2 SHARING TECHNOLOGY AND SERVICES

Banking has long been an industry in which the various members have been willing to share ideas with one another. This is rather rare in the business world. In fact, outsiders are frequently amazed at the willingness with which bamkers have let other bankers know the results of the work they have spent many years perfecting.

Perhaps this has come about because banking has had to share credit information to avoid a deadbeat from moving from one bank to another after he has damaged the position of the first institution. Be this as it may, the industry has developed a closeness of communication that has helped each individual bank avoid the problem of reinventing the wheel when another bank—even its close rival across the street—has taken the time, effort, and expense to solve a problem that is generic to the entire industry.

While bankers have been willing to share ideas, however, there is a much greater hesitation when it comes to sharing the operation of a facility that might save both or all the institutions a good deal of money if it were jointly operated.

This has become quite evident in recent years as technology exploded upon the banking scene. Many bankers readily admit that they could have saved a small fortune if two or more banks had gotten together to run a joint paper processing operation instead of having each bank own its own computer and handle its own transit and proof operation independently. The governmental agencies that regulate banks have allowed the banking industry to own stock of cooperative computer operations. This is a basic exception to the rule that banks cannot own equities in their own right. However, even this aid in the development of shared computer facilities has not done much to build a trend toward joint operations.

Some have held that the reason banks have opposed joint operation is the fear that another bank will learn too much about the other's customers and ways of doing business. There is a fear that the bank across the street will start with a joint operation, and then use the data it gains to raid its rival's customers.

Other banks take the attitude that "I want what I want when I want it." Therefore, they are not willing to join a joint venture for fear that their checks would have to wait at deadline time if another bank's material was being processed.

Whether for these or other reasons, the joint use of computers has not progressed too far in the industry.

However, with EFTS, remote terminals, and all of the other technological developments that EFTS has brought, there is even more reason for bankers to share. There is growing recognition by most bankers that the industry will not be able to cover the full cost of Point of Sale (POS) networks and remote ATMs unless each bank gives up the opportunity to go it alone and joins in a cooperative to share hardware, software, and line costs.

Yet here again there is a fear of joint operations.

Maybe the problem stems from the very nature of how cooperative ventures function. Every banker who has ever been in a committee with representatives of other banks realizes that matters cannot run that smoothly. Each bank's representative feels that he or she is not being useful unless he makes a suggestion on some area of the proceedings.

The result is that what might be a smooth venture is turned into one of lengthy compromise—simply because each banker feels that his bank must be represented in the final decision in some concrete way. The truth is that the best contribution the individual bank can make is to concur in the basic discussion and help it move smoothly toward the ultimate conclusion as rapidly as possible.

Sharing EFTS proposals, unfortunately, has met with this kind of opposition. This is a shame. If anything is clear in American banking today, it is that EFTS is already a part of the banking structure. Anything that can be done to reconcile the high cost of this change with our unique mixture of large and small banks is all to the good. One ray of hope is the trend toward ATM networks (see the next chapter). This is a good sign. The sharing of ideas and sharing of procedures should remain a part of our banking pattern.

5-3 CHOOSING AN ATM NETWORK

In response to competitive situations, bankers too often make quick decisions that have far deeper implications than they expect.

Giving away credit card service was one such decision—a number of banks found out that once they gave out credit cards which offered up to a two months' interest-free loan on every purchase, it was difficult indeed to get the public to give this up.

Similarly, the offering of the Negotiable Order of Withdrawal (NOW) account as a replacement for the interest-free checking account without asking the public to provide something (i.e., a fee) to the bank in return was another lost opportunity.

There was a time when banks could have persuaded the public to give up the return of the cancelled check as part of the price for interest on checking accounts. It will be far more difficult to achieve this goal of voucherless banking when the bank has no plum to offer the public as an inducement to give up the vouchers.

Now, an even more important decision is being made that could determine a bank's position in its community for years ahead: whether or not to join an automated teller machine network, and, if so, which one to join.

Again, banks are too often making this decision without thinking through the full implication of what it means when they choose which banks to join if they go into this network endeavor.

INDIVIDUAL IDENTIFICATION

One point is clear to many bankers—the ATM network they join has to give them individual identification in their own communities. If a bank joins a network that includes the competition across the street and the thrift down the block, then there are no locational advantages over any other institution. What good goes it do to set up an ATM in a great location when the competition's customers can uses the same ATM for their banking business?

Thus, unlike Visa and Master Card, in which the product of every bank is essentially like that of every other in the card group, many banks want to be in ATM networks that give them exclusive rights in the community. This is where trouble can start. A bank may join an ATM network because it offers an exclusive franchise and the exclusive opportunity in town for its customers to use the ATMs of the other member banks of the group throughout the nation. But once it joins such a group, it is almost impossible to disconnect.

First, the customers have been trained that their cards are good at a specific number of locations around the state or the nation. It is a terrible marketing decision to retract such a feature once it has been promoted.

Second, banks that join networks may find that they will be increasingly bound to these networks by common computer software and procedures. As a result, switching from one network to another becomes ever more expensive.

Joining a network involves accepting the approaches of that network's leaders in a number of areas—notably choice of system for point-of-sale terminals, banking in the home, automated clearing house decision, and a host of other decisions regarding automated banking.

In essence, banking is slowly becoming more of an electronic delivery system and less the local brick-and-mortar institution. The choice of an ATM partner may be made in haste, in order to meet the competition. In many ways, however, it is like a marriage that forces the joining banks to go down the road with the other banks in far more ways than just choice of ATM equipment and locations.

Decisions on whom ATM partners will be may well be the most important decision that today's management makes in terms of long range implications for their banks. It certainly deserves exploration of every aspect before being made.

5-4 THE NEED FOR TECHNICAL KNOWLEDGE

With the computer playing so important a role in our lives and in the operations of a bank, the day is quickly passing when a senior bank officer can function effectively without some knowledge of how to use this data processing miracle. We are increasingly finding that information we want and need immediately is readily available if we are able to handle a cathode ray tube. But that information is hidden from us if we must wait for a computer printout.

Happily, most top bank officers have come a long way from those not-so-long-ago days when they felt it beneath their dignity to even look at computer-generated data. (Several operations officers have indicated that until recently they had to take computer printouts and have someone type them up in the old style or even, in one case, hand write them on yellow pads, before the CEO would accept the data and utilize it.)

But now matters are going even further. Many bankers are proud of the CRTs on their desks, and they are often eager to show off their ability to punch up immediate data on the total relationship with a customer or the liquidity position of the bank. With a million dollars often earning as much as $500 per night, this ability to know a bank's position and utilize the funds instantly becomes a valuable asset whose lack can be expensive to a bank.

Fortunately, it is not likely to reach the point of the recent movie on international banking, *Rollover*, in which the hero, upon sneaking into the competing bank president's office, uses his knowledge of computers to break the code and find the disposition of balances that had been transferred from his own bank. But it certainly helps to have some "hands on" knowledge of computer utilization.

NOT BEING SNOWED

One of the major values of computer knowledge is to help the CEO or other senior officer make sure he or she is not being hoodwinked by the staff into having more equipment or more programs operational than is necessary.

There is a real "cover your rear" syndrome in most business decisions. The uninitiated in the world of data processing can often be talked into expenditures that are unnecessary simply out of ignorance and a fear that if the purchase is not made or the program is not developed, that executive will be criticized later for his failure to act. Knowledge of what is actually going on can frequently lead a banker to conclude that this program is really "The Emperor's New Clothes," and an expensive way of generating data that is either readily available in a cheaper form or is not needed at all.

Consider the company that had a rather simple financial structure. There were two hooks on the wall next to the president's desk. Over one hook was the sign: MONEY IN: over the other hook, the sign read: MONEY OUT. All paper was put on one of the two hooks.

After an exhaustive study by a consultant with extensive computer knowledge, this expensive concluding report was issued:

> This company should use two hooks—
> One for MONEY IN and one for MONEY OUT.

Without an honest consultant, think how complicated the company's book might have been.

Knowledge of computers can sometimes serve as a splendid defensive weapon; or to make sure that when he looks back, the banker does not have to say, "At least if I can do nothing else, I can always serve as a horrible example."

TOO MUCH INFORMATION?

While the chief executive officer can use some knowledge of computers, there is a question as to whether top managers are given so much information to digest that they cannot handle it, whether it is provided on yellow pads or on screens.

Richard Watt, senior vice president at United Banks Service Co., part of United Banks of Colorado, has commented that management information systems today offer too much information and not enough management. Calling this "information overload," Mr. Watt explains what his company has done to decrease that load for its bank executives:

> We are doing a couple of things which might be of interest. One is that we are striking out in the direction of presenting information in graphical form. We are finding that the Chinese proverb, "a picture is worth a thousand words," also applies to numbers. Therefore, we are presenting more information in graphical form, in order that managers, CEOs, and boards of directors can "see" the information we are presenting to them.
>
> A second approach we are taking is to create an information center. We are finding that only a relatively few managers have the types of analytical training that would permit them to directly access the mounds of data that most computers can produce in the flick of an eye.
>
> The information center is a place where users within the banks can call, describe their information needs, and where they are not met by existing reports, and the center will provide the information to the users, often within hours or days.
>
> A third approach we are experimenting with is to have various managers recommend to their immediate superiors information which they think their bosses ought to receive. We are starting with the current reports they now receive to see if we cannot cut back on those in terms of volumes, level of summarization, and graphical presentations.

Still, a top bank manager must know something about the capabilities of the technological wonders at work in his bank. And there is one thing about all the information now at their fingertips, no matter how overwhelming it might be—it's better than not enough information.

PART 3 The Human Side of Banking

The most important resource of any bank is its people. In many banking institutions, unfortunately, the resources are not all that plentiful. In others, however, there is a growing awareness that people can and do make a significant difference in organizations that are often essentially the same.

In addition, there is increasing acceptance of the principle that the personnel of a bank must be selected with care, given adequate training, and moved along to higher positions as their performance—and openings—warrant. This was not always the case, but it is happening in the majority of banks today.

Then there is the matter of management. Every financial institution must be managed; it is the degree or quality of management that can make a difference. Sad to say, the banking industry has not always been known as a bastion of brilliant management. It isn't that banks have been poorly managed so much as that they all too often have been inadequately or ineffectively managed.

This, too, is changing—and just in the nick of time. If ever an industry needed good management, it is banking in the mid-1980s. The turbulence in the financial markets virtually demands that a banking institution have a capable and savvy management team to navigate it through these stormy times.

6 People in Banking

6-1 WHAT IT TAKES TO BE A SUCCESSFUL BANKER

Banking has undergone a major revolution in its attitude toward trained personnel in the past twenty years or so. There has been a switch from the attitude that an outside education is not necessary for bank employment; today, banks are one of the more significant hirers of the graduates of our nation's business schools.

It is easy to understand the older banking attitude on a number of grounds. After all, most top bank officers of the last generation, and perhaps still a majority of today's chief executive officers, never went to college or at least never graduated.

The typical career path of a top officer of the typical American bank began by his being hired by the bank right out of high school. This was followed by many years of on-the-job training in all areas of the bank. Finally, those individuals with the best minds and/or the best ability to judge people became top officers.

The ability to make loans and get the bank's money back was the key responsibility of a CEO. It was generally thought that there was little or no correlation between formal training and the credit judgment that a top banker had to have. A good bank president generally could tell you the financial position and trustworthiness of most of his customers without looking at a single file of credit information. It was the ability to say "yes" or "no" on the spot with a high batting average of successful loans that made the top manager of the bank succeed.

This slowly began to change after World War II. More and more banks began to look to college graduates as potential candidates for the training in the bank. The reason was not that banking had become more complicated and the need for academic skills had become greater. Rather, the reason for the turn to college graduates was simply that opportunities for education in the United States had broadened. The individual who found it necessary to go to work right out of high school, and went right into the bank, was no longer typical in the late 1940s and 1950s.

The GI Bill, scholarships, tuition aid, job opportunities for students, the vast expansion of state schools, and a variety of other programs made it possible for most young people who had enough motivation to get a college education to find a way to finance it. The result was that the person who looked for work in a bank right out of high school was less likely to be the type who had the drive to get to the top. Thus, more and more banks decided they would have to hire college graduates if they wanted good potential officer material.

Time passed, and banks had to go a step further and start looking at graduates of graduate business schools and others with post-graduate training. Frequently, the best people were going for advanced training, and, if the bank wanted the best, it had to wait until they had the advanced degree, and then pay that much more for their services because of this added training. This practice was sometimes overdone. Many bankers report the disappointment they experienced in hiring the MBAs who had been trained by their universities to be top managers—but not necessarily to do the work to get to the top.

Be this as it may, banking is now at the top of those industries that hire graduate students and place them on a rapid track to the top.

TWO VIEWS

Has banking made a mistake? It is hard to tell at this juncture. Some traditional bankers look at what the new breed of MBAs has done to the industry and wonder if their textbook knowledge was actually a drawback. They see a banking industry that left the fundamentals of taking deposits and making loans and tried to move into a diversity of other services through the development of holding companies. They see an industry that is increasingly relying on technological devices that require specific technical training.

Similarly, new techniques such as liability management, under which many bankers felt they had no limits on how much they could obtain in the way of lendable funds if they would only pay the going rate for money, have left many traditional bankers shaking their heads. It was the high price paid for funds that had already been loaned out, and the difficulties of obtaining short-term funds at any price on occasion, that has caused trouble for many banks. The traditional bankers often observe that it was a failure to follow the banking basics that had been passed on from generation to generation, and their replacement with new techniques that looked good on paper but could not stand the test of the marketplace, that put so many banks into difficulty.

Others have responded that this is too strong a criticism. They indicate that banking is a far more complicated game than in the past. Handling routine data processing operations, making loans that involve complex computerized analyses of borrowers' positions, and a myriad of other banking areas now involve the use of skills that simply cannot be passed on from generation to generation of bankers.

They admit that some bankers became overwhelmed with their ideas of how much a bank could accomplish through diversification and techniques like liability management. Even so, they feel that it's impossible for banking to provide the complicated services and credits that today's customers need without a skilled staff of top officers who have had training of the highest level available today.

There is another, slightly different point that must be made. The job of the banker is a highly social one. He must mingle with his customers and understand them socially as well as in the office. If the bank contact officer does not have the training, background, and skills borrowers have developed in the past few years, he will be outclassed both professionally and socially. The business borrower who is highly trained and understands the social implications of credit, computer applications, and other complex issues does not want to talk business with a banker who is not trained in, and does not understand, these areas, even if the banker may be able to do an adequate job of lending and handling the task without such training.

The days when bankers could say in all honesty, "We don't hire college graduates, they just cause trouble" are certainly over for most institutions.

THE OUTLOOK TODAY

As banking tries to cut costs and remain competitive in a highly intense financial climate, we are apt to see a greater selection process develop. To fill jobs at the top, more and more highly-trained people will be hired who can see all sides of many academic, social, and economic issues, and hold their own in any circles in discussing and acting on these questions.

Yet, an increasing number of banking jobs are going to have to be middle-level jobs that will not need as much training. To hire people for these jobs who are overtrained for what they will have to do leads to unhappiness in the bank and higher compensation costs than are necessary.

Along with this, banks will continue to automate routine functions. This means that the numbers of middle management people now needed to supervise the staffs will be decreased. Middle-level bankers more likely than not will have jobs of public contact rather than management of other people who in turn have the contact with the public as we see now. And these people need more of an understanding of their communities and the problems that typical bank customers face than they need academic training.

Finally, the banking industry has its own training programs that are second to none. Frequently banks find that people who receive their academic training at night while in the bank's employ are more loyal and gain more relevant education than when they have their training before. This is especially true when the bank recognizes the effort the students are putting in and rewards them accordingly with promotions once they graduate. Thus, more and more bankers are looking at local universities, American Institute of Banking (AIB), and banking schools as a valuable resource that helps bridge the gap between having overtrained people and having middle-level staffs who cannot handle the complex issues that have entered today's banking world.

6-2 CARE AND FEEDING OF THE COLLEGE GRADUATE

Increasingly, banks are looking to college graduates and to holders of MBAs and other advanced degrees as their principal sources of talent for movement up the ranks. These highly educated individuals are also impatient to move up the ladder and frequently are unhappy with doing the routine tasks that must be handled.

As banks look to these educated people for their fast-track trainees, bank employees who have worked up from the bottom feel neglected. Some of them fight back by getting a college degree at night. Smarter bank executives realize that the potential of people who have this type of drive is just as good as that of people who came to the bank with their degrees already in hand.

Other employees just give up and assume that because they did not have the educational opportunities of the new trainees, they will be passed by throughout their entire careers. Many slink down into the state of complacency that such expectations can cause. They prepare themselves, not for 40 years' experience, but one year's experience 40 times. They rightly feel that the fast-track people are taking the opportunities that used to be theirs.

Be they BAs, BSs, MBAs, MSs, or whatever, banks now recognize that the basic core of future officer material is college graduates. However, bankers are also finding that not all those with degrees are winners. People have different views of what they want from a job and what they are willing to put into it, no matter how much education they have received.

One of the first observations reached by many banks is that potential employees can be separated into A personalities and B personalities.

THE "A" TYPE

The A personality is a go-getter. He or she wants to make it to the top and will work conscientiously and continuously to do so. This is the kind of person who demands a great deal of both himself and his employer. The person feels that he has been trained to make decisions. and he wants the salary, responsibility, and titles fast—or he will move to where he can get them.

Such an individual can be both a blessing and curse. He can be a source of ideas and inspiration for other staff members; at the same time, his strong, aggressive personality may grate on some people.

The greatest drawback of these A personality types, however, is that frequently they do not like doing the details that contribute toward the proper functioning of a bank. The CEOs and top officers who worked themselves up from the bottom recognize the importance of controlling paper flow, handling differences between employees, keeping track of customer waiting time, and the host of other little details that can make or break a bank. They realize that one smiling teller or one little courtesy can do more than a major difference in price of services to keep some customers loyal to the bank.

Unfortunately, some of the new fast-track college graduates look upon these details as beneath them; they want to concentrate on the "big picture." This is where they often get into trouble. When it comes time to become a top officer, the individuals who understand the details and the personnel problems usually make far better senior executives than do those who feel that such concerns are not worthy of their attention.

Some companies, such as IBM, have handled this problem by forcing everyone to spend time handling the details in a staff position before he or she moves up toward the top.

A number of banks, in their own way, are also trying to temper the aggressiveness of their fast-track employees so that they, too, understand the importance of the routine bank work and what it means to the overall functioning of the organization.

THE "B" TYPE

The B personalities present another type of problem. These are individuals who have been educated and who, in many instances, even have MBA degrees. But they have received this education, not because of unusual drive but because, as indicated earlier, so many people have an opportunity to get a college degree today.

However, The B people are willing to put in their eight hours a day and little more. They consider their free time far more important than their work time. At the same time they expect to follow a slow, steady, upward path just by being there, doing their job, and keeping their noses clean.

Handling such people can be difficult. Frequently, they expect promotions that A personalities deserve, without providing the bank with the value that justifies these promotions. Top management must explain to B personalities that they cannot have it both ways—they can either serve in capacities that do not require tremendous drive, or they can exert the kind of effort that merits promotion to top positions.

Just because an individual has a college degree, then, is not a passport to the top in banking or any other endeavor. This fact of corporate life should be made clear.

OUTSIDE AND INSIDE PEOPLE

Another problem that banks face in utilizing college graduates is that some of them want to become "outside people," while others want to be "inside people."

Outside people are the sales types. They like to go out and call on others, with a pocket full of change to call back to the bank to find out what is happening at home base. Inside people like a routine that is fairly steady. They come to the same place every day. They work in the same environment.

A bank should make sure that it is placing its new hirees in the jobs that match their personalities. An individual who likes selling and customer contact should not be placed in a computer room or at a desk handling credit analysis. If he is, he is likely to leave and waste all the bank's time and effort in training him. Conversely, an introvert sent out on business development calls is likely to keep the bank from moving ahead and may do damage.

The problem of separating the outside from the inside people involves more than just typing them so they have the proper job climate. It also involves rewarding people based on their worth in the bank and to the bank, rather than by the standards that the public sees.

One of the most difficult jobs a bank has is to keep people happy in the operations area, when they see that the outside people who go out and make the loans are rewarded with titles and money, while they stay in the background keeping the bank functioning. As one top CEO of a multi-billion-dollar bank put it: "Anyone can put on a dark blue suit and go out to lend money to one of the Fortune 500 companies. What I need are people who can keep the computer room humming and the paper flowing no matter what happens inside the bank."

An increasing number of banks are recognizing inside people with faster promotions and more money. In addition, they are posting salary ranges and providing other techniques that indicate to these inside people they are not being neglected. As a result, some insiders are beginning to realize that even though the loan officer may be given his title early so that he has more stature when he goes out to represent the bank, when it comes to the basic rewards of money and responsibility, the insiders are appreciated as much or more. Some banks are also becoming more generous with titles for insiders who handle operations and other staff functions. This lessens or eliminates the jealousy of contact officers whose promotions have always had to come rapidly for stature purposes.

NO MORE JOB SECURITY

Another change that is taking place in banking is the elimination of job security. Banking used to be an industry that did not fire anyone. Once the initial trial period was over, people could stay with the bank for the rest of their lives if they just kept out of trouble and did their jobs with a modicum of efficiency. This is no longer the case.

Banks are becoming increasingly willing to fire people who do not pull their load, even if these people have been on board for many years. Interestingly, banks find that they gain in several ways by firing people who are not doing their share. First, the bank no longer has the high cost of keeping people who are not doing their fair share of the work. Second, it finds that those who were not fired work harder and are happier, especially when the right people are fired. There is nothing so damaging to an individual's morale than to see someone goofing off and still enjoying the same promotions and raises. After a while, the hard worker decides it is not worth the effort if the slacker is treated the same way as he. There is a definite morale boost among those who are not fired when judicious firing takes place. They feel they are appreciated as good employees and their efficiency goes up.

In fact, some banks have found that by working people to the utmost, and firing those who cannot or do not want to keep up, they solve a number of problems:

- The deadwood weeds itself out.
- People start to earn their keep early in their careers, so the bank does not have the expensive process of training people for years in the hope that they will stay with the bank after they have received this costly training.
- By working people hard from the beginning, and then letting them go later if necessary, the bank can afford to hire people with potential who might

not stay on board. This gives the bank the opportunity to hire job-hoppers, people who often add a great deal to the bank with innovative ideas while they are employed, but who then get bored and decide to move on. Their departure may be regretted, but it isn't all that expensive to the bank.

- This procedure also gives banks more reason to end their former prejudices against women in officer ranks. Banks once would not consider women for promotion because they felt that after they were trained, they might leave to have a family. The bank would have wasted its expensive training. Now, however, if women also are worked as hard as possible while in training, banks can accept the fact that some of them may leave to have families, without feeling that they have been taken advantage of. These women, like the job-hoppers mentioned above, will have earned their full keep while on board.

  By itself, this is extremely valuable. Traditionally, two-thirds of bank employees are women and one-third are men. Most banks have tried to get the vast bulk of their mangerial talent from the one-third.)

Salary Aspects

There is another aspect of this policy that must not be ignored. If banks are going to work their people hard and let them go when they no longer are useful, banks cannot have it their way on salaries. Banking has traditionally paid less than other industries. This was accepted because people knew they had tenure once they had been employed for a certain amount of time. However, if banks are no more secure as places of employment than other industries and professions, then banks have to provide competitive salaries.

Also, with the growing complexity of banking, more people are moving from other fields to banking and from banking to other fields. They have discovered that the talents required to handle the paper flow in banking are little different from those needed to handle any other production process. Consequently, the mystique of banking has been removed—and it is another reason why bank salaries must be competitive.

EMPHASIS ON TRAINING

Since banks are relying to a greater extent upon college graduates as the backbone of their officer staffs and officer potential, the problem of training must be resolved.

In the past, when employees started at the bottom, on-the-job training was adequate for most individuals. "Following Furbisher on his daily rounds for months" was a good, albeit slow, way to learn. Now, however, banks cannot afford this approach. Furbisher has his own job to do, so the time he can devote to training is at a minimum, and he frequently resents taking the time to train new employees when he can do the job far more quickly alone. As a result, many college graduates who are involved in on-the-job training report that they feel they are neglected. Some find themselves doing routine, repetitive tasks like microfilming checks because no one wants to take the time to train them properly.

This is a sure way to lose good potential officer material.

A bank must have a formal training program if it wants to attract and keep good people. And the training of new employees must be considered to be as important a job to the people doing the training as is the carrying out of their own day-to-day functions. On top of this, a bank that wants its college graduates to learn banking must also give them responsibilities—even if it hurts the bank.

Top bankers report that time and again they have sat back and watched a trainee make a mistake that costs the bank good money, when an experienced employee would have halted the process in a minute. However, they felt that if the trainee has the opportunity to see the consequences of his mistakes, he will never make such a mistake again. (More on training will be found in the next two sections.)

THE MOBILE EMPLOYEE

What about the problem of losing good people once the bank has trained them and allowed them to make the costly mistakes that a good training process involves? What can a bank do to make sure that it does not serve as the educational institution for people who will work later on in other competitive banks in the same town or elsewhere in the country?

There was a time when tradition dictated that no employee once trained, would leave. Even in the 1960s, shock waves reverberated through many banks when an experienced officer left for another opportunity in another community. The idea of a banker leaving and going to a bank across the street was unthinkable. This, too, is no longer true.

Bank mobility is as great as the mobility of people in all other business fields. There are several responses that acute bankers give to this problem of mobility:

- There should be no reason to lose good people if the bank has treated them well, given them responsibility, and paid them adequately. If these people do leave, the bankers hold, it may well not be the bank's fault.

- If banks recruit at home, from those who know the community because they were raised there or went to college there, they are likely to get people who will not leave just because they want a better climate or a different geographical surrounding. Recruiting at home also helps make sure that the bank does not lose people for reasons it cannot control.
- Banks also feel that if they have worked their trainees properly, and have tried to get their value out of them from the beginning, then the loss of employees is not so hard to take. They will be losing people who have pulled their own weight or worked adequately while on the bank's staff.
- Some banks have developed teams to cover accounts, so that the customer feels loyalty to the bank and its team, rather than to the individual employee. Many bankers have left one bank and gone to another because they thought they were so good that they could bring the accounts with them. To their sorrow, they found that it was the bank's strength that attracted the customers, not their personal skills as bankers. Team handling of accounts can help ensure that the customers recognize where the bank's skills and talents lie.

A good banker does not worry about loss of talent. If the bank is really doing its job, it will not lose good people unless there is a reason. The banker also feels that the bank is better off without an unhappy employee whose heart is elsewhere.

6-3 THE TRAINING PERSPECTIVE

One of the facets that makes banking unique in American business is the tremendous amount of time and expense devoted to training.

There are various banking schools, ranging from the numerous chapters of the American Institute of Banking to graduate schools such as Stonier. Any banker who has not furthered his or her education cannot plead that there was no opportunity for growth.

The most important of the educational opportunities, in terms of impact on the industry, however, are the training programs that many major banks have for new employees who are considered to have fast-track potential. Bank training programs make the careers of employees who are lucky enough to be accepted to them. Throughout the nation, the top officers of many large and small banks are people who have been trained at banks is in New York, Chicago, Philadelphia, San Francisco, and other major city institutions.

In fact, the advice that banking instructors often give to their students is this: "If a bank has a regular intensive training program, and you have been accepted for it, grab the job no matter what the salary. You will get invaluable experience. But if the bank says, 'You will work with Gridley, who has 30 years experience in banking,' watch out. For Gridley usually doesn't want to be bothered training you. And even if he does, he may be a far better banker than he is a trainer of other bankers."

Unfortunately, banks that run intensive training programs have a major worry: the loyalty of the people they have trained.

TRAINEE LOYALTY

All too often, a bank will train a bright new empoloyee, at a cost of well over $40,00 or $50,000 by the time salaries, fringes, and training are added up, before the bank gets a day's work from the individual. If he or she soon leaves for another bank or institution—giving that other outfit the benefit of the first bank's efforts—the training institution loses out.

This is not a minor problem. Some banks find it far easier to hire from other institutions than to train people themselves. Frequently one visits a bank whose staff is bright, well-trained, experienced, and raring to build that organization. After questioning, it turns out that most of them have come on board from some other institution within the past few years.

When questioned on this topic, some training officers of major banks are complacent. They say that even though part of their training classes leave the bank, they remain friends of the bank that trained them, and the students often bring the bank business. In addition, a great many bank CEOs throughout the nation who were trained in city institutions use the bank that trained them as their major correspondent.

Some banks that train people feel that if their own bank cannot challenge this new talent as well as some other bank might and reward them as well, then their own bank deserves to lose the people it has trained.

TRAINING THEORY AND PRACTICE

Some training executives are not so sanguine, however. An increasing number of banks are mixing the training programs with actual work for the bank so that the trainees earn at least a part of their keep as they go along. Then, if they do leave soon after the program is over, the loss to the bank is not so great.

Another problem that disrupts banks even more is that after people are trained and given accounts to service, they sometimes take the accounts with them if they change banks. This is especially significant now that taboos against officers leaving one bank and going to another bank in the same town have largely broken down.

Some wish that the industry would develop more cooperative training schools so the cost of education would be borne more equally, and so that people piracy would be less costly to specific banks.

Yet, when one talks to the people who have moved from bank to bank, it may turn out that the people moving had a good reason for doing so. It appears that in a number of banks, the training program is far superior to the bank's approach to people once they are trained. And the beneficiary of this discrepancy between the training and the job is the rest of the industry, which gladly accepts these trainees once others have paid for their education.

6-4 TENDER LOVING CARE FOR TRAINEES

The banks that have had successful training programs and, more importantly, the trainees who say that they have gained a great deal from their training period, generally emphasize that one aspect stands out: trainees must feel they are doing something useful for the bank while they are learning what the bank is all about.

Telling a new trainee that he or she will spend a specific amount of time in each of several departments until he or she is fully familiar with its operations is a poor way to run a training program. This practice generally leads to all inputs and no outputs—a lot of effort but little positive results.

A better approach is to assign the new trainee a project that involves working in a department until the project is completed. The project should be broad enough for the trainee learns what he or she needs to know about that area of the bank. The project should also be meaningful. The trainee must feel that the bank actually uses the ideas and/or facts developed. Nothing is more demoralizing than to offer one's best and have it ignored or placed in a for-posterity file. In addition, the trainee should not leave until the project is finished—quick learners leave sooner and slower ones stay longer.

Some banks have found that trainees especially like these practical experiences:

- Time as a teller or operations clerk.
- Time on the phone trying to collect overdue installment loans.
- An assignment where, after the trainee fully understands a credit, he accompanies the loan officer on a visit to discuss renewal of a loan or any other matters. When the officer turns to the trainee and asks for his advice, this becomes a truly memorable and exciting moment for the new banker.
- Assisting with preparation of next year's training program and helping train the subsequent class. This tends to make the present trainees feel they are truly useful, and it gives those who have been most affected by the training program the opportunity to make it more effective, more pertinent, more exciting for future trainees.

Trainees must feel that top management knows they are there. A monthly dinner attended by all the trainees and one or more top officers on a rotating basis is a sure way to get feedback that can both solidify the bank-trainee relationship and also give the bank access to the fresh approaches these newcomers have developed.

AREAS OF CONCERN

There is no way that a bright, young trainee can be overburdened. The more work this person is given to do, the more he or she likes the bank and the job. Still, bank training officers suggest several areas of concern.

- Watch out when trainees are given the choice of which department they want to go into after rotational training. The trainee may pick the department whose people impressed him most, rather than the one where he will be most challenged and thus most useful.
- Trainees must learn that there are more routes to the top than just commercial lending. Too often they feel this is the only path to the top, and the bank loses their talent in other areas where they might be better utilized. Sometimes salary-range posting, to show that commercial lending is not the only lucrative area of the bank, helps solve this problem by encouraging good trainees to go into operations, trust, and other vital and exciting areas.

All this may seem like a heavy expenditure of time. But, the added cost and effort to make trainees feel that management cares about them is modest indeed if it protects the bank's investment and insures that the trainees stay with the bank once they have been trained.

6-5 MAKE ROOM FOR THE DIFFERENT DRUMMER

A bright MBA candidate, discussing his forthcoming job interview at Citibank with his faculty advisor, asked if should shave off his beard before the interview. The advice he received is well worth repeating.

> If you want that job so badly you can taste it, then shave off your beard. The very fact that you asked whether the beard would be held against you means there is doubt in your mind about its acceptance. If there is doubt, and your heart is set on Citibank, shave the beard.
>
> But if you are the kind of person who would not be happy working for an organization in which a beard makes a difference whether you are hired, then don't you dare touch that beard. If the beard is important enough to make or break you, it could mean this organization is too rigid and doctrinaire for you. You would be happier at an institution where more relaxed attitudes towards personal idiosyncracies would be the norm.

What that student did is unknown. What is known is that far too many good people leave banks because there is just no room for people marching to a different drummer.

This is most unfortunate today when banking is in the midst of change. The days are gone when a banker could say with conviction, "My motto is, 'never do something the first time.'" If ever banking needed to do something "the first time" it is now. If ever an industry needed people who can break the mold and bring innovative ideas to it, it is banking.

One would think each bank would have at least one iconoclast on the staff—a person who asks, "Why do we do this? What good is tradition for its own sake?" That is the kind of person who can shake up an organization and cause it to reexamine policies and practices without fear that openness and difference will cost him his job.

Another factor to be considered is that banking is becoming more and more like other industries. The processing of paper and data is little different from that in any other business.

Hiring people with different disciplines and experience produces ideas that can help a bank, just as hiring those whose lifestyles and attitudes are a little different do. This is the valuable perspective and contribution to be gained from outsiders.

It is now an accepted fact that community banks do extremely well in competing against giants; banks that join holding companies frequently lose their cutting edge in the competition against the independent across the street. Perhaps part of the reason is that large banks generally attract too many people who want to fit into a mold, and who interpret policy doctrines from headquarters more rigidly than top management wants.

Too often we see CEOs who are far more flexible than the people below who interpret policy and pass it down the line. Go to the financial district of any major city and you will see people who look alike—men in dark, three-piece suits, and women in tailored suits. Maybe a few more beards and a few more people who feel that banking is both a game and a challenge would help the industry in today's era of deregulation and intense competition for the public's business.

6-6 TOO MANY BANK OFFICERS?

As old time bankers look at young people still in their twenties gain the title of assistant vice president or even full vice president in some cases, they shake their heads in wonder. These veterans remember the days when to receive the title of teller was an achievement, and one did not become a full vice president until a person had a head full of grey hair.

Perhaps the rash of titles these days is an example of the greater cost-consciousness of the industry. Undoubtedly some banks give out titles instead of money. It is cheaper for the bank to have 20 full vice presidents each earning $17,000 a year than to have 18 of the as assistant vice presidents earning $20,000 a year. Many bank personnel officers have found that in a great many instances, young people are as content with the title as they are with the higher income.

Another reason for title inflation is that so many of the bank officers are contact people whose customers almost demand that they deal with people of "higher authority." The treasurer of a corporation holding a Senior Vice President or Executive Vice President position often is not particularly pleased if the person who visits him from the bank and handles his account is only an AVP.

A simple solution for the bank is to raise the contact people to higher titles so that they have easier going in their travels, and so that the customers do not feel that the bank is belittling their importance.

However, this growth in the number of people with titles has caused a number of problems inside the banks. Not everyone is satisfied with a bank that has so many top titled officers. The most unhappy are the older officers who worked long and hard for a title that a young individual is awarded after only a few short years. They feel that their lifetime's work has been degraded by the ease with which others have been given what they fought so long and hard to win.

Others who are unhappy are the noncontact people who frequently find that it is far more difficult for them to gain the titles that are given to the contact people, even if their salaries remain on a par with those who have received the promotions. In fact, in some cases, the operations people are paid more than people with higher titles who are contact people. However, the pay scale does little to eliminate the unhappiness unless it is well-publicized in the bank that pay ranges for operations AVPs are higher than the range for AVPs in customer contact positions.

Finally, the employees of banks that have not engaged in this new game of title inflation are unhappy. They see their colleagues in other banks walk around with titles that are far harder to earn in their own institutions. While they might understand the situation, in the eyes of most outsiders the people at the other institutions appear to be advancing faster.

These are all legitimate complaints. Some banks are trying to handle them by giving up many of the rankings and replacing them with more descriptive titles such as "data processing officer" or "personal banker." Such a policy, tied with more openness about what a certain job is worth in terms of salary range, can frequently smooth some of the ruffled feelings that many people—both new and old to the bank—have about today's rapid title advancement.

Still, while many managers recognize the trouble that rapid and widespread distribution of titles can cause, they also realize that they cannot halt the trend completely and go back to the days when a title was something received after long years of employment. After all, if one bank doesn't give the title, another bank will. And some good people will move to those other banks.

6-7 WOMEN IN BANKING

One of the more successful and valuable activities that banks are developing as part of staff training and updating is the weekend retreat away from the bank premises.

The location is usually an attractive one. This is because top management believes that if everything about the weekend is first class, the officers who are invited will feel they are first class, too. And it works.

Experience has indicated that this must be an employees-only occasion. When spouses are invited, it becomes largely social. And the interchange of ideas between people who seldom get together—which makes the whole meeting worthwhile—is badly diluted when each officer is worrying about whether his or her spouse is having a good time.

Recreation usually includes a tournament with a trophy awarded for golf, tennis, and fishing. This brings the bank team closer together than ever before.

The retreat, however, is by no means all fun and games. For the affair to be valuable, the business sessions must be intense and relevant. Otherwise the staff feels the get together is a boondoggle and, in addition, a real opportunity for education is lost. Also lost is an opportunity to air topics that simply do not seem to come up in the course of the normal work day.

At a weekend retreat held by the Cape Cod Bank & Trust Co., for example, the role of women in banking was the subject of a three-hour Saturday evening session.

Certainly nothing could be more relevant. In the past decade the number of women officers has jumped from about 3% to 30% of the entire officer staff of American banks, although only 1% of top management is female at the present time.

Certainly times have changed since the day when a personnel officer of a major Philadelphia bank responded to the question of discrimination against women with the remark: "What do you mean, discriminate against women? Why we never waste a man when a woman can do a job!"

But even today, the woman's path in banking remains a rocky one.

As James H. Rice, president of the Cape Cod Bank, put it: "We know women are as qualified as men. We know that they have every right to the same responsibility, titles, and salaries as men, but our problem is what to do when the customers prefer male officers and feel they are being belittled if a woman is assigned to their account."

Mr. Rice and other bankers readily admit that this problem does not necessarily apply just to women. Often, regardless of gender, an officer has to be removed from an account because the customer is not happy with the working relationship.

But the question the panel of bankers at the Cape Cod Bank focused on was what is it that often makes customers hesitate to work with a woman—in what situations does discrimination still exist and how might it be overcome?

The panel asked the assembled officers how they would feel about having to deal with women in various job situations. The response was revealing.

The consensus appeared to be that if the job is one in the public sector where equal opportunity laws mandate that a woman fill the position, and it seems highly likely she is there only because of her sex, then some might not feel comfortable doing business with her. On the other hand, if the job is with a firm whose sole concern is to select the candidate best qualified to represent them—whether male or female—then the feeling is that the firm's choice would instill confidence in the customer.

One feeling that came out of the panel was that aggressiveness and willingness to work pay off in either sex at any age. And bank after bank report of women who started at entry level jobs and worked their way up rapidly in management because of talent and a willingness to work.

Of concern to some is situations caused by women who make career decisions later in life, after they have families, and then expect to move up more rapidly than others who have put in more time and years.

The vast majority of women, however, simply report "Give me a chance and I'll show what I can do."

6-8 THE KEY ROLE OF OPERATIONS PERSONNEL

Every once in awhile, something happens in the banking business that dramatically points up the vital importance of those too often neglected people—the operations force of a bank.

Perhaps nothing in recent years has demonstrated this so graphically as the Drysdale Government Securities debacle. This was the case where Chase Manhattan Bank lost at least $270 million—and also received quite a bit of bad publicity.

Conversations with top officials of Chase indicate that the whole problem in the Drysdale case developed because operations people had to make decisions on the flow of tremendous sums of money without real knowledge of the intricate workings of the markets or of the liabilities involved. Put simply, the Drysdale affair developed because the people in that securities firm were able to pull the wool over the eyes of some securities transfers people at Chase and make them feel that a $1 million bond is a $1 million bond and is interchangeable with any other million bond, even though this patently was not the case.

It seems that the bonds that Drysdale borrowed had several months' interest built up in their coupons, while the ones they returned had just passed their coupon payment date. They thus had had the interest for half a year stripped from them, making the bonds worth less.

It was like borrowing a chicken just about to hatch a egg, taking the egg when hatched, and then returning the "empty" chicken.

The numbers point this up.

Drysdale had done about $4 billion worth of repos with Chase. Let's say they stripped each bond borrowed of five months' interest. At 16% a year, five months' interest on $4 billion comes out to about $267 million.

On paper, in retrospect, this looks simple. But who could expect an operations clerk who had never worked with bonds and their unusual way of figuring worth on an "and interest" basis to understand that one bond of a set donomination was not equivalent to another?

Failure to train operations people on basics like this can be expensive.

WIRE TRANSFER

Let's look at another example. A fast track Harvard MBA is hired by a bank as a lending officer. He puts on a vest and goes to a Fortune 500 company, where he makes a loan for $50 million that is almost certain to be repaid. He is considered an important risk-taker for the bank.

Meanwhile, down in the wire transfer room, someone else, who may have graduated from Trenton School of Taxidermy—has this problem:

A Telex comes in from Germany's largest bank: "$200 million being forwarded to you by Fed Wire by 5 p.m. for transfer to Seattle First for the account of Volkswagen."

The job is simple. Notice will be received by 5 p.m. that the German bank has put $200 million in the U.S. bank's account at the Fed, which will then be wired to Seafirst for the account of Volkswagen. The process involves knowing the security code and pushing a couple of buttons.

But 4:55 comes around and the funds have not arrived.

Does the transfer officer transfer the funds anyway and risk taking a full loss of $200 million if the German bank has changed its mind? Or does he refuse to send $200 million because the notice and funds did not arrive? This would risk alienating the valued German customer, who will be extremely mad and feel the bank does not trust him because his customer, Volkswagen, did not get the needed funds due to a tiny slipup in placing funds with us.

This is why operations people in wire transfer can burn out in three years. And can one question whether the lending officer or the wire transfer officer has a more crucial role in this bank—no matter the titles or salaries.

WHAT A DIFFERENCE ONE PERSON CAN MAKE

If any lesson is clear in the business failures seen in recent years it is that one person can make or break an organization.

The single individuals who decided to invest in long-term bonds and bet that interest rates would fall were the causes of several notorious problem cases in banking.

Operations is a similar situation. As the Drysdale case points out, it can be even more critical. One person, by a routine decision, can make or break an organization.

In this vein, it is interesting to note that the Operations and Automation division of the American Bankers Association has long emphasized the need to explain the rest of the bank to the operations and automation people—notably through its Business of Banking School.

Now, however, ABA is stressing the other side—explaining to the CEOs the role that operations plays in the bank and its critical posture in maintaining bank viability and profits.

The basic problem of getting operations people to be appreciated and to realize their own worth and significance to the bank still remains, however. It also remains difficult to get college graduates to accept the fact that jobs in operations are key to the bank and are routes to the top.

Perhaps a better understanding of what happened at Drysdale and what the actions of a few operations people did to the entire fabric of a major banking institution can help give everyone a better appreciation of where the vital decisions of banking are really made. The Drysdale case makes a good object lesson for future training programs.

6-9 WHO MAKES A GOOD LENDING OFFICER?

It seems that everyone wants to become a banker these days. College students frequently decide that this is the profession they want. It looks prestigious. There is a feeling that the student will quickly be in a major decision-making position—deciding who gets what loan and which company will have to do without credit accommodation. But these first dreams of glory are quickly dispelled as the interviewers come to campus and as students go to the banks looking for jobs. Realism quickly replaces the glamorous image. They soon learn that it takes more than a college degree to make a good lending officer.

What does it take to be an effective lender?

There was a time when social position made the big difference. Banks' loans were more likely to be made at the club than at the bank. People with the right background and contacts made the most valuable additions to the staff.

"Most bankers are picked by matrimony or patrimony" was the old saw with regard to smaller institutions—for people either were born to a bank or married into it. Now all this has changed. Banking requires technical skills. College graduates who are lucky enough to get into the training program of a major bank that leads to a lending position report that no work they did in graduate school or in their undergratuate educations required the rigor of the training programs in accounting and corporation finance that they had to pass before they could get their hands on the bank's money.

WHAT LENDING REQUIRES

But the question still remains. What makes a good bank lending officer? It takes more than just brains and willingness to work. When the most important requirement of lending is lending it so the bank gets it back, it takes a certain type of personality that does not freeze up and become overwhelmed by the responsibility.

One major New York bank, for example, wanted to figure out who made the best lending officers. To do so, they looked at some of the more creative credits that had been arranged, then tried to correlate the background of the lending officer with the loans. This was their conclusion:

The best loan officers are those from wealthy families who just do not give a damn. If they make a good loan—great. This gives them meaning and they willl take risks to develop new, novel credits.

If they make a poor loan because of their efforts at innovation, this does not bother them. Why? Because they feel secure enough that they do not worry about the bank's reaction. Thus they try to do their jobs without worrying about covering their own positions. Moreover, they can do ingenious work.

The next best group are those from the farm or small towns who went through college and somehow ended up at the bank. They try to do their best, and they also take risks to carve out creative financing.

They have a willingness to take risks, because they feel if the bank fires them because of their actions, they can always go home to the farm and forget banking and big city life.

The worst group, with regard to ingenuity and willingness to take risks, turned out to be typical middle class people who are climbing the ladder of our economy.

They are trying to do everything right so they can advance; as a result, they are unwilling to take the risks necessary to carve quality credits out of marginal situations.

In this regard, one is reminded of a major brokerage firm in New York that has turned down most of the students sent to it from state colleges where many students are the first generation to get a college degree, and more go to school at night than in the day.

"We find that people climbing the economic ladder today are just not motivated enough for the type of selling we need," is the way one partner of the firm put it. "The people who make the best people on Wall Street are those who were born rich, lost their fortunes, and want to get the money back so badly they can taste it."

The same partner put it another way: "You can tell a person has what we want when he or she will play poker all night for big stakes, take a shower and then come to work and trade or sell all day long without any sleep."

Maybe this all looks harsh for the typical student climbing the economic ladder who has nothing to sell but brains and a willingness to do hard work. But since the getting of the job is only a start, and since it appears that these unusual qualities may be necessary for success in lending or brokerage work, at least the students of today should consider these factors before they push for a position that they may not be best able to perform.

This is especially true when there are so many other areas of banking that badly need just what these people have to offer.

6-10 PRIMER ON PRODUCTIVITY

Bankers are slowly coming to realize that the future of their financial enterprises, perhaps the future of the country as well, depends upon productivity. Without a working force that expands output per hour and improves efficiency as time passes, any nation or any country or any bank is going to atrophy.

One reason for the productivity problem of this nation is an overemphasis on alllocating funds to other sectors of the economy, notably housing and consumer spending. If the lion's share of available funds is directed to consumption goods and building up our housing stock, less is available to help improve our capital facilities. Without modern capital in the form of new and efficient plant and equipment, improved productivity cannot be achieved to any great degree.

It is not just capital equipment that brings improved productivity, however. The attitude of the working force is also important. Workers who are anxious to aid the overall productivity of their bank or business firm are the greatest asset available—even more important in many instances than capital equipment. A working force that is anxious to please and is willing to do its utmost in turning out products and services, utilizing available equipment, is far better than a sluggish work force utilizing the newest of capital equipment. As every businessman-banker knows, a worker who wants to sabotage the procedure or slow it down markedly can always accomplish his goal by some means no matter how effective the tools he has to work with.

This is what makes the suggestions on productivity by Dr. C. Jackson Grayson Jr., director of the American Productivity Center in Houston, and formerly wage and price control czar under President Nixon, so significant. Dr. Grayson has pinpointed the employer's contribution to worker productivity down to three R's—Recognition, Responsibility, and Reward. Each has deep significance to the banking community.

RECOGNITION

Recognition has always been a key factor. Every employee wants to feel that he or she is appreciated and that good work is recognized. Nothing discourages the conscientious worker more than to see his promotion or appreciation kept on a par with that awarded the lazy worker. After a while, the firm sinks to its lowest common denominator. The productive workers find that they gain nothing from their hard work, and they, too, sink to the level of the routine.

Top officers may say that effective job completion is satisfaction in its own right. That may be true, particularly at the top of the ladder, where the CEO sees the bank's overall performance as a sign of his successful work. The lower echelons need more direct appreciation of what they are doing for the bank.

RESPONSIBILITY

Responsibility is a second key factor. Nothing brings out the best in an individual faster than the knowledge that the operation sinks or swims on his or her own decisions, and that there is no one up the line to whom the buck may be passed. All too often, however, responsibility is not fully given, and the worker knows all too well that his power to make or break the job is limited at a certain point.

This shows up quickly in the productive output and effort extended by the worker. Yet, it usually is possible to place more responsibility with people without creating problems so why not do it?

REWARDS

Rewards remain as much a motivator as ever. In banking, this is even more apparent. Bankers now recognize that a bank job is not a lifetime situation with tenure. Bankers are willing to fire people just as readily as are other business leaders these days. As a result, bankers must reward people adequately for the work they are doing—at least as competitively as other industries reward people. If the security of bank positions is gone, then the immediate satisfactions must match those elsewhere, or banks will not keep top people.

Dr. Grayson states that productivity is not solely a matter of capital investment, or even of worker attitudes. It is largely a matter of employer attitude and employer effort to bring out the best in people in the organization. What the Productivity Center director is saying is that productivity starts at home and begins with decisions far less complex and more human than one might expect when considering the abstract term of productivity by itself.

6-11 OVERSTAFFING

In today's banking environment, personnel costs are more important to the profitability of a bank than ever before. Yet it is common even now to find an overstaffed banking organization. More often than not, the overstaffing has occurred for years. It is almost a tradition.

Franklin National was the largest bank failure in U.S. history up to that time in the mid 1970s. One of the contributing factors was it excess staff. One analyst, for example, whose firm became wary of the situation at Franklin National long before others did, reports that his suspicions on cost control were aroused when he went into the new building the bank had built in the New York financial district. There he saw the amount of space that the bank had available for staff.

"Bankers hate empty space in their buildings, and we figured that with the square footage they had available, they had to employ a certain number of people to fill the space whether they needed them or not," the analyst stated. Evidence obtained later proved his estimate to be quite accurate.

Other bankers have become complacent on staff growth because the ratio of employees per million dollars of deposits stays steady.

What they frequently forget is that, because of inflation, $1 million of deposits is the equivalent of one-half a million 15 years ago. In addition, since more bank deposits are being purchased in the money market, it should take less people to generate a million in deposits now than in the past. The complacency that has developed on staff control is a serious drain on a bank's profits.

CENTRALIZE

The banks that recognize this problem of staff costs are doing something about it. A growing number of banks are centralizing talent in certain locations, with peripheral sites served by people whose jobs are only routine functions. Thus, the customer has to come to a central branch for credits and more complex services, but it is far cheaper than staffing every branch with expensive talent, when fewer people can handle the same work in a more central location.

Citibank in New York has even gone further. To service some locations, they have developed the vestibule branch. This consists of a module with two automatic teller machines, a desk for an account opener, and a cover to keep out the elements. The module is actually brought in hanging from a heliocopter and is placed on the selected location. Later, if the site does not work out, the heliocopter comes back and the module is moved to a different location.

As with pricing services to eliminate unprofitable accounts, bankers are also learning that they cannot be all things to all people in staffing—they cannot provide full service banking with top talent at every location. With the electronic movement of funds, and even banking in the home making routine transactions more convenient, banks can make the availability of top talent a little less convenient without alienating the customers they want to keep.

7 The Art of Bank Management

7-1 THE LONELINESS OF THE CEO

Management is an elusive science, yet perhaps more attention has been paid to it than any other aspect of business. The books and articles on management, including the management of banks, are endless—and the list gets longer all the time. Yet the level of management skills in banking is still not at an acceptable level, although it certainly has risen in recent years. This means there is still room—and need—for additional ideas.

IT'S A LONELY JOB

Ironically, many thoughtful bankers, who are at the center of their communities, involved in every civic and social activity of the area, sum up their lives as being extremely lonely. This is true, to some extent, for anyone in a managerial position.

Top bankers feel that in the community they are often set apart from the rest of the people, in the same way that clergymen are set apart. Those who come in for a loan often cannot escape a twinge of fear about the banker knowing too much about their lives. Even customers who have nothing to hide feel a little uncomfortable in the presence of the individual who knows so much about their finances and can have such a strong hold on their businesses and standards of living.

Employees, too, are not completely open with the chief executive officer in many instances. One bank president says: "I hate to have lunch with any staff member around bonus and salary increase time. The air is so thick you could cut it with a knife."

It is not only a social loneliness that nags at many bank chiefs. There also can be a professional loneliness, a fear they are falling behind in their rapidly changing industry.

CEOs of many community banking institutions who got their early training working for large city institutions think wistfully about the meetings they used to have with other Young Turks—criticizing the way things were done, suggesting changes, and generally arguing for hours over the state of the art in banking and bank lending policies. Those who came up through the ranks of the bank they now head had similar experiences working with equals in the bank and generally critiquing everything going on.

As CEO, these same people find that when they hold meetings, everyone sits waiting for their opinion. What they say can become law without the honest give and take that ideas should receive.

Equally significant is the feeling that the world outside of the local community may be passing them by. They look almost with envy at the young correspondent bankers who come to town and talk about the newest techniques in cost control, pricing of services, and credit evaluation; they feel they may never again have the opportunity to keep current with changes in the industry, given the time pressure of handling their jobs.

Being CEO of a banking organization these days is a tough job; and even being among all the bank's officers and staff people, it can be a lonely job. But it can be exciting, and challenging—and rewarding, as well.

7-2 AVOIDING TOUGH EMPLOYMENT DECISIONS

> How can we move Gridley aside? He has been our chief investment officer for 30 years. I know he doesn't believe in tax swaps and bond-loss planning. I know he keeps our portfolio overliquid and acts like we are in the 1930s. But he retires in only two more years, so we're just hanging in there until he goes.

This is how the CEO of a major eastern bank described how his bank sets investment policy. The policy was established to avoid offending the investment officer. Yet this officer should have been retired years earlier.

Similarly, a western bank has an extremely low loan-to-deposit ratio because the chief loan officer is proud of his no-loss record. He will sacrifice profits, new customers, and bank growth to maintain his unsullied loss posture. Again, the top officers of the bank hesitate to act. "After all, this man was here years before all of the present top management. How can we push him aside, even if he won't make loans in tune with the competitive environment of today?"

Another bank bought two different computers that could not interface. It had two officers who wanted different types of hardware, and the chief executive officer felt he could keep from offending either by buying both brands of computers.

Too many banks have a personnel policy geared toward not offending people instead of making the bank as effective as possible. The basic style of the chief executive who accepts this approach to personnel policy is "it's only a couple of years until Gridley leaves. We can wait that long to make needed changes."

In today's fast-paced banking world, this kind of policy simply cannot be tolerated. In fact, it never should have been tolerated at all.

This is an era of tough competition. The bank that cannot earn top dollar will not be able to pay the depositor top dollar. This, in turn, will lead to outflows of funds and further profit problems, eventually snowballing the original difficulty to the point where the bank's viability is threatened.

There is also a question of whether the bank can straighten up its act and get back into twentieth-century banking even after Gridley retires. Gridley will have trained a whole department to accept his outmoded ways of thinking and acting. What generally happens is that good people either leave or become like Gridley. The bank finds that the two years with Gridley's policies become two more and two more—all because no one wanted to offend an officer whose attitudes and policies were out of date.

No one likes to fire anyone. No one wants to uproot the life of an oldtimer who may even have been the first boss of the present chief executive. But banks face competition from new rivals, both inside and outside of the industry, that they did not have to face before. Among the advantages nonbank rivals have in starting fresh in offering banking services is that they have not lived for years with people whose policies have been bypassed by today's banking needs.

The adage "nice guys finish last" is true if the chief executive feels he must leave Gridley alone or risk not being a nice guy. Unfortunately, having to make unpleasant decisions such as removing Gridley is what being a chief executive officer is all about.

7-3 MANAGEMENT EGO—AND WHAT TO DO ABOUT IT

All sorts of things can go wrong in the management of a bank. When the problem is at the top, however, when the CEO or other senior officer is not as efficient as he or she might be, then steps should be taken to correct the situation.

THE MATTER OF EGO

Somone who rises to the top must have a substantial ego to have made it up there. But that human trait can get in the way of effective management. For example, a top officer who talks about his bank and uses the term "I" instead of "we" is usually making a true statement about the way the shop is run.

Personification has its place, of course. With the impersonality in banking, an individual who is identified with the institution sometimes makes the bank look more human. In New York City, for example, Joe DiMaggio has become so closely identified with the Bowery Savings Bank that when he did TV commercials for a coffee maker, people asked whether the Bowery had started selling coffee machines. But when the individual who personifies the bank is also the top officer, there may be problems that can demoralize the staff.

Consider the college graduate who joined a bank training program. After several years, the junior officer left, causing the bank to lose its heavy investment in him. The reason—even after training, the CEO made all the decisions and so the young banker felt he was just a puppet. He also pointed out that while that bank had worked aggressively to build a staff of good people, not one had stayed five years with the organization.

Ego gratification can be carried to extremes. One fairly large bank, for example, took an advertisement on a TV station carrying the Superbowl game—even though the market area of the bank was only a small fraction of the territory the station covered. The advertisement showed the CEO standing before the camera talking about his bank—a pure and simple ego trip, at the expense of both the bank's bottom line and the morale of the staff.

In another example, two men were competing for the top spot at a major bank. One used the team approach—"we are all in this together." The other utilized management by intimidation—people perform best when frightened into it. The former won, because his staff was willing to give their all for him when the board was examining the performance of the units each commanded.

There are many people who like to have a CEO who makes all the decisions. It makes days uneventful, and there is the feeling of security that no choice has to be made that could jeopardize a career. But most of the top talent will move away from such an institution, as do acute security analysts.

TEAMWORK

It is certainly difficult to analyze banks and decide which will be top performers and which will not be. Looking back, some of the banks picked as the brightest starts a decade ago have turned out to be the most disappointing. Beneath it all, however, the ones that have performed well year after year have largely been those run by a team. Top management is known in the community for its banking skills rather than for its public appearances.

Perhaps the first indication that a bank is comprised of team players rather than a star and supporting troops is whether the CEO refers to the bank as "we" or "I."

7-4 FRIENDS IN LOW PLACES

Talking about his management style the popular CEO of a solid organization set out the reason for the success he had achieved: "I have a lot of friends in low places," he explained. Having friends in low places does not mean that a CEO or other senior officer in a bank should not cultivate friendships with staff personel. It does mean that people from the bottom up know that you appreciate their efforts and do not take them for granted. This is a key to effective management.

Managers who try to get their staff on their side find their own work more effective. This is particularly true when someone comes in from outside the organization. There is the case of a new president who was brought in from outside the state to head a large eastern bank. The bank had been in great trouble. The first thing the new CEO did was to drop his briefcase in his office and visit every branch office of the bank. The CEO said that people were amazed. Many had never seen a top officer of the bank before. The boost to morale was nothing short of spectacular.

At a recent meeting of a major New Jersey bank, when officers talked about the former CEO, who was deceased, the first thing that came to mind was that he knew every guard in the bank by name and knew something about everyone's family or life which he talked about when seeing them. This man had built the bank from several hundred million dollars to several billion. Yet the first thing remembered about him was his relationship to people.

At one of the nation's top 10 banks, people still say that the reason one of the two candidates for the top job beat the other was that his staff would work for him day and night while the other's staff put in their eight hours and went home. The results achieved by the staff impressed the board.

7-5 IMPROVING COMMUNICATIONS

As suggested previously Section (7-3), it is important to have friends at all organization levels of the bank. Such friendships, imply that the lines of communications are open. And it only is with such two-way communications that it is possible to determine what really is going on throughout the bank.

Not that banks do not want open communications lines. Most banks are managed that way. But they could be run much better with more information about what people are doing, feeling, and planning. Top management often can gain valuable insight from others in the bank. But, if the staff fears the reaction to their views, they are likely to clam up.

WHY THERE IS POOR COMMUNICATIONS

One generally cannot blame subordinate officers and staff personnel if they tell the top officer only what they think he wants to hear. In some cases, their fear of honesty is valid. If the top officer does not like criticism and feels that anyone who criticizes him has bad judgment, a barrier is set up that is impossible to break down.

Far more frequently, however, the barrier is set up by the lower level official, who operates under the old fear that the emperor will put to death the bearer of the bad news from the battlefront. If an employee thinks some other individual is not doing his job, or that the bank's policies are poor in some area, he or she frequently fears that to tell this to the top level of the bank will bring a reaction that includes blaming the reporter of the news along with the perpetrator.

Even when the individual who does have something important to say follows the chain of command and tells an immediate superior, this superior frequently stops the upward information flow out of a similar fear.

Often, there is an attitude in banking (and in most business and government operations for that matter) that the smartest policy is to cover your rear. All too often, people rise to the top simply by remaining noncontroversial year after year. When promotion time comes, there is nothing negative to say about them. The price of keeping a clean record is frequently a refusal to get involved in decisions that might help the bank, but that also involve risk. The employee reasons, rightly or wrongly, that if he takes a risk and it succeeds, the credit fades fast; but if he fails, it is remembered for quite a while. Thus, there is hesitancy on the part of many employees to take any chances. One of the areas in which employees follow this don't-rock-the-boat policy is in talking to superiors about complaints, problems, and programs where they feel the bank may be making a mistake.

The result is that a bank frequently becomes a very political institution. Honesty takes a back seat to politeness, and the CEO does not find out matters that would be of major concern to him until far too late.

WHAT CAN BE DONE

On deeper examination of the problem, there is much the CEO and other bank officials can do to make the organization more communicative, with the bank and all its employees becoming major beneficiaries of the change.

It cannot be stressed enough that if the top officer of the bank bemoans the lack of honesty and communications, but does not really want to hear unpleasnt news about himself or his stewardship of the bank, little will happen. A phony campaign of openness in which suggestions bring no response will quickly become apparent to the staff. Worse is the case where the person who has taken up the offer of openness finds that a coolness develops on the part of the superior he talked to when he registered his opinion about some facet of the bank he feels needs improvement.

People quickly learn whether a communications program is honest or not. An insincere campaign can lead to even more secretiveness once the falseness becomes apparent.

The best way a top officer can show he wants constructive criticism is to act on it, even if it is only to explain why the suggested steps could not be taken. This must be more than simply sitting down with the employee at the time the suggestion is presented and explaining why it is not good. If no follow-up is undertaken to see if the suggestion has validity, then the employee is permanently squelched.

Listening to suggestions, following them up, and rewarding the suggester is a first class way of showing that openness is valued and appreciated, even if the ideas are not always accepted.

Accentuate the Negative

Far too often, an officer given the responsibility for developing a plan or program for the bank quickly recognizes what top management wants his conclusions to be. Whether it is analyzing the decision to build a new building, to offer a new service, or to expand geographically, the person with the assignment frequently knows what motivates his boss in initiating the study and what he would like to see the conclusions show. If the person assigned the task values his position and wants to move up, there may be just too much pressure to enable him to bring in a truly impartial report.

Top management can solve this problem, however, by requesting the preparer of the study to work up a second report that indicates only the negatives. In some banks, the individual reports to top management or the board, giving his basic presentation on the proposal he has researched. Then he makes a second presentation providing only the negatives.

This gives management the chance to see the adverse side of the recommendation. In effect, it forces the individual to draw conclusions on the issues instead of just on the desires and the personalities of his superiors in the bank.

Reward Positive Thinking

It is essential to try to end the cover-your-rear attitude that is prevalent in so many organizations. This can only be accomplished by getting the entire staff to recognize that when a decision or action involves risk, it is understood that the chances of succeeding are not 100% and, thus, that failure must be part of a banker's life.

No bank would appreciate a lending officer who had a perfect record of never having made a bad loan. This would indicate conservatism that has denied the bank many good loan opportunities. Similarly, a bank must indicate that if employees in other areas have not gone on a limb and had their share of failures on occasion, they have not truly served the bank in the best possible manner.

Just as in lending, an individual's spotless record on equipment purchase, trust decision making, portfolio investment, and other areas could be a sign of a conservative posture that may have robbed the bank of the chance for the gains that reasonable risk taking offers.

When a person is promoted who has been responsible for one or more failures in risky instances where success might have benefited the bank markedly, this shows the rest of the staff that bank management means business—it does not want top people whose sole principle is to cover their rears.

It would be best if the CEO could sit down once a year or so with each officer and each middle-management employee and just talk about what is going on in the bank. Such meetings, with no agenda and a cleared desk, can get people to give information that can be highly valuable and might not otherwise be available to top management. Even if this is impractical because the CEO cannot spare the time or does not want to buck his own chain of command, there is much that can be done to improve communications so that top managers can find out what is going on in the bank.

Opening the lines of communications can help a bank solve problems. More importantly, it will help avoid problems before they develop.

PART 4 The Financial Side of Banking

In the last few years, with the stock of many banks not rising even to book value, with the need for additional capital a problem at banks large and small, and with the squeeze on profits a fact of life in banking, every banker has become aware of the need to manage his institution's finances with skill and dexterity.

Not all banks have followed through on that awareness. Yet there has been a realization that with some effort, much can be accomplished. Seminars and lectures at banking meetings have reflected the situation and the desire of bankers to do something to help their institutions be stronger financially.

It isn't always easy, though, particularly when the economy doesn't cooperate. But steps must be taken to try to move up stock prices, to help find new sources of capital, and to loosen the squeeze on profits.

8 Bank Financial Management

8-1 CASH MANAGEMENT AT THE BANK

The old proverb, that shoemakers' children go barefoot, frequently applies to bankers and thrift executives as they offer cash management services to their customers. Their institutions are among the poorest when it comes to utilizing cash management techniques for their own operations. Just consider the case of the bank whose branches sent cash letters directly to the Federal Reserve—without letting headquarters know exactly how much was involved. As a result, a fortune was regularly lost in excess reserves on deposit at the Federal Reserve. Even in day-to-day operations, many banks and thrifts keep too much cash on hand.

Eugene Mann, a New Jersey-based consultant on operational efficiency in financial firms, reports that branch managers are never judged by how well they utilize cash on hand and how they keep cash to a minimum. But let a branch office run out of cash just once, and that branch manager's name is mud from then on. Consequently, the managers automatically overestimate how much cash they will need to be on the safe side, while the bank loses the opportunity to use those funds in overnight money market investments.

One solution is to study cash needs, just as banks study teller utilization, with the bank working cash down to a realistic minimum at each branch. Emergency supplies and the services of special couriers can then be made available at a few locations.

A further suggestion is to make arrangements with a local supermarket for its excess cash should an emergency shortage occur. For example, the bank may run short at the end of the week or just before a holiday. It is just at that time that the supermarket often is overloaded with cash and would like to get rid of some to avoid storing it over the weekend or holiday period.

Even with vault cash now serving to meet reserve requirements for all banks—Fed members and nonmembers alike—less cash reserve requirements are still so low that the effective management of cash can provide a substantial saving to the bank—just as reevaluation of service charges, elimination of free checks, and other steps to improve efficiency can generate bottom line benefits.

8-2 PRICING UNDER DEREGULATION

There was a time when running a bank was easy. A bank could borrow short and lend long. Since the cost of funds was zero for demand deposits and was kept very low on a vast portion of time and savings deposits, the profits rolled in.

All this has changed. First, the banks found that many people would not accept demand deposits as their basic bank relationship. A number of banks hesitated for a long time to pay the maximum on time and savings deposits; they felt that money would have to end up in the bank anyway, whether people placed it into savings banks, savings and loans, or any other interest-paying savings from. Even though the depositor pulled his money out of the bank, the savings institution placed it right back there.

But banks soon discovered that this meant that the economy was being financed by growth in velocity of money, instead of by growth in bank demand deposits. Individual banks also found that if they did not compete for the public's deposits by paying reasonable interest, there was no assurance that the thrift that got the money would put it back in their banks. A banker gained little satisfaction in knowing that while his bank lost the deposit, the savings institution did not take the deposit money out of the banking system, but put it in the bank across the street.

"Time and savings deposits are worse than demand deposits," bankers concluded, "but they are vastly superior to the real alternative—no deposits." The days of cheap demand funds ended. Demand deposits became like currency; the public kept just so much and no more.

What was next? Banks still could make money borrowing short and lending long. This was because of Regulation Q. Banks were limited in what they could pay on small savings and time deposits. So even at maximum rates the spread between costs and returns on funds still made the industry hum.

Then along came the 1970s and volatile interest rates that forced some relaxation of Regulation Q. Banks were allowed to offer higher yielding certificates of deposit lest the money flow elsewhere. And again they had a choice: either pay more or lose the deposit to the competition. The banks were between the rock and the hard place: high-yielding certificates frequently cost more than the banks earned on their long-term fixed-rate assets. The choice was to lose deposits or lose money on investing some of the deposits the bank attracted.

Fortunately, the development of flexible rate assets has helped to shrink this problem as the older fixed-rate loans have matured. Still, matching volatile rate assets with volatile rate liabilities still narrowed the spread and substantially reduced the chance for profits from playing the yield curve or the gap between maturities.

Finally, at the end of 1982, along came the ultimate blow: deregulation. This was in the form of permission to offer money market accounts—accounts whose rate of payment was limited solely by what the bank could afford to pay and (unhappily) by what the competition offered, even if it was above what the bank could afford.

Money market accounts grew from zero in mid-December 1982, when this deposit form was approved, to over $360 billion by mid-1983. The banking industry began to feel like the man on the deck of the Titanic who said to the steward: "I ordered ice, but this is ridiculous." It is all well and good to want a "level playing field" and an opportunity to compete in a gloves-off battle for the deposits of the public. But how do you make this competition profitable in today's banking environment?

To this question there are three answers: cost control, sale of new noncredit services, and proper pricing. Of the three, to the typical U.S. bank, pricing is the one with by far the greatest potential for successful results.

COST CONTROL AND NONCREDIT SERVICES

What can be said about cost control? If banks have volatile rate assets and liabilities and managing the spread has become the key to bank operations, the wider that spread can be made the better off the bank is. This involves cost control.

But cost control is like apple pie and Mother's Day. Everyone is for it, but it is not easy to make it more effective. Some banks have done thorough surveys of their operations to see what can be done to contain costs and limit the number of employees needed on the staff. Others have decided that maybe it is not necessary to reinvent the wheel—i.e., why develop separate computer programs when these are already available from correspondent banks, software houses, and service bureaus and can be installed without heavy development costs?

But little more can be said. All banks that are profit-minded are continually working on trying to control their costs.

Sale of new noncredit services is another area in which not too much advice can be given. One can readily see why banks want to market their talent, offer discount brokerage, sell insurance, and provide other noncredit services. After all, banks are limited in earnings on loans and investments by the rigors of today's need to practice asset/liability management and thereby to avoid taking chances through mismatching asset and liability maturities. They naturally would want to look elsewhere for income. And many of these fields, which were not open to banks in the past, look like the greener grass on the other side of the fence.

But are they?

Bankers have generated public trust through years of doing their jobs well and concentrating on these jobs. New areas involve the development of skills which takes time or the hiring of talent that is not accustomed to bankers' ways of doing business.

Certainly banking will be in the discount brokerage business, for example. But at what price? The banks that buy discount brokerage operations are paying a hefty fee for them, and some are going to find that they could have earned far better returns on their funds elsewhere. And those that have started their own operations may find that these can backfire to hurt their banks' image.

Certainly a discount broker states that he is only an order-taker and will not make investment suggestions. Yet, one wonders if this Chinese Wall between the banker and his client can be maintained. What happens to the public's image of the banker and confidence in him when a stock purchased through the bank plummets—whether the bank recommended it or not?

We saw what happened a decade ago, when the banks became so-called congenerics and offered real estate investment trusts, mortgage company assistance, and other nonbank services to the public. Frequently, they were a disaster. The people who ran the REITS often were entrepreneurial types rather than bankers. By and large the services just did not fit in banking, and the banks suffered heavy losses from some of these excursions into the other guy's territory.

This is not to say that banking should stick to traditional services and forget the expansion now being made available through the pioneering efforts of institutions like Citibank and Bank of America. For outside observers to conclude, however, that these nonbank services are going to be the salvation of the bank's bottom line in all-sized banks throughout the nation would be a naively optimistic conclusion.

Where can banks turn, then? To the proper pricing of the services they do offer.

PRICE VERSUS SERVICE

If there is any basic principle to be followed in analyzing banking under deregulation it would be this: Banking must, of necessity, change from an industry emphasizing service competition to one that emphasizes price competition. Fortunately, there are some good examples for bankers of other industries on the matter of service versus price competition.

Airlines and Department Stores

The airlines are certainly such a superb example. This is an industry that formerly had no price competition whatsoever. Prices were set by the Civil Aeronautics Board (CAB), with the result that an airline's prices, advertised time, routes, and even distance between and width of seats were controlled by the CAB or industry conferences.

What could one airline do to differentiate itself from others? It had to rely on food, friendliness of its people, speed of baggage handling, ticketing procedures, seat selection amenities, and other service criteria; yet, in their hearts the airline executives knew that with regard to what really mattered—speed and price—all airlines were alike.

But look at what has happened now under deregulation. New airlines have developed that offer minimum comfort, selling tickets on the plane, charging extra for baggage and food, and with people standing in crowded lines to race for the plane instead of having advance seat selection available. Yet the prices have fallen. The airlines that have undertaken the new policy of price competition instead of service competition have won away a large portion of the business and forced the traditional airlines to develop discount practices themselves or lose their customer base to the discounters.

Department stores are another example. Except for a few select stores, the days of free delivery, elegant sales help, and all the ambiance that shopping used to offer are rapidly disappearing. The public prefers a discounted price, even if it means crowded clothes racks, driving the family car to the back of the store and lashing the furniture to the top to get it home, and the other indignities that enable the store to lower its prices. To the public, though, it's the low ticket price that counts.

Competing on Price

Banking must face a similar decision: offer price competition or service competition. Deregulation, bringing with it the need to pay top dollar for money market fund deposits, gives most bankers a single answer: compete on price, even if it means letting service go by the boards.

But with this decision comes a basic principle that all bankers must keep in mind as they compete for the public's business: You cannot pay top dollar and kiss the customer's rump too! This means that if you are rewarding the depositor with a rate as high as he can get elsewhere, you do not have to cater to him in other ways too.

As far as the bank goes, if it is paying as much for a customer's deposits as it would have to pay to buy funds through the money desk or through any other available route, why give this customer special service? If the customer doesn't want to give the bank his money fund deposit, it can get the same amount of money elsewhere at a similar price.

And what this means is that banks should be doing a true soul-searching of pricing policies to make sure that every account is as profitable as possible, and that the public is not being given costly services that are no longer needed to attract their business.

It stands to reason: If you are paying nothing for a demand deposit, you can give an awful lot of service to win this money into the bank. If you are paying 5.25%, you can still give a good bit of service, because the deposit is a lot cheaper than alternative fund sources. But if you're paying top dollar for the deposit, why bother? If the services provided make the account a loser, you certainly don't need to have it on the books.

What it comes down to then is reevaluation of service charges, minimum balances, and the overall pricing policy of the bank. In an era of deregulation, this is where the banks must focus their attention if they want profits, to keep the stockholders happy, and the doors of the bank open.

REEXAMINING PRICING PROCEDURES

There are a lot of ways in which banks can reevaluate service charges, balance policies, and their operations to improve fee income and bank profitability. Yet, many bankers hesitate to become aggressive in pricing. They fear that if they raise prices for services, their customers will leave in droves.

With few exceptions, however, every banker who has marshaled the courage to do the job and raise fees has found that the fear was far worse than the reality. Certainly there were accounts closed, but in most instances these were losers that the bank was better off without having on the books. Seldom has a solid customer closed his account because of a rise in service charges. The customer knows that good bank service is expensive to provide and that reliability, accuracy, and a close bank relationship mean far more than a few dollars a month in saved service charges.

Bankers are sometimes surprised by the loyalty of their customers. At least one medium-sized bank has reported that when it raised minimum balance requirements in order to close small, unprofitable accounts, instead of having the smaller accounts leave, the majority of them found extra money—from relatives, from other bank accounts—to build up the balances and meet the minimums.

Banks that have raised service charges to exceptional heights have frequently found a substantial amount of public acceptance. This is so if customer contact personnel were told how expensive it is to handle an exception item; they, in turn, explained the cost of this service to the customer.

There are few, if any, horror stories of banks that raised service charges and then found their market share eroding seriously. Conversely, there are many stories of banks that priced services too cheaply and got swamped with unprofitable work they could not handle. Reevaluation of prices and customer policies—this is the key.

Some Specific Suggestions

What are some of the specifics that bankers have learned and started to implement as they have recognized this and have turned to new pricing policies as the way of maintaining profitability in an era of deregulation?

1 Learn your costs and charge enough to cover them. If a bank knows that its charges do not cover out-of-pocket costs, there should be no fear inherent in raising fees. If the customer does leave when the charge is raised, this will be an account that was unprofitable anyway.

2 Reexamine the value of your services to the public and charge accordingly. Take safe-deposit boxes, for example. A bank charges $10 or $15 a year for a box in which people keep their valuables—with the box located right downtown. The country club, however, charges $60 or $75 a year for a similar-sized box, located out of the high-rent district, in which to keep sneakers. Shouldn't the bank be able to charge more for the box it rents than it does?

   Consider exception items. What is it worth to a customer to be able to stop a check he has written? Isn't a certification of a check or issuance of a bank draft something no money fund can provide? One bank's $30 fee for a N.S.F. check is based on costs. And the bank indicates that if a customer will use the bank's services and open a line of credit, no N.S.F. checks ever need be issued by an individual, no matter how low the balance.

3 Review the list of customers exempt from charges. An officer likes to earn points with a customer by exempting him from the bank's normal service charge policy. But one customer here, one there, and little by little the bank has seriously eroded its fee income base.

One idea is to publish a list of all exempted accounts, along with which officer of the bank approved each exemption. When an officer finds his name on the list next to customer after customer, sitting in boldface for all bank employees to see, he is likely to become more careful, especially if the bank has a profit-sharing program.

4 Review the tremendous numbers of free services provided by bank officers, such as giving financial advice, helping customers plan their financial affairs, and simply listening to complaints. If a bank is paying top dollar for the customer's account, there is no need to throw in free services too. Why shouldn't the bank charge for its officers' time, just as a law firm charges for its attorneys' time and advice?

5 Reevaluate the need for each of a bank's branches. If a customer gets a top rate, he will be more willing to come to the bank for service than in the past, and less likely to expect the bank to come to him.

6 Consider why banks offer 24-hour service without charging a premium for off-hours banking. The convenience stores charge more for groceries than do the mainline supermarkets. Why can't banks have a rate schedule that charges more for after-hours withdrawals than for regular hours withdrawals?

7 Review the practice where every depositor can deal with a teller. Now that we are in this era of inexpensive electronic funds transfer, it is far cheaper for a bank to provide an ATM than to provide a human teller for routine transactions. Yet, experiments with denying the small-sized account access to a teller have generated tremendous adverse publicity and led to embarrassing retractions of policy. A different approach can work. A few banks offer free deposit and withdrawal service if an ATM is utilized, but charge a service fee if a human teller is desired. The choice is left up to the customer.

This makes bank pricing like that of the phone company, which charges far less for a call in which no operator is needed than for the operator-assisted transaction. The public has its choice, yet the phone company (or the bank) is compensated for the high cost of personal, nonelectronic service.

Rates and Service

Pricing is not all on the charge side. There is also the opportunity to make more money by acute handling of the rates paid on money funds.

Not all banks pay similar rates. Some pay a top rate only above $2,500 per account and only 5.25% on the first $2,500. Some do not pay anywhere near as much as others in the same community. But it appears that once an account has been opened, the public is not going to shop rates week after week. Published data show that some banks pay as much as 100 to 150 basis points less than others in the same territory without unusually adverse impact on deposit flows.

There are also people who will accept lower rates or even pay service charges for exceptional service. Personal banker service is an example—with many people willing to keep money in core deposits and not switch it to higher-yielding money funds just to get personal service.

One bank, the Burlington County Trust Company in New Jersey, is charging $375 a year for personal banker service. The bank already has a considerable number of people willing to pay the price for special banking services, coupled with one complete portfolio review a year.

Reexamination of programs, like the Gold Card of Wells Fargo in California, shows that it is not cheaper service that the public wants when it buys a combination package account. Rather, the customer wants to have the feeling that he is special in the bankers' eyes, that when he comes into the bank, his business means more than that of the regular customer. (Airlines have capitalized on this in their frequent-flyer programs. They offer free trips, special ticket counters, different boarding passes, even an effort to keep the middle seat empty next to a frequent flyer if the plane is not sold out. The feeling that the customer is special is generated and the loyalty of the customer to that airline is boosted markedly.)

SWITCHING FROM SERVICE TO PRICE COMPETITION

Will the banks succeed in switching from service to price competition? That's hard to say. But one thing is certain: Banks will have no trouble winning back the funds from money market mutual funds issued by nonbank organizations.

The fact that bank money market accounts have reached $360 billion from ground zero in half a year surely indicates that the public wants the convenience of dealing with the hometown bank instead of a brokerage firm's 800 number. They also like the federal deposit insurance (something the brokerage money funds are working to match). Also, in the minds of most Americans, financial transactions appear to belong at home and not at an impersonal organization in a distant city. On the other side of the coin, though, it is by no means certain that banks will have an easy time in finding enough profitable uses for this inflow of funds to generate good profitability on this exceptional deposit growth.

Banks do have advantages over money funds in this regard since they can chose between local lending and money market investing of the funds, while nonbank money funds only have the latter opportunity. Remember, money funds have for years earned a good return just on the 40 or 50 basis point spread charged depositors. The banks have the opportunity to incorporate this amount into their spreads and still be competitive with nonbank money funds.

The key, then, is pricing. Bankers must recognize that they have no reason to give the bank away to any customer whose account is replaceable with funds from a number of other sources at similar cost. They have to end the feeling that friendliness is the key to banking. The customer frequently has shown that rate means more to him than friendliness, so why should favors be a one-way street?

Banks also must recognize their strengths—that many customers need the bank and its services far more than the bank needs them. Customers will pay what these services are worth and cost to deliver.

If we have learned anything from the bank problems of the early 1980s, it is that earnings—not capital, not territory, not image—are the best buttress a bank has in trying to remain independent.

Opportunities to build bank profitability still are strong. But the banks who want to build profitability in today's banking jungle must look inward. They will find that reevaluating pricing, getting rid of unprofitable accounts, and charging what a service costs and what it is worth will be their shining lights as they work to enhance the most important goal of a viable bank—a strong bottom line.

8-3 THE IMPORTANCE OF OPERATIONS EXPENSE

As bankers examine what determines high performance in a financial institution today, they are increasingly coming to the conclusion that the key is internal. The bank that looks inward and controls costs is the one that is likely to do best.

The reasoning is clear. Core deposits are getting more difficult to obtain. Thus, most banks have concluded that they often must rely upon purchased funds as the basic raw material for lending and investing. In turn, reliance on purchased funds means that a bank has no control over costs of funds—the marketplace determines what the depositor must be paid on his certificate of deposit and what the other bank must be paid on federal funds.

Similarly, on the asset side, banks are coming to the conclusion that they must utilize variable rate pricing on virtually all loans and keep investments fairly short. With today's volatile interest rate structure, the bank that has locked itself in with fixed-rate assets can be subject to a serious earnings squeeze as rates rise.

Certainly some banks will be willing to risk locking in fixed-rate loans, and others may still have core deposits that are not interest rate sensitive. But more and more bankers are finding that both assets and liabilities will float with going rates—and thus that costs of funds and returns on funds often will be beyond the control of the bank itself.

This leaves the gap between money costs and returns as the area in which banks can improve their performance. Widening this gap involves giving major attention to the large and small costs of operation.

PAYROLL EXPENSE

Cost control covers many areas. Naturally, if a bank cannot control the costs of funds, the second most significant area—personnel costs—becomes the leading point where most emphasis can be placed.

Bank employment today offers no particular status advantage over employment in an office, or even in a department or grocery store. So the advantage of wearing a white shirt in a bank has disappeared. Thus banks have to pay with money instead of status. And bank salaries must be competitive.

As shown earlier, if salaries are to be competitive, then banks no longer have to offer the advantage of not firing people if they are incompetent or if they are no longer needed. Firing has become as much a part of the bank way of life as it is in other industries. In fact, many banks report that instead of hurting morale, the firing of people improves morale, if the right ones are fired. The remaining people feel they have made the cut and are still on board while the bank has been weeding staff—a sign of approval to those remaining.

Thus, banks are becoming less traditional and more aggressive in their personnel policies. And the result is that sizable savings on employee costs can be achieved while actually improving rather than diminishing the effectiveness.

BRICK AND MORTAR

Another area in which banks can achieve substantial cost savings is in the utilization of buildings. Any bank that undertakes the construction of a new building today without looking first at developments taking place in remote banking does so at its peril.

Look how quickly changes have come in the delivery system of banking services. It was only a decade ago that First Federal Savings & Loan of Lincoln, Nebraska experimented with letting customers make deposits and withdrawals at the check-out counters of the Hinky Dinky market chain. Yet, today, automatic teller machines, point-of-sale terminals, and the other aspects of remote banking are commonplace.

In addition, banking in the home is at the same take-off stage that remote teller operations were a decade ago.

Brick and mortar are expensive and may tie up capital that could be better utilized backing earning assets.

The bank that keeps its old buildings, modernizes them, economizes on space, and plans for the day when fewer and fewer people will actually need to be in the lobby, and when more routine bank functions will be automated, is doing a tremendous service to its bottom line.

Keeping personnel under control and watching space requirements interact with each other. The bank that has more space than it really needs is always under temptation to hire people to fill the space it has.

WATCHING FLOAT

Another area in which substantial savings can be generated is float control. In the case of nonmember banks, this has not been a significant factor in the past, as they have had to keep heavy reserves in cash and at correspondents anyway to meet legal requirements and to pay for services.

Now this is changing. Services are being charged for in hard dollars far more often, so that excess reserves at correspondents or at the Fed are simply a drain on available earning assets.

Thus, banks are reevaluating their float management. They are cutting down holdings of excess cash. And some are even operating so close to the minimum on cash that they have emergency courier service available to move money from branch to branch if needed.

There is even thought of an arrangement with a local supermarket so that as indicated above, when the supermarket has too much money while the bank may run out, the bank can obtain cash from the supermarket, rather than having the cash flow the other way as is traditionally the case.

THE LITTLE THINGS

Big items such as personnel, buildings, and float control are not the only places where savings can be made. Small savings can add up quickly. Some areas in which bank funds erode in driblets and quickly add up to torrents include:

- ***Equipment*** Does every new piece of equipment that comes down the line have to be purchased or rented by a bank? Is there any control on purchase of staplers, typewriter paper and carbon paper, clips, forms and other small items that mount up quickly? Does the bank make sure that the paper it purchased does not end up as the paper on which the employee's son writes his term paper?

  Mort Saul, the comedian, used to say: "Remove white collar crime from the office and you remove from the worker the last vestige of job satisfaction." This may be true, but it is not the job of the bank to be a stationer for the homes of its staff.
- ***Paper*** Paper itself can be recycled. Some banks have developed programs of separating scrap white paper from other garbage, with the paper company collecting it and recycling it at tidy profit to the bank.
- ***Xeroxing*** How many copies of each document are really needed? Does the bank monitor its duplication and make employees feel there is a direct connection between their conservation of bank resources and their supervisors' opinion of them?
- ***Travel*** Are trips to most conventions really necessary or are they continued because of tradition? Does the person attending a convention have to justify in advance what he or she will get out of it?

  Is there recognition of how expensive travel is today and that a normal round-trip fare across the country, for example, can easily exceed two weeks wages for an officer? Does the bank work with travel agents to get best prices on travel? (For example, returning Saturday morning instead of Friday evening may save as much as one-half the round-trip fare.) Do people who attend meetings have to justify their attendance afterward with reports of use to the rest of the bank, so the trip is not just for the benefit of the individual?

- ***Phone*** Here is an area where real abuses can take place if a bank does not have controls. Not only does the bank bear the cost of the calls, but it pays for the time of the people who are sitting and chatting with friends and relatives all over the nation.

  If there is no audit of long distance calls, a bank is looking for abuse. A phone sitting on a desk is an invitation for an employee, a part-time janitor, or even a customer to sit down and make a call.

  What about calls returned to people the bank does not even know? How often does an officer find a long distance call message, return the call, only to find the bank has paid for a call to do someone else—an unknown party—a favor?

  The AT&T split has accelerated the entry of new phone companies, offering systems and long-distance rates in competition to the Bell System. The services provided by new companies should be explored.

- ***Others*** Do people turn off lights? In one major Midwestern bank, the chairman always turns off his light when he leaves his office. When asked about this, an officer responded about his chairman's habit: "You would turn off the lights too if you owned 55% of the bank's stock."

  Employees share more interest in such little items of cost control as turning off lights, curbing excessive purchasing, etc. when they are stockholders or on a profit plan. But it is up to management to make people feel that their successful performance includes keeping little things in mind, just as the chairman remembers his light switch.

  What about lunch hours and entertaining? Is it abused or does the officer's long luncheon out of the bank really bring in business? All too often what occupies a lunch, takes up two hours and leaves the officer groggy all afternoon from too much food and a cocktail or two, could have been handled in a 10-minute phone call.

BOTTOM LINE

Cost control can be abused, to be sure. In some instances the cost of keeping costs under control can exceed the savings available. And if employees are made to feel that cost control is part of their job and something that will be rewarded (instead of supervisors just criticizing those who are wasteful), a bank can build savings over time that add up bit by bit to a substantial level.

Remember: interest expense cannot be controlled; returns on loans and investments are largely beyond the banker's control; and pricing is set by competition in the vast majority of instances. This leaves cost control as almost the only game in town in the bank that is trying to build its bottom line results.

8-4 MANAGING THE BANK'S CAPITAL POSITION

To most bankers, capital adequacy has been something like the human appendix: it is only thought of when it causes trouble.

A bank can go on and on, earning profits and serving the community without any thought given to capital, until suddenly the examiners tell the board and the management that capital is inadequate. Then, just as the person who gets appendicitis finally devotes his attention to nothing but this problem, the bank thinks of little else until the capital problem is solved.

What makes it more difficult for banking is that adequate capital is almost impossible to define. There was a time when the regulator followed the rule-of-thumb that the bank should have a dollar of capital for each $10 of deposits. (One explanation given is that it was simple: the examiner had 10 fingers. And if the bank had the bad luck to have a one-armed examiner, it would have to keep a capital ratio of five-to-one.)

But as time went on, regulators and examiners modified these rigid rules. They recognized that each bank is considerably different from the others. A bank with a high degree of liquid and solid assets can operate safely with a much lower capital-to-deposits ratio than would be required of a bank with less liquid and more risky assets.

The result was that bankers could have a so-called trade off. Either they could operate with conservative assets and a high degree of leverage, or, if they wanted to have more risky and higher-yielding assets, they could have to have a stronger capital position.

Beneath all this, however, capital still remained a bargaining problem between the bank and the examiner. There have been no exact rules of capital adequacy since the old ten-to-one ratio died. As a result, the banker told to raise more capital could either ignore the request for a while, or he could fight back and indicate that he wholly disagreed with the examiner.

Since there was little the regulator could do as punishment except take the drastic step of closing the bank, the banker knew he could get away with a weak capital position at least for the present. Eventually, though, he would have to raise more capital—especially if the bank wanted some special approval from the regulators, such as a new branch or an acquisition or merger.

But otherwise, until recently, banks found they could ignore the capital issue with impunity for a good period of time.

EXAMINER ATTITUDES

Matters have changed in the last few years, however.

One factor that has made bank capital adequacy a more nagging problem has been a tightening of examiner attitudes. Whereas in the past 15 years, debenture capital grew in favor, now regulators are more frequently requiring that any new capital be equity.

This, is far more expensive for banks to raise. Debt capital sale merely requires the bank to offer the investor the going rate on debt funds, and the interest cost is a tax deduction to the bank. But equity involves giving the new investor a piece of the bank, which means he gains the average return on equity that the bank is already earning. (And, if the stock sells below book value, it costs the old shareholders even more than the average return on equity; the bank is getting less than a dollar in new funds for each dollar's worth of book value it gives out to the new investor.)

Further, with the notoriety of several bank failures recently, the regulators appeared to have become more inflexible again in their "primary" capital requirements—comprising only equity, loan loss reserves, and non-redeemable debt—pushing for a fixed ratio of about 6% capital-to-deposits.

Where in the recent past a bank could have a capital ratio that was fairly low, if it were a well-run bank with good diversification, the regulators have been asking community banks to keep this new ratio no matter how well run the bank is.

COMMON SENSE ON CAPITAL

The reaction of the banker to this new conservatism in capital adequacy has been twofold.

First, bankers have tried to get examiners to relax their new standard by indicating that in the particular case of their bank it was not necessary. Bankers have recognized that the reason why larger banks can get away with smaller capital-to-deposits ratios than community banks need has been because they have diversified assets and liabilities and have matched maturities of these assets and liabilities in order to avoid earnings squeezes in periods of volatile interest rates.

Second, banks developed controlled growth programs. They realized that growth without profit leads to double difficulty. It adds to the need for capital to back augmented size, while it does not add to retained earnings. Thus, more banks have accepted the strict doctrine that if deposit growth is not profitable there is no reason to court it.

Happily, this need to restrain the growth of the bank is being relaxed by brand new developments taking place in regulatory thinking. Regulators are finally recognizing that capital by itself is not the basic protection of deposits that it appears to be in theory.

To be sure, capital provides the extra cushion of assets over and above deposits that serves to protect depositors' funds if the bank is in trobule. But, if a bank operates in a high interest rate environment, and it has fixed-rate mortgages and other long-term assets whose value has dropped by one-third or even more, due to rising interest rates, how much real protection does even an 8% capital position provide this institution?

The strength of the bank depends then upon its ability to continue to operate without having large deposit drains that must be met by selling assets off at distress prices. In other words, it is the fear of illiquidity that can harm a bank far more than anything else.

Even a highly capitalized bank can not survive a so-called silent bank run under which a substantial proportion of deposits are withdrawn over a period of time because of losses that must be taken on sale of assets. Conversely, a slimly capitalized bank can survive happily if deposits remain stable; for there is no need to sell off depreciated assets at a loss in the latter case, and the bank can hold on to them until they mature and return to book value.

Based on this recognition that liquidity means more than capital adequacy, one can hope that the regulators will modify their new posture on the fixed capital ratio.

However, capital adequacy remains a problem for some banks. All that has really happened is that standards have been modified. The basic issue is that if a bank grows, it needs more capital.

8-5 WHY BANKS DO NOT USE TAX SWAPS—AND WHY THEY SHOULD

Tax loss planning, or doing so-called tax swaps, is about the greatest opportunity given to banking by Congress and the Tax Code. They allow a bank to deduct bond losses from normal operating income without limit. In effect, the Internal Revenue Service (IRS) eats up about half of all losses for a bank in the 50% tax bracket.

If tax swaps are so good for banks, however, why do so few bankers use them? Well, there are four basic reasons:

1 They do not have the earnings to shelter, so tax savings don't mean anything to them.
2 They fear the impact the tax loss will have on their capital positions.
3 They fear the public's and the investment community's reaction to the announcement of these losses, something they do not have to face if they don't take their losses but just keep depreciated bonds on the book.
4 They do not understand them.

GENERATING PROFITS

The first prerequisite for a tax loss program is to have income to shelter. A bank that is not paying any substantial amount of taxes has little reason to want to realize tax deductible losses. There is a good deal a bank can do to beef up income enough to make tax swaps valuable, however.

First, banks must remember that they have the right to carry back 10 years and recapture any taxes paid on income for a full decade. Tax losses that bring back home money long since paid out to IRS are sweet indeed.

In addition, banks can switch income from tax-exempt to taxable form by switching from by switching from tax-exempt bonds to higher yielding taxable ones. Granted that today the spread between taxables and tax-exempts has narrowed considerably because of a dearth of buyers for municipals, and a rise in the variety and number of tax-exempts being issued. Even so, any improvement at all in yield by switching to taxables from tax-exempts is valuable if the swap procedure is going to negate any tax liabilities on taxable bonds anyway.

A bank can also reexamine its loan loss reserve program, and look at other discretionary decisions that may be slanted to bring more income now as another way to build income, so that tax losses taken on depreciated bonds can be valuable. Normal steps to improve earnings by rethinking pricing, lending policies, efficiency, and other traditional banking decisions also can help.

There is another possibility, albeit one that many frown upon: detaching future coupons on bonds and selling them now at a discount. While legal, this practice is considered to be poor accounting and reporting policy.

This procedure generates income today at the expense of income tomorrow, and it overstates income to a degree because the coupons' income has not yet been earned. Thus, some acccountants and auditors raise their hands in horror at the suggestion.

Others, though, look at this as a legitimate way of generating income today so that tax swaps can be utilized, and so that past tax losses can be used to offset current income before the tax loss provisions expire. They also can push the losses into the future, because the bonds with detached coupons, if sold, will have to be sold at a loss later on due to their missing coupons—so that tax loss benefits can be transferred to the future when profits may be high enough to make them more valuable than they would be today.

But a word of caution: if profits are not there after all of these procedures are considered, tax swaps do no good. Deducting losses from operating income when there is no operating income is impossible.

CAPITAL QUESTION

Another reason why so many banks do not do tax swaps is that they fear the impact on their capital positions.

This is still a topsy-turvy world of regulation. One bank has bonds that have depreciated. The bank does nothing about it. It holds bonds in its portfolio and waits for them to mature in the distant future.

Because the bonds stay in the portfolio, the regulators say that these bonds are worth what the bank paid for them and do not have to be written down. Thus, there is no charge-off against capital, even though if the bank needed funds and had to sell these bonds, it would have to take a substantial loss at that time.

A second bank, however, does make tax swaps. It realizes its losses, improves its income-generating potential by reinvesting the proceeds and the tax saving in new, higher coupon bonds, and it has a new portfolio marked much more closely to market—so that if it has to sell bonds, it will not have to realize the losses that the bank that just sat there and did nothing would have to take.

Yet the regulators and examiners say this second bank has impaired its capital by taking the losses and thus it may be subject to pressure to raise more capital because of this impairment.

This is crazy. The bank realizing its losses is a far more profitable and stronger bank than the one with its head in the sand. Yet regulators act as if the exact opposite were the case.

Banks that are under pressure because their capital positions are not up to regulators' standards (whatever these may be) thus hesitate to do tax swaps because of the impact on capital. Many know they would be better off rather than worse off making tax swaps, but what regulators say still carries a great deal of weight.

Happily this situation is changing.

The Federal Home Loan Bank Board has ruled that when savings and loans sell depreciated mortgages, they can write off the losses over the remaining life of the mortgage instead of immediately. In this way, the S&Ls can improve income by reinvesting the proceeds without impairing their already thin capital positions.

Who knows? Maybe bank regulators will soon also take the same enlightened attitude. Some top regulatory officials admit privately that they are more relaxed in demanding stronger capital positions when a bank has done tax swaps and improved the strength and worth of its bond portfolio thereby, than when the bank has not done so.

Be this as it may, the problem of impairment of capital does remain the most substantial drawback to tax loss planning because of the short-sighted rules of regulators and examiners that still apply today.

PUBLIC OPINION

A third issue, that of public and investor attitude, is a lot easier to handle than is the problem of the regulators' attitudes towards tax swaps and their impact on bank capital.

Those bankers who fear public reaction to announcement of losses and worry that investors will turn away from the bank because it has announced higher losses should take heart. This can be completely overcome and the taking of losses can be turned into a positive feature instead of a drawback, if explained properly.

At least one large bank sent a letter to shareholders and the public that included the following paragraphs:

> The bank recognizes the hard reality that present levels of inflation and interest rates are expected to remain with us for some time. Therefore, management has decided to take steps this quarter to improve earnings prospects in the fourth quarter and the year ahead. We have elected to take significant losses on bonds previously acquired at lower rates of return and to reinvest the proceeds at today's high levels.
>
> The improved earnings realized will recover the losses during the year, while increasing the bank's operating earnings substantially.
>
> In addition, this strategy raises the liquidity of the bank, improving our ability to handle rate volatility, and affords us the opportunity to restructure the bond portfolio in light of uncertain markets over the next few years. This action, coupled with our ongoing program to control all categories of operating expense, will return us to an upward trend in earnings beginning in the fourth quarter of this year.

It would be hard for a depositor or stockholder to read this statement without feeling better about his work. The announcement and explanation help get the public to realize that the reported losses are a sign of strength, not weakness.

What about shareholders and investors? Do they look at tax losses caused by selling depreciated bonds and downgrade their opinion of the organization?

Investment professionals do not. They know what tax loss planning can do for future bank earnings.

According to a study by bank analysts at The First Boston Corp., a bank can take 10–15% of a full year's earnings in security losses, and the hit will not hurt its stock price in the market, provided the bank will use the loss to enhance its portfolio. In other words, as long as the losses and replacement bonds make portfolio sense the bank will not be hurt. Naturally, as earnings improve following the tax swap program, stock prices should move upward.

BOTTOM LINE

The only snag is the unwillingness to take tax losses because the bank and especially its board do not understand them. Hopefully, this chapter will change things:

One bank CEO put it this way:

> I explain my tax swap plans to the board, and then I tell them it is just like taking the penalty on an old certificate of deposit to get my money back so I can reinvest it at higher rates today.

When I put it in such personal terms, board members begin to understand better what we are trying to do.

Accounting techniques cannot be expected to change enough so that banks that do tax swaps avoid the problem of announcing these losses while those that hide them can avoid the issue. But this is certainly a valid goal.

While many banks continue to hesitate to use tax loss planning, those that do continue to smile at the result and the splendid impact on bottom-line earnings. Bank executives and their boards must fully understand what tax loss planning involves, what the implications are, and especially by how much the benefits outweigh the disadvantages. Until they do, this valuable tax feature will remain one of banking's least utilized opportunities for profit enhancement.

8-6 TAX SWAPS ON BONDS MAKE SENSE

One of the mysteries of commercial banking is why banks pay more income taxes than they have to. No one wants to pay taxes. There is no benefit to paying more than the legal minimum. Yet, in bank after bank, the opportunity to reduce tax payments by tax-loss planning on bonds (otherwise called tax swaps) is passed by year after year. Banks pay their taxes when they have profits. But when they have losses, they hide them so that no one can know about them, even though the government is willing to absorb 50% the loss.

What makes this even more poignant a situation is the fact that so many banks have large losses on their municipal bonds.

Many state and local governments are offering their tax-exemption power to corporations, home buyers, students in need of loans, and others. The result has been such a proliferation of new bonds that interest costs have soared, and so older bonds with their lower coupons have declined sharply in value.

There is talk now of changes in this structure. These changes might include reducing the ability of state and local governments to share their tax-exemption feature with corporations, banks, and other credit users by limiting the sale of industrial revenue bonds. There has been an end to the practice of advance refunding, under which local governments borrow money before they need it on a tax-exempt basis and invest it in U.S. governments until that time to take advantage of the interest rate spread.

There is also talk of replacing tax exemption with a federal subsidy for state and local facilities that are thought to be worthwhile, with the borrower then selling taxable bonds. It is felt that such a subsidy would be cheaper than the loss of revenue that impacts the federal government when tax-exempt bonds are sold.

But this is in the future. For the present, the state of tax-exempt bonds, coupled with high interest rates, have made the value of bonds in bank portfolios decline sharply. The laws now in force make it worthwhile for banks to sell these bonds and reinvest the proceeds. As matters now stand, the IRS will absorb about one-half the loss, thereby making the tax swap truly valuable for the bank if it reinvests both the proceeds of the sale and the tax savings in new municipal bonds that offer today's higher yields.

MOTIVES

Why are banks given the opportunity that no one else has to deduct bond losses from normal operating income in determining tax liabilities? The answer involves an understanding of the pivotal role that bank investments play in motivating economic activity, especially in a time of recession. As every investment officer well realizes (although they frequently wonder why no else in the bank seems to realize it) bonds are the residual use of bank funds.

When loan demanded is weak, the investment officer gets the money to invest. But at such time, interest rates are low and bond prices are high, so his opportunities to put the money to work in attractive low-cost investments are limited.

Later, however, when loan demand picks up and the bank wants the money back for its lending people, the investment officer is forced to sell his bonds. Yet at this time, improvement in economic activity has brought higher interest rates and lower bond prices. Thus the investment officer buys high and sells low. (This may explain why so few investment officers are picked to be the new CEO. The board wonders: "How can we choose someone who buys them when they're high and sells them when they're low?")

Why is the bank willing to make its investments a residual use of funds? The answer is that the bank wants to serve its market area, and loans are personal and local while investments are impersonal. The bank that turns down a loan request because it does not want to take a loss on its bonds may be losing a customer and his balances forever.

What many banks do is keep bond investments extremely short and liquid when the investment officer does get the funds. In this way, the losses are less when the bonds must be sold to meet reemerging loan demand.

This, however, is just what Congress does not want. If banks keep investments extremely liquid in recessions, the economy does not get the benefit of the impetus to economic activity that would accrue were the banks to be aggressive in their investment policy.

The economy would be far better off were the banks to buy longer-term municipal bonds that finance schools, roads, and other facilities than if they restrict investments to short-term Treasury bills.

To help commercial banks be more aggressive at such times, the banks have been given the ability to deduct any losses, taken later on such bonds when they are sold, from normal operating income—a privilege offered no other group of institutions or individuals in the nation. This means the IRS eats about one-half the bond sale loss in a bank earning average income levels.

Since 1969, this privilege has been tied to a parallel feature: any profit on bonds is subject to normal tax rates rather than to capital gains rates, so that banks can no longer pay capital gains rates on profits but deduct losses from normal income as was the case before 1969. Since banks generally have losses on bonds rather than profits, this is a low price to pay for the privilege of deducting bond losses from normal income in determining income tax liabilities.

With this feature of deductibility of losses from normal income, the stage is set for creative tax planning in the bank.

HOW IT FIGURES

The hypothetical swap presented below is far too elementary. It does not include transaction costs, and it assumes, incorrectly, that new bonds with their par price and current coupon sell at the same yield as do older, discount bonds that banks and others are trying to get rid of. But the advantages of a tax swap, as set out below, are so great that even when the numbers are tempered with reality, there is still enough value in them to justify the bank realizing its losses on depreciated bonds with the expectation that the benefits from doing so will be unbelievably large!

In our example, the bank has a municipal bond with a 4% coupon and 20 years left to maturity.

Since interest rates have risen considerably, this bond naturally would sell for far less than the price the bank paid for it, and for far less than the price at which it is on the books. A yield book would show that this 4% bond now would have to sell at a price of $768.90 (for $1,000 principal) to offer the buyer at a going yield of even 6%. If nothing was done, the bank would hold the bond, earn $40 a year, and receive $1,000 back in 20 years when the bond matures and is paid off at par.

Consider the same bond in a tax swap situation.

First it is *very* important that a bank have profits against which it can realize its losses for a tax swap to work. Too many banks have developed tax swap losses and then found that they did not have the income that needed to be sheltered and that could thus make the tax swap valuable.

It must be added, however, that a bank that has reported income and paid taxes in the past decade can use a tax swap to generate a loss and recapture the taxes paid for as far back as 10 years. This also can make a tax swap work, even without adequate current income.

But if there is some present or past income to be sheltered, the bank realizes a loss by selling its 20-year 4% bond at price, which would be $768.90 per $1,000 of principal in a 6% rate environment, for a loss of $231.10.

If the bank is in a 50% tax bracket, this means that the actual loss after the tax saving is half the $231.10 or $115.55.

The bank now reinvests the $768.90 and the tax saving of $115.55 in new bonds. It can invest the tax saving along with the proceeds, because this $115.55 consists of actual dollars that do not have to be sent to the IRS any more. They are thus now available for bank usage, when they would not have been available to the bank had the tax swap not been taken.

Important: the $884.45 must be placed into new fully priced tax-exempt bonds with a current coupon or the tax advantages are dissipated. If the bank bought other bonds selling at a discount, it must be remembered it would have to pay normal tax rates on the capital appreciation. But if it gets all its yield through the higher coupon on new municipal bonds selling at par, the yield is all tax exempt.

This is what makes a tax swap work: the loss is fully deductible. However, the reinvestment is exempt from taxation, because the profits all flow to the bank through new higher coupon tax-exempt bonds.

With interest rates at 6%, the bank reinvests its $884.45 (the $768.90 plus the $115.55 tax saving) and it earns now a coupon yield of $53.06 (6% of $884.45), which means the bank is earning nearly one-third more on its money than it earned when it received a coupon of $40 a year.

This is a 32.65% increase the bank's yield. That is what a tax swap does.

There is a price, of course. The bank now has only $884.45 principal value of bonds instead of $1,000. And 20 years from now it will only get back $884.45 instead of $1,000. But, looking at the present value of $115.55 20 years from now in a 6% rate environment, the present value of this loss is $36.07. In other words, if $36.07 was put away away at 6% today, in 20 years we would have the $115.55 needed to make up the amount necessary to bring the principal back to $1,000.

Put in its simplest terms, then, a bank must give up $36.07 to earn $13.06 a year more in coupon income for 20 years than it would otherwise earn. This is a return of 36.65% a year on the investment.

No wonder so many banks have determined that, by using tax swaps, they can improve earnings and earn back their losses in several years, with all further profit improvement being to the shareholders' benefit.

8-7 A PROFIT PLAN SHOULD HELP THE BANK, TOO

"We made a good profit last year, despite low loan demand, by selling bonds that had appreciated sharply." This was the boast made recently by a bank CEO. Further examination showed that the policy about which the CEO bragged, really did not make sense.

The bank was operating with a loan-to-deposit ratio of about 20%; the CEO indicated that there were few loans available in the community to raise that poor ratio. In addition, he stated that the main use of the bank's funds was selling Fed funds to other banks—with Fed funds then running at 20 to 25% of overall assets of the bank.

Why, then, did the bank sell bonds that offered yields of up to 15%, only to pay taxes on the profits, and then place the remaining proceeds into Fed funds that yield around one-half what the bonds brought home?

There was a simple answer. The bank's investment officer knew that officers' bonuses were tied to profits. The only way to generate more profits in that bank was to realize capital gains by getting rid of the high-yield bonds. Thus, the CEO had given the indication that this was in the bank's best interest. In actuality, it was a lousy policy for the bank. However, it was a good policy for the officers who wanted their bonuses and did not much care what happened to the bank in future years.

Unfortunately, this is a recurring problem in banks that have developed incentive programs. Profits can be whatever the bank and its top staff want them to be:

Loan officers who want to generate profits can take on loans that have a higher than satisfactory prospect of going sour, but that can generate income today.

Auditors and loan reviewers who want higher profits for higher bonuses can place loan loss reserves well below what the correct figure should be.

Investment officers can take profits when they are not in the best interest of the institution. But as long as profit plans are developed that stress current income, no one can blame the officers who generate income and let tomorrow take care of itself.

NO PROGRAM

Perhaps this is why some banks frown so strongly on profit incentive programs. They feel that by offering such incentives, they are making the officer corps supersensitive to present income at the expense of the future of the institution. Even so, there are few mottos as effective as: "What's in it for me?"

Maybe the problem is that some banks have set up profit plans without refining them to a degree that encourages actions that work for the long-term advantage of the bank. Many observers feel that one problem with the United States industrial complex is that managers are judged on immediate results. This encourages them to think only of today's profits, and not undertake capital spending that might dampen present income but generate future revenue. A major reason given for this emphasis on the immediate is that it is what the public and investors use to judge management performance. If managers were judged on the way they prepare their companies for the future, instead of being evaluated on present income, profit generation, and a rise in stock prices, there would be less emphasis on today at the expense of tomorrow.

Because of its more flexible accounting possibilities, banks are most susceptible to this. The bank that sold its high-yielding municipals and placed the proceeds in Fed funds, and paid a tax for the privilege of so doing, should serve as a horrible example of the need for long-range planning in profits as well as in other aspects of banking.

8-8 BANK ANNUAL REPORTS—FACT OR FICTION?

The annual report of a corporation is the most revealing regular document the company issues. In commercial banking, the significance of the report is even greater. After all, a manufacturing company has, as its principal obligation, the fostering of the well-being of its shareholders. But for a bank, there are far more publics than just shareholders who must be well served. If a bank gets into trouble, the entire community is affected. And if a bank is not doing its job well, the depository and people dependent upon bank credit are the sufferers.

It would appear, then, that there are a number of groups concerned with bank performance and so are interested in the bank annual report. They include:

Stockholders who are anxious to protect their investment and benefit therefrom.

Depositors who want to make sure that the funds they have placed in the bank are safe.

Borrowers who want to be sure that, when they come in for credit, the bank will be able to grant it.

Employees who want to be sure of the viability of their employer.

Regulators who have to be sure that the banks they supervise are safe.

The banking industry and especially competitors and those banks that might want to join this institution in merger or in a holding company.

And the analysts, last but not least, who must make sure that they are recommending the best investment vehicles to their clients.

Yet despite the importance of bank statements, one can still question whether these documents are really adequate to serve all the people they are intended to serve.

Unfortunately, bank annual reports and other financial statements can be skewed in many different ways to accomplish many different goals of management. There may still be a lot of truth in the old story that an accounting firm hired is the one that answers the question, "What is two and two?" with the response, "What number did you have in mind?"

One cannot simply blame the bankers or the accountants. In an era in which honest differences may develop, it can be difficult to generate exact data that all could agree upon. But the fact that many of the problems stem from honest differences of opinion rather than attempts to skew data in one way or another does little to help those who must depend upon bank reports for actionable data. The warning must be accepted that bank reports are only a beginning; the interested party must dig beyond the printed page to learn what he or she really wants to know.

THE SIZE OF THE BANK

The first area in which bank data can mislead is the issue of size of the institutions. One might think that size is something that cannot be adjusted to please the management. Unfortunately, this is not the case. Banks can add window dressing to their statements. And there may be times when they are forced into a situation that bloats the balance sheet to please good customers.

Window dressing, by itself, is a simple procedure. The statement that a bank publishes includes uncollected funds as well as collected funds. Thus, two banks sometimes exchange large-sized checks just before statement day. The result is that in the annual report, each bank is considerably larger both in deposit totals (including the new deposit from the other bank which was uncollected) and in checks in process of collection. Shortly after year-end, both totals drop back down as the crossed checks clear and the banks settle back to their normal size. In the meantime, each bank looked better on statement day.

The procedure reached a point where one year the Comptroller of the Currency waited until January and then asked for a call report based on late December figures rather than December 31 totals; a number of banks were shown to have expanded rather rapidly in the last few days of the year.

Another way in which window dressing takes place is when a good customer decides to reward certain banks with large deposits for statement day, even though these deposits are kept elsewhere during the rest of the year. For example, a major company may wish to help the local bank look good at year-end, even though the basic funds are usually kept in a much larger city for corporate convenience. Thus money is wired home on December 31 and back out on January 2, distorting the size of both banks concerned.

Not all window dressing is the banker's fault or at the banker's bidding. There are companies that borrow over year-end to make their own liquidity ratios look better. If, for example, a company has $1 million of short-term assets and $1 million of short-term liabilities, its quick ratio is 50%. If over statement day, however, it borrows another $1 million and just leaves it in the bank, it raises the ratio to 67%. This procedure also makes the bank look bigger in the process.

Finally, since much of a bank's total deposits consist of float by the normal flow of payments, a bank may look far bigger than it really is just in the normal course of business.

Bank size, then, can be almost anything on statement day. Consequently, some bankers have specialized in making their banks larger for annual report purposes than is actually the case. Others, however, have hesitated, either out of a feeling that this is an unnecessary distortion, or because they fear that they cannot get the same deposit growth results every year; therefore, they might look good one year and terrible the next in terms of bank growth.

Because of this situation, a number of good analysts try to get averages of daily figures, rather than a picture of how the bank stands on the last day of the year. They feel this is a far better picture of a bank's true assests and liabilities.

Quality of Deposits

Another problem that analysts face in determining bank size is the quality of bank deposits in terms of loyalty.

An annual report is only a good indicator if it can be used as the basis for prediction of future results. But all too often a bank's picture on statement day has distortions in it that will alter the totals dramatically in the near future. A bank that uses a gift program to generate deposits may or may not find that these deposits stick to it beyond the minimum time required. Pots and pans can hype a balance sheet. But how long will that hype last?

Similarly, a bank can build deposits by offering extremely attractive rates on hot money. But this money will leave just as quickly as it came in if someone else offers a better yield at the short-term certificate's maturity date.

Also, deposits may be political in nature. A bank may have obtained deposits from a company or a public body on a temporary basis in payment for past favors done. The bank, then, is sold, and the new owners expect that they have obtained a sizable core of deposits, only to find that much of this money leaves when those to whom the repayment for favors was due have given up control.

THE BANK'S LIQUIDITY

The question of bank liquidity has assumed prime importance in recent years. Most banks that have faced difficulties have done so because of liquidity squeezes rather than capital problems. A key factor is similar to one discussed under the topic of size—the degree of loyalty the depositor has to the bank.

In addition, banks frequently have given false pictures of their liquidity by not adequately breaking down assets and liabilities in the annual report. Gone are the days when an observer could look at the loan-to-deposit ratios and tell by this whether the bank was liquid or not. Loans can be long or short term in nature, as can investments. So, unless a bank does a breakdown of the maturity of investments and the nature of the loans, a bank with a low loan-to-deposit ratio may look good but may actually be highly illiquid, because of a locked-in position with long-term bonds. At the same time, a bank with a high loan-to-deposit ratio actually may be fairly liquid because of the short-term nature of those loans.

What makes the liquidity issue more complex in today's environment is the fact that so many banks are practicing active liability management—purchasing funds to meet loan demands and deposit outflows. Thus, a breakdown of the character of deposits is mandatory for a proper determination of the bank's liquidity. Without that breakdown, the librarian should head automatically for the fiction section as soon as the report arrives in the mail.

THE BANK'S PROFITABILITY

The key area where bank reports can be skewed to provide the "numbers the management has in mind" is profitability.

There are various reasons why banks may want to bloat profitability or to shrink it. While one can quickly think of illegal means of altering profits—such as the backdating of the switch of investments from the trading portfolio to the bank portfolio so that recent bond losses could be hidden—there are a large number of strictly legal steps a bank can take to alter profitability figures. What is worse, the bank that is honestly trying to boost profitability by taking valid and worthwhile actions may look worse for the present than the bank that ignores the opportunities that exist to improve long-range profits.

For example, if a bank feels it is generating too much profit, and wants to store a little away for next year, so that its profit growth pattern is more stable, some of the actions it can take are prepaying lawyers' fees, insurance, pension plan contributions, and other expenses. The banks can also speed up routine maintenance that can be expensed instead of capitalized. A few banks have been more ingenious, including several that have simply loaded up the postage meters in late December to tuck away dollars for the next year.

More technical, but also more significant, are the decisions on depreciation of assets acquired through foreclosure as well as depreciation rates on the bank's own building and equipment. And there are some banks still holding common stock they acquired years ago in foreclosure that are on the books at a tiny fraction of their true worth today.

Conversely, a bank may depreciate assets at as rapid a rate as possible for tax purposes and write them off far more slowly for accounting purposes to make profits look better to the public.

But the two most significant areas in which profit data must be taken with a grain of salt are determining the reserve for loan losses and valuing the bank's investment portfolio. Observers of banking are frequently amazed to see the press and the general public look at a bank and feel that it is improving substantially; in effect, all it has done is alter its policy with regard to these two areas.

LOAN LOSS RESERVES

The basic rules of loan loss reserves are well known by most bankers. Simply stated, as long as the IRS permits a bank to deduct a certain amount from profits to be set aside as a reserve against possible loan losses, a bank would be foolish not to build this reserve up to the maximum level allowed. If it does not do so, it must pay taxes on the revenue—a distasteful step that is easily avoided by the building of reserves.

The problem, however, is that the level of loss reserve the IRS allows and the level the bank feels it will actually need to cover losses (called the valuation reserve) are almost always two distinct amounts. Banks handle this by establishing a valuation reserve that reflects the amount the bank feels it will need to cover future loan losses. If this is less than the IRS allows, the bank breaks the rest of the allowable reserve into two categories— a *deferred tax* portion, placed under "other liabilities" on the balance sheet because it will eventually have to be paid to the IRS if, the bank feels, loan losses are not as great as IRS loss reserve maximums would cover; and a *contingency* portion, placed just under undivided profits, because it really reflects profits the bank feels it has earned and will record later but has set aside to reduce tax liabilities today.

If the bank feels it needs more valuation reserve than the IRS allows, it pays taxes on earnings and then sets money aside as a "tax paid contingency reserve." If it is proven correct and the reserve is needed to cover losses, it will recapture the taxes paid and use both the recaptured taxes and the contingency reserve to meet losses.

Reserve Guidelines

Banks do have guidelines as to how much to place into the valuation reserve, based on past experience, evaluation of economic events, and a review of the loan portfolio. These figures on loan loss reserves to be taken must also be approved by the bank's independent auditor. Yet there is still plenty of room for controversy or disagreement. After all, who can honestly tell which loans will go sour and which will not? If a bank wants to skew earnings upward or downward, its decision with regard to its loan loss valuation reserve can play a major role in reaching the profit goals desired.

This can work in both directions. A bank that wishes to keep earnings totals high may keep its loan loss reserves down and accomplish this goal. Sometimes, however, such a bank is later forced to build up the reserve by the regulators or the auditors, or management may feel it has to correct a mistake. This can lead to a downward restatement of prior years' earnings—a true indication of how correct the librarian was who placed the report in the fiction section.

Conversely, a bank may wish to keep earnings lower for some reason. It may want to have ammunition in reserve for profit growth in the next year. Or management may want to write off all past lending mistakes, bite the bullet, and get a fresh start for the next year with valuation reserves built up enough to cover all losses possible (with the bank getting the opportunity later to recapture these reserves into profits if the actual loss record is not as gloomy as the forecast).

A new management may wish to clean out all the mistakes of the old chief executive and air them publicly by building the loss reserve at the expense of profits. In this way, the new CEO starts with a clean slate (and also his figures on profit look good compared with those of the last year of prior management).

To the observer reading the annual report: Look deeper than the immediate numbers if surprises in later years are to be avoided.

REALIZING BOND LOSSES

The second major area in which profits can be distorted by management action involves the tax loss planning that leads to sales of depreciated bonds—a step that makes a bank look worse but actually will allow it to become far stronger both now and in the future.

A quick summary of information discussed earlier on tax swaps shows how this apparent distortion takes place. A bank has an obligation as part of its reason for being in business to make loans when the local people want them. Investments thus are made generally when loan demands are weak and are sold when loan demands pick up. But this also means that the bank is buying bonds at times of slack credit demand when interest rates are low and bond prices are high; they are forced to sell them when interest rates have moved up due to increased demands for funds and bond prices have fallen.

The bank is willing to buy high and sell low because it wants to serve its community. Moreover, it feels it will get back the losses on its bond sales through quarter income on its loans and the correlated deposits and business its local borrowers will bring it. But even so, banks are likely to keep bond investments extremely short term when they are made, so that the switch back to loans can be made with a minimum capital loss. The shorter the bond, the less the price decline for any given rise in interest rates.

As far as the government is concerned, however, it wants banks to be aggressive in the bond market when loan demands are weak and to buy longer-term issues which help finance schools, hospitals, and the various other facilities that the nation needs and whose construction can help cure the economic slack. To encourage banks to be more aggressive in their bond investments at times of economic slack and weak loan demands, then, the IRS has allowed banks to deduct their capital losses on bonds sold from ordinary income for tax purposes! Since banks are generally in a corporate tax range of close to 50%, this means that the government is absorbing almost half the loss that banks must take by selling depreciated bonds.

A bank that sells its depreciated bonds and reinvests the proceeds and the tax savings generally can improve earnings substantially, especially if it invests the proceeds and tax savings in new tax-exempt bonds that are selling at par with current, higher coupons. In such a situation, it can deduct the losses on the old bonds from ordinary income for tax purposes and pay no income taxes on the new higher coupon bonds it is buying. (If it buys depreciated bonds with lower coupons, however, this is poor policy. The depreciated bond provides part of its yield through appreciation to maturity, and this capital gain is subject to normal income taxes for a bank—as an offset to the deduction of capital losses from normal income for tax purposes. Buying a new, higher coupon bond at par avoids this problem.)

The smart bank thus sells its depreciated bonds, takes its tax savings, and reinvests the saving and the sale proceeds. The result frequently is that a bank can improve earnings enough to pay off the loss in three years or so, and then have the new higher stream of earnings from then on that reinvestment in higher coupon bonds provides (See articles on tax swaps earlier in this section.)

Distorting the Picture

This is where the accounting techniques required by the regulators distort the picture. Basic to an understanding is the fact that if a bank has a bond that has depreciated in value and it merely holds it, it keeps the bond on its books at cost and never recognizes the loss. If, however, the bank sells the bond, it must write off the loss and also erode its capital position by the amount of the write-off.

Common logic would show that the bank that sold the bond and wrote off the loss would be stronger than the one that did nothing. This is because it would have its bonds priced realistically, with prices on the books realistically indicating what the bank could get for its bonds in an emergency if it sold them to meet a liquidity squeeze. In addition, the bank would have its tax saving available as investable funds, which would help generate a higher stream of earnings from the procedure. Yet the bank that realized its losses has to show the losses on the books.

The other bank that did nothing now sits with a portfolio that is valued at far more than could be obtained in an emergency, it has no funds generated by tax saving, and it has a lower level of investment income yearly because it did not do a tax swap. Still, its earnings posture is stronger on the statement because it did nothing with its old, depreciated bonds.

Before the mid-1970s, a bank would report both operating earnings and net income, with operating earnings the more significant indicator. Thus the bank that did do tax swaps would look better on the indicator that counted most—earnings on loans and investments; and few would look at the decline on the bottom line in net income, caused by the bond sale. Now, however, banks must report one bottom-line number. So the banks that have taken their losses, strengthened their portfolios, and built up their earnings generation capacity are forced to report poorer earnings on the bottom line and poorer capital positions than the banks that did not take this acute step.

Accounting standards being what they are, no wonder so many banks do not take advantage of this real benefit the IRS has given them in an effort to help the economy. They feel they cannot afford the publicity of the negative impact on reported earnings and capital, even if they recognize in their own minds that this is merely cosmetic and reflects the exact opposite of what the tax swap did for their bank's future profitability.

INTERNATIONAL ASPECTS

Those who work with banks that have international departments have another concern: how funds flow from office to office to take advantage of tax laws and regulatory requirements in each country in which the bank operates. Some banks have been accused of parking profits in the nations with the lowest tax rates: they feel that this is the only reason why some international banks have reported such a large percentage of their income as coming from abroad and from specific nations.

This is a far more complex issue than even domestic bank accounting; but it further indicates how difficult it is to predict bank profits and performance in years ahead from data available today.

To be fair, some banks have tried extremely hard and effectively to make their annual reports into realistic documents that point out pitfalls and potentials that serve as the best available indicators of where the bank is going in the years ahead. Others, unfortunately, continue with business as usual.

On balance, the bank annual report remains like the pretty face on a girl seen at a mixer dance. To make a long-term decision based on this one factor can lead to misery later. But at least it serves as the initial means of attracting attention and encouraging the necessary deeper investigation.

9 Bank Stock

9-1 THE PRICE OF YOUR BANK'S STOCK DOES MATTER

Bank stocks have become an enigma in recent years. Price has lagged well behind performance—unless performance has been bad. As many bank stock analysts have observed, the price of a bank's stock generally does not reflect how well the bank has been doing.

Except for some of the larger money centers and regional banks, people hold on to the stock they have in a bank. It might not be a spectacular performer in the market, but it is there. Fortunately, in most cases, shareholders do not evaluate their bank stock in the same way they do other investments; the shares are something special, perhaps to pass on to one's heirs.

This kind of attitude, however, is changing as the financial marketplace itself changes. Moreover, bank executives who simply do not care what happens to their stock price, and thus leave it the same year after year, exhibit a rather callous attitude toward the shareholders. It may be that some bankers hold such a view because they feel they really are the bank and that the shareholders are some amorphous mass that shows up once a year at shareholder meetings, if at all, and which must be sent an annual report and possibly a dividend check.

One of the most frequent complaints of bank officers is that they boosted earnings substantially, or raised the dividend, or declared a substantial extra dividend—and the stock price did nothing or even went down on the news.

What these bankers should realize is that the day-to-day share price, if set by an independent dealer, must reflect supply and demand at that time rather than anything going on in the bank. Thus, even if the bank has good news to report, if at the same time a major shareholder wants to sell his stock or an estate is settled and a large block of shares must be liquidated, the stock price will go down rather than up.

Thus, many bankers feel share price action is unrepresentative of real bank worth. Many bankers then think they can do a better job of setting share price than the marketplace can. This makes them able to rest easily even though they are both chief executive officer and market-maker in the bank's stock, a dangerous legal conflict of interest.

There are also those who really like their stock price to be low. They are steadily buying in shares for board members, for the pension fund, and for other insiders such as the employees represented by the stock option plan. To these bankers, the more shares they can collect at attractively low prices, the happier they are. In many institutions, over time, the shares have become more and more closely held because of such actions.

CAPITAL NEEDS

Is such a policy fair to the bank and fair to the bank's shareholders? For the bank itself, it may have seemed to matter little whether share price is high or low. But this is no longer true. If banks want to grow, they need new capital. If the shares of the bank have remained static for years at a low price-earnings multiple, it will be extremely difficult now to get present shareholders or anyone else to invest in new shares needed to back the bank's deposit expansion.

Other cases of the impact of unfulfilled capital need can be even more striking. Consider one bank where there top officers and the board decided a new building would be a splendid idea. When it was finished, the regulators came in and said the bank needed more capital because it had converted so much of its liquid funds into new fixed assets. However, the bank was unable to raise more capital because of the share performance through the years. Eventually, it had to sell out to a holding company that promised to pump more capital into the bank, even though the board and officer staff wanted to remain independent.

SHAREHOLDER EQUITY

The question of equity for the shareholders is even more important.

While in certain years a bank's stock may do well, the far more likely story has been of share price remaining fairly static in the banks with closed markets. Openly traded stocks have at least had the opportunity to experience price advances to match bank performance improvements.

What the banker who makes the market in his desk and keeps the price steady or low is doing, then, is saying that those who hang on to the stock are holding an investment of growing intrinsic worth, if there are rising earnings. But, if a shareholder has the misfortune to want to sell or to have to sell out at any time, he or she will probably not get a price that reflects the rising worth of the investment.

Since banks generally have lower percentage dividend payouts than do industrial companies, because they need the capital to back growth, this maintenance of a fixed stock price thus harms the bank shareholder in two ways: (1) the shareholder does not get the dividend growth that shareholders in other ventures would as profits rise: and (2) the shareholders of the closely held bank is denied the rising market price that otherwise would be likely to develop over time in reaction to rising earnings retained for future use in the bank. One wonders, then, why anyone would want to hold the shares of such a bank or buy into the corporation.

SHAREHOLDER LOYALTY

Banks used to be able to count on the loyalty of their local shareholders. This loyalty is no longer as deep as it once was.

As tender offers come in from the stock of the bank from foreigners with ample dollar holdings, or as other bidders come in who want to take control of the bank, some bankers have been surprised and very unhappy over the "disloyalty" shown by their shareholders. It appears in these cases that stockholders, while apparently happy with whatever action the bank's management took, really were not too happy with share price action. When a reasonable offer came in that involved a price well-above the going price on the shares, these supposedly loyal shareholders jumped at the opportunity to get out of their investment.

9-2 WHAT SHAREHOLDERS WANT

Owners of a bank's stock want earnings to increase every year, of course. Earnings are, inpart, a result of effective management. However, outside forces, over which the management of a bank has no control, also impact on the bottom line.

Beyond the earning picture, however, there are a great many things that management can do to make the bank's stock more attractive than it otherwise would be with the same level of earnings. Fortunately, many of them are simple to implement.

SURVEYING SHAREHOLDERS

A number of bankers are taking the somewhat unusal step of surveying their shareholders to find out just what they want. Some of the responses have been amazing: people who have held bank shares for decades report that they were never before asked their opinions on anything to do with the bank.

One benefit of such surveys is that the bank can determine whether the shareholders prefer a more generous dividend payout or whether they would rather that the bank pay out less and reinvest more. If a bank has a large number of rich stockholders who pay out as much as 50% of their dividends in taxes, a lower payout/higher reinvestment programs would be preferred. These shareholders hope and expect that the reinvestment will raise the stock price and bring about capital gains. Then, if the shareholder sold the stock, the tax would be substantially lower.

Specifically as a result of surveys and conversations with shareholders and analysts, bankers have learned several basic strategies that appear to work to raise the multiples in most instances.

PRICE RANGE

Studies have shown that most investors, for some reason, like stocks that sell in a moderate price range of from \$10 to \$20 a share on the low side up to \$70 to \$80 on the high side. Below the \$10 price, investors seem to feel that it is a cheap stock and not representative of quality. Above the \$80 figure, the price seems unreachable.

There are two possible solutions in this situation. If the stock is too cheap, a possible reverse split may be undertaken. This may be difficult, as few companies like to call in two shares and issue one in their place. The other alternative is far more palatable, however. Many bank shares are in the \$100 range and even well above that. Bankers generally find that if a 3-for-1 split takes place on a stock selling at say \$150, the resulting three shares frequently end up selling at above \$50 rather than at that level. The split makes the issue more attractive.

RIGHTS OFFERINGS

With infrequently traded stocks, it is hard for the public to figure out what the value of the stock really is. Thus trades sometimes take place at extremely low prices because of the lack of sufficient and current information as to what a stock is worth.

If the bank makes a rights offering to its shareholders, however, it can accomplish two things. First of all, it can raise needed equity capital. Second, by setting an offering price, the bank itself can tell the public what it feels the stock is worth.

Naturally, the price cannot be set so high that the stock purchase is a poor value for the shareholders subscribing to new stock. This would quickly be denounced by market-makers and analysts, and the issue could well be a flop. If an inactive market is causing the stock to sell at a multiple below that on stocks of similar banks in the region, however, the price established in the rights offering can be used to bring the multiple back up to that of other banks. The stock price would thus be raised a number of points.

As an additional step, some banks offer annual rights offerings to their shareholders, setting the price somewhat higher each year than it was the previous year. In this way, the bank can establish a trend of steady increases in stock price. As long as earnings rise to validate such pricing, the bank's board can offset the vagaries of the thin market for the stock that could lead to price flip-flops bearing no relationship to earnings.

STOCK DIVIDENDS

To impartial observers, frequent stock dividends of 4 or 5% are useless. They merely involve creation of new pieces of paper to represent the same proportionate ownership of the bank, and they give the trust department the nuisance of distributing the paper and worrying about handling fractional share problems.

One would think that a 4% stock dividend would just lower the value of each outstanding share of the stock by 4% to offset the dilution, leaving everyone where he was—except for the bank's expense of handling all the paper. Not so. As indicated earlier, what frequently happens is that a modest stock dividend can be distributed without having the stock price decline. This means a 4 or 5% increase in the market value of the shareholders' equity positions.

To those requesting information about the dividend policy, some banks reply: "We give 9% annually—5% in cash and 4% in stock." A corporation finance teacher might tear his hair at that statement, but the public evidently likes it. In fact, some banks report that when they have surveyed their shareholders and asked specifically what they would like to see, high on the list of requests are frequent stock dividends.

BUYING IN YOUR OWN STOCK

Holding companies have another means available to influence their stock price: having the holding company buy in outstanding stock to use in future acquisitions.

This provides two benefits to present shareholders. First, it raises the price of the stock on the market today, as the banking holding company itself is an important buying force in the market. Second, it means that there is less dilution when new acquisitions are made. The bank's own stock purchase plan has raised the price-to-earnings multiple, thereby reducing the number of shares of stock that must be paid out in an acquisition to meet any particular level of market value required by the selling shareholders to complete the deal. If the holding company had not bought in stock ahead of time, it would have had to issue new stock for the acquisition. Therefore, it would have taken more shares to reach a certain amount of market value of shares offered, because the price-to-earnings multiply and thus the stock price would have been lower.

AUCTIONS

Some banks have found that a stock auction is a way of raising the price of the stock when there is a thin market. Once a year, such banks announce that an auction is to be held in the lobby of the bank and that those who wish to sell or buy shares can place them or bid for them in the auction.

In some communities, all the banks combine to have a cooperative auction, so that the sale of various banks' stocks at one time brings in more potential customers. Bankers report that these auctions bid up the price of the stock and give the bank trust department and other large holders an opportunity to peel off large numbers of shares without seriously depressing the market. In addition, the auctions also frequently set the tone of the market and the approximate price range within which the bank's stock trades for the entire year until the next auction is held.

9-3 DO YOU REALLY WANT A MARKET FOR YOUR BANK'S STOCK?

Most banks, and certainly most community banks, have stocks without any real market. The president of the bank sometimes makes the market for the stock in his desk, and all potential buyers and sellers come to him to make the trade. Frequently, the stock stays static in price for month after month.

"The last trade was at 60," the president may say, "so I think that this is a fair price. Carried to its logical conclusion, if all trades are at the price of the last trade, then the stock never moves from the price it came out at when the bank was chartered.

Other bank CEOs take a more fluid approach. They simply sell the stock at a certain percentage of book value. Then, if the bank does make money and retains it, the stock at least goes up so that the holders of it are rewarded for the bank's performance during the time they were shareholders investing their capital in the institution.

Some bankers go even further than to arrange for the trades at the last trade's price or at book or a certain percentage of book. They develop lists of potential buyers of the stock. Then, if an individual shareholder does decide to sell, the bank president can call up the top person on the list and say that some stock is available at the established price. That person's request—which may have been on the books for months or even years—can now be filled.

Having a waiting list for stock gives patent evidence that the stock price is determined artificially by management and not determined by supply and demand.

The very fact that stock is not available when someone wants it indicates that the price is too low. Otherwise, the price would be bid up when demand surfaced until the shares rose high enough in price to clear the market.

Thus, many discussions on stock have little relevance for the typical smaller bank. Bank shares are a small nuisance that must be handled when someone dies and an estate must be liquidated, or when someone leaves town, needs money, or otherwise initiates the rare situation that a sale of stock must be made. For most of the year, the stock and its price means nothing to the CEO, or anyone else for the matter, as they go about the day-to-day job of running the bank.

MAINTAINING THE STATUS QUO

To be honest, many community bankers like this situation and have no desire at all to change it. There are reasons for this:

1 Having no market for the stock means that there is one less worry for the banker. If a bank's stock is traded and the price is reported regularly in the local press, people call in and ask what is going on and why the stock has or has not moved. In effect, they are questioning the CEO's actions in running the bank.
2 A bank whose stock is quiet and inactive has no reason to care too much about dividend policy. If the shareholders remain quiet, or at least "sullen but not mutinous," then why bother with paying out large dividends to them? Neither a generous dividend policy nor a stingy one will make a big difference in the bank's activities. In addition, by having a small dividend payout, the bank can generate the capital needed for its growth internally—and keep the examiners from questioning the bank's capital adequacy at the same time.

With holders who are quiescent and with no active market, the bank needs to provide far less information than is the case if there are active market-makers who want to know what is going on. Far better for the banker to have shareholders to whom owning a piece of the local bank is an emotional decision rather than a financial one, for then there are few who challenge what the CEO says.

In this era of deregulation and relaxed regulatory and legislative attitudes toward bank structure, there is a far more significant reason why many bankers like a situation under which there is no active market for their stock. They feel this is the best way for present management to keep control of the bank and to avoid having an outsider come in, buy up the bank's stock, and take over. "Let sleeping dogs lie," these managers say. "Don't stir up interest in our bank from outside by doing anything to develop a market in the stock." Or, to put it as Bert Lance used to do when he was at the Office of Management and Budget: "If it ain't broke, don't fix it."

Thus, community bankers who do not have active markets for their stock generally are happy that way. This is one major reason why so little has been developed in the way of broadening investor interest in the shares of community banks.

IMPROVING THE MARKET

There is, however, good reason today to rethink this complacency towards the market for a bank's stock. While the motives of the banker in wanting a quiet market are understandable, the shareholders and the bankers themselves may be better off if the bank does make the effort to develop a true market for its stock in which the shares are traded regularly and price is set by the supply and demand of the public at any given moment in time. For example, there is the question of whether the bank is really being fair to the investors where there is a policy of no active market for the stock.

"Wait a minute," many bankers will respond. "Our stock sells at a 10 to 12 multiple of earnings, while the stocks of major banks sell for one-half that amount. Our stock sells for book, even double book, or more, while the stocks of major banks sell for a fraction of book in many instances. The bank that sells at book or more is rare among money center institutions. How are we punishing our shareholders by our policy of making the market in our desk?"

On the surface, there is no answer to this statement. The community bank generally does sell for a higher price relative both to book and to earnings than does the larger institution. However, there are many issues involved. First, the people who hold the stock frequently have paid more for it than those who bought larger banks' shares in terms of book and earnings multiples. So the fact that the shares now sell at higher prices does not reward the shareholders any more. It just means that they started at a higher plateau and remain at a higher plateau.

Far more important is whether the CEO or anyone else has the right to say that shareholders have been rewarded enough in terms of the price of their stock when the marketplace may well provide an even higher return.

As indicated above, if there are people who want the shares and cannot get them without a long wait, then the holders are truly entitled to a higher price for their stock than is presently available.

In addition, there is the question of what happens when a big block must be distributed because of an estate problem or because someone has lost interest in investing in the bank.

A bank whose stock has no real market can truly hurt the shareholders who are forced to liquidate. These shareholders are at the mercy of management or of anyone who is willing to place enough capital into the organization to buy up their shares.

Thus, the individual who may have been happy with the stock for years will become extremely unhappy when he wants to unload it. This is because the lack of market for the shares will directly and seriously affect what he is paid for his position when he wants to sell or must sell his holdings.

Also, a bank that does not have an active market for its stock does not get the opportunity to distribute share ownership throughout the community. Nothing makes customers more loyal to the bank than owning stock in the organization. The statement stuffer that says "Put your money where your money is," or in some other way indicates that the bank wants depositors and borrowers also to be owners of the bank, can do more for bank business and profit development than most other activities.

A broad market for the stock enables the bank to generate this community ownership that otherwise is extremely difficult to obtain.

Management Gains

From the viewpoint of the CEO himself and top management, however, there are two major reasons why an active market for the bank's stock is in their own best interest as well as in the best interests of the bank's shareholders.

First is the issue of lawsuits. This is a different world today. In the past, if someone bought something and it went down in value, they would say "damn," and do nothing about it. Now, people say "sue."

Bank officers who make the market for their own stock are placing themselves in a position of conflict of interest that can truly come home to roost if someone does buy the stock and then takes a loss on it or of someone sells and then finds that the bank sold out at a much higher price at some date in the near future.

An open market in which buyers and sellers set price leaves the CEO completely free of legal implications. A market in which the CEO determined the price does not.

THE TAKEOVER SITUATION

Most important is the issue of takeovers of the bank. While, as indicated above, many CEOs feel that by having an inactive market for their stock they can avoid takeovers because it is too hard for someone to come in and buy control, many others are beginning to realize from sad experience and analysis of developments in the marketplace that the truth is just the opposite. The best defense against unfriendly takeover of the bank is to have a broad market in which the stock sells at an attractive price.

If there is anything the community banker fears, it is an unfriendly takeover. Nothing is worse than to be running the bank and then have some outsider come in and buy it and then institute the new golden rule (i.e., he who provides the gold makes the rules).

But unfriendly takeovers are not haphazard events. Two basic situations come to the forefront when discussing what leads an outside force to try to take over a bank.

First, if the bank has a large block of stock in few hands and the holders decide to sell out, the bank becomes a natural target for a takeover. It is far easier to buy out the shares of one or a handful of individuals than it is to make a tender offer to pick up small pieces here and there from holders in a bank with a broad market and many shareholders.

Second, a bank president may feel that he has a close family of shareholders and that the biggest shareholder is his biggest supporter. One family that owns 50 to 60% of the shares can give great confidence to the CEO that no takeover will take place.

But people change. An individual may die and his heirs may feel that fresh management is needed. The family may decide to invest elsewhere, especially with the low dividend payout that most community banks offer. This big block may turn against present management in some other way that can cause the bank to be sold out from under present management's nose. A broadly held bank stock, with no one having majority control, is thus far more conducive to the maintenance of independence, and a broad market for the stock can make this broad ownership far more feasible.

Another Takeover Reason

A bank may look attractive to those interested in taking over if the price of the stock is fairly low. There is nothing that deters a potential buyer of a bank more than to have the stock sell at so attractive a price that no offer will be accepted unless it is far more than the bank is worth.

The people who buy a bank under unfriendly terms are generally taking a risk: They have to take over a building that is probably far less efficient than a newly constructed building would be. They must take over the low-yielding old mortgages and other fixed rate assets that are not worth their book value today because of the higher level of interest rates in the economy. Core deposits are becoming increasingly scarce, so the bank is providing no base of cheap deposit money to the new buyer .

What the bank taking over another bank gets, then, is basically the good will in the community, the management, the staff, and the board. If these people are hostile to the takeover, it makes acquiring a bank under unfriendly terms a difficult job indeed.

But if the bank is selling at a price so low relative to real worth or potential of the institution, then it is worth fighting these hurdles. The unfriendly takeovers that have been initiated have usually been in cases where the stock had been kept so low that even offering the shareholders a portion of what the holdings were really worth would have been an improvement over what the stock was selling for under old management.

This is the point: a bank whose stock sells at an attractive price is far less likely to be a candidate for raiders than one whose stock has been allowed to languish and thereby become a bargain for the taking. Since an active market for a bank's stock helps improve the price markedly and thereby helps avoid such unfriendly takeovers, it must be concluded that to management and shareholder alike, developing a market for the shares of the stock makes sense in this era of deregulation.

For more on making a market for your bank's stock, see the next section.

9-4 DEVELOPING A MARKET FOR THE STOCK

There does seem to be a general movement or trend toward developing an active market for a bank's stock. There are several reasons for this:

- Investors get a much fairer shake when the stock is actively traded. The fact that inactively traded stocks usually have a waiting list of potential buyers indicates that the holders should be getting more for the shares they do sell. There is no surer way of wiping out a waiting list of buyers than to raise the price that they must pay for the shares until the market is cleared.
- The bank with an inactive market has trouble liquidating a big block of shares when some holder dies or decides to get rid of his position.
- The bank with inactively traded stock has not developed local ownership of the bank's shares to a great degree. Yet local ownership is the best business developer available, since people like to bank with the institution that they personally own.
- Banks whose top officers make the market for the stock are subject to lawsuits due to the potential conflict of interest.
- Finally, and most important to many executives, banks that have large blocks of stock closely held are really more subject to unfriendly takeovers, rather than less so. If a holder of a large block does decide to sell out, it is far easier for an outsider to gain control by taking over this large block than by going out and picking up shares in small amounts from various holders.

In addition, the closely held stock usually sells at a lower price than is established on the stock with a broad market. And the higher the stock price, the less attractive that institution is to potential takeover specialists and outside investors. They much prefer undervalued banks.

BROADENING THE MARKET

Since there do seem to be compelling reasons for a bank to broaden the market for its stock, what can be done to accomplish this?

To develop a broader market, the mandatory prerequisite is the desire of management to make it happen. Without management's cooperation, no such broadening can take place. Once management has decided that it is in the best interest of both shareholders and the bank's staff to have this broader market, management must work to develop outside market-makers so that shares no longer are traded in the president's desk.

This is not always an easy job. Many banks have had shares traded in the president's desk, despite the CEO's own desires, simply because no decent marketmakers could be found.

There are market-makers and there are market-makers. Some banks have discovered that the only investment dealers available were people who were willing to take shares on consignment at a tremendous markup. In essence, these dealers would be willing (1) to hold shares that present holders wanted to sell, and (2) to use the bank's list of people interested in buying in order to bring buyer and seller together. But the dealer would not put up any capital. He would only hold the shares. And he would pay for them only if he found a buyer who provided him a nice profit over the price he offered the seller. If no such buyer was available, the dealer would simply return the shares to the unhappy potential seller.

This is no service. A bank is far better off having its president make the market and arrange for buyer to meet seller without any commission or spread. In either instance, the seller only gets his money if an actual buyer is available. When the bank makes the deal itself, however, the seller gets the full amount—not an amount substantially discounted by the dealer's commission.

Thus, the bank must find a market-maker, or preferably several market-makers, who will actually buy outright all stock offered. Finding a market-maker who will act as principal and put up his own capital can be difficult. After all, the market-maker borrows most of his capital, as do automobile dealers, mortgage bankers, and other middlemen. And capital is expensive. If a dealer has bought some bank stock and he cannot sell it for several months, the spread between buy and sell price must be pretty substantial to cover the interest cost of carrying the stock and the costs of the dealer's operation.

The bank that wants to get a good market to buy, sell, and position its stock must do everything possible to facilitate active trading in the bank's shares, so that the dealer sees the light at the end of the tunnel. In other words when the dealer buys shares he should have a good chance of selling them in the near future.

Here are steps a bank should take to facilitate active trading in its stock:

- The market-maker must be given fair treatment. He must be given the opportunity to handle all trades that develop in the stock. All too often the bank's officers will only give the market-maker the small pieces. When a big block is traded, it will be handled inside, with some friend of the bank or board member getting the opportunity to pick up the shares at an attractive price. If the market-maker does not get all the business he is unlikely to want any of it.

- The market-maker must also be given the opportunity to do other business with the bank. This does not mean he should be given preference in handling bank trust department business or trades in the bank investment portfolio if his prices are out of line. If he is competitive, however, he should have a chance to bid on the bank's business. In addition, he should be given the feeling that the bank wants to do business with him in other securities because of the close relationship in handling the bank's own shares.
- The bank should provide the market-maker with all available information that is relevant to him with regard to who the big holders are, who has shown an interest in investing, and who might be selling out his shares. Only with such information can the dealer make a truly active market in the stock.
- If at all possible, a bank should have a dividend reinvestment and employee stock option programs that buy shares on a periodic basis. If the dealer knows that there will be a demand for the shares every quarter or semi-annually to fill the needs of the reinvestment program of the Employee Stock Option Plan (ESOP), he will be willing to be more aggressive in his own positioning of the stock. The dealer must understand that he can get out of his shares—and thus get his money back, plus hopefully a profit—on a periodic basis.
- A bank should work with the dealer or dealers to make the stock as attractive for trading as possible. This should involve letting the bank's customers know that they can buy shares of the institution and how to get them. It should involve stock splits and stock dividends to create activity in the stock and also to keep the price in a range that is attractive for potential investors. It should make sure that the price of the stock is quoted in the newspaper and that people know they can buy the stock. If local newspapers do not consider publishing stock prices as being newsworthy enough to insure free publication of the information, the bank should take advertisements to keep the public informed.
- The bank should develop a shareholder information service so that both present holders and potential holders can get maximum information on the bank, its performance, and the potential for healthy stock appreciation.

Shareholder information, incidentally, should be a two-way street. The bank should learn what its shareholders want in the way of dividends, splits, and the like. In sum, shareholder relations should be considered a separate facet of the bank's operations. As such, it must be handled actively, just as investments and customer development require active considerations. It should not be thought of as a nuisance that comes to mind once a year when the annual shareholders meeting is held.

9-5 DEALING WITH THE MARKET-MAKERS

Once a bank has decided on policies that will improve the price of its stock, the next job for bank management is to develop good relations with the brokers, dealers, and analysts who make a market in the share.

The market for bank shares is frequently an extremely thin one. Purchase or sale of about 1000 shares of stock can move the price up or down to a marked degree. Frequently, bank shares are depressed because of the liquidation of just one large block by a single owner. Conversely, they are boosted by the demands of only one individual or institution to gain a solid position in the stock.

This is both a problem and an opportunity. It is a problem because if a large holder becomes disenchanted with the stock it can knock the price down enough to hurt the image of the institution. But, because most bank shares are traded in such a thin market, something that makes even a few large investors take an interest in the bank, can bring about a decided improvement in share price.

This is where bank stock dealers and analysts come in. It is they whose boosting or bad mouthing of the bank can make the difference. One cannot overemphasize the importance of the bank share dealers and the analysts who work for dealers and institutional investors in determining the value of shares on a day-to-day basis.

To be sure, if these individuals are wrong in their estimates of bank earnings performance over the long run, there is nothing they can do to alter the impact of the fundamentals on investors and bank share prices. For the immediate time period, however, they can be a potent force for good or bad.

WORKING WITH BROKERS

The care and feeding of brokers and dealers is not easy. Some of them are extremely sensitive because they feel that some banks have tried to put one over on them by giving them false or misleading data in the hopes of winning a higher demand for their shares than otherwise would be justified. Others, sad to say, have become rather arrogant because of the power they have over share prices and, thus, over the immediate fortunes of the bank. For example, one analyst for a New York brokerage firm proudly bragged about how he went out to see the top management of a bank in the Rocky Mountain area. "They kept me waiting for 20 minutes before they would see me even though I had an appointment, so I shorted the stock." Such as approach, selling a stock short because of a real or imaginary insult, is a gross abuse of the analyst's power and a breach of his responsibility. But this is the type of problem that does occur and that bankers must be prepared to face. It also helps explain why banks are so cautious and courteous in dealing with analysts when they visit.

Recently, this has been applied even to more highly visible stocks. When the management of a major food company refused to provide more than routine, already-published data to security analysts after the analysts had come halfway across the nation for a company-sponsored junket, the analysts returned home and immediately issued negative reports on the company—just because of management's attitude towards the investor community.

"Our trader had over $100,000 invested in that bank's stock, and the president of the bank wouldn't even come up one flight of stairs to meet him," is the lament of one analyst at a regional brokerage firm discussing a certain local bank.

Bankers, then, must meet analysts and brokers and understand how they operate, what information they need, and what data can be legally provided. To neglect this function can be extremely dangerous to the bank's share market.

PERSONIFICATION

It is natural to personify the bank so that people feel closer to it. Then, if a customer thinks of taking a negative step such as moving his account, he often feels that he is letting "Sam" down—not just letting the bank down. In the same way, a banker who gets to know the analysts and traders who make a market in his stock and stack their reputations on their opinions of the stock, finds that these market professionals also appreciate the personal relationship.

This can be carried too far. For example, some banks that hyped their stock in the boom period of a few years ago found, to their sorrow, that their stocks went down just as fast as they had gone up. That is because when the analysts thought all the profit had been milked from a stock's movement, they recommended other vehicles.

The bankers who had hyped their stock by frequent analyst meetings, heavy press efforts, and other means later reflected in many instances that they would have been better off not trying to boost their multiples of price-to-earnings in the first place. When the prices went back down again, they were left with new buyers who were unhappy at their capital losses and with employees whose options had been issued at high prices not likely to be seen again for quite a while.

Thus, the courting of analysts and dealers must be done with care. Keep in mind that over the long run there is nothing a bank can do to make its share price rise above what is justified by the bank's present earnings and its future growth and profit potential.

However, the bank can at least make sure analysts and brokers give the bank every benefit of the doubt. After all, it is the recommendations of analysts, and the building or lessening of trading positions by dealers, that basically determine what share prices will do in the immediate period at hand.

WHAT BANKERS SHOULD DO

In summation, to keep the dialogue between brokers, analysts, and bankers at the healthiest possible level, bankers should:

1 Meet the analysts and dealers. Know who is risking his capital and his reputation on the bank's equities. Understand what they are doing and how they do it.

2 Provide honest information to the public and the investment community in every way possible, Make sure there are no surprises when quarterly and annual reports are released. If there is bad news coming, let everyone know it as soon as legally possible.

   Good news needs immediate publicity, too. Nothing maddens a professional in the market more than to find the bank coming out suddenly with new information that makes all expectations and analyses considerably off target.

3 Be fair to the brokerage community. It cannot ask the brokers to make a market in the stock and give all the juicy large trades to insiders without going through the market. It is discouraging to a dealer to have made a market and stood up for a stock month after month in a thin market, only to find that when a large block becomes available or desirable, the bank arranges the deal itself through the trust department or the investment department.

Not giving the brokerage community a chance to bid on the transaction will hurt a bank in the long run.

4 Make sure the brokers and dealers who are analyzing and reporting on the stock and making a market in it should have a chance to bid on the rest of the bank's security business. Again, brokerage professionals become extremely upset when they are asked to make a market in a thinly-traded bank stock, but when the bank has a large block of listed stock to trade for the trust department, they go to some large national firm instead.

5 If the local broker is not making the same market as the national firm, or if execution is poor, the bank must by law go elsewhere. But the local market-maker simply wants a chance to compete for the business and show he can do it as well as other firms. This is a reasonable request.

WHAT BROKERS WANT

Brokers and analysts hope bankers will turn to them for advice on security matters. They have a better feel, in many instances, than the banker does as to whether the dividend should be raised, a stock dividend paid, more information provided, etc. To ignore the advice of the professionals, who see a great many banks in the course of their business, is also a mistake that can be costly in terms of share price action.

To repeat, many dealers report that the establishment of a dividend reinvestment program is a solid move. It gives market-makers the assurance that one, two, or four times a year there will be a demand for a big block of the bank's stock to fill the dividend reinvestment plan's needs. This, in turn, makes the market-makers more aggressive in their willingness to position the bank's stock, for they know that there will be a periodic demand for a certain number of shares. This means their capital won't be tied up in shares that they'll have little chance of selling without taking a serious loss on the transaction.

Perhaps most important, brokers and analysts want bankers to recognize that they are partners of the bank in the serious job of marketing and positioning bank shares. If the bank just does not concern itself about the process by which the bank stock market operates, it is not likely to see its shares reach the potential they otherwise might. The banking industry relies heavily on the personal relationship of banker with customer. To fail to have a similar relationship between banker and broker so that both can work together in the best interest of the shareholders is both ironic and short-sighted.

9-6 THE PROBLEM WITH REVERSE STOCK SPLITS

A bank with some half-million dollars in assets had to sweat through the following situation.

The bank had seen its stock decline sharply in price in recent years. Part of the reason was stock splits and dividends that can naturally lower market price. In addition, a bear bank stock market took the shares down even further with the result that the stock was selling below $10 a share—a category some institutions believe gives the entire organization a poor image.

The concern of the bank was not only that it did not like having its stock quoted at something below $10 a share. It was also that there was a dollar spread between bid and asked in the dealer quotes for the stock. When this is added to the normal retail commission that dealers place on bank share transactions for individuals, it makes the price of moving in and out of the stock extremely expensive. In fact, by the time the typical individual is through meeting the spread and paying the in and out commission, a person who wants to trade the stock has to see it rise 25 percent in value before he can break even and start to make a profit.

Facing this situation, the bank's management wondered whether a reverse stock split might not be the thing to do. This would raise the price of the stock up over $10 but under $40 (which appears to be the range of share prices for bank stocks that is most popular with the public and so attracts the greatest interest). The hope was that if there were a one-for-two split, the dealers would still keep a dollar spread between bid and asked.

This is the kind of dilemma that banks sometimes face that is difficult to settle.

THE IMAGE IMPERATIVE

Many who have looked at the idea of having a reverse stock split have frequently felt that the disadvantages of such a move far outweigh the advantages. Bank share pricing has a psychological effect, and a reverse stock split can result in a strong negative response from the investing public.

At first, one might ask what negative impact could there be from a reverse split that brings one share for two outstanding. Yet more than the $10–40 price range, the public dislikes the thought of something being taken away from them by the bank.

Stock splits and stock dividends often cause great public satisfaction, even when there is no dividend increase accompanying the action, and the real result has as much significance as changing a ten dollar bill for two fives. The public likes it because it thinks that it is getting more paper.

A reverse split breeds an exactly opposite reaction. In addition, reverse stock splits have had to be used by troubled companies in reorganization that have substituted new stock for debt. The increased stock outstanding caused by the recapitalization has made the individual shares worth so little that a reverse stock split of four or five to one has sometimes been necessary to get the stock out of the penny stock category.

Bankers fear that if they do a reverse split, they will be categorized as being in the same kind of trouble. The first issuers of debenture capital in the 1960s faced a similar plight when they found that many investors still remembered the 1930s when debentures were only issued by banks in trouble and were sold to the Reconstruction Finance Corporation.

For many banks, then, reverse splits simply do not work. There is little a bank can do to improve its stock price immediately, except to maintain good communication with analysts on what the banks is doing, develop stock purchase plans for employees, and institute reinvestment plans for shareholders. And, of course, most important, concentrate on improving earnings.

PART 5 The Business of Banking

For all that is happening these days to alter the face of banking, there are essential ingredients upon which the business is based.

The keystone is the lending function. Sure, people expect a bank to provide a safe depository for their funds. And they expect (perhaps demand is a better word) a decent return on those funds. Yet if things stopped there, the banking business would be severely limited. What makes a bank a bank is the lending function. How well the function is run goes a long way in determining the success of a particular institution.

Over the years, lending has been enhanced and segmented. Some banks can be classified as retail banks, where much if not all of the business is with individuals. Others are more commercially oriented, dealing mostly with business firms. Most banks, however find they must go after any business available in their market area.

A further extension of all this is correspondent banking. While there has been less emphasis on correspondent banking in recent years, lately the concept has been given a new lease on life.

At the bottom of such efforts is the need to build a deposit base. After all, without deposits, a bank cannot lend.

Affecting each different aspect of the business of banking is the current competitive environment. Competition from other banks in all location, from thrifts, from credit unions, from financial institutions such as American Express, and from organizations such as Sears, is changing how banks conduct their business.

10 Lending

10-1 MORE EFFECTIVE LENDING

Not many years ago, lending, along with the safe-keeping of deposits, were the major functions of banks. They were unique services setting banks apart from other financial institutions. Then competitors began to get into the act. All sorts of firms are taking deposits these days, and all sorts of firms are making loans of one kind or another. A growing number of these firms, incidentally, are operating without the restrictions and the safeguards—and the reserves—required of banks.

Still, regardless of the changes taking place in banking and finance, lending (and deposit-taking, too) are central to a bank's reason for being. How well a bank does in performing these two key services will, to considerable measure, determine if a bank succeeds or fails.

Lending is a risky business. It should be. The loan officer who makes no loans that turn sour probably is not doing his job adequately. Conversely, a loan officer who makes too many bad loans is an even worse problem. The banker's goal is to achieve the proper balance—to manage the risks, to serve the bank's community of customers, and to contribute to a healthy bottom line.

AGGRESSIVE HANDLING AND PROBLEM LOANS

How do today's bankers feel towards aggressive lending and investing?

There is considerable conservatism in the industry, and several solid reasons for it. Bankers heed the aphorism "fool me once, shame on you; fool me twice, shame on me." Many have decided that once they get out of unprofitable loan situations, they will not put themselves in new ones. The aftermath of the major problems banks have had with domestic loans is one such instance. When bankers see their past loans turn sour, they become highly conservative about making new ones.

The international banking situation intensifies this conservative trend. Think of the outrage that many bankers must feel as they look at their international loans that are not being serviced with interest, much less being repaid on schedule. To add insult to injury, the banks are then told they must lend these foreign borrowers even more, lest the borrowers default on the entire debt.

One lesson that many bankers are relearning to their sorrow is that the so-called strong borrower is really the difficult one, while the small, weak borrower is frequently the best credit. The strong borrower who takes a giant loan from the bank knows that he now has the bank by the jugular rather than the other way around. The borrower's inability to repay would hurt the bank as much as it hurts him. In many instances, it is the small company that worries most about repaying. The small company knows that the bank can harm it far more than it can harm the bank, so the mutual dependency which forces banks to renegotiate terms and be more benign in enforcing repayment does not exist.

DEFAULTING ON DEFAULTS

There is a third force making banks extremely cautious in placing new loans on the books, no matter what is happening in monetary policy: the courts and lawmen are refusing to enforce the bankruptcy laws. Lenders are not allowed to repossess the farms, homes, and other property on which the borrowers have defaulted. It is a 1930s mentality—the lender is an ogre and the person who borrowed the money is a poor, suffering soul, no matter what he spent the money on or how ill-developed his financial planning was when he borrowed the funds. The injustice can be tremendous. The news media portrays the banker as the mean Simon Legree, forcing people off the land. The borrower is the poor, abused citizen. Yet think what would happen were the banks to carry this a step further and not allow their depositors to withdraw their money because the borrowers were not paying and the courts were not enforcing legal steps to gain the saver his reimbursement.

The reaction of lenders seeing this trend must naturally be to retrench on new loans. Their attitude is "Why should I make more loans when I am in such an inferior position if I try to collect on the ones I have already placed on the books?"

As is so often the case with social legislation and programs to protect the weak, the weak are the losers. Many banks will not make new consumer loans to the poor because the bankruptcy laws are so skewed in favor of the borrower if the loans default. The losers are people of marginal credit who would be serviced if the banks had stronger legal recourse when their gambles on their borrowers failed.

Similarly, strong consumerist legislation leads to lessened willingness to issue credit cards, make small loans, and otherwise take chances.

10-2 THE HAZARDS OF FLEXIBLE-RATE LENDING

An increasing number of loans are being made on a flexible rate basis. (The next section of this book discusses variable rate mortgages, for example.) At the same time, however, some bankers are beginning to worry about the impact this concept has on the willingness and ability of borrowers to pay interest changes and to repay the loans themselves.

It is all well and good to tell a borrower that he or she can get a loan provided it is tied to the Treasury bill rate or some other index that reflects going interest rates. But when the bank then sends the borrower an announcement that the rate is going up by 2, 3, or even 6%, as has been the case in some instances, the consequences of the borrowing agreement becomes clear indeed to the customer.

Many people find that when their flexible rate loans rise in yield, they simply can not pay them. The number of defaults on mortgage loans is higher than at any time within decades. Higher rates on flexible rate business loans are also leading to more problems in repayment and to more defaults.

The banks have no choice. By making new fixed rate long term loans, they would merely be setting the stage for the same troubles that many banks and thrifts now face with fixed rate loans made in the past at rates as low as 5 or 7%. They also recognize that by passing on the interest rate or so-called money risk to the customer, they are taking a new, different risk upon themselves: the risk of default on loans caused by the uncertainty and burden that flexible rates impose on the borrower.

REACTION AND ACTION

The reaction of some bankers has been to prepare for the worst in making loans, that is, to make sure that the borrower can stand the possible higher cost of financing even before the original loan is placed on the books.

One banker from Ohio, for example, recently indicated privately that he now examines a potential mortgage borrower and makes sure that he can qualify for up to a 50% increase in mortgage interest *before* the original loan is granted. If other bankers take this attitude, not only will many borrowers find themselves saddled with the money risk inherent in an environment of flexible interest rates, but, in addition, their ability to get a loan in the first place will be hampered. This, then, is another way in which the new emphasis on giving the saver a going rate on his funds is finally imposing on the borrower the full cost of the credit accommodation he wants.

One solution to this problem, at least for mortgage loans, is to extend maturities instead of raising the amount paid per month when interest rates rise. This keeps the payment steady, and thus more affordable. However, the result could be a structure of reverse amortization, under which a loan becomes larger in size and longer in maturity until it reaches unrealistic proportions.

This was not a major problem when home prices went up and up. The bank had no fear of the collateral being worth less than the amount of the loan outstanding. But, as high interest rates and house price increases have slowed down, bankers worry that a long-term loan whose outstanding principal keeps rising because the interest payments do not match going rates on mortgages, could result in the bank being owed more than the value of the property!

At such a point, the borrower may just walk away—as has been done with so many automobile loans whose collateral value quickly went underwater because of rapid depreciation of the value of the car.

10-3 RETHINKING THE MORTGAGE MARKET

After years of an on-and-off attitude toward the mortgage market, many commercial bankers seem to have decided to go back into the home loan arena. Traditionally, the feast and famine nature of the mortgage market has brought with it sharp fluctuations in housing start rates and in the fortunes of those involved in the home building industry.

The way the market had been structured, the banking industry cannot be faulted for blowing hot and cold on mortgages. In many states, usury ceilings were set so low that most banks found it would have been a waste of bank assets to make mortgage loans for many years. Corporate bonds and other investments yielded much more than banks were allowed to charge on mortgages. Even when it was not a usury ceiling that prevented the banks from charging going rates for funds in home liens, there was at least a tradition of low mortgage rates. The bank that tried to make home loans at rates that were competitive with what it could earn elsewhere often encountered terribly bad publicity.

There were times when business loan demand was so weak and alternative investments so low in yield that bankers made all the mortgage loans they could. But for much of the banking industry, the commitment to mortgage lending seldom lasted beyond the next economic upturn. For lengthy periods, banks were all but out of the mortgage market.

Not surprisingly, this pattern has been unsettling to home builders and real estate brokers whose livelihoods depend on availability of mortgage money. Indeed, many of them have tended to feel that the commercial banks were a lost cause and that they should concentrate on thrift institutions and other nonbank mortgage lenders for their sources of funds.

RATES FINALLY CATCH UP

What has caused this change of heart towards mortgages in so many banks? First, bankers have been finding that mortgage rates have risen to competitive levels. The public is much more receptive to market rates than formerly was the case. They have learned that a high interest rate mortgage is better than no mortgage at all.

Second, with regard to usury ceilings, the same attitude is finally penetrating state legislatures. Many have recognized that an unrealistically low usury ceiling on home loans means that financial institutions just do not make any loans in those states. Rather, they place their available funds into mortgages out of state, where usury ceilings are more realistic or do not exist at all, or else they place their money into corporate bonds and other investments whose yields vastly exceed the usury ceilings.

ALTERNATIVE TO BUSINESS LOANS

Many banks are finding that other uses of funds are not as attractive as they used to be. Business loan demand sometimes is not as strong as banks would like. And corporate treasurers often are not loyal to the bank; they borrow at tight money times, when the bank is short of funds, yet they desert the bank and obtain much of their credit needs from other sources when money is plentiful.

The corporate treasurer's reasoning is clear-cut. Bank rates have greater stability than open market rates on such instruments as commercial paper. So, if rates rise, commercial paper rates rise more rapidly than do bank lending charges. This is when corporate treasurers move into bank loans. Yet it is the very time when banks are trying to cut back on their lending.

Conversely, as interest rates fall, paper rates fall more rapidly than do bank charges. The treasurers thus move back to open market sources to obtain cheaper funds—at just the time when the banks could use their business.

Consequently, a number of banks are beginning to look at the stability of the mortgage market as preferable to the fickle nature of many corporate customers.

VARIABLE RATE MORTGAGES

Many bankers are particularly excited by the potential of variable rate mortgages (VRM).

In the past, the consumer had the benefit of taking advantage of both sides of the business cycle. If interest rates were low when a mortgage loan was placed on the books, the bank found that the customer stayed with this low yielding loan for the life of the loan. The bank was hurt as interest rates rose. Bank costs of funds would rise, while the return available on this mortgage loan would remain fixed at the low yield prevailing at the time when it was made.

If a loan was placed on the books at a time of high interest rates, the borrower frequently found it advantageous to pay off the loan and refinance it as soon as interest rates fell. Thus, the borrower had the advantage of a "heads I win, tails we play over again" approach to his home loan. This, in turn, made many bankers reluctant to make heavy commitments to mortgage lending.

Now more and more institutions are looking at the VRM to provide a satisfactory solution. Under the variable rate mortgage, the amount the borrower pays each month remains the same. However, if interest rates rise, more of the monthly payments goes into interest and less into repaying principal; if interest rates fall, more goes into amortization payments and less into meeting the interest payment. The amount of the regular payment that must flow into the interest component of the loan goes up and down as open market interest rates rise and fall.

Banks like this, since it gives them an opportunity to make home loans whose yield is equal to that available on other investments. As a result, the banks that have started offering VRMs find themselves willing to place far more into mortgages than other banks will. They no longer fear being locked in with low yielding loans at a time of rising interest rates.

There are two other features of the VRM that both banks and many borrowers like. First, they are extendable, so that if an individual wants more money for any purpose, he can refinance his mortgage, just as long as the principal value of the home remains well-above the amount borrowed. This makes the home mortgage into a line of credit that is available to the home owner, yet one that costs far less than a consumer loan would. The bank is happy because it is getting return on its money that moves up and down with open market rates. The borrower is able to count on his bank as a source of consumer credit at very attractive rates through the extendability feature of his mortgage.

A second feature of a VRM is that the loan is assumable by the new owner if one person sells his home to someone else. Again, the bank likes this, because as long as it is getting going rates on its mortgages, it does not care who the borrowers are. It is only when a mortgage is on the books at a low interest rate that a bank dislikes having the new buyer of the house assume the mortgage. In such a case the bank, would prefer to use this opportunity to get its money back and invest elsewhere to raise its yield. But, if the yield goes up and down automatically anyway, this objection to assumability disappears.

As for the home owner, he is thrilled to have an assumable mortgage. He knows that when he wants to sell his home to someone else, the sale can not be thwarted by a lack of mortgage money for the potential buyer.

Real estate agents love the assumable mortgages, too, because they know that the home can be sold to someone else without the possibility of having the sale killed because of the lack of a mortgage for the potential new buyer. Thus, real estate brokers have been big boosters of variable rate mortgages, and they have been good helpers in talking potential home buyers into accepting this type of mortgage loan.

A BOOST TO CROSS-SELLING

If commercial banks are not in the mortgage loan business, the field is left open to the thrifts. Moreover, the thrifts are moving into commercial banking areas, and they can use mortgages as a selling tool if a bank passes on mortgages. However, those banks now back in the mortgage market avoid being at a disadvantage in competing for the full service retail banking business against the savings banks, savings and loans, credit unions, and other organizations that are gaining more and more power to service the public's financial needs.

The return to the mortgage market makes good economic sense for bankers looking for good uses for their available funds. It also makes excellent market sense in a financial environment in which everyone says "what's mine is mine and what's yours is negotiable." The institution that can get the public's first business and then cross-sell its other services too is the one that will end up with the lion's share of the retail market and the revenues available from it.

10-4 BORROWER QUALITY OR SIZE?

The lessons of the last several years have left America's commercial bankers with a dilemma—should they stress the quality of loans, or should they instead try to court the middle-sized company whose credit quality is frequently poorer than that of the giant?

The stress on quality is easy to understand. Banks were badly burned over the last couple of years through large-sized loan losses. Bankers who had never seen a large loan loss problem in their entire careers found that loans do have risks. As they looked at their troubled real estate investments, their energy loans, and the other credits that got into trouble, they decided "never again." From now on "we will stress quality in our lending; the yields on loans just do not make it worth taking the risks that we have experienced recently."

This helps explain the decline in bank loan demand. Banks have become much more cautious as to whom they will lend money than has been the case in the past. But another reason for the decline in bank loan demand called for exactly an opposite solution.

THE MATTER OF LOYALTY AGAIN

Another factor limiting bank loan demands has been the attitude of large borrowing customers. Many of these firms came to the banks and demanded funds when credit was tightest, but turned away from banks when credit became easy and the banks were looking for loans to make. One can understand the economics that have motivated these large corporate borrowers.

When loan demand is strong, credit conditions are tight, and interest rates are high, the banks offer two advantages over the open market to those in need of credit. The rates banks charge generally do not go up as high as open market rates do. And, vastly more important, because of a feeling of loyalty to customers, banks make every effort to fill their credit demands no matter how tight money is, even if it involves selling securities at heavy losses and depleting liquidity to low levels.

Thus, the large companies come to the banks when loans demands are strongest and add their requests on top of the others.

Yet when credit conditions are slack, these same large borrowers either turn back to the money market for funds or they find that bank lending charges do not drop as low as open market rates do (just as they did not rise as high). In easy money periods, credit is available everywhere, so loyalty means little or nothing.

The bankers thus feel that loyalty is a one sided issue—with the banks providing loyalty.

MIDDLE-SIZED COMPANIES

Faced with this dual-edged policy of the large corporations, many banks have decided that the only answer is to stop stressing loans to these borrowers who can go elsewhere when credit eases, and to give more attention to the medium-sized companies that can not tap the money and capital markets—and thus remain dependent upon the banks even when credit is easy. Consequently, there is quite a change in the marketing attitudes of some bankers as they recognize that these medium-sized companies will be more loyal at both extremes of the business cycle, simply because they have no place else to turn.

The medium-sized companies generally are not as interest rate sensitive as are the large companies. They want and need loyalty more than they need a rate that is a quarter to a half a percent lower than they might find elsewhere. Since they have not developed the complicated techniques of cash mobilization to reduce float that many large companies have developed, their collected balanced are generally larger than those of large companies relative to the size of borrowings.

But this leaves the bankers with the dilemma. The same medium-sized companies that are more likely to be loyal to the bank and are more willing to pay somewhat higher rates for funds and keep larger balances are also the companies whose credit standing is generally lower than that of the giants and whose loans are therefore somewhat more risky.

The bank lending officer must then decide whether to stress quality to reduce the chance of more loan losses, or whether to stress the courting of these medium sized companies whose loan demands will remain stronger through all phases of the business cycle, but whose credit quality is likely to be lower.

It is a real dilemma. But from this vantage point, it appears that as banks experience slack loan demands, and as the need for earnings increases, more and more of them will forget their loan loss experience of the past few years and aggressively seek these new medium-sized borrowing customers. They are tired of being loyal to corporate treasurers who forget their own standards of loyalty whenever alternative opportunities came along for getting money cheaper. While the medium-sized borrower may require more risks, bankers hope to make up for this through better pricing, plus a customer loyalty that will smooth out the peaks and valleys of bank loan demand.

10-5 THE INSIDER LOAN DILEMMA

Loans to directors and key officers is an area where many bankers feel they are damned if they do and damned if they don't. The days are long gone when a bank could make loans at preferential rates to insiders and not worry about the quality of the credit because the borrower was a member of the bank's board. If anything, banks are being extra tough on credits of board members and key officers because they *are* directors of the bank. Every bank fears the adverse publicity that is generated when a loan to an insider defaults, no matter how honest the bank officials were in their credit evaluation process when the loan was placed on the books.

This explains why many bank executives feel that the insider loan must be at the top of the loans on the books in terms of quality and that no preference at all should be given on rate.

But sometimes the banks and especially board members can go overboard on this concept. Many directors question whether they should borrow at all from the bank on whose board they serve. They are concerned that a commercial relationship of any kind will be considered to be an insider transaction, which could cast bad light both on the bank and the board member undertaking the transaction. To avoid any taint whatsoever, many members have decided that when they are serving on the board of one bank, their financial business should all be conducted with some other institution.

In the long run, this is extremely unfortunate for both the bank and for the board member. As a general rule, a board member was picked because of his stature in the community and the role he had played in helping the bank to prosper by giving it the lion's share of his business. If the bank and the director sever commercial relationships because the individual has now joined the board of the bank, the bank and the individual are relinquishing the very link that brought them together.

The bank suffers because it loses the business of its own board member. And the board member must suffer also; after all, he selected that bank in the first place because he liked its service, the talents of its staff, and its rate schedules. If he must then move to some other institution because he happens to be a director of the first bank, he loses the ability to use the facilities of the bank he is serving.

Banks and directors must draw a fine line on insider loans without denying them altogether.

WHAT CAN BE DONE

Some board members have taken the attitude that they will undertake any transactions with the bank they serve as long as they would not be unhappy seeing all the details of the transaction published in the local newspaper the next morning. This is a good way of letting your conscience be your guide. If the board member considers that what the newspaper might say about his loan or other transactions and feels that this would not hurt his business or his stature in the community, then he can go ahead with the transaction without the slightest fear.

While many bankers find that they can reconcile the problem of conflict with regard to borrowing by making sure that there is no preference given to them in rate or in credit evaluation, there is another area in which bank directors worry: Because they are on the board, they may learn a great deal about their competitors that can be useful to them in business. If a competitor comes into the bank for a loan, and the board member learns all about his business transaction, this can be a decided plus to in the director's nonbank business dealings.

Thus, some directors try to maintain strict standards on knowledge as well as credits. They feel that if they do not, the bank will lose the business of competitors when they join the bank's board of directors, just as the bank would lose their own business if they were overstrict on insider relationship standards.

Insider information can be just as important as insider loans in determining bank ethics. Bank board members recognize that this, too, is an area in which they must walk a fine line between their two roles as bank directors and as businessmen who operate and compete in the local community.

10-6 LENDING BY COMPUTER?

Now that computers have become smaller, cheaper, and more prevalent in banking, many bankers are wondering if their lending operations should be on the computer.

Most banks have automated loan reporting and record keeping, both for commercial loans and consumer loans. But the question bankers are asking themselves now is whether the actual decision-making in the lending process should also be computerized. Should the judgment of the individual lending officer be replaced or supplemented by a decision that is pumped out of a microcomputer when the relevant data about the borrower or the company is pumped in?

There are certainly reasons why lending by computer should get some attention from today's banker. The evidence shows that in many instances, the computer can help make better decisions, if the right data is put in. In this regard, all bankers and all other users of data processing equipment forget at their peril the old adage "GIGO"—garbage in, garbage out.

Just look at the possible results. Instead of spreading sheets of 114 lines, a good program can reduce the evaluation to examination of several gradations or even one number. And, as reported by Donald J. McGowan, Senior Vice President of the Conifer Group of Worcester at a Loan Management Conference of the Massachusetts Bankers Association, the results of computerized loan evaluation can be fantastic. Mr. McGowan reported that at the National Lending School, a number of cases of companies needing loans were presented and the students were required to predict which would fail. Of the mere mortals who predicted success rates based on the cases, 67% correctly predicted which companies would go under. But of the examinations made by the computer, the accuracy was 97%.

Still, it is possible to look at such results and still be skeptical. After all, can lending really be quantified and placed on a computer? Most bankers would respond to this question with a resounding "no."

MAKING A LOAN BANKABLE

The problem with computerized lending is that the basic goal of a lending officer is not to predict failure but to make a proposal "bankable" when it otherwise would not be so. The job is not to look for trouble, but for ways to avoid trouble. Remember the old fable of the CEO who visits the lending officer in a remote branch who has been with the bank for many years:

"How long have you been a lending officer?" the CEO asks.

"Forty years" is the response.

"How many bad loans have you made?"

"None," the officer replies proudly.

"Then you're fired."

The obvious point is that if someone can lend for 40 years and not make a bad loan, think of the solid loans that have had to have been turned down in order to produce such a record of perfection.

Lending, then, is a creative art, rather than a straightforward approach to a potential borrower. Creativity cannot be programmed into a computer.

On top of this, bankers today report they are trying their hardest to develop relationship banking under which the lending officer sells the entire bank and knows its whole operation. No such relationship approach can be programmed to give the officer a computer print-out that says "yes" or "no" even if an evaluation of the risks inherent in a potential loan can be so quantified.

THE ART OF LENDING

Virtually all CEOs and lending officers now accept the premise that lending is an art. A good lending officer knows that no amount of caution and examination can prevent the bank from being taken if a potential borrower wants to engage in fraud on his application. This is why a good lending officer lends by looking at the eyeballs as much as he looks at the statement. No computer can handle this issue and challenge.

Top lending officials add that the best education comes not from spreading the sheets but from adversity. No lending officer is fully trained until he or she has been through a full business cycle and seen what happens to a perfectly fine balance sheet as the economic environment deteriorates.

This is a major reason why so many lending officers scoff at the idea of computerizing the lending decision.

Lending officers see three basic factors in a potential borrower's situation: management, the industry's economic situation, and the data on the individual company. Of these three, the only data that can be placed into a computer formula is the historical information.

The keys to lending bank officers hold are thus the ability to interview and seek out an understanding of the strengths and weaknesses of management, the ability to evaluate the future economic environment and its implications for the specific industry of the potential borrower, and a willingness to become deeply involved in understanding the borrower's operation as a going concern rather than as a balance sheet. This is why so many lenders put communication skills, evaluation of people, and a breadth of economic understanding way above ability to analyse financial statements in importance when they are picking lending officers. All in all, it helps explain why computerized lending programs have not played more of a role in the industry.

LESSONS FOR THRIFTS

The same factors that make computerized lending less significant as an innovation in banking than some had hoped should serve banking in good stead as savings banks and savings and loan associations begin to develop the new commercial lending authority they have been given.

The same complexity of lending that makes it difficult to quantify credit data and make decisions on a machine means that institutions, such as the thrifts, that are new in the commercial lending field, will also take considerable time to develop the culture of the field.

Thrifts can certainly buy away good bank people to establish and run their commercial credit operations. But it takes a lot to get top credit people to leave their banks. And it frequently is not just one person who makes or breaks the commercial lending operation. Rather, it is a team that has worked together and that can analyse difficult situations and bring about a consensus.

The difficulties involved in the Penn Square National Bank of Oklahoma City failure show what happens when lenders make decisions without checking the credit with people who have been through adversity and are wary. One can wonder how well many thrifts will do without a tradition of lending and a cadre of people who have been tested in the fire of tough lending periods.

Both in setting up a commercial lending department and in developing new techniques for lending, tradition, and people skills mean far more than new technology and desire to lend.

THE VALUE OF COMPUTERIZATION

What then, is the value of the new computerized approach to lending? Should it be completely ignored?

Acute bankers answer this in the negative. Computerized credit evaluation programs can serve in several valuable ways despite the drawbacks:

- They can serve as red flags on a lending proposition, pointing out that the computerized analysis of the data shows problems that may not have become obvious to the lender.
  In many instances the examination of what the program points up may prove that the red flags were groundless. But it certainly forces a reevaluation when problems show up that might otherwise remain hidden.
- Computer programs can help in grey areas. Credit scoring on personal loans shows that the computerized program can indicate characteristics of the individual that correlate with his or her ability and willingness to repay a debt. Age, sex, employment, marital status, residential location, ownership of a telephone, and a few other factors correlate well with ability and willingness to handle debt. To be sure, there are problems here of violating compliance laws on lending if too much reliance is placed on such data. In many instances, lenders are happier utilizing subjective factors instead of scoring programs for the very reason that they can not be blamed for quantifying the lending decision and discriminating against any specific group based on groupings that are too specific.

- They can serve to affirm the lending officers' decision and give him confidence that he has done the right thing, especially in pricing to compensate for higher risk situations.

In the long run, however, lending remains more of a relationship situation than a yes or no decision process.

Many banks do not like to make long-time customers take the time and effort to fill out the lengthy applications that are frequently necessary to computerize lending. And customers who have always had an informal evaluation often resent the new techniques that quantification of lending require.

In many respects, banking remains a people game in which the one-on-one relationship of the banker and his customer has always been the glue of the relationship. The large and small banks that have forgotten this fact have forgotten it at their peril. And the young Turks who have thought that they could computerize the operation have frequently found that nothing in banking is that black and white.

Certainly computerized models can help, as indicated, through giving the officer a chance to second guess, to reconfirm his thinking, to seek out hidden problems and to price better based on the risk factors the model points up. But banking remains a game in which the best way to get and keep a customer is through the process of working with a situation to make it bankable if at all possible—that is changing the situation to fit the decision, rather than making the decision fit the credit data presented.

11 Corporate Banking

11-1 WHO'S CALLING THE TUNE?

The relationship between banks and their corporate customers has always had the appearance of a cat and-mouse game. Banks certainly need corporate business. And, while there are changes going on in the financial marketplace, corporations need banks. Yet the two often vie with each other to maintain the upper hand. At this point in time, it would seem that corporations are on top. How long this situation will continue is anybody's guess. But that does not mean that banks have no cards to play.

Corporations rely on bank credit when it is cheaper, and then turn to open market funds sources, such as commercial paper, as soon as rates in the open market become lower than bank lending charges. When rates turn up again, and bank credit again becomes the cheaper route, these same corporations return to banks to borrow—usually without the slightest embarrassment over their seeming disloyalty.

Unfortunately, the bank is the loser in this shifting process. It must maintain its ability to service corporate customers even though they turn away from the bank when credit is easing and rates are cheaper elsewhere. In effect, what the banks are doing is standing by, ready to provide funds just at the times when credit is tightest and demands for funds the strongest. Yet the customer can turn elsewhere when rates fall and credit eases, even though that is the time when the bankers could really use the loan business.

A LESSON FROM THE RAILROADS

One might make an analogy between the utility industry and the railroads.

The utilities formerly gave reduced rates to those customers whose overall demands for electricity were the greatest. They felt that the utility could gain economies of scale in providing service to these customers. Included were both industries and individuals who were induced to build all-electric homes by the low overall electric rate provided to a home utilizing no other energy source.

Thanks to OPEC, the utilities have found this to be crazy economics. They must have enough plant capacity available to provide the peak power needs of the huge users as well as to meet the peak needs of everyone else, even though this peak power need may be only a couple of hours a day or a few hours a year (such as on super hot days in summer, when all air conditioners are at maximum usage). Now, the utilities generally use a rate based on amount of power used at peak times. In this way, those who use the power at peak times and who thus require the utility to have all its capacity available, are the ones who help most in paying for peak capacity.

Conversely, the railroad community lines got into trouble by following the reverse of that rule. The railroads gave the cheapest rates to commuters, who used railroad facilities for two two-hour peak periods five days a week, and then ignored the railroad the rest of the time.

The railroad needed all its cars and terminal facilities to meet this peak 20-hour a week demand. Yet the commuters who required this heavy investment were given the lowest rates. Those who used the railroad at times when excess capacity was available were charged maximum rates. It did not make sense, and the railroads that offered commuter service generally found they were running a losing operation because of it.

What does this mean for banks? Should a movie theater charge its lowest rates on Saturday evening when everyone wants to go and its highest rate on Monday afternoon, when the theater is almost empty? Certainly not; it should be the reverse. Yet banks charge companies that only come to borrow at peak times their lower rates and charge the individual who remains a customer all the time a higher rate for money.

Of course this can't be completely turned around. The costs and risks of placing small loans on the books are far heavier than the cost and risks of lending to large companies (if the cyclical nature of the corporate demand is forgotten). Yet bankers can be more selective in their pricing of corporate loans because it is the cyclical nature of these demands—appearing when funds are scarcest and disappearing when credit again becomes available—that requires greater capacity, and thus makes the entire bank operation more expensive.

But why have the corporate treasurers been able to be so fickle in their relationships with the banking industry? Why have they been able to move into bank loans when credit was tight and commercial paper rates were higher than bank rates, and then leave the banks at times when the banks could have used the loan demand? When credit eases, corporations often decide to fund into the long-term bond market and move back into commercial paper.

One can easily see why a corporate financial officer would want to play this game. But the real question is: why he is able to do so? The answer, sad to say, is that the banks allow him to.

In other words, the banks have simply allowed company treasurers to walk all over them:

Banks want loyalty, yet they get disloyalty.

Banks want loan demand when credit is easy; yet they find customers leaving them.

Banks want loan demands to be postponed and moderated when credit is tight; yet they get their heaviest corporate demands for credit just then.

LOSING THE BALL

Why do banks let corporations call the tune? It is because of the practices and policies of bankers toward corporate customers.

There is only one reason why banks find the commercial paper market a major competitor in granting credit to the larger companies able to tap the paper market. The banks provide the back-up lines of credit that make it possible for these corporations to utilize the paper market! Were the banks unwilling to provide this back-up line of credit, then many of the corporate borrowers would find themselves forced to rely on bank loans in easy as well as in tight money periods. Without the back-up lines of credit, the commercial paper market would be closed to corporate borrowers.

Not only do banks provide back-up lines of credit, they in effect tell the commercial paper market that they will assume responsibility if the borrower's credit standing deteriorates. After all, banks know that if credit standing does decline, the paper market will then become closed to the borrower. Yet banks stand willing to take over and pay off the debts to the commercial paper buyers.

Bankers are often pictured as willing to lend an umbrella when it is sunny and then take it back when the rain starts. But with regard to lines of credit, bankers are really the people who carry around the umbrella all the time when the sun is out; but when the rain starts, they give the umbrella to a friend and the banker gets wet. Instead of being appreciated for this, the banker looks foolish.

On top of all this, the banker appears to let the corporate treasurer take advantage of him on the deposit side too. Bankers say they perform all their services and give all the credits because the bank gets balances from the customer. Yet, as most bankers will admit privately, many of these balances are not worth much at all, because they are largely float. Corporate treasurers have learned zero balance accounting under which they know how long it will take for checks issued to be cashed. Accordingly, they place the funds in the bank just in time to cover them.

Conversely, and with banker help, they are able to collect funds faster on the checks received, and deposited through techniques such as the lock box and wire transfer of funds. As a result, the bank on which the check was written gets little or no float either.

Some bankers have determined that certain accounts are not profitable, when actual collected balances are utilized instead of book balances. Yet most of them have not had the courage to force the customers out of the bank if they will not raise fees or keep more idle balances.

Occasionally, a banker will figure the true worth of the corporate balances and tell the customer in no uncertain terms that either he sweeten the pot or he gets out. Sometimes this works; but sometimes the customer leaves. All too often, though, even after the bank has figured out that the account is unprofitable, and has confronted the customer, it is the banker who backs down and refigures the account because he doesn't want to upset things.

11-2 DANCING TO YOUR OWN MUSIC

Bank-corporation relationships are not indestructible. So, banks simply cannot alienate the corporate customer, no matter how healthy the economy, nor how well-off the bank. Banks are in the business of providing financial services and lending money. Banks should serve the financial needs of their corporate customers—but they should set the terms of sale, and not the other way around. Some terms banks should set are discussed below.

PRICING BASED ON COMMITMENTS

Pricing must be based more on commitment of the line of credit and less on actual utilization. Use is bound to be erratic while the commitment can be long-term. If a bank gives a line of credit and agrees to meet the present needs and growth needs of a company, the bank must be ready to serve the company whenever the need arises. This means that the bank cannot lend the money that the company may need later to another company now, since it cannot get it back when the company with the commitment needs it.

A bank can only pull liquidity down to a certain point and can only buy so much new money through liability management. Thus, if a company has a commitment, it may preclude lending money to some other potential borrower. Therefore the company with the commitment must be charged accordingly. The price of stand-by commitments has been increasing in recent years; it is a distinct possibility that the charge for lines of credit will rise even higher.

DOUBLE COUNTING BALANCES

All too frequently, bankers have told borrowing customers that they must keep balances, only to have the same balances do double and triple duty—backing the loan, backing account activity, and compensating the bank for other services rendered. This has been happening because the banker has allowed it to happen. As one banker put it: "If I let a customer in my store buy a shirt for $5, or buy the same shirt and a tie, also for $5, the customer will naturally take both."

Bankers are learning to require idle balances to back their loans and lines, and thereby eliminating double counting. Since many companies that are required to keep idle balances simply borrow more to cover these balance requirements, some bankers are turning to profitability analysis instead of balance requirements.

They recognize that if the borrower borrows an extra amount to meet his balance requirement, then the bank must run this extra deposit amount through the Fed and meet reserve requirements on it before it can relend its own money that its customer has borrowed to meet balance requirements. On top of this, the bank must keep capital backing for this new deposit which is really the bank's own money borrowed and redeposited.

Thus, many banks ask a certain fee and allow it to be met in other deposit or fee form. This approach of profitability analysis enables the bank that gets fees to realize a better return on its loans without as much in reserve requirements or capital needs.

Where the customer does want to keep a balance, more banks are accepting a noninterest bearing time deposit instead of a demand deposit. This lowers reserve requirements, and it also makes sure that the deposit is idle and does not do double duty in backing account activity and other service usage provided by the bank.

REPRICING SERVICES

An idea whose time has come is a repricing of services so that each service stands on its own. All too often, bankers have allowed a customer to utilize the service of a division of the bank for little or no cost, because that customer keeps balances elsewhere in the bank or buys another service. This means that the same balances are used as the excuse to allow free or cheap service all through the bank.

Now banks are doing account analyses on every service and balance to make sure that each service provided is paid for. Even if a customer has a good balance in one area of the bank, the customer is being informed of what the services he is asking for cost and how much of that good balance elsewhere has been allocated to meeting this service. Customers are informed that their accounts are not providing sufficient returns for the bank, and that new services beyond this point will require new fees or higher balances.

CROSS-SELLING

Recognizing that the customer is likely to need the bank more than the bank needs the customer, many banks are demanding, not requesting, a share of all the company's business. The feeling is that if the bank does not get a share of the trust business, the officers' and employees' personal accounts, and the company's investment business, then the bank need not provide the same loyalty as in the past. Again, as indicated, each of these services is costed out and made profitable in its own right, not just thrown in for the balances on hand.

More bankers have come to the conclusion that if their corporate customers will not meet the terms specified, then it is simply time to give up the account. No bank will give up an account without trying to get better fees or balances first. But, if the customer is adamant, then perhaps it is time to part company. A customer whose business just puffs up footings without adding to profits is not worth having.

11-3 CONCERNS OF CORPORATE TREASURERS

In all this discussion of the bank-corporation relationship, it would be well for bankers to consider the viewpoint of corporate treasurers. And they do have definite views and real concerns.

After all, changes in banking mean changes for them. Moreover, there seems to be an increasing number of bank failures in recent years, including the failures of some rather large institutions. The new competition, the new deregulatory mode, the blurring of distinctions between depository institutions all present problems for corporate financial management; they mean increased opportunities, as well.

Consider the specter of bank failure. Treasurers of smaller companies assure themselves that if each account is $100,000 or less, they have nothing to worry about since FDIC insurance covers deposits to that amount. There is, however, reason for caution because each name, not account, is insured to $100,000. Therefore, if a company has a $75,000 time deposit and a $75,000 checking account balance in the same bank, it is insured only to $100,000 on both. More important, many companies cannot keep individual bank accounts under $100,000 and meet operating needs without tremendous inconvenience.

On the other hand, few treasurers realize that if a company owes a bank money, the loan is offset against the company's deposit in the failed bank before determination of the amount the depositor has locked in the bank. Therefore, because of this right of offset a company that owes a bank more than it has on deposit there, comes out unscathed in case of failure of the bank.

Some corporate treasurers complacently point out that they use zero-balance accounting, so they never have anything in the bank but float. However, if a bank goes under, when checks that the customer deposited and that are in process of collection eventually clear, the money is held in the bank subject to the same delays and loss potential as any collected balance in the bank at the time it went under.

MORE THAN SAFETY

The stability of banks is not the only reason for selectivity in banking today:

- Treasurers fret that if they maintain relationships with banks facing liquidity squeezes or capital shortages, these banks will be unable to expand their loans or extend lines of credit when the treasurers need them.
- A treasurer may want to sell CDs in the secondary market before they mature. But if they are not the obligation of a bank with a prime name in the money market, he may have to accept a substantially lower price.
- If he is aware of weaknesses of certain banks, an alert corporate treasurer has more muscle for bargaining on yields. One customer, for instance, demanded and got 60 basis points (.6%) more in yield on a 90-day, $50-million CD than stronger banks were offering. It was worth $75,000 to him.

- The disenchantment with banks has caused many of those institutions needing funds to keep their yields on CDs well above those of bills. Investors confident of their banks' liquidity and solvency have taken advantage of this situation with little risk by switching from bills to CDs.

CORPORATE TREASURER JUDGMENTS

Financial managers are far more sophisticated, at least about judging banks, than they once were. They use new tests to determine where to take their banking business. Some of the approaches are discussed below.

Liquidity

Capital adequacy is a poor test, since one big loss can erode capital quickly. Analysts favor liquidity as a test of solvency because that test notes whether the bank matches short-term liabilities with short-term assets. Too many banks have courted trouble by taking short-term, money-market funds and placing them in long-term loans. Then, when the investors wanted their money back, either because of anxiety or a wish to make other uses of the funds, the banks faced a liquidity squeeze.

An analysis of liquidity also helps redefine capital adequacy. If a bank appears to be undercapitalized relative to deposits, yet many of its assets as well as liabilities are in short-term money-market instruments, the corporate treasurer knows that the institution can collapse both the assets and liabilities quickly and thereby sharply increase the capital-to-deposits ratio.

Loan Yields

A pattern of comparatively low loan yields for several years show that the bank either has been overcommitted in mortgages or has a poor collection record. Either condition damages earnings and hurts the capital position. Conversely, a history of high loan yields indicates an aggressive bank that has generated profits from areas like construction loans at a time when few banks were so profit-conscious.

A long record of high loan yields indicates a profitable, capital-generating bank. But since these loans are illiquid, the bank should be supporting them with long-term deposits, like demand and savings deposits, and not with volatile instruments as CDs, Eurodollars, and federal funds.

A good test using loan yield is whether the bank's yields have moved with interest rates. If they have, the bank is a liquid one that is able to turn over old loans for new ones.

Charge-Offs

A bank with large charge-offs of loan losses but low loan yields is a bank that has been chasing marginal credits and offering them the prime rate. This is a danger sign. While the losses develop, the bank is inadequately compensated for the higher risk.

Overhead

Another red flag is high overhead relative to operating earnings (from two to five times after-tax earnings, according to banking authority David C. Cates). This means that the bank is inefficient. Its unprofitability can eat up capital quickly when interest-rate margins narrow in slack periods,

Funds Borrowing

Double leverage, that is, when both a bank and its holding company borrow funds to provide capital for the former, is yet another danger signal. The holding company's need for high dividends to meet its debt obligations can force the underlying bank into a too aggressive dividend payout policy, leaving inadequate retained earnings for building capital.

Regulatory Signals

Corporate treasurers also scrutinize signals from the regulators. When a regulator turns down a bank's request for a branch or for approval of an acquisition and offers the reason that the bank is not strong enough to handle the growth, large depositors should take warning.

The concerns of corporate treasurers are often valid ones. They should also be concerns of the banks.

11-4 KEYING IN ON CASH MANAGEMENT

Meetings of cash managers have been growing in importance for several years now. In the past, the conference, centered around how to get more out of the bank for less and how to pay slowly and get funds faster. Different topics have now moved to center stage.

Certainly, more efficient handling of funds has not disappeared from the cash manager's agenda of important topics. But it has declined in importance, as most of the new cash collection and disbursement tricks of the trade have become more commonplace and understood.,

As cash management ideas are discussed, such experts as George White, who left Chase Manhattan to form his own consulting firm, explain to financial executives that float time is not as important as the overall cost of handling collections and payments. Although a corporation may lose float, it still may be more profitable to switch from a paper to an electronic payment mechanism.

The issue of float and quicker collections will become less significant when and if banks can pay interest on corporate checking accounts.

One issue corporate financial officers disagree on, as has been brought out in many recent seminars at banking meetings, is whether rate means more than loyalty. Many financial officers do not care about the best rate or the lowest service charges. They want to maintain their bank relationships so that credit will be there when their companies need it. Others, however, have changed banks frequently as some banks have raised service charges while others have not.

Some corporate treasurers are beginning to favor up-front pricing of banking services, rather than having to meet balance requirements. Companies often forget to include the cost of meeting bank balance requirements when they figure out the cost of their products. With up-front pricing, they can compute the cost of banking services just as they determine other costs of doing business.

The failure of Oklahoma City's Penn Square Bank NA, the effects of this failure on several large banking institutions, and the fear that the FDIC may not completely reimburse large depositors when a bank fails are on the minds of many cash managers. Corporations are concerned about whose certificates of deposit they can trust.

This concern has led to such programs as brokered CDs under which CDs of many banks are packaged, and a buyer can obtain more than $100,000 worth of CDs without exceeding the federally insured maximum at any one bank.

MORE CAREFUL FUNDS PLACEMENT

One thing is sure—corporate treasurers no longer feel that a bank is a bank. They are far more careful about where their money goes and far more willing to switch balances than ever before.

What worries some observers is that corporate treasurers may equate size with safety. They may move funds to bigger banks on the theory that the FDIC cannot let a giant institution go under.

Of course, larger banks are not necessarily safer. But what people think is true can be more important than what is really true.

Development of deregulated bank deposit accounts has allowed smaller banks to compete and regain funds that had flowed into the nonbank money funds, and through them into large-bank CDs and corporate commercial paper. But treasurers' uncertainty about bank quality could spur another reversal, with funds again moving from the small to the large institution. This would have a major impact on concentration in the banking industry and on the U.S. system of large and small banks working together to serve the nation's credit needs.

For more about the relationship between banks and corporate treasurers, see the next section, "The Corporate Treasurer and the Banker."

11-5 THE CORPORATE TREASURER AND THE BANKER

One of the age old facts of life in banking has been the tug of war between the banker and the corporate treasurer. The banker has always tried to get the best out of the corporate account, both in balances held and in fees paid for services rendered. The corporate treasurer has tried his best, in turn, to get a free ride—to get his bank service paid for through float, so that the actual cost to the corporation would be minimal.

In years past, the corporate treasurer has generally been the hands on winner. More often than not, this has been the banker's fault. Just listen to this conversation:

BANKER: We have done an evaluation and have figured out your balances relative to the services you are using and we find that your account is unprofitable. Either leave more balances or pay us fees.

CORPORATE TREASURER: Nuts. We won't do either. Now, what are you going to do?

BANKER: We will go home and refigure. Maybe we can make your account look profitable by a different analytical approach.

To add insult to injury, even when the banks have been sure the account was not profitable, the bank still bent over backwards to service the corporation. Listen to this conversation:

BANKER: Schmidlap Oil's account is unprofitable. It costs us far more than it earns us. And they won't raise balances or pay us fees for service rendered.

OUTSIDE OBSERVER: Why don't you give up the account, then?

BANKER: What? Lose Schmidlap Oil? They are one of our major accounts in the bank!

With such an attitude on the part of the banker, no wonder the corporate treasurer looked at the bank as a pushover and tried to get away with paying the bank as little as possible, either in fees or balances.

Now this has all changed. The banking industry has faced enough of a profit squeeze so that bankers can no longer afford to lose money on each account and try to follow the proverbial approach of making it up in volume. Each account must pay its own way or the bank will soon be out of business. No longer do the banks have the lush noninterest bearing checking accounts to subsidize everyone else. And the steady deregulation of the industry makes each dollar of deposits tougher to win and more expensive every day.

Up to now, however, even with a greater realization by the banker as to the importance of the profitability of each account, the corporate treasurer has still been in the driver's seat most of the time. He has developed sharp cash management techniques that have enabled him to compensate the banker with float and otherwise push those collected balances, on which the banks make their living, down to a minimum.

Again, it must be added from the outset, that much of this pressure to work collected balances to a minimum is caused by bank policies. Bank pricing of balances and account analysis techniques leave a great deal to be desired in many cases.

Corporate treasurers have used the system. In paying bills, they have been as slow as possible, using techniques like remote disbursement that involves paying people in the East with checks written in the West and vice versa so that float time before payment must be made is the greatest. Yet, in collecting funds, they have been developing new techniques that get payments collected far faster than in the past through lock boxes, direct sending of checks and other collection speeding techniques.

This has had a two-fold impact on the banks. First, because of better cash management techniques, the treasurers have had less need to borrow from banks.

Second, because pricing of bank deposits in the account analysis has been less attractive than moving funds away from banks, because of the assessment for reserve requirements and frequently because of less aggressive bank competition in the certificate market, much of the saving in funds that corporations have been able to generate by aggressive cash management has been placed into money market securities—not deposits.

Acute cash management techniques have also enabled the corporate treasurer to keep track of the funds that he must keep in balances so effectively that he is able to shift them from bank to bank to cover balance requirements. Thus, the banks have fewer instances of corporate balances that are above the minimum requirements to pay for activity. This means fewer balances that provide the extra gravy of a return to the bank over and above the minimum needed to cover the cost of service.

What hurts the banks even more is that knowledge of cash management techniques are spreading steadily from larger companies on downward to smaller institutions. In the past only the largest companies utilized acute cash management programs and the remainder left idle balances that provided a cushion of profit to the bank. Now, most mid-sized and even some small companies are hiring aggressive cash managers who are working balances down to a minimum and slicing the bank profit from corporate accounts to a minimum.

What is encouraging, though, is that this trend appears to have gone about as far as it can go. In other words, the techniques of acute cash management and balance paring appear to be known by most companies by now.

Far more important, however, the lower interest rate levels make it less profitable to cut bank balances to a minimum and play the float for all it is worth. Corporations can no longer make yields of upwards of 15% on the investment of funds freed by aggressive cash management. Thus, the role of cost of fund handling and the economies that banks can offer through electronic payments approaches are weighing more heavily in corporate treasurer's decision making, while the yield available from pulling the funds out of the bank quickly are meaning less in the evaluation.

This also means that banks will have to be prepared to show corporate treasurers how they can be better off by leaving more funds in the bank and not working so hard to reduce float.

This leaves the strong conclusion that the corporate treasurer has bested the banker through much of the past because he has been willing to become more aggressive while the bank has all too often relied upon outdated pricing schemes and balance requirements. The bank now has an opportunity to get a better position in the tug of war with the corporate treasurer than he has had in the past. But this will not come without effort.

Conditions are ripe for banks to play a stronger hand in the bank-corporate treasurer tussle, but it is up to the bankers to make this better position materialize. Better pricing, more thought as to what the treasurer really wants and is willing to pay for, and new techniques of electronic money flow will be the key to banker improvement in this tug of war.

11-6 GAINING A BETTER POSITION WITH CORPORATE TREASURERS

Each bank that has developed a cash management program, such as lock box collection systems, is, in effect, telling the corporate treasurer: "You give me a small balance and I'll help you rob all the other banks of large balances." The end product has been that banks have not gained too much profitability from corporate accounts in recent years, and banks have had to turn to the less sophisticated corporations and the consumers for the backbone of their profits.

Now, this is changing. For the first time in years, it appears as if the banks are gaining a better position in the bank corporate treasurer tussle.

What is bringing this about?

Bankers found, for example that when they tried to offer new services, such as direct payment of payroll, the treasurer laughed in their faces.

The banker should have realized that he was fighting a losing battle:

"Look," the banker would say to the Treasurer. "You are now paying your employees with checks. You send out the checks and you have the use of the funds for the three or four days before the employees cash these checks.

"What we are offering is a new program to have the employees get the funds immediately, so you lose the use of the money immediately. All we ask for this service is $1 a week per employee."

The banker was left wondering why it was so hard to sell direct payroll payment and use of the automated clearing house.

But the passage of time has given the banker an answer to this question of the corporate treasurer: "What's in it for me?"

With the steady rise in the cost of providing payroll service, the inexorable growth in urgency to get away from paper and develop paperless, more efficient corporate operations, the bank's offer to take over payroll preparation with all its handling and operational costs makes the fee involved of handling this through the automated clearing house more reasonable and acceptable every month. And the decline in the interest that can be earned on the funds saved through float that accompanies payroll checks and their physical distribution to employees makes the value of retaining traditional means of payments far less than it was when interest rates were almost double today's levels.

Thus, banks have a real opportunity to earn a profit from providing a service for a fee because they are now offering what the corporate treasurer wants and needs. In effect, the bank's goal and the corporate treasurer's goals have become similar.

CAREFUL ACCOUNTING

Carried further, banks are finding that not only can they offer something that is of value to the treasurer and offers the bank a chance for a service fee too, they can expand this service further by capturing the extra income that is available through providing even more service to the treasurer.

Treasurers report that with the value of float declining in the lower rate environment, what means more to them than almost anything else is the quick and accurate reporting of transaction data. Treasurers want to know which checks have cleared, what balances are available, and what bills have been paid or are outstanding. Again, this is data that the bank can provide and with which it can earn a decent return.

It is becoming more common to see electronic payment of bills from company to company, and what the treasurer wants is efficient recording and reporting of data on trade terms, invoice numbers, and other invoice details.

Again, this is an opportunity for banks, both large and small; for the automated clearing houses can help even the smaller community bank provide this type of service to the corporation utilizing the bank for its financial operations.

If this added service coupled with lower interest rates were not enough to calm down the aggressive cash management techniques of the corporate treasurer, the Federal Reserve's (Fed's) efforts to speed float and reduce the value of remote disbursement also is aiding the community bank.

Corporations are learning that the Fed is not willling to let them play games with balances after they have written checks on them. This makes the banks' willingness to provide efficiency and added invoice data, albeit at the expense of float, an even more worth while service than would have been the case had float time not been curbed by the Fed.

SOMETHING FOR EVERYBODY

One can understand the motive of the corporate treasurer. He is judged by his ability to cut costs and improve profits of his company. When the treasurer can show added yields on money market investments caused by the rapid flows of funds around the nation to curb balances to a minimum and free the most funds for short term investment, he is the hero in his organization.

Now the immanent development of interest on corporate checking is likely to help relax the treasurer. He will be able to earn as good a return leaving his funds in the bank as he could moving them into the money market—especially as banks get rid of the obsolete clipping of the account to cover their own reserve requirements.

Interstate banking—as it comes along—also will help the treasurer to relax, as he will not have to concentrate balances with so much effort in order to obtain a decent return on them. He will be able to leave them in the same institution even if spread around the nation.

The growing need to develop paperless transactions has already given the banking industry a tremendous selling point as it tries to offer something of value to the treasurer that he will be willing to pay for. And pay he will if he can get the efficiency and data that bank handling of corporate payments is prepared to provide today.

What this basically means, though, is that banking is becoming more of a service operation in which income stems from selling services, rather than from the spread between costs of funds and return on funds, or the spread that can be generated by borrowing short and lending long.

This is a world of flexible interest rates on both assets and liabilities. Therefore, the bank that can widen the spread the most between asset yields and liability costs, through efficient operations, will be the winner; while the bank that can earn income from operations that do not involve lending and investing funds will be an even greater winner.

The greatest opportunities to banking lie in the bank-corporate treasurer relationship. Happily, the fact that the banks have been the losers so long in the conflict with the corporate treasurer has largely been the fault of both bank pricing and a financial environment that encouraged the corporate treasurer to curb his bank balance to a minimum. Now both of these conditions are changing. Banks are becoming more acute pricers. The decline in money market yields, coupled with higher costs of paper handling, have made the corporate treasurer ever more willing to use bank services and pay for them.

The result, then, is that with today's banking and financial environment, the question of who is winning the bank-corporate treasurer battle can be answered categorically: If the bank is pricing correctly and offering the services the treasurer wants and needs, both parties are bound to be winners.

11-7 FEES MAKE MORE SENSE

There is no reason for a corporate treasurer to want to both pay for bank services and back his loan activity with compensating balances. If a corporation cannot earn more on its funds by using them in the business than it can earn leaving them as balances to compensate the bank for loans granted, then the company really should question whether its operations are profitable enough to justify continuing.

This is especially true when it is remembered that the bank generally subtracts a healthy portion of the balance on deposit first to cover its reserve requirements before evaluating the earnings credit that the balance generates. Thus, even if the bank gives a return on balances that matches the present level of money market rates, the actual value to the corporate treasurer is 20% to 25% less because of the subtraction for reserve requirements.

This is why some acute banks do not subtract this amount. They feel that this reserve requirement is a price of money that should be born by the borrower, not by the depositor, if the bank wants to build deposits against the competition.

But even here, if the corporate treasurer cannot earn at least as much using funds either in his business, or in the money market, as he can by leaving them in the bank to back loans, then something is drastically wrong with him or his company.

What reason does a corporate treasurer have to compensate the bank with balances under such circumstances?

Basically, the corporate treasurer is sloppy and does not realize how much his decision to keep balances is costing his company; or, far more likely, he realizes that his bank is sloppy. If his bank is sloppy on pricing, then the treasurer can usually let the same balances do double or triple duty—backing the loan, backing all activity, and paying for a call on bank service and advice, too.

Generally, he also recognizes that the bank is not going to be as precise in analyzing collected balances as it is in making sure that fees are paid. Therefore, the compensation to the bank can be whittled down without any complaints developing.

BANKER'S VIEW

A sharp banker should recognize that a corporation willing to accept payment by balance compensation and not demanding fee payment for services received is generally expecting that it will benefit from the situation. Bankers themselves have good reason to want balances replaced by fees:

- Balances, unlike fees, must be backed by capital, and most banks do not have any excess of capital available these days.
- If a bank is a member of the Fed, having the balances means that the bank must keep higher reserves at the Fed than otherwise—and for nonmembers this means higher reserves in vault cash and at correspondent banks. Fees need not be backed by reserves.

On top of this, the bank has the bookkeeping costs and the added work of handling the balances. But fees are simple and provide income directly instead of indirectly. Some bankers respond that if they do not get balances, they have no money to lend to others. But usually this argument does not hold water.

If a customer must keep balances in the bank to back his loan, he generally has borrowed this money as part of his original loan. This means that the bank gets back as balances its own funds that it loans out—only with added reserve requirements and capital needs attached because the same loaned out money comes back to the bank as new deposits.

Why, then, do banks still rely so heavily on balances instead of fees? Largely because of tradition. Smart bankers, however, are recognizing that they are better off with fees than balances to back their loans, even though it makes the bank look smaller. When they see a treasurer who still pushes for balances instead of wanting a fee basis, they realize that he often wants a balance compensation approach because he thinks he can pull the wool over the banker's eyes and pay with balances that are either all float or that would have had to be in the bank anyway.

It's about time the tide has begun to turn.

12 Retail Banking

12-1 MAKING SMALL RETAIL ACCOUNTS PROFITABLE

"If you could offer one new service to help build your bank's profits, what would it be?" That is a tough question, and there is probably no single answer that will apply to every institution. But here is one surprising response that certainly merits consideration: *Rediscover the retail customer.*

The answer is really a variation of the old adage, when everyone else zigs, you should zag. Applying that to banking, it seems that almost every bank in the country is stressing the so-called middle market at the expense of the smaller retail customer.

It is hard to define what the mid-market really is. Perhaps the best way would be to say that a mid-market business customer is one with annual sales of between a measly $10 and hefty $500 million.

But one thing is certain: Banks are downgrading their service to the small retail customer in their search for the mid-market. Some banks are removing tellers, setting high minimum balances and service charges on small accounts, and closing accounts that are felt to be too small to be profitable. Then there is Citibank, where there are special teller lines for those with $5,000 or more.

One cannot blame banks for doing this. Most small accounts are not just profitable; they cost more than they are worth. And now, with banks paying going rates for money—either through money funds or the money desk—banking has become a game in which a bank knows it can buy all the funds it needs and need no longer count on the small, unprofitable account as a source of lendable funds.

In the new banking where rates have replaced services as the basic magnet for funds, catering to the small account that costs more than it is worth has to stop.

SMALL ACCOUNTS CAN BE PROFITABLE

Before banks give up on the retail customer, there is a question as to whether the public will pay for banking services, thereby making it profitable to the bank to continue its provisions.

Look at some of these examples:

- In the Miami area, a bank decided to close all accounts that did not keep $5,000 on balance. Instead of having their accounts closed, however, a great many people simply found ways to build their balances—they asked their relatives to combine their funds, they consolidated accounts, and they got up to the minimum balance to keep the account in the bank. In essence, they felt that staying at an exclusive bank was worth it.
- When banks have raised service charges and said customers should go elsewhere if they do not want to meet these higher charges, as a general rule, complaints have been minimal. There have been very few accounts closed as service charges were raised, and most of the ones that have been closed had been very unprofitable anyway.
- In Moorestown, New Jersey, the Burlington County Trust Company has developed a personal banker program similar to that at other banks trying to appeal to the upscale customer. It offers personal consultation on investments once a year, special treatment in handling routine banking service that some other personal banker programs offer, and the aura that the customer who gets this service is special in the bank's eyes—a very important factor. But the facet that makes the Burlington County Trust Company's program different from the other personal banking programs is that the bank charges $375 a year for it, and there have already been about 50 people who paid to obtain the service.
- Banking has a good deal to learn from the Merrill Lynch cash management account and similar full service programs that charge a hefty annual fee. This charge is solely for the privilege of having all financial transactions tied together in one account, with the worry of moving funds for varied transactions removed from the customer and taken over by the bank.

  The key is that people will accept a lower rate on their savings and pay higher service charges and fees if they feel they are special in the bank's eyes and can get the service they need and want without a hassle.

Banks have certainly seen that the affluent customer return from the brokerage firms to get money market fund service when banks were allowed to offer them. And it seems likely that banking can keep a lot of other business that might go elsewhere, while still making a profit on it, if the bank charges enough.

Evidently there is a mystique about having your business at a bank instead of some other financial institution. Many people will pay a lot more than one might think to get that special feeling that they are served by a bank.

In many instances the banks have been kidding themselves when they think the public will not pay more for a bankers' attention.

Look at safe deposit boxes: Banks practically gave them away, with the result that people pay 10 times as much for a locker at the club in which old sneakers are kept than they pay for a bank vault of similar size, and in a downtown location, where their wealth is stored.

The special companies that have developed high-priced safe deposit boxes have found that the public will pay many times the price of a traditional vault if a few extra services are added such as broader hours of operation.

Thus before giving up so much of the retail business, one can wonder whether bankers might be better off trying to make the traditional retail business more profitable. Not only could this make a new profit center out of a service that used to be a loss leader, but it can avoid the problem of what happens to banking's political base if the people who used to rely on banks are forced to go to credit unions and thrift institutions for their financial service.

There are just so many people who want and need financial services. If the banks give up one great segment of this group without first trying to make it more profitable, it may have turned away the proverbial bird in the hand for the two in the bush.

12-2 SERVICES MUST SATISFY NEEDS

How can a bank get the public to use a new service and build its volume high enough to generate profits? This perennial problem in the industry is made even more difficult by the diversity of new banking services being offered under deregulation.

One basic way is personal selling by bank people on a one-on-one basis.

Contests to get employees to sell a bank service work, too. They have induced many people to try credit cards when they feared them, to open trust accounts, and even to give their date of expiration on their auto insurance policy so the bank could sell the customer its own policy. Nothing makes an employee more anxious to sell a new service to a customer than a reward for the sale.

A second approach is the basic one of price. This is extremely important in this era of electronics, under which the old way of doing business is just too costly for the bank.

Bankers first induced the public to give up the passbook for no passbook savings by offering a higher return on the nonpassbook account. And they have induced the public to use ATMs instead of tellers by substituting service charges for transactions that involved seeing tellers.

Finally, banks have enticed people to try new services with offers ranging from $2 to use an ATM card the first time, to the use of gift items such as televisions and all the other goods that fill the ads banks put in the newspapers.

But the key to selling a bank service remains the public's real need for that service. Without it, there is little likelihood of success.

THE MATTER OF NEED

As an officer at Citibank once stated: We don't worry when people go to other banks for all their banking services. But once they need an international service, they have to come to us. And then we start cross-selling until we have the full account." In essence, need made the difference.

Similarly, with regard to automated teller machines, one banker in Colorado told of the job he had selling an affluent customer on taking an ATM card. Nothing happened until his son went to college and found that there was a machine on campus that could provide him with emergency cash. His personal campaign did the job on Dad, and he got the card.

PRORATION

In the same vein, bankers who look at the new cash management accounts with skepticism should realize how valuable they are when there is a need to transmit securities in a hurry for a tender offer. Maybe a little explanation here is in order.

When a company puts out a tender offer for stock, there is usually a final day of acceptance of stock. But there is a far earlier proration date, the date the securities must reach the bidder to be guaranteed that any shares at all will be accepted.

To small shareholders, this can be a raw deal. The tender is usually for well above the market price of the stock, and thus it is usually oversubscribed. The company bidding usually wants only control and not 100% of the stock.

The bideer thus sets up a proration date, and thereby says that only shares reaching the bidder by that date will be included in the pool of securities being accepted if the issue is oversubscribed. Thus if 4 million shares reach the bidder by proration date and it says it will take 3 million, it takes 75% of each tenderer's shares. But those who miss the proration date only have their shares accepted if the offer is not fully subscribed and more shares are needed.

Proration dates for some reason are set unreasonably soon after the announcement of the offer. Getting to the vault, mailing the stock and hoping it will arrive is a pretty rotten procedure. If the individual is away from home for three days, the whole offer is unavailable to him.

Here is where a cash management account can do the job. The broker already holds the stock, and, on receipt of a phone call from the customer, wires the acceptance, arranges the transfer, and deposits the proceeds in the money market fund—all free!

Does this make a cash management account pay for itself over and over again? You bet it does.

And as banks begin to offer securities brokerage services, handling securities and tenders of them should be one important service included if the banks are to win this cash management account business back from the brokerage community.

Again, it proves the point: need makes a service work.

HOME BANKING

How about banking in the home?

Right now, many observers wonder whether the public really needs it. After all, telephonic bill paying, an early form of banking in the home, has not done all that well.

But what about the combination of banking in the home and the money market accounts? With limits on the number of third-party transactions per month, can't home banking be used to switch funds from the money market account to a regular account just before the check is written or the bill paid? Isn't this a way of getting maximum yields on a money fund account that, in effect, has no minimum size check? Money market accounts may actually help build the need for banking in the home, and justify the cost over and over again in the added interest earned.

The job, then, is to make sure there is a need, and not just a new gimmick that is shiny and intriguing. If a need develops once, the customer generally becomes hooked, and he makes more and more use of the service which, in time, makes the new service vital to him.

12-3 THE POTENTIAL OF FEE INCOME

The changed emphasis of monetary policy and partial deregulation of the banking industry has forced banks to reexamine their traditional sources of income. In this reexamination, community bankers in particular are coming to the conclusion that they must be tougher and more acute in their use of service charges than ever before.

The change in monetary policy started in October 1979, with the so-called Volcker Revolution. At that time, the Federal Reserve gave up its efforts to establish interest rates in the nation and switched to a policy of trying to better control the money supply. As a result, there has been a far greater volatility of interest rates than in the past, with the prime rate swinging up and down by a factor of over 10% in a matter of a couple of years.

This has caused bankers to reexamine their loan pricing and investment policies. The banks, thrifts, and other lenders that continued to make long-term fixed rate loans after the Volcker Revolution found themselves locked into assets whose yields were stuck at times when interest rates soared; as a consequence, the cost of funding these loans and investments also soared.

Borrowing short and lending long was the basic problem behind the vast bulk of bank failures in the recent past.

But, in addition to being squeezed by borrowing short and lending long, institutions also got killed another way in this new world of volatile interest rates. Banks that had locked in long-term deposits in certificate form also were under a tremendous profit squeeze as interest rates fell and the returns earned on certificate funds declined.

Thus, bankers have largely switched over to a new approach of gap management, under which assets and liabilities are matched to a far greater degree so that the bank is not killed by either a rise or a fall in interest rates.

However, while eliminating the money risk that interest rate changes formerly brought to the bank, gap management also eliminated the profit that had come from riding the yield curve through borrowing short and lending long, and earning profits from the differential between long- and short-term interest rate levels. So banking institutions have had to look elsewhere for income to run the bank and maintain their profit as replacement for the income formerly earned by borrowing short and lending long in periods of rising yield curves.

THE 80/20 RULE

The second area in which banking has had to reexamine its source of income is in the determination of who provided the bank's profits. In the past, most banks traditionally relied on the old 80/20 rule, i.e., 20% of the depositors would provide 80% of the bank's income.

This rule was valued because Regulation Q and traditional bank policy involved keeping interest rates low. This, in turn, meant that the saver got rates well below market interest rate levels, and the borrower obtained cheap funds because the saver was being paid below market rates.

The savers suffered, but the bank was balanced because the savers subsidizing the borrowers.

Now this, too, has changed. The savers have decided that either they get going rates for their funds or they will take their money elsewhere. The switch of over $240 billion into money funds of the brokerage firms and other nonbank providers of this service that took place before December 14, 1982 was a solid indication that the banks could no longer keep savers' funds if they were not able to offer going interest rates on these monies.

The fantastic growth of bank and thrift money funds since the deregulation of rates on December 14, 1982, with the totals exceeding $400 billion in the first year, is ample proof that the banks can keep the savings of the nation—but only if they pay going rates for this money.

It also brings two conclusions that cannot be ignored. First, borrowers must pay what money is worth if they are to be accommodated. Second, banks must look to other sources of income if they are to prosper. Banks can no longer count on the underpayment of interest on savings as a basic source of profit any more.

Thus, these two separate trends—the Volcker Revolution and the deregulation of rates—both point to the banks' needing a new source of income. And that source has to be noncredit fee income because there is no other source available at this time.

Certainly banks can help maintain their profitability through the strict control of costs. And industry analysts look to banks that keep noninterest expense under control as the best ones for investment potential. But this is only part of the game. Expanding noncredit income is the second part of the forward plan of the aggressive bank today. This means a total reexamination of bank service charges.

CHARGING FOR SERVICES RENDERED

For community bankers in particular, noncredit income and service charges come as a hard lump to swallow at first. This is because bankers think of themselves as friends of the community, and they hesitate to impose service charges that may weaken this friendship. Thus, many banks have kept charges far below what they should have been. In other instances, the banks have made so many exceptions to their service charge policies in order to immunize certain customers from the service charge policies that the source of income was riddled with holes anyway.

If the community bank has made a costly mistake in the recent past, it has been this gingerly approach to service charges. The bankers who have bitten the bullet and reexamined and raised service charges have found out that it has not been as adverse a development as they once thought. And the resulting increased service charges and elimination of exceptions to these charges has been a boon to the bottom line.

What bankers have been finding is that even in an era of deregulation under which there is tremendous price competition for deposits, the public wants quality and will pay for it.

John Glenn, the astronaut, was once asked what was it like flying around the earth in a capsule. His answer: "All I could think of was that there were 763 moving parts in the capsule each of which was built by the low-cost bidder."

Similarly, the public recognizes that it keeps its basic wealth in the bank, and it wants a quality service in handling this wealth. Banker after banker reports that when service charges have been raised and quality maintained, there is practically no response from the public, and it becomes almost a nonevent. The bankers then wonder why they did not do this before.

Other changes to heighten bank profits also have been accepted with far less unhappiness than had been feared. Banks have raised the minimum size of an interest-bearing savings account. The expectation was that the number of these smaller accounts would drop sharply. In many instances, they actually have gone up. Now, these same bankers have decided that in addition to eliminating interest on accounts below $100, they will also service charge the small accounts that have excessive activity, even though they are not paying interest on the accounts in the first place.

Other banks have raised minimums. They have also automatically closed the accounts that did not meet these minimums, sending the depositor a cashier's check for his balance. What some report is that instead of having the accounts closed when the notice of this new policy is given, people consolidated their accounts to meet the new minimum. In at least one case, Jefferson National Bank of Florida, this was true even though the minimum size account was raised to $5,000!

The Girard Bank in Philadelphia (now called Mellon East) has imposed a policy of charging $30 for a check written on insufficient funds for the past several years. Instead of having the customers leave, the result has been an acceptance of this charge for an exception item because the bank had the foresight to explain its costs and policy to its employees who, in turn, have explained it to the customers. The result is that instead of cursing the bank along with the customer when the customer complains about this charge, the bank teller explains the banks costs and suggests that if the customer is not willing to compensate the bank for its full cost of doing business, maybe the customer belongs in some other institution. The explanation works and the accounts are usually saved while the fee income builds up.

So, by putting some backbone in service charges and by being willing to lose the accounts that do not meet bank minimum standards or are unwilling to pay these charges, the banking industry is able to build income to replace revenue sources that have disappeared. And, since the smaller bank has far less opportunity to build new, more exotic, sources of income, this reliance on service charges is a tremendous boon to the acute community institution. In many instances, service charges are far more important to small banks than to the larger institutions that also face this new earnings squeeze from the volatility of rates and the end of the 80/20 policy.

A QUESTION OF COMPLIANCE

The question arises of whether banks can charge a lot more than they traditionally have charged without facing public resentment and possible lawsuits—both of which could injure the community bank's reputation. This is especially cogent when we remember the new world of banking compliance, whereby the banking industry must meet certain standards of community service and nondiscriminatory pricing to avoid legal action.

The answer is that there is nothing wrong with making service charges compensatory, and there is no reason to fear legal action just as long as the bank is consistent. The bank must assess the same charges against all customers, not just a few or most customers.

Certainly a bank can make exceptions to its service charge policy if there are reasons that are in the interest of the bank. For example, it is not necessary to throw out the accounts of teenagers that have only a few dollars in them under a policy of higher minimum balance banking—if the teenagers have parents with substantial balances in the bank. However, an account analysis of the parents should include the child's account in it to insure that the family as a whole is not getting preferential treatment.

The key is simply this: any policy is legal—no matter how unpopular it may seem at first—if it is consistent and the bank does not make exceptions for reasons that cannot be justified on strictly economic terms.

Now, however, there is a new development in the United States: so-called lifeline banking. This is where everyone is entitled to a minimum banking service just as everyone is entitled to minimal electric service, even if the customers do not meet minimum standards for such service.

Here, banking will have to be careful to insure that minimum service means just that—and these accounts should not be allowed to do more than deposit of a paycheck and withdrawal of a few checks a month—unless the customer is willing to pay the going rate for bank service above the minimum.

Unfortunately, our banking system has evolved to a point where charges are so cheap that services are actually wasted. For example, kids use a bank account and a checkbook to pay for a 35 cent pack of gum, when the bank pays 50 cents to clear the check. People also use the bank account as a safe deposit box in high crime areas—taking out $10 each morning to get through the day, and costing the bank several dollars in teller and handling costs by doing so. And people keep separate bank accounts for several different purposes, each of which is so small that the bank loses money on it when one combined account could be profitable.

In the past, a bank could make these high costs up through playing the yield curve on investments and generation of high income from the 20% of profitable accounts. But with these two sources of profit eliminated, each account must stand on its own. Service charges and other stricter requirements are the basic way of achieving this.

12-4 LEARNING FROM ACCOUNTS THAT LEAVE

Both authors have closed checking accounts—in different banks and where the accounts had been active for years. Both of us had similar experiences—closing the accounts was just too simple.

We stopped using the accounts, waited until we were sure of the balance to the penny, wrote checks for those amounts, and waited for the statements. In time they showed up with balances of zero and each with a little notation stamped: "Closed Account." That was all. One account had been open for 19 years, the other for eight. In both cases, the relationships with the banks were ended—and it was done as impersonally as that.

Should we have expected more? Well, there had been little personal contact with either bank through the years. Still, checking with each other later, the impersonal closings of the accounts had us both feeling that the banks would go on just as happily as before; that they cared as little about either of us when we closed the accounts as they did when we had opened them. But what a lost opportunity for those banks, and for banks generally when accounts are closed.

Suppose either of the banks had had a policy of sending a survey to all those who had closed accounts, asking why they had been closed? Might the replies not tell management a lot about what was right and what was wrong about the bank's policies?

Top bankers often bemoan the fact that they do not know what is going on inside their organizations. An account being closed provides one opportunity to get some information from someone who would probably be completely honest. Many banks conduct "exit interviews" with departing employees to find out what they really think about the bank and the work. Couldn't a bank give this same opportunity to departing customers?

Some banks do have a policy of sending a letter to all closed accounts, but for another reason. They want to be sure that the customer closed the account and that it was not done by an enterprising employee who wanted the funds and found it easier to close an entire account that had been inactive for a month or two than to juggle an active account to make the books balance. But to have a seemingly satisfactory business relationship and then to have it end without learning why is just plain foolish.

It must be noted that banks are not alone in this. People buy cars and then never hear again from the auto dealer. The smart few send letters after a couple of years to say that it might be economical to trade now that the car has had its third anniversary. And realtors act like your closest friend while they are selling you a house. But as soon as the papers are signed, most disappear. The few who do follow through are generally the ones that get the listing business when the house is subsequently sold.

In banking, a few sharp bankers have followed up on lost business and have been able to win it back.

People usually close an account for two reasons: either they are insulted so often they recognize it, of they move away from the community. If they have been insulted (or there has been some incredibly bad mishandling of the account), bank management should certainly want to hear about it. An exit survey mailed to all the closed accounts might not only point out bank weaknesses but also bring back some of the accounts that left.

Even if an account is closed because of a move, it may be that with today's credit cards, ATMs, and a host of other EFT programs, the bank could even hold on to some of the customers—but only if the bank understood why the account was being closed and what the customer now needed in the way of banking service.

12-5 SERVE THE CUSTOMERS YOU CAN AFFORD

Part of the new lean and mean approach that bankers have had to take is development of greater selectivity in terms of which customers they want to serve.

This is a tremendous about-face for many banks. There was a time when banks wanted to be all things to all people, and the industry was loaded with institutions that spent fortunes telling the public how friendly they were and how anxious they were to please the public, no matter how small or crazy the request.

This is no longer the case.

Bankers have been forced to be more and more selective. The bank that in effect tells some customers that their business is no longer desired, by charging so much for services that the customer gets the point and leaves, is becoming the model that others follow.

What has happened? What has made bankers so much more selective in soliciting customers and in fighting to keep them? And much more important, what are the means that have been used to become more selective, and what have they done to bank bottom-line profits?

SENSITIVE SPREAD

Two forces have combined to make acute bankers more selective in the business they want to win and keep. One is spread management, and the other is the difficulty in obtaining capital to back bank growth.

Spread management, as indicated earlier, is a direct result of changes in Fed policy and in the volatility of interest rates.

Bankers formerly considered that one basic way of making money was to borrow short and lend long. With an upward sloping yield curve, this was a profitable approach. For banks paid low rates on funds in the short end and lent them out at attractive yields in longer term loans.

But Federal Reserve emphasis on controlling the money supply and letting interest rates go where they may made this a dangerous game.

It is all well and good for a bank to borrow short and lend long when short rates are 10% and long rates are 15%. But what happens if the bank has made a long-term loan at 15% and rates rise to such a degree that it must be funded with short-term funds that can only be obtained at a cost of 20%?

Smart bankers have looked at this problem and determined that their solution, if they wish to survive, is not to gamble on rate differentials at all. Rather they match maturities of assets with maturities of liabilities, so that if rates go up, they both pay more and earn more at the same time. But if rates go down, both their costs of funds and yields on funds decline simultaneously too.

The resultant spread management makes a bank a safer institution than it would be if it gambled on the gap between short-term and long maturity interest rates. But it does put considerable pressure on that spread between costs and returns on funds to make sure that it is as wide as possible.

EARNINGS CRUCIAL

A second reason why bankers have had to become more selective in accepting business is the difficulty in generating capital to back growth.

Bank stock prices in most institutions have remained well below book value. This means that any new sale of stock, if feasible at all, has to penalize present shareholders—the actual owners of the bank—to reward those being enticed to provide the bank with new capital funds.

Thus, bankers have to do what they can to reduce the need for new capital. And prime among the steps available is to limit growth to that which is profitable and can generate its own new capital through retained earnings.

This is common sense. If a bank grows, it is told it must gain new capital to back that growth. But if the growth is not profitable enough to generate its own capital, then the bank is merely becoming bigger for its own sake, and soothing the egos of its officers and board members at the expense of shareholders. Selected growth is the key. It cannot afford to serve all customers who would like to utilize its services.

SAVER VERSUS BORROWER

Which customers should a bank solicit? A first rule that should be drawn is that banks (and thrift institutions alike) must start by reversing a policy of several decades that the borrower comes first and must be catered to at the expense of the saver. For in today's banking environment, proper action involves the exact opposite.

Public policy in this nation for the past 20-30 years has been to encourage home ownership and borrowing to finance cars, vacations, and other activities and goods, all at the expense of the poor, hapless saver.

Interest rates were kept low, through public policy and through Regulation Q, so the borrower could get the money he wanted as cheaply as possible. This meant, of course, a lower return for the saver.

On top of this, tax policy encouraged borrowing instead of saving. For the borrower found his interest costs deductible, while the saver found that the earnings on his hard-earned funds were taxed.

Inflation made a further mockery of saving. In nominal terms, the saver earned his 5¼% or so (then subject to taxes) but in real terms, with inflation rising to a high of 18½%, the saver was being robbed of his purchasing power by a factor of as much as 13¼% a year (the 18½ minus the 5¼ earned on his passbook savings). And then he was subject to tax on his so-called interest income to boot.

The financial institutions (and some in government) have finally recognized this inequity, and we have seen interest rates paid on savings move up to such levels that even after taxes there is something left for the saver today.

This means in turn that the borrower has to pay far more for his funds than in the past, and many feel this is a violation of the "American way."

But the saver has determined that either he will get a going rate on his funds or he will provide no funds at all to the banks and thrift institutions. As the banks and thrifts have learned this, they have become far more willing to pay top dollar for savings and to earn these high-cost funds by charging borrowers top dollar as well.

In sum, the prestige customer used to be the borrower; now it is the saver!

But even recognizing that the borrower must pay the piper to reward the saver better, there is further selectivity that can be developed in determining which customers a bank wants.

As indicated earlier, most bankers now recognize that 20% of their customers have provided about 80% of the bank's profits. But the 20% are getting restless. So the bank must do its best to reward and solicit the 20%, even if it means discouraging banking business from the 80%.

What are the criteria for determining which accounts are in the desired 20% and which are in the 80% area? First and foremost in today's environment is size and amount of activity that requires personal attention.

The cost of maintaining an account has become so large with current labor and transaction costs that banks just can't afford to handle extremely small accounts, unless the customer is willing to cover the high cost of serving such deposits. This explains why so many banks are instituting service charges on accounts that fall below $300, $400, or an even larger minimum balance.

On top of this, banks are beginning to assess service charges for active use of smaller balances, charges that are more aggressive than in the past. Who would have thought that banks would service charge savings accounts with more than a certain minimum number of transactions per month? Yet this is happening. Who would have thought that banks would be looking into service charging those who have excessive entrance into their safe deposit vaults? Even this is being discussed.

Now banks are looking at service charging those who demand the services of a teller and are not willing to use automatic teller machines with their inherent cost-saving features for the bank. Not all banks are going as far as the Philadelphia bank which charges $30 for a check written on insufficient funds. But we are seeing banks assess higher and higher charges on active, small accounts to make the customers bear more of the cost of handling these unprofitable deposits and of servicing highly costly exception items.

What about borrowers? Even here banks are recognizing that they have to worry about bank profitability rather than borrower happiness. Thus charges are rising and, far more important, standards are rising as to whom the bank will accommodate. With the permissive personal bankruptcy laws today and far more customer defaults than ever before, banks have to be very selective in determining who will be given funds.

REACTION BY THE PUBLIC

What about public acceptance of these charges, fees, and requirements?

Almost universally, bankers report that people accept them and recognize that banks also have to make a profit.

The public accepts fees and higher balances. In some cases the key is to make the charges simple, so that the customer can still figure out his account. A simple charge of $5 a month for bank service can do more to generate income while keeping the customer happy than might a complex service charge that costs less but takes a computer to decipher.

What will this do to banking's image as servers of the community? Will it hurt the bank's political standing and lead to lawmakers favoring competitors, notably credit unions, that take on the small account?

One must conclude that this trend has taken place anyway, and that banks have been really hurt in their fight against credit unions and investment bankers for a "level playing field." How much more harm can be done?

Some bankers also worry that today's small account will be tomorrow's big one. If the bank turns the customer away, it will have no chance to serve him later.

This is a risk that banks are taking. But they also must make enough profits today to remain viable. And losing money now so the bank can serve these potentially profitable people later is just not a sensible approach in an environment of spread management and the difficulties in raising capital.

12-6 CROSS-SELLING BANKING SERVICES

The cross-selling of services is perhaps the most valuable marketing weapon available—and it can be used by any bank.

Once a customer comes into the bank for one service, there is a pretty good chance that he or she can be sold on other services that the bank offers. As most marketing officers report, this has a snowball effect. Once an individual is using the bank for several services, there is almost nothing that can get the customer to move his account elsewhere, other than a real rift with the bank or the physical movement of the individual from the community. Even with regard to the movement of the customer from one town to the next, the newer developments in electronic funds transfer are eliminating the inconvenience of living in one community and banking in another.

If bankers are to cross sell their services to the public, however, the first step that must be taken is to get the bank's own staff to know what the bank has to offer and to interest the employees in cross selling. All too often, individuals come into a bank that has been pushing a certain service in its advertisements, only to find that the tellers and other contact people know nothing of the ads, much less the service advertised. A customer may walk into a bank that has reversed policy and started to build up its mortgage portfolio. But when he talks to the platform officers, he finds they have not been informed of the switch. The result is that at the same time as the bank is spending its advertising dollars to woo new home loan customers, the platform officers of the bank are telling live prospects to go across the street to the savings and loan because the bank isn't interested in home loans.

There are some marketing people who feel that it is not the responsibility of all bank contact people to understand the bank's services, or what the customer can develop in the way of new accounts and relationships. They believe, for example, that a teller is a teller because of accuracy and intense purposefulness of handling the bank's money quickly and without error. To make the teller think in terms of talking the customer into using a new bank service at the same time as the teller is trying to keep the lines moving and avoid an over or short position at the end of the day is just too much. They feel that each individual should have his or her one function, and that to make everyone into marketing officers by cross selling the bank's services is not possible without giving up something else that should be accomplished.

Regardless, there is a great deal that a bank can do to make sure that the public does know what the bank has to offer and what is appropriate for the individual customer.

Some banks see that guards and telephone operators are among the first to understand and know about the bank's newer services. After all, they are the first individuals that outsiders contact and the first people who handle the queries of bank customers as to whether something can be done. If a guard sends the individual to wait on a long line in front of a platform officer, when he could have handled the situation himself, the customer is inconvenienced—and the bank has lost an opportunity to build its relationship with that customer. Similarly, a phone operator who must switch the customer from individual to individual to get a simple answer does little to build the bank's stature in that customer's mind.

The basic problem in any organization is always communications. And communications means not only an understanding of bank policy but also a full understanding of what the bank is and does.

To most people, their banker is the teller or the local branch manager. They know little or nothing of higher management at a distant office. Luckily, this problem does not exist in smaller banks, today. But as these independent banks grow, and as banks join into larger organizations, they face this communications problems. Cross selling involves knowing what the bank does. If banking really is to rely on this concept as a potential for growth and profitability, it must make sure the employees, from top to bottom, know their bank. Otherwise the public never will.

12-7 PRICING SERVICES FOR PROFITABILITY

Gap management, or the coordination and synchronization of assets and liabilities, has become extremely important to bank profitability.

In an environment of uncertain interest rates, banks are taking great risks in trying to make money by borrowing short and lending long or borrowing long and lending short.

Most banks and thrifts that have suffered losses over the last few years were locked in with fixed rate assets as interest rates rose, squeezing profits to zero and below.

The situation is brought home in a sign seen in a bank investment department:

GOOD NEWS AND BAD NEWS
First the Bad News:
We can't predict interest rates.
Now the Good News:
We finally realized it.

Banks are avoiding playing the yield curve and are trying to match assset maturities, to a far greater degree than ever before. This means, however, that bank profits will depend on the width of the gap between asset yields and liability costs.

Widening the gap, in turn, depends on three factors: efficiency in operations, selling non-credit services for fees, and realistic pricing of bank services.

EFFICIENCY OF OPERATIONS

Efficiency of operations needs little comment. The lower a bank can keep its non-interest expense, the better off it will be.

Many analysts view low non-interest expense as the finest test of managerial effectiveness. Cost control, limits on personnel expense, effective management of occupancy outlays and the other non-interest expenses are keys to the generation of profit.

SELLING NONCREDIT SERVICES

Selling noncredit services is an increasingly important aspect of bank profit generation.

Banks have talent available in many areas. And they are beginning to sell the use of this talent in cash management, investments, pension program development, and the like, for fees, instead of giving them away or offering them for deposit balances. Frequently, balances disappear or are used to back so many services that there is no profit left.

The day is not far off when bankers, like lawyers, will have pads at their desks to help keep track of the time devoted to customers, and will charge for the use of their time.

New services such as discount brokerage are another way in which banks are trying to sell their capabilities for a fee. If anything proves that the public wants to transact its investment business through a local bank, it is the way bank money funds have soared since after such services were legalized. Now banks are trying to capitalize on the opportunity to gather in the securities transaction business of individual customers through discount brokerage operations.

REALISTIC PRICING OF SERVICES

The real key to bank profitability—in an environment in which gap management imposes restrictions on the ability of banks to make profits through borrowing short and lending long—is in pricing services.

Banks that have experimented with more efficient pricing of services have been happy with the results. To recap previously presented material:

- More and more banks are raising minimum balances and closing accounts that do not meet these minimums. The outcome frequently is not the closing of an account but rather a building up of the balances.
- More and more banks are service-charging very active accounts; and customers are paying the charges, apparently recognizing that account activity costs the bank money.
- Banks are service-charging exception items far more heavily, with the cost of a returned check reaching as high as $30 in some cases. The public can understand that if it costs a bank so much to handle an exception item, an abuser of the bank's service must pay for it or be unwelcome as a customer.
- Banks are charging more for the use of a human teller than for an A.T.M., thereby encouraging the public to switch to the less costly form of service.
- Banks are charging more for credit cards and reducing the extent of the "free ride" to avoid interest charges between day of purchase and day of payment.
- Most important, banks are finding that when they raise general service charges, cancel special exemptions from charges, and otherwise make services pay their way, customers do not object. Few and far between are the bankers who report that a general advance of service charges resulted in the loss of profitable accounts.

Along with this, banks are learning two other facts:

- People are less unhappy with service charge increases than they are with a complicated charge policy. Customers would rather pay a high rate that is standard—fixed each month—than to have to deal with a complex formula that leads to different fees each month and messes up the checkbook.
- People want to feel that they are "first class" customers, that they are considered special; and they will pay for such consideration.

Efficient bankers, then, are turning inward to a far greater degree than before to look for talent to sell; they are charging for non-credit services, and pricing traditional services more aggressively. As they do so, bankers find that the rewards show up directly on the bottom line.

13 Building Bank Deposits

13-1 SOLICITING DEPOSITS

Without deposit growth, a bank actually loses ground. There must be some growth simply to keep pace with the competition. There must be substantial growth if the bank is to prosper and be successful in the financial marketplace. It is essential, then, for a bank to concentrate on increasing deposits—no matter what the condition of the economy or the proliferation of eager and resourceful competitors. A bank must be more resourceful, more competitive, and do what it can to build its deposit base.

A LITTLE INGENUITY

Bankers can obtain certificate of deposit or money market account funds if they pay enough for them. But the key to a high performance bank in this era of volatile interest rate movements is whether it can place a sufficient share of its money in interest-free demand deposits, NOW account funds, and relatively low-cost passbook savings.

This represents a shift from past bank thinking. There was a time and not long ago, when only demand deposits were considered to be cheap funds and any payment of interest for deposit growth was frowned upon.

Now passbook savings and no passbook 5½% minimum interest accounts are considered to be manna from heaven. Even NOW accounts, which many bankers once feared so strongly, have turned out to be one of the cheapest sources of funds. Interest on checking makes the depositor "sullen but not mutinous," and he apparently is willing to keep a great deal of money in the bank earning a minimal rate instead of moving it to a much higher costing certificate, as long as he has the convenience of writing checks on the balance.

But how can you obtain new core deposits in a high interest rate environment?

Some bankers have about given up. They look at historical data and conclude that each bank's market share remains about the same in its community no matter how hard it tries to be something different and more attrractive to the depositor. Others have decided that buying growth through new programs just is not worth it. The deposits they receive are small, and frequently cost more than they are worth. This helps explain why so many banks first turned to free checking and then gave it up when they saw the types of accounts that free checking brought in.

In spite of all this, some novel approaches are being tried in the fight for additional deposits:

- One bank determined who were the most affluent people in town who banked elsewhere and then made them offers of seats on the board. Getting someone on your board is the first large step to getting him to move his accounts over to your bank as well. Of course, this idea could get out of hand; after all, you don't want more directors than employees.
- Other banks have tried to pick up large balances by going to customers of competitors and explaining the advantages of cash management and money market investment. If a customer who has been sitting with a large balance in his bank is told by a different bank that there are ways of using these funds more profitably, he may make a move. The target here is the customer of the bank across the street who maintains a large idle balance. If a bank can explain to the customer how he can mobilize his funds more effectively and earn a good return on idle cash, the customer is likely to become upset with his own bank for not explaining this to him. While the new bank will not get too great a balance of hard core funds, since it will be helping the customer put his money to work in money market instruments, what it does get will be at the expense of the bank across the street.
- Some banks are developing new services in the hope of winning new balances from the competition. One bank has recently started a department to serve people with changed family circumstances. The department, staffed by a widow who had to learn the financial facts of life the hard way, helps other widows, divorced people, and other people with changed financial circumstances make the necessary financial adjustments. This is like a personal banker program taken one step further. Moreover, it wins the type of balances and people the bank wants to attract.

What about restoration or raising of service charges? Does it lead to an outflow of core deposits?

This fear that future profitable core deposits will be driven away by service charge increases today is one that inhibits many bankers from raising service fees. But in the current environment, the majority apparently feel that banks have to buy most of their funds anyway. And it is cheaper to buy the money needed by paying going interest rates than to buy it a little at a time by subsidizing the small depositor—whose reason for keeping his modest account with you is because he can get the service for far less than it costs you to provide it.

13-2 SOLICITING THE LARGE DEPOSIT

Generating deposits involves acceptance of the fact that demand deposit growth will be limited in the years ahead. And banks must fight for time and savings deposits.

Attracting the time deposits of the smaller saver will be difficult, too, because many other institutions and instruments are fighting for the same pool of money. Other banks' thrifts and nonbank financial institutions will provide even more intense competition for the savings of the public by offering rates as attractive as possible on deposits as small as can be practically handled.

A bank must also fight harder for the large-size deposits of companies and institutions. The savings available from the general public won't provide sufficient funds to meet all the demands likely to be placed on the bank for credit accommodations in the years ahead.

This gives banks two problems: (1) generating income strong enough so they can afford to pay top dollar for certificate of deposit funds; and (2) finding ways to attract this larger depositor into placing some of his liquid balances in the CDs instead of channeling virtually all funds except a small payroll account into money center institutions.

Both problems are solvable, however. Many community banks are successfully working on them today.

EARNING TOP DOLLAR

As indicated, if smaller banks are to compete for large-sized deposits, they must offer rates that match the return offered by larger institutions. This, in turn, means earning yields that also match those earned by major money center banks.

The local business firm must recognize that the rates charged for his credit accommodation have to be the same as in major cities; after all the local bank has to pay as much for the money it lends out as anyone else does. The days are past when compensating balances were not necessary or if they were required could be double-counted and triple counted as backing for account activity, bank service, and as balances for the loan too.

Some banks have gone the further logical step and determined that since such balances must be idle balances, why require them at all? Why not replace them with a fee structure that is fully compensatory, so the bank does not need to tie up capital, backing deposits the customer does not want to hold anyway?

COMPETITION FOR DEPOSITS

The bank that has determined that it must earn competitively so it can afford to pay competitive rates on certificates has thus surpassed one major hurdle to gaining the deposits needed. If it can afford going rates on CDs, obtaining negotiable CD funds may not be as difficult as initially believed.

Before going out and soliciting high-cost CD funds, the bank should see what it can do to obtain the money it needs in cheaper ways. If the bank still needs CD money to fund its operation, however, it may have to turn to local and more distant companies to solicit CD funds. This is not an easy route to take. The natural inclination of a corporate or municipal treasurer is to place his money in only large institutions. The advantage of using the bigger banks is twofold in the treasurer's mind:

- He or she feels that the larger bank's CD is far more liquid and salable in case the funds are needed before maturity; and there is a fear that a smaller bank that finds itself in trouble may be allowed to go under while the larger institution will be rescued because of the impact its failure would have on the region and on the entire banking industry.

This second fear has been somewhat reduced by the current $100,000 FDIC ceiling on accounts. Now a local corporation can place that much in a local bank with impunity. But if a bank wants more than $100,000 from a corporate or municipal treasurer, the greater strength imputed to large banks, whether real or imagined, becomes a barrier to CD solicitation.

APPROACHES TO TAKE

What can a bank do if it wants and needs CD deposits from corporations and other large fund holders and finds these roadblocks in its way even though it is willing and able to pay going rates for money? There are several possibilities:

- Banks that have major corporations in the region or whose local government units have sizable amounts to invest have a real opportunity to go to these treasurers and point out that if they do not place funds into local banks, then the local banks will not have the money available to make mortgage and consumer loans to these institutions' own employees. The simple pitch of self-interest can do wonders to obtain large CD balances.

- If a chain store has a branch in town, a bank can go to the distant headquarters to explain that without funds deposited in the local banks, the banks in turn cannot finance the people who work for and patronize the company's stores. This also helps do the job of getting CDs placed.
- Some banks have found that many local corporate customers still do not practice active cash management. Banks can explain to them the benefits of such policies. This is under the theory that they will find out sooner or later; and if the bank has been the one to educate them they will remain more loyal than if the information is first learned from a distant competitor.
- A number of bankers have found that a topnotch way to get CD deposits from both local and more distant companies is to simply ask for it. What these bankers report is that frequently corporate treasurers do not even realize that a particular bank wants their CD funds and will pay competitive rates to get them. And the treasurer is happy to oblige when asked.

13-3 GETTING GOVERNMENT DEPOSITS

In this banking jungle where customer loyalty has been eroding steadily, one area where the depositor has remained extremely loyal to the local bank has been in the solicitation and maintaining of state and local government deposits.

Corporate treasurers appear willing to kill their grandmothers for an extra basis point of yield on their liquid funds. Individuals have become more and more willing to move their funds to another bank offering a higher money market certificate yield. Even the old reliable treasury tax and loan account funds now must pay interest. The bank unwilling to pay going rates for such funds loses its treasury balances in a day. But state and local deposits have remained loyal. Bankers trying to win public balances away from other banks have generally had little success in this solicitation.

YIELD CONSCIOUSNESS

It must be noted these public deposits are not always a bargain. Gone are the days when municipal treasurers sat with large demand balances in local banks, waiting until the funds were needed for some pre-planned expenditure. Money is too valuable to take this approach.

Consequently public deposits do not come cheaply these days. Usually, the municipal treasurer wants the highest yield available, and asks the various local banks to bid on the funds, with the veiled threat that if the local banks do not offer as attractive a yield as Treasury bills, then the funds will be moved into the bill market.

Local and state treasurers are also learning the tricks of the corporate treasurer on cash management and float usage. In the City of New York, for example, municipal officials determined that it takes firemen about two days longer to cash their payroll checks than it takes policemen. Thus, they place the funds in the bank to cover firemen's checks two days later than they place them in the bank to cover policemen's checks.

SOCIAL GOALS

This is not the entire story. While banks frequently find that municipal and state treasurers are as acute in utilizing spare liquid funds as corporate treasurers are, in many cases the municipal officials go further. They demand not only top yield from the local banks, they also want the banks to use the funds in a manner that aids the community or the state.

Even though the officials like to remain loyal and will give preference to local banks over placing funds in the impersonal money market, they want to make sure the banks are using the funds to help the community or the state. A number of states have surveyed the role the various depository banks are playing in the mortgage market, in rebuilding cities, in education loans, and in other areas felt to be socially desirable. The implied threat is that if the local banks are not using public deposits to serve the community, then there is no reason for the public body to keep these funds at home, and they will be transferred elsewhere.

PLEDGED SECURITIES

As if this were not enough, banks usually find that their public deposits must be backed by pledged securities. This by itself bothers many institutions. They feel the pledge security requirement separates some depositors from others. "Why," these bankers ask, "must we take some of our assets and pledge them as collateral for public deposits while the rest of our deposits do not get this extra security?" In the case of default, the pledging of some assets to back public deposits means there is less backing available for the rest of the bank's deposit structure.

There is also the cost factor. Sure, the pledges consist of Treasury securities or of securities of that state, and banks generally hold such securities anyway. But when securities are pledged to back public deposits, they can not also serve as a liquid reserve to back other deposits.

As for the local securities, they sometimes bring another cost factor into consideration. When a state requires that banks buy bonds of that state to hold as pledges behind state and local deposits, it creates a much stronger market for the state's securities. This means they can be sold at lower yields than otherwise would be necessary based on their quality and the volume outstanding.

This is just what the state is trying to accomplish by specifying the use of securities of that state as pledged security requirements, as it does cut the cost of state finance. The losers are the state's banks who otherwise would be able to get a better yield on their investment funds.

THE OTHER SIDE OF THE COIN

Thus, some bankers have looked at the total cost of soliciting public deposits and decided they are not worth the trouble. This negative analysis is by no means typical of all solicitation of public deposits. In many instances, public deposits have major advantages:

Public bodies do try to keep the funds locally, so there is less chance of their being moved to another institution—if the local bank is willing to pay competitive rates or rates reasonably close to what distant banks offer on time deposits;

There is still some profit potential in holding public depository demand balances. Not all accounts have been worked down to zero balances; and

Most banks are local institutions, and they want to play a role in the local economy. They bid on local bonds, aid local causes, and they seek to serve the financial needs of the local public institutions.

This is all part of the service that keeps the community bank strong and keeps other customers loyal to the local institution. Beneath it all is one simple fact: a deposit is a deposit. If banks are to obtain money to lend and invest, they must obtain deposits. State and local deposits, albeit not as profitable as some other deposits, are still a basic source of bank funds that cannot be ignored.

STRATEGIES

Banks now offering different things to public bodies, in an effort to either keep the account loyal or to win it away from other banks. For example,

> Bankers are becoming more and more willing to buy the unrated bonds of municipalities if there is a chance of getting the public body's deposit along with it. This is true of both local banks trying to win the account from the bank across the street and of more distant banks trying to break into the community.
>
> Banks are offering public bodies new services, including unemployment compensation accounting, municipal tax billing, payroll preparation, direct deposit of payroll, and bond servicing facilities. These are attractive enticements for the movement of an account.
>
> Banks are establishing offices in more distant communities under the more relaxed branching and holding company legislation being enacted in many states. Such banks have started to look at the deposits as a potential source of the kind of large-sized balances that are usually necessary to make any new office profitable without a lag of several years.

State and local government units still look to local banks as their basic depositories. And the local loyalty of citizens makes it difficult for an outside bank to obtain public balances from a state or community, no matter the enticement.

Keeping money local is a highly sensitive political issue. Even banks that have established branches in other communities find that as long as the home office is located elsewhere, the new bank is felt to be a carpetbagger from the viewpoint of gaining public deposits; it usually has little success in competing against the bank whose principal office is right in town.

Although most bankers look upon public deposits as the last bastion of loyalty in a highly competitive banking environment, prudent bankers are taking nothing for granted. They are declining public deposits when their studies show that maintaining them is unprofitable to the bank. But when they feel the balances do add a dollar value to the bottom line, they are working hard to keep state and municipal financial officials happy. And while they count on loyalty to give them that little extra edge in maintaining local public deposits, they are also not above talking to officials in other towns to see what the bank can do to woo some of their balances away.

Good bankers knows that no bank can take any account for granted—no matter where it is located or how long it has been with the bank.

13-4 THE POTENTIAL OF RETIREMENT ACCOUNTS

A great many of the developments in both the business environment and on the financial scene are truly propitious for bank generation of new retirement accounts. A glance at what banking is trying to do today to stay competitive shows that growth of these retirement programs is in the best interest of a bank's bottom line.

Some of these economic developments that make Individual Retirement Accounts (IRAs), Keogh Plan Accounts, and 401 K salary withholding programs so much more attractive to the public than in the past include social security problems, less reliance on government, and lower inflation.

SOCIAL SECURITY PROBLEMS

With the adverse publicity that the Social Security system is getting, many people are more interested in generating their own pension programs than in the past. There are two reasons for this. The first is that many fear that Social Security will go under and they are thinking more of protecting themselves by establishing and building private pension programs.

Second, others recognize that while Social Security will not go under, benefits may well be pared as time passes. They are looking to private pension programs as a more important supplement to the benefits that may be obtained from the Social Security program.

As background, there are many economists who have worked on the question of what public pension programs do to the willingness of the public to save privately for old age. One might think that a rise in government pension programs would reduce the amount that people save privately, because they feel they are covered by the government.

However, studies have proven just the opposite. If the public feels that it has little or no protection for the future through government programs, then the futility that sets in makes people feel they will have to work all their lives anyway, so why save if retirement is not possible. Still, if there is some governmental protection, then these people have hopes of a decent retirement program, and they supplement it privately to make it better.

This means that the talk of reducing or taxing Social Security benefits makes Keoghs, IRAs, and 401 Ks more attractive as replacement vehicles.

LESS RELIANCE ON GOVERNMENT

There has been a decided switch in the feeling of Americans away from a certainty that the government will always protect them over to a recognition that it will not and that they will have to protect themselves.

The firing of the air traffic controllers by President Reagan was in the view of many a watershed decision. It made people recognize that they are not as important as they would like to think they are.

On top of this, the willingness of the government to allow companies like Braniff Airlines to go under without bailing them out gave further proof that government protection would not always be available—even in an emergency. This is a decided switch from the viewpoint of the past. It also makes the establishment and building of private pension holdings even more important to Americans than was formerly the case.

LOWER INFLATION

The decline in inflation and the fact that borrowers must now pay a positive rate on interest for money borrowed is another force aiding the buildup of private pension plans. Investors are switching from the tangible assets that did so well in inflation to the financial assets that shine in a period of high real interest rates (after inflation), and in an era of less inflation such as the present. Consequently, private pension programs look far better today than placing money in condominiums, diamonds, land, and other tangibles.

Thus all systems should be "go" for private pension plans in today's economic environment.

BANKS VERSUS OTHERS

But what about the competition between bank and nonbank programs? Again, it appears that banks have some decided advantages.

In an environment of high risk and well-publicized failures of financial and nonfinancial institutions, there has been a tendency to turn to the more stable institutions as respositories of funds. This aids banks in their fight against brokerage firms and other outlets allowed for private pension fund money under Keogh, IRA, and 401 K.

On top of this, the fact that bank competition generally charges service fees and commissions helps banks get the funds.

Furthermore, capital gain tax benefits do not mean anything to private pension plans, because they are not being taxed at the present time. So the steady return and assured principal of a bank program means more relative to, say, placing funds in a mutual fund than would be the case were taxes to be levied, enhancing the value of capital appreciation, subject as it is to lower taxes than those assessed on normal income.

The banks do, however, have a tax advantage in their private pension programs; for the rulings indicate that interest on the money borrowed to buy an IRA is decuctible, while the income earned is not taxable. This gives the saver a decided arbitrage possibility, if his bank is aggressive in pushing this feature.

While all the above features should mean that banks will continue to garner the lion's share of private pension money under these three plans, the plans have an advantage for the bank too in that most savers want fixed rate programs rather than those with variable rates. This means that banks can generate fixed cost money to fund the loans and investments that they want to make at fixed rates without subjecting themselves to an interest rate gap problem that could be expensive if interest rates rise sharply again.

Bankers have a very valuable marketing weapon in their fight for profitability in the new and expanded private pension programs. Those who have been in these programs for years recognize how rapidly small amounts deposited each year can add up into large, attractive accounts.

14 Correspondent Banking

14-1 HOW CORRESPONDENT BANKING IS CHANGING

Correspondent banking—the voluntary alliance of a bank with one or more other banks that offer either complimentary services or services in other geographical areas—has been a fact of banking life in the United States for several generations. It has helped provide a breadth of services that was needed under the independent unit banking system with its restrictions against interstate banking. But all that is changing.

Banks with long-time ties to other banks are reevaluating these connections in an effort to determine what is best for them. Much of the tradition that has surrounded correspondent banking is going by the boards as banks adjust to today's competitive environment.

TRADITION VERSUS PRACTICALITY

Because the social side of correspondent banking meant at least as much as the business side, a bank that kept balances with another institution seldom thought of changing this relationship. After all, one basic purpose of the connection was to have friends around the nation whom a banker visited when traveling to major cities and who visited him in return. The net result was a night out in both locations. The correspondent officer knew how to pay for tickets to sporting events and cultural activities and how to pick up a dinner check.

On those rare occasions when these ties were broken by a new officer who felt they were not worth the price, pressure was quickly put on management and the board to reestablish them. (One Pittsburgh banker remembers going to Boston to close an account. He closed it, but by the time he had returned to Pittsburgh by train, the Boston bank's representative had flown in and gone over his head to have the account reopened.)

There was good reason for the correspondents to expect that their parties would bring in balances. Most smaller banks kept accounts at a great many correspondents in many cities. They feared that if they did not have balances with most large banks, they would be left out when business was being referred to their communities by these large banks, they could not get the specialized advice these large institutions offered, and they would not be invited to the parties.

Today, the traveling representative of the major bank is no longer a person whose social graces take precedence over his banking experience. The correspondent must know credits, automation and operations, marketing, politics, and other banking and nonbanking skills. Moreover, the traveling banker is sometimes a highly trained woman who accepts the loneliness and awkwardness of continuous travel as part of the price of moving up in the bank hierarchy.

Both men and women in banking find that correspondent banking is a solid route to the top because the correspondent officer must know so much and must be able to make important decisions on the spur of the moment.

More significantly, correspondent banking is changing because the respondent banks find that the old ties are no longer strong enough to offset the competitive changes that have come into banking. Community banks often find that they are fighting head to head against their correspondent for the same business—a situation that is sure to split long established relationships. Moreover, changing delivery systems and cost structures are altering correspondent relationships as never before.

As a result, tradition no longer plays a major role in correspondent banking among route bankers. Those who rely on established relationships merely because they always have done so are discovering that this can be an expensive and unfortunate way to operate.

THE NEW RIVALRY

Some correspondents have always tried to serve their respondent banks while also competing with them for the same business. Consider the case of a banker who worked for a major New York bank. The banker met an acquaintance at the Holiday Inn in Kalamazoo, Michigan. "What are you doing here?" the friend asked.

"Mondays, Wednesdays, and Fridays, I call on the correspondents to get their balances. Tuesdays, Thursdays, and Saturdays, I call on the business firms to steal the accounts," the banker replied.

Correspondent bankers have always known this to be the case. What has made matters worse today is that many large correspondent banks are trying to expand their territories, and thus are competing against respondents far more than ever before.

In addition, the large-sized customer is relying more on commercial paper for borrowings and money market deposits surplus funds. At the same time, large money center banks that provide correspondent services are moving into the mid-market—the area that has up to now been largely served by their correspondents—for business. The large correspondents recognize this problem, and most are leaning over backwards to avoid rifts with their respondent banks.

In some cases, the correspondent department is not allowed to have contact with other credit departments of the bank so that a true hands off attitude exists. Others give the correspondent the business whenever there is a conflict between the two institutions. However, many community bankers report that just the opposite is true.

In some instances the large money center bank has gone further and told smaller banks, including those with as much $100 million in deposits, that their accounts are no longer worth serving and that the relationship will be severed. To a bank that has relied on the correspondent for the handling of all its check processing activity, this can be devastating. It must rapidly revise procedures and find another servicer compatible with its system.

Many banks are not taking all of this lying down. Some are looking to other nonbank processers that do not compete with them to handle the kinds of things correspondents used to handle. There are a number of large banks that have always operated with a noncompetitive status as a major marketing weapon: These banks are finding their correspondent business on the increase. Finally, now that mandatory reserves are a fact of banking life, an increasing number of banks are looking to the Federal Reserve as a new provider of correspondent services.

PRICING

The whole issue of pricing, coupled with the changing cost of providing bank services, is also playing a major role in the reevaluation of correspondent services.

The ever-increasing efficiency of computer technology is making the provision of data processing services increasingly competitive. More service bureaus and facilities managers are beginning to compete for the bank business than ever before. Also, the reduction in the cost of computing is causing many banks to reevaluate the desirability of doing the job themselves.

Since banks are reevaluating and paring down their reserves, correspondents are charging more for the services they formerly provided free because of the large balances maintained. With the correspondents charging for services that used to be free, the respondents are reevaluating whether they (1) want the services provided by the correspondent, (2) might do better buying them elsewhere, or (3) should provide them for themselves.

On top of this, many banks are reexamining how much they need to leave in correspondent banks. Banks are refining their own cash management to more effectively use their idle cash.

14-2 FINE-TUNING CORRESPONDENT RELATIONSHIPS

With all the changes taking place and all the consolidations going on, it would seem that correspondent banking should be on the decline. In some respects, this is true. There are fewer correspondent relationships, and a smaller percentage of total bank resources are dedicated to correspondent banking. But the concept is not about to die. In many ways, because correspondent banking is becoming far more selective, the relationships today are stronger and more beneficial to all participating parties.

EMPHASIZING PROFITS

At Small Banks

Most smaller banks readily admit that they had no profitability analysis programs to determine whether the correspondent balances they were maintaining were worthwhile and justified the cost. No wonder the large banks were so anxious to woo them; some small banks could leave idle correspondent balances that contributed significantly to the correspondent bank's profits.

On the other side, few large correspondents did honest cost studies either. They assumed the profitability of the respondents' balances and seldom checked to see if these balances were really worth it. Thus, some sharp smaller banks were able to get far more from the larger banks in services, aid, and social benefits than their balances justified. To the better run smaller banks, correspondent banking was a fool's paradise, in which they could get far more than they paid for. However, on balance, most respondent banks did not know what their balances were worth and the large banks found correspondent banking a truly profitable business.

Now, because of the growth in check clearing through the Federal Resesrve (the Fed) and automated clearing houses, bank can be more selective as to where they keep balances. With high interest rates, respondent banks are finding it more valuable than ever before to weed out unprofitable correspondent accounts and only keep those that truly are worthwhile.

When Federal funds trade at 4%, a respondent bank can be far more lax with regard to leaving balances around in various banks than it can be when funds rates are in the 12% range and every $100,000 pulled from correspondent balances and placed into the funds market can earn $35 overnight.

At Large Banks

As for the larger banks, they too have reason to be more selective with regard to the correspondent balances they accept.

Bank shares are frequently selling at such low prices that it becomes almost confiscatory to sell more equity, and debt capital sales are limited by market resistance, high interest rates, and regulatory pressure. Hence, larger banks recognized that deposit growth has to be profitable growth (i.e., earning the bank a decent spread over cost, or the growth is not worth it. What good does it do to expand deposits at the expense of high operational costs only to find that the bank now needs more expensive capital to back this deposit growth that was of marginal profitability in the first place?

Consequently, larger banks are becoming more selective in their willingness to accept correspondent balances, just as they are becoming more selective in viewing all deposit growth. The result is that the smaller banks who used to utilize correspondent services without leaving balances high enough to justify the relationship are being told to pay fees, raise the balances, or take their business elsewhere. This is quite a change from the old approach where anyone who brought in a dollar of correspondent balances from any bank was a hero, no matter how costly the services were that the respondent demanded once it had opened the account.

For Both Large and Small

The key, then, is profitability analysis on both sides of the correspondent relationship. The smaller banks want to make sure they are getting their money's worth for balances. The larger banks are costing out services, including advice and consultations, to make sure that the balances are sufficient to compensate for the overlines, clearing, and services provided.

CONCENTRATION COUNTS

Formerly, a respondent bank needed a correspondent in each major city through which it sent its checks. This is no longer so vital. Now balances are left in the banks that offer the best service, the most generous and loyal overline relationships, and the best advice, no matter where they may be.

On top of this, the respondents realize that they need fewer accounts. By concentrating the balances they do leave at correspondent banks into fewer banks, they can demand more service from the banks they continue to rely upon. The concentration of balances makes each account kept in correspondents that much more worthwhile to the larger banks.

Respondents thus have fewer major correspondents than in the past. But the banks at which they do keep major accounts are earning these funds by service, not by accident of geographical location. As the result, correspondents are competing against each other for the balances of potential and actual respondents that appear likely to be profitable, regardless of where these banks happen to be located. A bank in the midwest may have its lead correspondent in New York, Chicago, another large midwestern city or even in the southeast or west. The quality and price of service has become the main determinant.

REGIONAL CORRESPONDENTS

Another aspect of correspondent banking today is the growing efforts of regional banks in offering services to smaller banks. And why not?. The well-managed regional bank can do just about everything a money center bank can do. The fact is that they are moving in while some of the major banks are turning away correspondent customers.

Not all the money center banks are moving away from correspondent services, of course. A number are responding by trying to regionalize their operations. The correspondent bankers they send out are often from the region they are serving. They are headquartered in major regional cities such as Atlanta or St. Louis rather than New York. And these traveling bankers try to offset the New York image by claiming that the "Backstabbers who want to go nationwide" are in other departments and that "we are offering correspondent services like always."

Regional correspondent relationships are covered in more depth in the next chapter.

THE FUTURE OF CORRESPONDENT BANKING

Those who feel correspondent banking is a dying art forget what is perhaps the most important factor assuring its survival: small banks need the services of the larger banks today more than ever.

When banking was a fairly simple profession, correspondent services were not vital, except for check clearing. But now, with electronic funds transfer, more complicated lending and investing patterns, and far greater demand for overlines and participations, bankers need their correspondents more than ever before.

It is possible that correspondent banking will serve as the alternative to more concentration of banks into branch and holding company systems. It enables the smaller bank to offer more complex financial services without having to join a larger branch or holding company network as prerequisite.

Correspondent banking may well serve as the lifeline for independent banks that want to remain independent in the maze of increasingly complex banking services and the ever greater geographical expansion of larger financial institutions.

14-3 CORRESPONDENT BANKING GOES REGIONAL

Pervasive among bankers in every area of the country is the belief that interstate banking is on the horizon, with New York banks in particular suspected of ambitions for territorial expansion.

Maybe this fear of New Yorkers is the reason and maybe not, but one major change in the convention circuit this year has been an apparent downgrading of the role of New York correspondents and an upgrading of the regional correspondents instead.

The key insight to be gained from the increase in the role of regional correspondents is that they can do everything a New York bank can do. Regional correspondents regret that it often costs them 25 basis points more to borrow at money centers than major banks must pay, so they must pass this charge on to respondent banks. Otherwise, they feel they can do everything for a respondent that anyone else can—and the community banks evidently agree that this is so. More and more of them say they have drawn down their New York balances and rely more on local correspondents.

The fear that the Fed will become a major participant in correspondent banking is not widespread among community banks. Many correspondents expect the Fed will underprice to get business when explicit pricing of correspondent services begins. Even so, they believe the Fed will get the "trash items" and private correspondents banks will still get the lion's share of respondent business.

"Who wants to do business with the government when you can deal with people," is the way one observer put it, reflecting the widely held view that the

Fed works in rigid ways. The feeling is that this rigidity will deter bankers from switching from their traditional correspondents over to the Fed.

As for New York banks, it is widely believed that Citibank is poised to become the first truly nationwide bank. Wherever it has credit shops, for example, they are on corners of shopping centers or at stand-alone locations, so drive-in windows can be attached if the operation is expanded to full-service banking.

As for Chase, there are some who say it is trying to court larger banks which it believes would participate in a national holding company network, just as correspondents years back used correspondent relations to develop alliances with banks that later joined statewide operations.

By knowing bankers through correspondent relationships, it is argued, you know the people, the loan policies, and the management, and you will find no skeletons in the closet if the banks eventually are linked in some way.

Some community banks have reacted to the prospect of nationwide banking by joining in cooperatively owned banks. They believe thay can eventually provide themselves with enough services to eliminate the need for any large bank relationships anywhere.

The New York banks are not sitting back. They are responding by trying to regionalize their operations. The correspondent bankers they send out are often from the region they are serving, with their headquarters located in a major regional city like Atlanta or Miami rather than New York.

But with interstate banking on so many people's minds, this shift from relying on New York banks to relying more on local banks in places like Lincoln and Omaha probably will continue in every state—at least unless or until the community banks come to the conclusion that they can compete in a interstate banking environment.

For now, the emotion connected with anticipation is far stronger than the actuality, and the feeling of tension between majors and community bankers remains strong. Consequently, the feeling pervades that sticking close to home for correspondent relationships makes good sense.

15 The Competitive Environment

15-1 DON'T LET THE COMPETITION RUN THE BANK

Far too often American banks determine their policy decisions on the basis of what the bank across the street is doing rather than based on what the bank itself should be accomplishing.

It takes a great deal of self confidence to merely stand back and watch the bank on the next corner start offering a service the public obviously likes. If the bank down the block offers a service at a certain price, and to match it will eat heavily into profits, then the real question is whether we do the same because they have done it or whether we just decide to let the business go.

FIRST STEP

Before a bank can decide how to react to competition that seems unrealistically underpriced, management must first make sure it is not kidding itself as to how cheap the other bank's service really is. It may well be that instead of finding that the other bank is pricing its service below realistic cost levels, our bank is just too expensive in its own methods of operation.

A bank, for example, may feel its costs are under control because it has maintained a fairly steady number of employees per $1 million of deposits. Yet if it examines what has happened to its deposits, it may find it is switching from active demand and savings deposits to relatively stable time certificates of deposit. Since these certificates can be handled with a small staff, the higher proportion of savings certificates to total deposits should allow a reduction in number of employees per $1 million. Thus, if the bank is staying steady in this ratio, the institution is becoming relatively more inefficient. The conclusion may well be that the reason the other bank can offer rates and services that our bank cannot without subjecting ourselves to loss is because they are more efficient as producers of bank services.

It certainly is worthwhile using the new competition from the bank across the street as an opportunity to reexamine our own operation to see if the rest of the industry is passing us by in efficiency.

ALLOCATING COSTS

But what if we find that other banks are not more efficient and the reason they offer lower cost service honestly appears to be a willingness on their part to offer these services under true cost levels? Must we match the competition now? Again the answer first turns to an inward examination. Once the bank has done some soul-searching to determine if it is efficient in cost control, then it must decided how it wants to allocate costs over the specific business it is trying to get or that the competition wants to take away.

The whole concept of pooled cost of funds come up at this point. After all, a bank must determine how much its money actually costs it before it can decide if meeting the competition is worthwhile.

As a bank tries to determine what it costs to obtain the funds it is lending out and investing, the choice made as to how to account for funds determines how much it must charge for its services. And what happens is that frequently wishful thinking determines our decisions.

If a bank wants to increase its loans and it needs new funds, it may well find that the only way to attract them is to offer higher rate certificates of deposit. Should the bank sell these certificates and then evaluate the new loans based on what the new money costs? Or should it assess against the new loans the average cost of funds in the bank—including some of the money obtained in cheaper demand deposits, some medium priced savings funds, and some high cost savings certificates?

Frequently, a bank finds that the competition can offer cheaper services and cheaper loans because it is figuring on an average cost of funds and is in effect subsidizing the new loans with low cost funds already in the bank.

The acute banker, however, may decide that this is a poor approach. The demand deposit funds are already in the bank anyway. To fund the new loans, the bank has had to attract marginal funds which are more expensive.

If it did not want the new loans, it would not need the new, higher cost money. Thus, the acute bank uses the marginal cost approach and assumes that the new loans must earn enough to cover the cost of the new, high cost deposits that must be solicited. If they do not, then why bother placing them on the books just to meet the competition from the bank across the street that may be using a pooled cost of funds approach?

Telling It As It Is

Thus, many banks have come to a conclusion of serious import: They have honestly examined their costs. They have figured what money actually costs them. And they have decided the bank across the street is offering a service they cannot match without causing their own profitability to suffer.

What should the bank do next?

Here, the possibilities are frequently more optimistic than one would expect. Many bankers report that by talking to customers honestly, they can get them to understand what the real facts are. And these bankers report that people are often more understanding and less anxious to push for the last penny than is feared.

Corporate treasurers, for example, have a reputation of being willing "to kill their grandmothers" for 1/100 of 1% lower cost or higher yield. Yet treasurers become pretty reasonable when a bank knows what it is doing and actually can present realistic cost figures, explaining why the bank cannot meet the lower costs some other institution may be offering.

First, however, the bank must meet the prerequisite of knowing its own costs. If it comes to a treasurer to state that the account is being offered at as low a price as possible, and that the bank across the street must be losing money with the rates it is advertising, it better be able to prove it. It cannot simply rely on hunches. Even if it brings in general figures, like the Federal Reserve's functional cost analysis data, the acute corporate or municipal treasurer has already seen the data and will not accept it as applying to this particular bank.

What bankers usually report is this: if you know your costs and can explain your basis for pricing to the treasurer, he will be sympathetic. He does not want his account switched to a bank that is losing money on the service.

The corporate treasurer knows that if another bank has won the business by undercutting its own cost structure, that bank will either skimp on service or will soon come for a reevaluation of the price. And the treasurer wants to face neither alternative. Thus, he is frequently willing to stay where he is, if the bank truly can explain why the offer made by the competition is unrealistic.

Individual depositors react similarly. Frequently, a bank will be the only one in town that does not offer free checking when all the others do. Yet its officers and platform people can convince the public not to go elsewhere. This involves making them realize that a bank does have costs, that the service fees are reasonable, and that the other banks giving the service away cannot possibly profit thereby.

The result often is that people decide to stay with the "quality bank" even though it involves a higher cost of doing business.

Sometimes bankers report that it is not the price that makes the difference but rather the way the service is offered. For example, in one community the hold-out bank that retained service charges while the others gave them up found it was not so much the cost of the account that bothered people as it was reconciling the checkbook when a service charge was added on each check moving through the bank. A simpler service charge form that avoids the uncertainty can clear up much of the objection to retention of the service charge in the cost structure.

Ultimate Choice

A bank can reevaluate its costs and prices. It can talk to customers, and it can try to make them understand why the competition is "giving away the bank." But, if all this fails to resolve the problem, the bank has two choices: (1) It can go along with the other bank's pricing schedule and let the guy across the street run the bank. (2) It can stand up to the customers who come in and demand the same price as the other bank charges and who warn that if they do not get what the other bank offers they will move their account.

To take the latter course, it must respond to the threat of the customer's moving the account: "Can you find the other bank yourself. Or would you like one of our young trainees to accompany you and make sure you get inside their door?"

In many instances, this is the most profitable approach the bank can take. Any alternative involves loss of earnings, the using up of scarce capital to back deposits that are unprofitable, and running the bank with a goal of large footings rather than profitable operations.

After the Account Leaves

What generally happens when people move accounts to take advantage of the better offer across the street?

Sometimes it becomes a real loss. The loss leader deposit, over time, becomes a profitable account. Here the customer who moved when our bank did not feel his account was profitable enough to keep later on does build balances and fees and justifies the other bank's having given away the service for awhile.

In other cases, the bank that maintained its standards comes out smelling like a rose.

There have also been cases in which people went to the other bank and came back in a few months with hat in hand to reopen their original account relationship. They found that while the price elsewhere was cheaper, so was the service, or a convenience disadvantage more than offset the price advantage. In these instances the original bank was justified in maintaining its standards.

Finally, there are other banks, and especially thrifts, that have offered unusually low prices to get into a new business only to revert to standard prices after they had been in it awhile.

Competition and Profitability

What conclusions can be drawn? The bank that sees the competition "giving away the bank" has a difficult but not impossible job in meeting the challenge. If anything is clear, the worst alternative is just to meet the price of the competition simply because they have established this price level.

In many instances a bank is far better off letting the customers go across the street than in providing a service at a loss and in the bargain using up bank capital that could better be utilized in backing more profitable activity.

Certainly a bank may fear that by not competing today it may be sacrificing profits in later years. Today's unprofitable business given up might be tomorrow's profitable business, if retained. If an account is not profitable by all reasonable methods of reckoning, and it looks as if it will not be profitable in the reasonable future, then there are far worse alternatives than letting the business go elsewhere.

The most important factor is knowing the bank's own cost structure and internal operations and having the confidence in these factors to let business go if the bank truly feels it is unprofitable. To do anything else is to engage in one of the worst sins a bank's management can sanction—letting the guy across the street determine pricing and so run the bank.

15-2 MOTIVATION AND BUSINESS DEVELOPMENT VIA PROFIT CENTERS

One of the toughest problems a top bank executive faces is motivating his people.

Too often, the CEO and his immediate managers feel they are working as hard as possible motivating the bank and making it go; while beneath them is a group of employees who are dragging their feet, doing just enough to earn the weekly pay check and no more.

Yet in other banks there is a feeling that the whole staff is part of a team that is doing its job and working to make the institution prosper.

What is it that makes one bank function as a team while another is a group of people that has never welded itself into a unit?

RECOGNITION

Bankers who have had success in winning the employees over to an attitude of giving the bank their all frequently report that the number one prerequisite for gaining employee support is recognition of those who do their jobs well.

Employees often feel that, to top management, they are merely bodies floating around the institution. They believe that whether they do their jobs well or poorly means little or nothing to top management and therefore little or nothing to themselves either.

Bankers who have molded their staffs into well functioning organizations report they spend a great deal of their time in getting to know staff people by name, getting to know what they are doing, and especially in learning when they have done a good job, so that recognition can be provided. In some banks, top managers have a stack of cards with pictures of each employee on them. Spare time is spent trying to connect pictures with names, so that the CEO can say good morning to an individual by name instead of giving the usual grunt of recognition that frequently is the only contact between a top officer and an employee.

In smaller banks, this is not necessary. Everyone knows everyone else. But even so, there are banks where top management will conduct regular ceremonies at which outstanding performance is recognized with a gift of cash or some other item, and more important, at which the outstanding people are recognized in front of their peers.

This involves not only rewarding the people who have brought in the top amount of new business, but also rewarding those whose jobs do not normally lead to tangible signs of outstanding performance. For example, a teller who has done his work without trouble and with considerable customer satisfaction for a period of time will not be likely to have anything on his record out of the ordinary. It is up to management, however, to find out whose day-to-day functioning is frictionless and super satisfactory so that recognition can be given. Nothing motivates other people more than to see a good individual rewarded for quiet, faithful service that usually would go without such notice.

However, this type of recognition ceremony is not enough. Even the annual review by the immediate superior is a difficult means of motivationg workers, for usually it is a routine process that does not differentiate one employee from others also doing competent work.

This helps explain why a growing number of banks have divided themselves into profit centers. By making each section of the bank responsible for its own share of bank profits, it is easier to see which groups, and then which people in those groups, are doing the best work and thus deserve the greatest rewards.

THE PROFIT CENTER

Many banks have some kind of profit center approach. The various line departments are assigned a cost of funds and given a value for the business they bring in.

Then the bank can determine how profitable each line department is. On top of this, if the bank really has developed its profit center plan, the managers of the superior line function units are given a pool of bonus funds to distribute to their employees as they feel justified—then each employee in the unit is personally rewarded based on his or her contribution.

It is more difficult to develop a profit center approach for staff and support positions, as they do not bring in dollar revenue to the bank. But even here, some banks try to break down the costs of their operations and set goals, the achievement of which will lead to recognition and extra money.

Profit centers are a means of dividing the bank into smaller units, so that each individual feels that he or she is working for that unit and not just for the whole organization. In this way, the employee can see goals that are far more tangible than would be the case if the only measurement of performance were overall bank profits. Hopefully, an attitude is generated that the fate of the unit is directly dependent upon each employee's own work.

At the same time, the profit center has led to serious problems in some banks. These problems result from the very nature of the profit center concept—for it makes the goal of the individual the achievement of maximum returns for his profit center rather than for the bank as a whole. And frequently achieving maximum return for the profit center is accomplished at the expense of the well-being of the overall institution.

This is the major pitfall in the profit center approach.

It is logical to expect that if an employee is judged on how well his or her profit center operates, then this is all the employee will consider. Yet, if we are to make goals that are meaningful, the bank must be broken down into smaller units for each employee in establishing these goals.

Solving this paradox is the job of top management as it establishes its goals. If it sets goals for the profit center that do not also bring top profit for the whole bank, then it has no one but itself to blame if the employees work only for their own center and do not care about the overall bank.

Guides to Profit Center Goals

What are some of the guidelines that management must consider in setting up profit center goals? Bankers who have had success with the profit center approach include these criteria:

Make the Goal Realistic for Each Unit. There is nothing more discouraging for an employee than to feel that the goal of his unit is far more difficult to meet than that of other units in the bank.

If a branch is located in a thriving, growing community, it is obvious that it will be far easier for that branch to generate new deposit and borrowing business than will be the case in a branch located in a static or declining urban core. To set goals that do not take the environment and potential of the community into consideration is to turn off the enthusiasm of those employees who feel that their goal is much more difficult.

This establishment of goals must apply within a unit bank or in a headquarters, too; it is not just a problem for branch networks. All too often, the contact officers and employees who deal with the public are rewarded for bringing in new business, while those who work in the back feel neglected because they have no opportunity to generate tangible results for the bank.

A good profit plan will provide rewards for smooth operations or minimal errors in a routine job that are as substantial as are the rewards provided for bringing in new business. A bank must see the value of smooth functioning operations and the cost of errors, and reward good employees in this area just as it rewards new business generators.

Make Sure Costs Are Realistic. In today's banking, nothing is more significant than the cost of funds. Yet too often in a profit center structure, no account is taken of the fact that some branches or units bring in low cost demand deposits while others are bringing in high cost certificates of deposit.

Branch managers who are responsible for their own profit centers frequently report they are frustrated in trying to motivate their people to reach the center's goals. This is because the cost of money used in determining their unit's profitability is given to them by general management—unrelated to the actual cost of funds in the branch.

If a branch is assigned an average costs of funds in measuring its profitability, and this average cost includes all the bank's deposit funds—from demand deposits to time certificates—then the people in that unit have no reason to try to obtain cheaper funds in their deposit solicitation.

Thus, the profit center determination must include a realistic cost of the funds attracted in each unit. If a unit is obtaining cheap funds or inactive demand deposits, that unit should be accorded a lower cost of funds than is assessed against the unit buying high cost certificates or taking in low balance checking deposits that generate a considerable amount of monthly activity.

In this regard, a well designed profit center approach makes the officers and employees of each unit far less anxious to please customers by giving them free checking accounts through exemption from service charges than would otherwise be the case.

Similarly in placing loans on the books, the profits of the unit must be judged based on the net profit of the loans generated, not just the gross profit. If a loan offers high yield but has high risk of default, the unit must be judged on the cost of default potential rather than just on the immediate yield. And if a loan requires high servicing costs in the banks, this should be taken into account in measuring the profit center that generated it.

The Center versus the Bank. Most important, a profit center must be set up so that employees actually work towards the best interest of the bank.

There must be rewards for generating corollary business that goes to another unit. Far too often we hear horror stories of the employee who has the opportunity to sell a customer a trust account or a new type of loan, but who doesn't bother to do so because the credit would go to some other unit of the bank. His feeling obviously is that the bank starts and ends with his own local profit center.

Thus, the employee and his center must be rewarded for business generated for other units of the bank too.

Tied in with this reward for generating business for other units must be a training program that explains to each employee what other services are available in the bank. It is amazing how often an employee lets an opportunity to help his bank gain new business slip through his fingers because he did not recognize that the need of the customer could be filled by a service offered by another area of the bank.

Some smart banks have started at the place of maximum public contact—the guards, the phone operators, and the tellers—to explain what services the bank offers and what they involve. These are the first people who hear the questions of the public. Frequently they can generate solid business for the bank by merely knowing who is the right person to see for the service desired, whereas sending the customer to the wrong office would lead to a run-around and a disgruntled person walking out the door.

Successful Profit Centers

A profit center approach is necessary to make the goals of the bank bite-sized for each employee. Otherwise he just does his day's work without any regard to whether it is really helping or hurting the institution. But unless it is properly structured, a profit center plan can backfire and lead to more troubles than it solves. An employee can become myopic and see only his own unit and not the best interests of the bank.

Banks that have successfully utilized the profit center approach report that when it is structured so the employee can see both his own unit's goals and also the overall goal of the bank, it is one of the best techniques available for making each employee feel he or she is an important part of the bank's team.

15-3 SALES SKILLS ARE NEEDED IN BANKING

At a national meeting of sales training executives not long ago, only a couple of banks were represented. One would think that with the changes taking place in banking, with deregulation, with the need to sell new accounts, with discount brokerage service, with broader bank electronic services, and all the other ways in which banking must get the public to accept change, that bankers would come out in droves for a meeting to discuss selling and sales training.

Perhaps there are so many marketing programs available exclusively for bankers that they do not have to go outside the industry and mingle with other sales professionals to gain the ideas they need for today's new environment.

But it would also appear that one reason for the lack of bankers is that bankers do not consider themselves to be salesmen. They feel they are banking professionals to whom selling is subsidiary to the knowledge of their skills in priority.

Yet, with change coming so fast, such thinking could well be a mistake. For if there is any real weakness in banking, it is that sales and marketing have not kept up with technological change. For example, if one looks at all the new ways that banks have developed to cut the need for paper copies and make the bank more efficient, it is not technical problems that are holding back their utilization. Rather, it is marketing difficulties: an inability to get the public to accept these services with their advantages for both the bank and its customers.

Not that everything is wonderful in sales outside banking either. One of the greatest problems brought up by the sales trading people was a lack of communication in both directions—from production and management to sales and then back from the salesmen to the production and management people.

What are examples of this?

First, the vast majority of training executives admitted when questioned that their companies never ask the sales people their opinions of the products being sold, what the customers think of them, and what changes should be made to provide products more in tune with what the public will buy. In other words, the sales force is sent out on a one-way street. It is out to tell the company's story, but it is not there to learn what the company should know—despite the fact that salespeople have regualar contact with the most important people to the company, its customers.

Conversely, when asked "Have your salespeople gone through the entire operation so they know what they are selling and who can handle suggestions and complaints?" they generally answered "No."

Most salespeople sell products without having spent time learning how they are produced, how they can be improved and how prices are established. Yet they are the ones who bear the burden of customer complaints and who must explain why things are the way they are and where to turn to get needed changes.

In this regard, bankers are finally learning that the most important service a customer wants is to have someone who cares when a mistake is made and who can correct it quickly and properly.

This ombudsman, or personal banker, is the key to customer satisfaction, and his role is becoming more important as routine banking becomes automated. The customer now sees his banker less often, except for the correction of errors and for transactions more complex than deposits and withdrawals.

KNOWING CUSTOMERS

Another area in which salespeople need education is in understanding the customer's product. If a salesman knows the company he is dealing with, he has an air of confidence about him in discussing the customer's problems that in turn gives the customer confidence in him when he turns to discuss his own service offerings.

This is why smart companies like IBM, American Bell, and many suppliers of hardware to banks spend fortunes training their people to understand banking as a business.

As bankers sell their own services, one wonders whether bank representatives should first learn more about the individual companies they are dealing with, to help differentiate the bank's personnel from those of other banks. For ability, availability, and continuity of calling officers coupled with professionalism is generally at the top of the services wanted by corporate customers.

Another area needing more attention is for companies to give greater understanding to employees of where the organization is going in this hectic world of deregulation. More mergers and changes in functions of both banks and nonbank organizations are taking place today than has been the case for decades. Giving the staff some indication of where the individuals may fit in our changing world is the key in keeping a happy work force.

In this regard, it is good to note that at many recent bank meetings, representatives of airlines and other industries that have faced deregulation have been scheduled to tell what this meant to their companies and to them personally. They can give an indication of what deregulation might therefore mean to banks and bankers.

Do bankers consider themselves salesmen? Everyone is selling all day long—from the person explaining a new ATM service at a demonstration site to the CEO trying to ingratiate himself with a prospect and make him feel that his bank will do things that no other bank can possibly do with such charm, efficiency, low cost, and willingness to please.

Routine banking is becoming more a function of the computer and the friendly approach means more than ever before, as we try to get the public to overcome its fear of the computer, even on a first solo flight on an ATM. This means that the people who do have public contact will be more and more important, handling more complex and difficult issues.

Brokerage firms, thrifts, and the new financial conglomerates certainly feel that selling is an integral of their operations, for they are trying to sell the public on moving its business away from the banks. Banks now are getting the freedom to fight back. But having new powers and selling them to the public are two different animals.

15-4 QUALITY AND IMAGE HAVE A ROLE IN BANKING

As banking faces rate competition never witnessed before, the question arises: Is there any place for quality and image in banking today?

Bankers have begun to understand that you cannot pay top dollar and give the customer special service, too. If you are paying the same interest on money market deposit and Super NOW accounts as the competition, you do not have to throw in special free services.

In the past, the quality and quantity of service was a way to reward customers when you legally could not pay them enough in cash. Now that you can pay whatever you want, why give out special services too?

Some bankers respond: If we don't give special service, then we won't get the customers to leave their dollars with us.

Others reply: Why bother? If we need money, we can just go to the money desk and buy it. Buying federal funds, certificates of deposit, Eurodollars, and other money market instruments available to banks, large and small alike, will still be cheaper than paying top dollar to a local customer and giving him special service to boot.

This explains why some banks are now charging fully for each check written, each deposit, and every other service provided.

But the issue still remains: Is quality worth anything today or are we going to see banking become like a row of discount stores on a main highway—blaring price and ignoring service and quality?

To many thoughtful bankers, quality does remains important; moreover they feel the public will pay for it.

They look at the brokerage industry in which both discount houses and full-service brokerage firms offer the same execution but at markedly different prices. The key is that the service difference is tremendous.

Banking may well have to work the same way. There will have to be one rate of interest payment for the full-service account, and a higher one for accounts getting just routine service.

But this means a bank will still have the job of getting the public to feel that this bank is special and has a quality of service that justifies high service charges or lower interest payments for deposits.

When rates were kept low by deposit-rate ceilings, banks tried to differentiate their product from that of other banks in order to attract deposits. Now product differentiation will still be necessary for banks that want to justify charging more or paying less.

This is not an impossible task. People will pay more or accept less interest if they feel they are getting a better product. After all, a mixed-up statement or an error that shuts down our credit limit on our credit card makes us more unhappy than a couple of cents less interest.

Some banks will emphasize rate as a means of gaining growth. Others will try to stress the value of quality—that the real financial professional does not quibble over a few cents but thinks of the quality of service he is getting. Similarly, an ad for a Mercedes-Benz or Rolls-Royce seldom screams the price; rather, it stresses that the car is so quiet you can hear the clock tick.

UPGRADING STAFF

If a bank decides to stress quality, it must provide it. This means getting the entire staff to work on error-free service and personal attention. It also means the bank must do some research first to see if it is worth providing such service.

This is a world in which service is hard to achieve, and in which the impersonalization of computer operations frequently is the only way to make service delivery efficient. Thus, many banks will find that providing quality service will be just too expensive relative to what can be earned on these services in charges and through lower interest rates.

They may well end up just saying, "O.K. we will be like everyone else. Just stress rate as a drawing card to the public and not offer special services and attention such as financial counseling, handling securities, and the like."

Still, it is nice that bankers now have a choice.

PART 6 Relationships

Banking institutions are not islands unto themselves—even though someone who has just been turned down for a loan may argue the point.

Certainly, there are relations that the bank has with employees, shareholders, and customers. These relationships are covered in the sections dealing specifically with those topics. Three other important relationship areas are discussed here: The government, the public, and society as a whole.

The relations a bank has with government are dictated by the laws and regulations affecting banking, at all levels of government, Compliance is a necessary part of conducting the business of modern banking. But the relationships a bank has with government entities can be much more encompassing, affecting the legislation that is, or is not, passed.

Public relations is one of those things that occur regardless of what a bank might do. Loan rates, the opening of a new office, a robbery, a merger—almost anything involving a bank—has an impact on the public. Whether the news is good or bad, a bank can help itself by putting its best foot forward.

Finally, banking is part of the fabric of our society. As such, it must act responsibly—and responsively—to the needs of society.

16 Government Relations

16-1 WHO INVITED THE REGULATORS, ANYWAY?

This may be the age of deregulation in banking (see Part 1), but that does not mean that government has less than a major voice in running a bank. Some level of government will be involved in the bank—whether the bank has a state charter or a national charter, whether it is large or small, or whether it is a member of the Federal Reserve. No matter what happens, that will continue to be a fact of banking life.

When businessmen are asked to name their number one nemesis, it is almost always government intervention in their operations. Bankers in particular feel that government involves itself in almost every decision they make. The trend towards government influence in credit allocation decisions certainly tops the list of ways in which the federal and state governments have tried to play more and more of a role in banking decisions in the recent past.

All too often, however, the intervention is the result of banker actions actually begging the government to come in. As this happens, the bankers who do ask for government interference forget that once government gets into the act, it almost never leaves.

The broad recent use of Regulation Q and rate regulation in general was originally pushed by institutions that did not want competitors to pay higher rates even though they could afford to. Once in to regulate the competition's rate structure, the government naturally stretched out and regulated the institutions that wanted their competitors hobbled.

THE COMMUNITY REINVESTMENT ACT

A recent example of this is the Community Reinvestment Act (the CRA). The CRA started with few if any precedents, so the government was hard pressed to establish guideposts as to what banks should do to meet the standards. To a large extent it was other financial institutions that came along and gave the regulators a set of guidelines to apply to financial institutions.

In fully one-third of the cases in which complaints were lodged against bank branching, merger, and other requests for expansion in which failure to meet CRA standards was used as the reason for protest, it was other financial institutions that lodged these complaints.

The motive is obvious: A bank or thrift wants to keep another institution from branching into its territory. The CRA is available to prevent the expansion if the applying bank has not met CRA standards. Thus, the opposing institution digs in, finds a reason why the applicant has not met CRA standards, and temporarily or permanently blocks the expansion.

In doing this, the opposing institution helps build precedents and standards that the regulators can use on others. This helps the regulators develop a set of criteria which then is applied against all institutions—including the ones that placed the CRA complaint in the first place.

There was a state bankers convention a few years ago at which the president of a college that had taken no federal money spoke about how he was able to run his college without government interference because he took no federal help of any kind. The bankers cheered. The next day at lunch, a regulator stated that after cheering the college president, they went back to business as usual, and about 10 bankers came up to him asking for restraints on competitors.

There was one savings and loan official who did not go along with this. When asked why he opposed government help to bail S&Ls out of low-yielding mortgages, he replied: "I went into the S&L business because I like the private sector. If I wanted to be a government employee, I would have gone to work for the government."

16-2 DEALING WITH GOVERNMENT OFFICIALS

It is important for bankers to work as closely as possible with government regulators and legislators. This is one of the few ways to get the banking point of view considered and/or get regulations and legislation to be less harmful to banks.

On the federal level, only the largest banks can spend much time or effort in Washington. The national banking trade associations, such as American Bankers Association and the Independent Bankers Association of America, serve as worthy surrogates. However, all banks can and should deal with such elected officials as Senators and Representatives.

Unfortunately, the banker's side is sometimes overlooked on the state level. Yet state legislative and regulatory action often presages what happens on the national level. It is too important not to make sure banking's story is told—and heard.

ON THE STATE LEGISLATURE FRONT

Bankers frequently complain that their legislative environment is unfavorable because legislators do not understand what banking is all about.

Too often there is truth in this lament. Legislation is sometimes passed that is really unfavorable to banking and that restricts the ability of banks to do their job. This legislation ranges from unrealistic usury ceilings to bankruptcy laws that favor the borrower over the lender, to branch and operational restraints that are applied to banks but not to their competition for the depositor's dollar.

Why do banks frequently do so poorly in dealing with the legislature? The answer in large part stems from the fact that many bankers have never tried to know their legislators or tried to get the bank viewpoint across to them. Thus, the elected representatives are left with the stereotype of a banker as being a rich, self-important individual who does not think of or understand the public interest—simply because so few bankers have made the effort to tell their story as it really should be told.

Similarly, the bankers who ignore a candidate running for office because he is unknown to them or because of his perceived views may later regret it if that candidate wins. "Why didn't you come and see me during the campaign when I could have used your help?" the legislator asks.

"I didn't think you would win," the banker replies.

Commercial banks have been far less ready to invite members of the legislature to be part of their convention programs than have other financial industries. There is a feeling that if a legislator, say chairman of the banking committee, is invited to the state convention at some nice resort to give a speech for a decent honorarium, it might look like bribery, something bankers want to avoid.

On the other hand, there is the fact that when the legislative representative does come to the convention, he or she meets the bankers and spends time with them. If there is one point that can be made with certainty, it is that once bankers get the opportunity to tell their side of the story to the lawmakers, they can win far more friends in the state capital (and more favorable legislative results) than they can when lawmakers feel that bankers do not have the public interest at heart.

Familiarity breeds respect and understanding. Bankers, sad to say, have a long way to go in developing this familiarity among their lawmakers.

COMMUNICATING WITH THE GOVERNMENT

The situation is not all bleak. Many bankers and bank associations have been making a sincere effort to develop ties with legislative representatives. There are more banker-legislator dinners at which the bankers are the hosts for the legislators of their district, and the banking association's program is presented for evaluation.

How can bankers get lawmakers to attend such dinners? The answer is to schedule them at a convenient location when the legislature is in session.

In addition, and far more important, bankers are beginning to arrange meetings to visit new lawmakers as they take office. Sometimes a bus junket will be scheduled with all the major bankers of the district coming to the capital together for a breakfast or luncheon meeting with the lawmakers of the district. And more bankers are inviting legislators to their conventions to serve on panels and present their own views.

(Additional ideas on meeting with legislators are discussed in Section 16-4, "Meet with State Legislators.")

BANKERS AREAS OF CONCERN

What do bankers want as they talk to lawmakers with this single voice? What are the issues on which they want the members of the legislature to understand their position and help them create a legislative climate that can allow the banks to thrive and to serve the public better?.

Each state has specific issues that are of concern to bankers. Yet, there are a number of general issues, which are discussed below, that appear to apply to virtually all states. These principles are tenets that bankers are seeking to get through to lawmakers as the basic foundation of any legislative agenda.

The first item to be considered is getting lawmakers to understand the virtue of a free market. They should be made to understand that a bank is merely a conduit. If the bank is not free to charge top dollar on its loans and services, then it cannot pay top dollar to the saver and depositor. In other words, legislators must overcome the attitude that a bank is a big bag of money, beholden to no one, and get the realistic understanding instead that a bank is merely lending one person's money to another.

The next issue is getting the lawmakers to recognize that in today's world, the borrower will have to pay more for credit accommodation and cannot expect rates to become extremely low again. Since the saver wants top dollar and is willing to leave the bank for the money fund and direct investment of his funds if he does not get it, the borrower in turn must pay top dollar so the saver can get his just reward.

When lawmakers generate sympathy for the borrower and feel that banks should be making loans for cars, starter houses, and other credit that the public wants at rates well below what big quality corporate borrowers pay, these lawmakers must recognize that there is no big bag of money available to fund such cheap loans—the money must come from underpaying the saver, who frequently is poorer than the borrower.

Another issue to be considered is the recognition that those who are in trouble in repaying their loans should not be given special treatment, if this means that the bank in turn is unable to pay its saver. It is the saver's money that has been loaned to the farmer, homebuyer or businessman who is in default; to deny the bank the opportunity to utilize fair legal standards to gain repayment or repossession of property is robbing not only the bank but the people who entrusted their funds to the bank.

One last issue should be considered: Lawmakers should understand that broadened powers of all institutions are part of today's financial climate of deregulation. Most important in this regard, they must recognize that it is in the public interest to allow deregulation with its more intense price competition, just as free market competition in any other segment of the economy has led to lower prices and better service for the public.

It is important for bankers to have their legislative representatives understand that when a bank charges for each service, closes unprofitable offices, and otherwise reduces the level of service offered, it is because the bank is paying top dollar for the public's funds. Without doubt, most people would rather have a higher rate of payment on their accounts than receive special service because the bank is not allowed to give them what they really want and need—hard dollars-and-cents payment for the funds entrusted to the bank.

The more closely a banker knows his lawmakers, the better the rapport will be. And once the banker gets the opportunity to tell his story as it really is, any legislative representative truly interested in the best service to his constituency will have to recognize that there is a healthy dose of economic reality and justice inherent in it.

16-3 COMPLYING WITH GOVERNMENT REGULATIONS

Regardless of what one thinks about government regulations or how they got there in the first place, a bank must comply with the regulations or face the consequences. And with so many regulations impacting on banks, it is easy to have that nagging feeling that maybe the bank is doing something that violates the new laws and regulations imposed on the industry from Washington and the state capitols.

To makes matters worse, there are many times when trying to meet compliance requirements of one regulation automatically forces the bank into violation of some other compliance law.

As a result, top officers in many small- and medium-sized banks complain that they spend more time making sure that they are following all the rules and regulations covered under the broad term "compliance" than they spend doing their basic job of taking deposits and making loans and investments.

A deeper analysis of compliance regulations reminds one of the old adage: "What you fear most never happens—something else does." The proper analysis of what compliance laws require and how they can be simply handled has led many bankers to the conclusion that meeting compliance requirements is mainly common sense and preparation. No exceptions for anyone, rather than a series of complex rules, should be the governing factor.

In essence, careful planning on compliance and recognizing that compliance requirements do exist and must be met is the basic prerequisite for getting over the compliance hurdle. Once that hurdle has been cleared, the banker can go back to running his bank the way he feels it should be run.

SIX AREAS OF COMPLIANCE

What are the basic areas in which compliance requirements impact back operations? They are:

- Truth in Lending.
- Regulation B—The Equal Credit Opportunity Act.
- Regulation E—Electronic Funds Transfer.
- The Fair Housing Act.
- State laws—especially usury laws.
- The Community Reinvestment Act.

Of these, the first five differ from the sixth in that the banks are subject to civil liability. What this means is that failure to meet the requirements of the legislation can lead to class action suits instituted by those who feel discriminated against. Civil suits do not limit the settlement claims that the courts can require.

The sixth law, the CRA, has no civil liability requirement. But regulators find this to be one of the areas of greatest public concern. Consequently, they dig deeply into the question of whether the banks are serving their communities adequately under this law.

What are class action suits? Legally, they involve an individual who thinks he has had his legal rights violated and who sues on behalf of all the people felt to be similarly mistreated. The law allows a class action because one individual could not afford to pay the legal costs of handling a suit in his own behalf when the amount involved is modest.

Who would sue to recover, say, $15,000 if the legal costs were $200,000 to win the case? Therefore, the law allows an individual to sue on behalf of an entire class. Then, if the case is won, the court awards the legal fees from the settlement made to all class members, so that the individual plaintiff must only bear his small proportionate share of the cost of the suit.

This is basically fair. Without class actions, how could an individual get justice for a grievance, unless that grievance were so huge that the plaintiff could afford his own lawyer? In other words, without class actions, companies could do almost anything they wanted, because no individual stockholder, customer, or member of the community would find it economically worthwhile to seek legal recourse.

The problem with class actions, as with virtually all consumer protective legislation, is that they can be abused. For example, an individual lawyer may find that a small infraction of the law has been practiced by one bank. The infraction can involve a mistake in the fine print on the truth-in-lending disclosure form, or something of this nature. The lawyer may then find one person who has been affected and sue for this person on behalf of the entire class of borrowers. The result is that the bank not only is subject to the possibility of a large award against it under the appropriate law, but, far more important, it has the heavy legal costs of defending itself against the suit—no matter how tiny the infraction or how spurious the suit is.

Some banks have taken the response of generally settling out of court simply because the cost of defending the case is higher than the cost of settlement. But others have taken the view that if they settle just to avoid legal costs, they will become sitting ducks for further lawsuits over other slight infractions of the law, so they fight.

The best defense against such suits, however, is to make sure that the bank is in compliance with the law in the first place. This is not that difficult to achieve if the bank is willing to take the issue seriously and develop a program that covers the bases that lawmakers and regulators are interested in.

INSURING COMPLIANCE

What should a bank do to insure that it is in compliance on these six legislative areas?

- The bank should have a written policy on compliance, indicating that it understands the law and intends to follow it.
- The bank should have a written set of procedures on meeting the policy standards it has set and a control program to make sure that its policies and procedures are carried out.

These steps place the onus of proving that the bank is in violation on the regulator and the class action lawyer.

NO EXCEPTIONS

If it is so easy for a bank to meet compliance requirements by thinking of them, then why do so many banks get into trouble on compliance? The answer is that they break their standards trying to do a favor for one or two customers, and news of this is learned by others. In other words, consistency is the key to meeting compliance requirements. A bank cannot make an exception to rate, service charge, or quality standards for one customer without risking a suit or a regulatory determination that the bank is in violation in handling others. Trying to be nice to a couple of people by eliminating service charges or accepting lower lending standards without adequate business reasons may leave the bank open to suits that it is discriminating against the rest of the bank's customers and potential customers.

This does not mean that all loans must be treated identically or that all accounts must have the same service charges. The customer with a large balance or the account that controls a considerable amount of corollary business in other accounts naturally can be treated differently. But the bank has to be prepared to explain why it is giving preference to some customers over others.

HANDLING COMPLIANCE PROBLEMS

Suppose the examiners indicate a compliance violation. Experts feel that the best thing a banker can do is to sit down immediately with the examiner and talk it over, indicating where changes will be made and where honest disagreements can be settled. Once the report is on paper, it is far more difficult to change than when it is a matter of friendly discussion between the examiner and the bank compliance officer.

Experienced compliance officers also report that when there is a problem, it is much easier to call a correspondent who has a similar problem and talk things over with him or her as to how to handle the matter than to call a lawyer. Another banker who has had a similar problem can offer suggestions for easy solution long before the stage is reached of hiring an attorney.

Since every bank must have a compliance program, why not adopt cooperative efforts to avoid having each bank do what the other banks have to do also? For example, each state bankers association could have a compliance department that goes through the laws and develops checklists and procedure books that can be used by all the banks in the state.

Alternatively, there could be an informal "old boy network" within each bank letting the state association know when an unusual compliance problem has appeared, so that the others could be warned and can avoid a similar problem. And there could be frequent dialogue between the bankers of the state and their regulators to help clear up misunderstandings on compliance, so that the issues can be resolved and the best public interest served, long before matters get written down and legal action develops.

Most banks want to meet compliance requirements and really have their hearts in the right place on the issue. The problem is the complexity of the regulations and the varying interpretations of different examiners who come into the bank.

As with so many disagreements that develop in business and personal relationships, the key is communications. And the most important step bankers must make is to show the lawmakers and regulators that they do want to meet all compliance requirements and are trying their best to do so. If, through their policies, procedures, and control programs, bankers can honestly demonstrate that they take compliance requirements seriously and are doing their best to meet them, this should substantially lessen the adversary attitude of some regulators.

16-4 MEET WITH STATE LEGISLATORS

"Hi Joe, how's Suzy?"

"Hi Ed, has Laura left the hospital?"

"Hello Eleanor, glad to see your plurality soared."

This is the way James P. Murphy, executive vice president of the New York State Bankers Association, stood at the door and, from memory, greeted each and every one of the 200 or so members of the state's legislature who showed up for the association's annual legislative dinner in Albany.

The association had top bankers on hand to greet the legislators. Far more important, the tables were arranged by district, so that bankers could get to know their new legislative representatives and renew acquaintances with returning members.

The basic aim of the dinner was to get the legislature to know the bankers and to have them learn the legislative program of the association for the year. That program included:

- Permanent deregulation of consumer deposit-interest-rate ceilings.
- Permanent deregulation of artificial interest-rate ceilings on consumer loans.
- Tax reforms aimed at removing inequities and promoting growth.
- Authority for banks to offer a full range of investment and insurance services.
- Deregulation of the pricing of bank trust services.

DEDICATED

The legislators present certainly could not take issue with those goals. The association's legislative program recognized, for example, that other industries also have a full right to encroach on banking services, so the public can have better competition. The banks just want the right to fight back in a fair battle.

The most important thing a legislative member who cares about the public interest has to keep in mind is that frequently the saver is poorer than the borrower, yet he has been taken advantage of for many years through artificially low interest-rate ceilings.

Therefore, the new world in which the saver gets more and the borrower has to pay more for credit may well be more in the public interest than the old conditions under which the saver subsidized the borrower.

This, plus an emphasis on the value of free market competition and the fact that we will have to pay fairly for our banking service, were all the association wanted to get across to the 200 representatives who showed up for dinner.

To the banking industry in particular, getting a better chance to meet legislators must certainly be valuable. All too often in the past, bankers have remained aloof. At the same time, thrift people and credit union representatives gained familiarity with their legislators and thus got their story across far more effectively.

It may be that dinners like New York State's do not draw as much enthusiasm from the lawmakers as the bankers would like. But legislative members have to eat, and this helps swell attendance at a banker-legislator dinner if the night is right and the location close to the Capitol. Grover Whalen, who used to be the official greeter of the City of New York, could get a ticker-tape parade of millions for any visiting celebrity on Broadway at noon on any weekday whatsoever.

"They are all out to honor that great celebrity—luncheon," Mr. Whalen would explain.

But a legislative dinner sure can help cement ties between bankers and people who can be pretty important to the bankers—and who should be given every opportunity to know what the bankers think.

DISCUSSIONS OUTSHINE THE PROGRAM

Naturally at any meeting like this dinner the conversations in the halls at cocktails and over dinner are more informative than the scheduled program. The dinner in Albany was no exception.

Some of the interesting topics discussed (and heard by the legislators) included these:

With banks now paying top dollar on savings, many local lawmakers want it all—they want top interest, pledged securities to collateralize their deposits 100%, and they want the local banks to provide all of the services they need for the community without service charges.

How can a bank provide all of this? Only by losing its shirt.

And if there was any topic discussed at the meeting in Albany, it was that banks have to learn to turn away accounts that are not profitable—provided the bank really has done its homework and determined that the account really is not profitable when float and value of collected deposits are accurately determined.

One banker explained graphically why he formerly had had to work so much more frenetically in the brokerage industry than he now does as a banker.

"In brokerage, if you don't sell something today, you don't earn anything today. In banking even if you don't show up the money keeps on earning interest. It's a nice feeling." Of course, these days he would have to add that if you don't show up, the depositors still keep earning top dollar on their accounts, too—which is why banking is not the easy game it used to be.

The Independent Bankers of New York State joined with the New York State Bankers Association at a dinner as invited guests and friends rather than as adversaries. Finally, the bankers of the nation are realizing that the real enemy is not each other but the opposing industries that want banking's turf.

With deregulation and broadened powers, many present thought the time would not be distant when all financial industries could combine more in presenting issues to lawmakers and keeping the nation's financial environment operating efficiently.

Upstate bank presidents said they had nothing to fear from the encroachment of New York City banks in their territories.

"They come in to set up offices, their staffs live 50 miles away and are changed frequently so they don't know the people, and they take all of the loans we have turned down. So why should we worry about them?" was the way it was put by one president whose bank is right across the street from a New York City bank's upstate branch.

Then there is the old joke where two partners in the garment industry were out fishing. One says to the other:

"Sam, I just remembered our safe is open."

"What's the difference, we're both here," was the reply.

Happily this Albany meeting indicates that banking is finally learning who its friends are and where emphasis should be placed.

It must be great for bankers from institutions large and small to sit down with lawmakers over cocktails and dinner and find that finally they as bankers agree on what they want and need and no longer leave the legislators with the feeling, "If they can't ever agree among themselves on what they want, how can I do anything to help them."

17 Public Relations

17-1 IT HAS TO BE PLANNED

A bank is involved in public relations by its very existence. The image, the relationship a bank presents to the public is there whether the bank does anything positive or negative. There simply is no way of avoiding the impressions the bank makes on people. That being the case, a bank might just as well put forth the best possible image. After all, positive feelings will help a bank far more than negative feelings.

Effective public relations, however, is no easy matter. And the existence of an extensive department devoted to spreading the good name of the bank is certainly no guarantee that relations will be positive. Citibank drew considerable criticism in recent years when it instituted a 50-cents-per-month charge for unused credit cards and when it required low-balance customers to use an ATM instead of a human teller. Regardless of the business sense of those two moves, the bank was greeted with derision in the press and some subsequent loss of business. The two policies were reversed rather quickly, but not before the damage was done.

One would think that such gaffes could be avoided. Many are, but sometimes the impact of news or policies on the public is overlooked. More often, perhaps, the impact is misjudged. Still, it is important to consider the effect on the public of what the bank does. It is important to maintain good relations with media representatives. And it is important to plan and institute a public relations program for your bank.

DETERMINING GOALS

The first step in planning a bank's public relation program is to determine the goals of the program. Some bankers feel that just having the bank's name in the media frequently is enough of a public relations goal. They feel that the basic role of public relations is to have the general public recognize the bank's name, and keep it in the back of their minds. Then, it is hoped, if people think of a bank because they need some service, they will think of this bank because the name is somewhere in the recesses of their minds.

This is the way many consumer goods companies look at their advertising as a means of establishing an image so that when a product is seen at the point of sale, it is immediately recognized, and, hopefully, purchased.

Most banks go further, they have more complex goals for their public relations programs. However, a bank must be honest about what it wants to achieve from its program. A number of bank public relations officers privately admit that the real goal of their bank's PR program is not the furtherance of the bank, but the glorification of one man or, at most, a handful of top officers.

At times this might not be so bad a policy for the bank. If a bank can personify itself, so that the public gives it a human feeling, this may help business. And some banks have found that a good public relations program can be built around the image of the CEO, so that people think of the organization as "Charlie's Bank" rather than just as "A Bank."

More to the liking of most PR people, however, is a broader "cult of personality" that tries to build the stature of a great many employees in the eye of the public.

By stressing different functions of the bank and different people from the bottom to the top, the PR program in some banks has been developed to give a feeling that the bank is staffed with professionals all the way through. Such a program has a side effect of boosting the morale, not only of the people chosen to be publicized, but all the people of similar rank. They feel that the bank appreciates to a greater degree what people at their level do for the institution.

Many report that the result of such a program is that whenever a bank representative, such as a lending officer or a member of the correspondent division, calls on a potential customer, the air of professionalism that the bank has tried to develop is carried with him, and it takes his job of selling the bank that much easier. Such an air of professionalism helps in bank employee recruitment drives, too.

Another goal that many banks have in mind as they plan public relations programs is a legislative and regulatory one. In the present environment, decisions in Washington, D.C. and in the state legislatures have a tremendous impact on the viability and operations of the commercial banks of the nation. Bankers feel that if their side of every story is better known by the public and by the lawmakers, this can help prevent adverse legislation and help encourage laws and regulations that can smooth the bank's path to its goals.

Public relations can help here in several ways. Naturally, a program that explains the bankers' side of any public issue can help a great deal if the explanation is plausible and not one-sided. On top of this, many banks try to develop an image as good public citizens through their actions and public relations programs.

INVESTOR RELATIONS

In some instances, a valid goal of a public relations program might be to improve investor relations and boost the price of the bank's stock. By keeping a relatively high share price, the bank hopes to accomplish several things:

- It makes it easier to sell new capital if this is needed without shareholder dilution:
- It keeps disgruntled shareholders away—nothing angers the typical shareholder faster than a depressingly low price of his investment.
- It helps keep the staff happy. Employees with stock options have every reason to want the price of the bank's stock to move up and remain attractive.
- A good stock price is a wonderful offensive and defensive weapon in mergers and acquisitions. The bank, whose share price is relatively high in relationship to its book value, is less likely to be a candidate for tender offers and takeover attempts. At the same time, the bank whose stock is selling at a good multiple to earnings and at a premium over book also has an easy time inducing shareholders of other banks to switch and merge.

However, there is no automatic correlation between bank public relations, bank performance, or anything else and what bank share prices will do over the immediate future. The stock market is a psychological world of its own. Good P.R. people fear that a bank stock whose price is artificially hyped by a good public relations program will move back down in price just as quickly when the intense campaign is over, or when the investment community feels that the stock has moved up all it is likely to and no more quick profits can be made by buying the stock.

COMMUNICATING GOALS

More and more American banks are establishing public relations departments or at least are appointing one officer to be in charge of public relations work. But all too often no one in top management has given this department or individual any idea of what the bank hopes to accomplish with its public relations work. There is always the quick response that the bank wants to keep up its image in the community and that anything nice that can be said about the bank in print or on the air is all to the good. And sometimes public relations is justified simply because a written story about the bank in a newspaper is far more credible in people's minds than a bank advertisement saying the same thing, and is far cheaper.

Bank P.R. people respond to this emphasis on number of inches of copy about the bank or number of mentions on the television screen by saying that if a bank really wants ample press coverage, all it needs is a good embezzlement or a number of spectacular robberies.

Mere press coverage is not enough. A bank needs to use this public awareness to strive for some goal. This is where many public relations people feel they have been abandoned. They are not told what the bank wants them to accomplish with public relations. The goals of public relations programs must be spelled out—and communicated to those responsible for the public relations function.

17-2 HANDLING THE MEDIA

One of the most difficult jobs of banks and bankers often is handling the local news media.

Bankers are considered to be "the establishment" in most communities. And, as the establishment, anything that can be said that is negative about a bank is what reporters call good copy. It pleases the readers and listeners who sit at home to hear that the bank, with all its supposed power and wealth, has some trouble or other.

This helps explain why every bank defalcation, every slip-up in operations, and any other development that might embarrass a bank receives considerable attention. At some other kind of institution, the same type of situation might be downplayed or not covered at all.

The press also includes a number of people who have developed a hostility, not only for the bank, but for all businesses. Thus, there may be an effort on the part of some reporters to point up every development they feel is anti-consumerist or in some way in opposition to what they think is the best public interest. Consider these items:

- Should a bank develop a new program of pricing services that eliminates giveaways and makes each customer pay his or her fair share of the cost of bank operations, this is written up as a means of "hurting the little man."
- If a bank buys new equipment that may help it serve the customer more efficiently and for more hours per day, some reporters will complain that it leads to concentration of banking into fewer institutions, because others cannot afford the equipment.
- Should a bank take a step that forces the community to put its financial house in order, some call it putting pressure on the community for the benefit of the bank.

What is forgotten in these stories is that the bank has to be efficient in its operations to stay viable. This involves reexamination of pricing if services are being offered too cheaply. It involves investing in capital equipment to make the bank more efficient (just as the reporters' newspapers and radio and television stations have done).

DON'T FIGHT BACK

One of the saddest examples of this problem was brought out by the president of a major bank in New York State, located in a suburban county of sophisticated newspaper readers.

A long-time officer had disappeared with a considerable amount of money, and the bank received a call from a major New York newspaper about the matter. The president's response to the reporter's questions was simply: "This is an internal matter. We are sad, for he was a long-standing friend, and we wish to make no comment about this."

The next day the tabloid (now out of existence) told several hundred thousand readers: "The president of the bank reported 'that man was never any good anyway. We should have gotten rid of him long ago.'"

"What do you do next?" is the question many bankers ask when they see such a reporting.

In this case, the president of the bank decided the best thing to do was to forget the entire thing. If he asked for a retraction, it would just keep the story on the front pages for a couple of days longer. On the other hand, if he gritted his teeth and turned to other matters, there was a good chance that the public would forget. Most CEOs would agree this is all that can be done.

In another instance, the top officer of a major southern bank was accused of political manipulation and bribery in a nationally syndicated column. The man was innocent, but the concern and worry wore him down. When the retraction was finally published, it was in a little box back near the sports pages in local newspapers. Obviously, the fact he had not done these things just was not as newsworthy as the accusations that he had.

DEFENSIVE ADVERTISING

Faced with this type of problem, some banks with branch networks have found they must place advertisements in every local newspaper appearing daily or weekly in the communities the bank serves. In many instances, it is not because they feel these papers draw business, since many of them are simply throwaways to surround the weekly supermarket advertisements. Rather it is for defensive purposes to keep them from trying to dig up some dirt on the bank that would simply damage the bank's reputation. There is, on the other hand, a feeling among some bankers that any publicity is good publicity. They follow the old adage: "I don't care what you say about me, just spell my name correctly." These bankers think all that publicity and advertising and an entire public relations program can do for a bank is to get the people to know the bank's name. Then, when people are looking to change banks or to initiate a new service, they will think of this bank because its name is in the back of their minds, just as makers of retail products want public familiarity with their names.

Most bankers, however, are a little more discriminating in their attitudes toward publicity. They like news media attention, but they want it to be favorable or they do not want it at all.

POLICY GUIDELINES

Thus, some banks have developed internal policies that can help generate favorable publicity and avoid the type of anti-bank reporting described above:

- Senior management must be in agreement before anyone talks to the press about any issues of consequence. And the closer the bank sticks to the real story, the easier the job will be.
- To avoid misunderstanding and to protect employees, all inquiries by the media concerning any bank related activity should be reported immediately to the proper central official responsible for press relations.
- Each bank employee must understand that members of the press are generally "on the record" at all times.
- If the report to be published is of a financial nature, it should be screened by the bank's counsel to make sure it complies with the Securities and Exchange Commission and other regulations.

DOES IT LOOK GOOD?

Most important, both bank officers and bank directors must look at publicity for the bank and for themselves as a background constraint on their decisions and actions—almost like a conscience.

Bankers worry about conflicts of interest. Bank directors especially wonder whether they can serve a bank as a director and at the same time remain one of its major customers, that is, borrowing money and otherwise utilizing the bank's services. Some bank directors report that they have developed a simple principle toward their relationship with the bank (a principle that many bank officers also follow): they will do anything at all and will develop any relationship with the bank in any area of business—as long as they would not mind seeing a full report of what they did appear on the front page of the local newspaper. If they would be unhappy seeing a report of their activity appear there, then they will not undertake the transaction.

17-3 MAKING THE MOST OF ANNUAL MEETINGS

A bank and its management must be on the alert to take advantage of developments that can mean positive public relations for the organization. Consider the annual meeting. Today, many banks are looking at the annual meeting as an opportunity. Yet not that long ago, most bankers feared the annual meeting and tried to get it over with as quickly and quietly as possible.

Back in the 1950s, a major New York bank held a meeting that lasted two minutes and 12 seconds from beginning to end. It is hard to see how all the legal formalities can be accomplished in that short a time, but it was done. The bank's chairman boasted about his short meeting and tried to chip off a few seconds each year.

In addition to running short meetings, most major New York banks would schedule their annual meetings at the same time or at the same time as some other popular company had its annual meeting so that the corporate gadflies had to choose between them and could not attend too many.

To be sure, there was a good reason to want to avoid having some of these individuals present, especially the ones who would buy one share of stock so they could attend and then would disrupt the meeting with silly questions and proposals that truly made little sense for banking or any business.

But there were still many others, such as those corporate meeting gadflys, the Gilbert Brothers, whose questions generally were pertinent and in the best interest of the banks. And when banks and other institutions did their best to stifle people like these, it was simply a case of the employees, that is management, trying to squelch the owners, that is, the shareholders, so that the stockholders got the message that mere investment of money gave no real rights of power unless the shares held were large enough to insure a seat on the board.

MANAGING THE ANNUAL MEETING

Opportunity Lost

Now many bank managements take an entirely different attitude toward the annual meeting. They are far more secure in handling gadflies and take the opportunity of the questions that these people ask to get across the bank's position on delicate issues, such as social goals of management and equal opportunity compliance.

Sometimes management is disappointed when sensitive questions on these topics do not come up. In such cases management is proud of its record, has prepared a good answer to each expected sensitive question and hopes to be attacked on such topical and sensitive issues because of the good light it feels it can put the bank in through its response.

But far more important, good managers look upon the annual meeting as an opportunity to get good press coverage and publicity on the performance of the bank in general and a chance to tell the bank's story to people who might do the institution some good.

How can a bank use the annual meeting to its best advantage? Most basically, the bank can be sensitive to shareholder needs in setting the time of the meeting.

Then the bank must get the shareholders and the attending press to understand the bank's recent solid performance. Unfortunately, most bank annual reports come out about the same time, so that good results of a bank may be buried among the reports of several institutions published that day.

The annual meeting can personalize the data and get it added attention. If a bank has taken losses on bonds or has had earnings declines for good and sufficient reasons, the annual meeting is a time to get public understanding of why this happened and why it makes the bank stronger rather than weaker, if this is the case.

Management can use the opportunity to get shareholders to meet top staff officers.

Banks can get shareholders to learn about trust services, Keogh plans, and other facilities that may not be understood; it is hoped the press will pick up this data.

Additionally, top management has an opportunity, not frequently available, to learn what the public feels about the bank. If comments and questions are truly accepted and mulled over later instead of being viewed as hurdles that must be jumped as gracefully as possible and then forgotten, a bank can learn a lot about itself from the shareholders' questions and areas of concern for the future of their organization. Finally, management can use this opportunity to talk about stock price performance and market characteristics, such as who makes a market and how to buy or sell the shares—something many bankers hesitate to talk about in printed material because of fear about the complex securities laws.

In sum, the annual meeting is a real opportunity to show how good the bank is to a group that wants to hear it—and to the general public as well.

17-4 EXPLAINING THE BANK'S POSITION ON TAXES

In their effort to overturn the withholding of interest and dividends a couple of years ago, the banks and the thrifts may have won the battle. But they may have lost the war.

The heavy campaign in which the banking industry engaged to win reconsideration of withholding unearthed a lot about banking operations—notably in tax treatment of income—that might have been better left outside of the public spotlight.

The problem of banks with regard to taxes is that they have been doing what really has been in the best interest of the nation, and the banks have paid in other ways for the low level of income tax rates that the industry enjoys. But the reasons for this are rather complicated and difficult for the layman to understand. It is far easier for the local newspaper or television station simply to report that banks pay much less income taxes than most of us and to leave it at that, than to go into a deep explanation as to why.

Bankers must also recognize that, all other things being equal, bankers are people that the rest of the community "loves to hate." After all, how can you love someone who not only lends you money, but then wants it back? Everyone who has ever had to make a payment on a loan forgets that the banker made him the loan; all he sees is the need to fork over money to the bank. Therefore, the borrower relishes seeing the banker in the limelight in some adverse way or other.

No wonder banks have a problem of gaining public understanding of what makes their tax rate so low. So anything that the individual institutions can do in their advertising and promotion to explain this would be all to the good.

REASONS FOR LOW TAXES

What are the reasons that banks pay such low taxes?

First, banks are just like all investors who benefit from investment tax credits, and other incentives given to encourage capital spending. Here banks have a story to tell that should be easily understood. For without capital spending, there is no growth in jobs and income in the nation. Thus, all benefit from such activities as the banking industry's leasing operations, and the tax benefits the throw off.

Second is loan loss reserves. There is an old adage, "It only takes five minutes to train a lending officer. But it takes a couple of years to train him so the bank gets the money back."

If the public wants banks to make loans only in those instances in which there is no chance whatsoever of default (lending the umbrella when it is not raining and asking for it back as soon as the rain starts) then no loan loss reserve deductions will be needed. But if the public wants banks to take risks in its behalf, the risk of loss should be subject to tax benefits just as the profit achieved is subject to tax payments.

In other words, you can't give half the profits of your business to your brother-in-law and then forget about him when you have a loss. If he shares the profits, he should also share the losses.

Tax Exempts

Tax exempt bonds, provide the most significant reason why banks do not pay as much in taxes as other industries. Banks are right up there at the top in purchasers of state and municipal securities.

How can a banker explain to his community that it is really in the community's best interest that the bank is buying municipal bonds and is cutting its tax liability down thereby? One way is to make a chart that shows what the local community would have had to pay for money had the banks not bought these bonds (indicating maybe what the rate would have had to be had the community have had to sell taxable bonds instead).

To show taxpayers in the community what would have happened to tax rates if municipal bonds were not a legal vehicle might bring home the point of the value of bank tax exemption to each and every one of them. In simple English, had the banks not been offered tax exemption to buy the bonds, the higher cost of finance would have been borne by the public. Therefore, by accepting a lower yield on investments because of their tax favored status, the banks are saving all taxpayers a bundle.

Tax Swaps

There is also the matter of tax swaps. Banks save a lot of taxes by selling depreciated bonds and deducting the full loss from normal income, whereas no other industry or individual is allowed such tax preference.

Why are banks given this privilege when the rest of us can only deduct losses against capital gains after a nominal ceiling of several thousand dollars is reached? Again, it is because of what banks do for the rest of us through this policy.

Banks are the middlemen between the Federal Reserve and the economy; as such, they play an important role in stabilizing the economy. No other industry operates under a regulatory structure that involves heavy restraint at one time and exhortation to expand at others.

The result, though, is that banks are encouraged to buy bonds when interest rates are low and bond prices high, and then must sell them when the reverse takes place. Banks should buy bonds when prices are high, since this encourages recovery. Then, the bonds should be sold when prices are low, to stem inflation.

Buying high and selling low may be great for economic stability, but it is sheer madness for the banks. So our tax laws allow the banks to deduct their bond losses from normal income as a means of encouraging the banks to undertake this rather irrational practice. The rationale is that if the government shares the loss, the banks will be that much more willing to undertake this needed but expensive policy, just as people would be more willing to make risky investments if the government absorbs one-half the loss when the investments turn sour.

In sum, the banks may pay less in taxes, but they pay in other ways that benefit society just as taxes do. This position must be explained to the public whenever the opportunity arises.

18 Banks and Society

18-1 THE SOCIAL GOALS OF BANKING—AND WHAT TO DO ABOUT THEM

Until recently, one rarely heard any comment on the social goals of commercial banking. Banking was considered a business, and, like any other business, its goals were the safety of depositors' funds, the meeting of the sound fund needs of the community, and the generation of a fair profit for the bank's shareholders.

Now, conditions are entirely different. Bankers are constantly under pressure to make loans to the poor, to undertake financing of socially-needed projects that may be substandard financial risks, and in other ways reallocate their available funds. Social goals are the target, rather than the traditional financial goal of making loans consistent with the best possible combination of low risk, income, and liquidity.

Commercial bankers have recognized that they must now alter policy to meet some of these social goals. In progressive banks, many projects have been undertaken and much time has been devoted to social goals, as opposed to traditional economic and financial ones.

ENVIRONMENT AND ECONOMIC GROWTH

Without question, one basic reason why banking is only now faced with the need to place priority on social goals is that the American economy itself has just switched from an emphasis on economic growth over the newer emphasis of the impact of this growth on our environment. This new emphasis on "Gross National By-product" is partially the result of the publicity being given consumerism. To a large degree, it is the result of the deterioration of the quality of our environment as the nation automates agriculture and more people are concentrated in urban areas. As the nation turns to introspection of its economic growth, the value of mere economic expansion by itself is being questioned. The banks have come under fire because (1) all businesses have been under fire, and (2) banks have been leaders in the fight for economic growth and industrial development within their communities.

In certain areas, bankers have already begun to turn their attention to the steps necessary to make economic growth as pleasant for the people as possible. The growth in antipollution loans has been impressive, and bankers have also been leaders in rebuilding their communities from the economic ravages of recession.

As bankers push for community growth today, they are recognizing that far more planning goes into economic growth than merely inducing industry to come in. Some of the newer areas gaining consideration include:

- When a new industry is persuaded to come in through tax concessions, does this unduly penalize the companies that are already in the community by forcing them to bear part of the new firm's tax load? Likewise, when the tax concessions expire, will this industry become economically unviable without the tax aid? In many cases, a company that otherwise would find a community uneconomical for its plant, because of transportation or resource difficulties, is induced to come in by tax concessions. Then, when these concessions run out, the community is left with a sick plant—because it was improperly located in the first place to gain the tax concession. When industry is attracted, does the banker make sure that he is working to attract the type of industry that best fits the available labor supply in the community? Does he work to provide the necessary public transportation and recreational facilities that can help make a new industry a success in the town or does he simply worry about getting the plant in town and leave it at that?

PUBLIC DEPOSITS

Another development that has forced bankers to emphasize social goals more than in the past is the changing attitude of public officials regarding the basis on which banks will be chosen as the recipient of public deposits.

In the past, the choice of depositor for treasury tax and loan account balances was based solely on the basis of equitable redistribution of treasury collections through the banking system, consistent with safety of the deposits. State and local government deposits have been allocated on the basis of geographical convenience, tradition, political considerations, and other diverse forces.

Now, however, more attention is being directed to the question of whether public deposits should be allocated to the financial institutions whose lending and investment policies best match the goals of the various governmental units. The results have been such proposals as reallocating tax and loan balances to financial institutions, notably savings and loans, which in turn direct these funds to the mortgage market. Another thought is that more government deposits be placed in minority banks to be utilized for minority personal loans and small business loans.

THE IMAGE FACTOR

Another major force leading banks to reconsider their attitude towards social goals has been the banker's new worry over his public image.

While bankers had little reason to worry about public attitudes in years past, they have found that this is no longer the case today. Banks have been subjected to television programs and articles that disseminate absolutely incorrect information, i.e., the suggestion that bank trust department investments should be undertaken for social goals even if it is against the wishes of the beneficiary of the trust, or that banks have callously neglected the poor and utilized unscrupulous collection techniques when loans to the poor have been made.

The banker is too often the whipping boy who must take the blame when the public's desires for credit accommodation cannot be satisfied. This is a basic factor harming the industry's image when tight money conditions are necessary to fight inflation.

One area of potential borrowing that is hurt most when credit demands cannot all be filled is home mortgage borrowing. Until recently, home mortgages have been low priority. They have a relatively poor yield and are unable to generate useful compensating balances. The banks have continually stressed other loans over mortgages, as have other financial institutions. The home mortgage, however, is considered something sacred in the United States, like God and Motherhood, and the bank's denial of mortgage applications has certainly added to the image problem.

Bank earnings reports have also seriously hurt the industry's image. While other industries, with few exceptions, are generally hurt by tight money, banks in tight money eras have reported earnings that have been up as much as 78% over the previous year's figures.

WHAT TO DO

While all the above would indicate that a bank should be doing more in lending to the poor, making loans of high risk for rehabilitation of decaying areas, and undertaking other tasks of social change, the dilemma of the banker is far deeper. From the public's perspective, the banks should be undertaking any and all projects of social betterment with the vast sums they have available. The analysis above indicates that banks no longer can eliminate social goals from their policy considerations in the way that many have done in the past. Yet bankers also recognize that the proposals that banks do more for their communities without regard to the riskiness of the ventures assume that bankers are rich people who own the funds they are lending and investing and who are failing in their responsibility to the poor.

What types of loans do improve society and the local community? A bank that makes loans for a low income housing project in 1984 may be called a slum lord in 1994. A bank in an area that has too much housing or where land and labor are not available may do more harm than good to the housing market by emphasis on mortgage loans in an effort to fulfill a social goal. It may merely pump so much money into the market that home prices are bid up above the level that most people can afford to pay. But enlightened self-interest involves training people for financial work whose own background has been alien to urban business activity. If the banks and other business firms do not take the necessary steps to train people and develop their talents, it is the communities the banks service that will suffer.

In addition, a bank cannot sit idly by when its community needs economic rehabilitation, when new business in the community needs a start and when other programs to aid the community maintain its strength or gain new strength lag for lack of financial backing. For, if the community is not strong, neither can the bank retain its strength.

Finally, a bank must recognize that the search for Gross National By-product and higher quality of life involves financing of the environmental improvement programs. Enlightened self interest of the bank involves loans and charitable gifts in these areas, undertaken under the broad principle that a stronger community environmentally is a better community in which a bank can do business.

The solution to the dilemma, and each individual banker's choice as to how to walk this tightrope between banker's responsibility and social objectives, is one of the toughest dilemmas the banking industry faces. Each banker must try to meet his responsibilities to his depositors, his stockholders, and his community on a day-to-day basis. At the same time, he must make sure that his basic decisions are consonant with the new and ever-changing social goals of the commercial banking industry.

18-2 MAKE SURE CHARITY IS VIABLE

Banks always have been pillars of their communities. After all, they help both business and individuals achieve their goals. A prosperous, growing community can contribute toward prosperous and growing banking institutions.

That does not mean that all banks have been successful in their relations with the communities in which they are located. Sometimes the management of a bank overlooks things they should do to help out. Sometimes they may be too uncaring when there is a need to foreclose on property. There may also be times when special interest groups ask for too much or state their positions too loudly. But, by and large, banks have done rather well in this area.

Still, effective community relations can sometimes be difficult to achieve. Moreover, as in almost all aspects of the banking business these days, there are new and insistent pressures that can make good community relations hazardous and risky. This certainly is the case in the area of charitable donations.

A couple of years ago, William W. Watson, president of the Bank of St. Joseph & Trust Company of St. Joseph, Louisiana, sent the following letter to the president of the Merril Lynch Ready Assets Fund in New York:

> Dear Sir:
> As your firm is now soliciting deposits from our trade area, we felt certain you would want to take your share of civic responsibility here in St. Joseph and actively participate in all the things that make our economy prosper, resulting in the production of the funds you solicit.
>
> Since a larger corporation such as yours undoubtedly operates on a strict budget, I am taking the liberty of assisting you in preparing your annual budget by chronologically listing the activities you will want to include in your program (for the coming year).
>
> JANUARY
> 1. Year's subscription to ten newspapers for the nursing home.
> 2. Cocktail party for farmers in conjunction with equipment dealer.
> 3. Annual dues for Rotary Club, Development Association, Farm Bureau, and other civic associations for your officers.
> 4. Annual contribution to local Boy Scouts.
> 5. Contribution to Cotton Producers Association to aid them at their annual convention.
> 6. Donation to high school band uniform fund raiser.
> 7. Donation to local DAR Chapter.
> 8. Purchase of 10,000 suckers for children of customers.
> 9. Send several officers to seminars to learn about Community Reinvestment Act.

The letter then lists February and March expenditures of a similar nature and concludes:

> I suppose you understand what I am talking about by now, so I won't spend any more time on this. Have to get busy with my program for the Rotary Club and be prepared to answer a lot of questions about Money Mutual Funds.
>
> Very truly yours,
>
> William W Watson
> President

Most bankers feel they are doing a reasonably good job of serving the community, keeping the economy viable, and supporting every charity in sight. Meanwhile outside competitors, both banks and nonbanks, come in and drain away the community's savings for investment elsewhere.

INTERESTS AND SELF-INTEREST

Mr. Watson's underlying point is: "If you steal all our money, how can we do the job we have to do in our communities?" There are several answers to Mr. Watson's implied lament. But on top of the list is the stark realization that a bank cannot be all things to all people when the public is so interest-rate sensitive. Banking could fully serve its community. The local bank could pay for band uniforms and nursing home subscriptions and all the rest. But it could do this because the depositors of the bank in some ways were subsidizing the bank in the same way the bank subsidized the community.

Implied in the acceptance of savings rates on core deposits or no interest at all was the feeling that making a bank deposit was serving the community indirectly through the bank, that the bank was a conduit for the funds to community services.

The saver no longer feels this way. If told that his failure to keep funds in home area will lead to less ability of the bank to serve the community in the numerous ways Mr. Watson lists, the typical saver is apt to reply: "Well, tough for the bank, and tough for the community. I want top dollar on my money." And if the bank has fewer and fewer core depositors subsidizing its community service, it can no longer continue to give this service.

This does not mean that a bank should give up altogether on the type of activity that Mr. Watson describes. There are many times when there is real value to the bank in them.

Enlightened self-interest is the key. If aiding the Rotary Club or the Boy Scouts leads to a stronger community that can generate new deposits for the bank, then the expenditure is worthwhile. Similarly, if the bank finds that its public service does draw in and retain deposits and inspire people to keep money at home in reciprocation for the bank's aid, this is a valuable use of bank funds too.

However, the real key in Mr. Watson's letter is that each charitable expenditure and community service contribution must be examined to see if it really does help the bank and is not carried out simply through a sense of tradition.

18-3 COORDINATE CHARITABLE DEDUCTIONS

To organize and rationalize their policy, aware bank managements have begun to coordinate all charitable contributions, no matter how small the amount. A budget is made up in advance, listing major contributions to be made during the year, minor gifts, and any other charitable contributions the bank wants to make. Exceptions and new requests then must all be channeled through one knowledgeable individual, who can determine whether this new contribution is really worthwhile for the bank.

The result can be a major saving of bank funds without any loss of the real friends that contributions are intended to develop, or any slight to causes the bank wishes to encourage and support.

Banks also find that the amount of time devoted to community projects can get out of hand. A senior banker in a moderate-size community may find himself on a dais three or four nights a week. Frequently he is also wondering what he is doing there eating rubber chicken and smiling at a group of people in the audience who probably are the same ones who were at the meetings he attended each of the last three nights for different causes. Sure, most, if not all, of this is done on personal time. But the bottom line is that it wears people down and makes them less effective as bankers and as people.

Some bankers have warmed to the jocular suggestion that the bank give its chief operating officer (CEO) the title of "Assistant Cashier and CEO" so he can go home at night, while someone else—with the title of "Chairman" or "President"—represents the bank on various platforms. While this may be a little too obvious, some banks have solved the problem by hiring a prominent community figure whose task it is to represent the bank at various civic and charitable functions.

Other banks question the value of these social functions altogether. They are willing to put in time on committees to help get the new hospital wing, the airport expansion, and the like. But they feel that sitting on the dais at the ceremonial dinner afterwards is not necessary. They also feel that while some would see this as denying them the credit that they and their bank deserve for the work they have done, the key people will also have been on the working committee and will know what has been accomplished and who deserves the credit.

Sometimes charity becomes a competitive matter among banks, with one bank serving on a committee or contributing to a cause because the other bank is doing it. This soon becomes a zero sum game as everyone gives up too much time and money.

Therefore, top bankers are reexamining their contributions of time and money with an eye toward greater selectivity and better targeting. This squares with their efforts to be more selective in deposit solicitation, lending, and the other areas of banking in this era of intense competition for survival and profits.

PART 7 The Bank Board— A Hidden Resource

The Board of Directors of a bank—any bank, large or small, money center, regional, or community—is a resource that can be of great assistance to the organization. This is not as true in other business firms. But a banking institution is unique in the world of business, and so, to a great extent, is its board.

Unfortunately, in too many cases, the bank board is a hidden resource. Or it is underutilized. And, sad to say, the bank board in some instances may be weak and of little consequence because of the kinds of people who are members.

Fortunately, all those problems can be corrected. The right kind of people can be chosen. After all, membership on the board of directors of a bank is an honor. The board should be brought into the mainstream of the organization, with the skills and knowledge and contacts of the members put to good use. The combination of an excellent staff, an effective management team, and a wise and capable board of directors makes a banking institution almost unbeatable.

19 Making the Board More Effective

One of the most potent bank resources that all too frequently is left to lie dormant is the talent and abilities of the bank board. More often than not the board member does little but come to meetings and rubber-stamp the decisions of management.

Many board meetings are almost ludicrous. Material for the meeting is distributed shortly before the appointed time, so that not too much advance study of the data can take place. And once the meeting starts, matters are rammed through like the proverbial steamroller.

The board thus does little to determine the course of the bank. And board members themselves often feel that their role in furthering the bank's goals is slim indeed.

This is not only a sad waste of board time, it is a terrible waste of bank potential. Directors can and should do a great deal to chart the course of the bank, and to make sure that the CEO and his officers are doing the job the bank needs done.

One can see why board members accept this minimal role. They have been picked by the CEO himself in many or most cases. Thus they fear that if they make too many waves, they will not be renominted in future years. Hence they go along with this don't rock the boat philosophy out of fear of losing their seat on the board. Because of this, the position they do fill is of far less value to the bank than it could be.

Then there is the tremendous *potential* liability a bank director has. There are countless stories of board members being held personally liable when there is a problem in the bank that the board should have seen and handled.

Ignorance is no excuse under the law. As Harry Truman pointed out, "The buck stops here." Problems that require reimbursement to the bank of funds because of improper action, or failure to act, can quickly become the personal financial problems of board members.

Maybe most directors try to forget their personal liability, or feel that the assessments and charges to board members by bank regulators that they read about can never happen to them personally. But down deep every board member knows the liability he or she really faces.

Yet few people turn down board membership. As one bank analyst put it so poignantly: "If you are a garbage man, you are a garbage man. But if you are a garbage man and a bank director, you are something in the community. You are one of the town's leaders."

The fact that banks are seldom turned down by those asked to be board members makes the board's potential for service to the bank extremely high.

The bank can garner the best talents of the community to its ranks through the offering of board membership.

Most banks do have top-quality boards. They include the business and professional leaders of the community.

What then is the missing link? Why are these board members, who are so anxious to serve the bank, frequently so ill-used by the bank itself in planning and in enhancing the effectiveness of day-to-day operations?

THE NEED FOR COMMUNICATIONS

There are many banks in which the answer to this question is a sad one: The ineffectiveness of the board stems from a fear of the CEO and his top staff that the board will intrude and make too many of the bank's decisions if it is given more adequate knowledge of what is really going on. There is little that can be said in situations like this except that the CEO and other senior officers who fear their boards and try to keep them docile are frequently overreacting and are operating under a false premise.

Certainly there are individual directors who like to take over on occasion. But most board members are too busy trying to run their own businesses to run the bank part time too. When an individual does try to take over from his or her position as a board member, the rest of the board is quick to put these people down and remind them that the CEO and other officers were picked and paid to run the bank.

Drawing the assumption then that bank executives and the board *want* to work together to get the most out of the board's available talents, the reason the board accomplishes so little in many situations boils down to a lack of communication. Put simply, no individual board member can do the job he or she is sworn to do, and is able to do, when the total commitment and source of imputs is reading a data packet delivered once a month and a two-hour meeting in which a great deal of perfunctory material must be handled and voted upon.

As a result many top banks are trying to make outside directors far closer to the staff through informal meetings, luncheons, dinners and breakfasts that keep individual board members posted on what management is thinking about on a more frequent and informal basis. Some board members do not have the time for this. But the ones that do find that their effectiveness as bank directors is boosted tremendously when their weekly schedule includes meeting the CEO or one of the bank's officers where ideas and problems are discussed informally.

Another result of these meetings is that directors find that board membership becomes a two-way street. In addition to learning what top management is thinking about, board members also find that they are able to provide inputs to management that might be considered impertinent or out of place if provided at a regular board meeting instead of in this informal manner.

Equally important are the meetings that board members can have on an informal basis with officers below the top. Frequently the board member can serve as a kind of communications link between the CEO and his staff, a link that may be difficult for the CEO and his officers to establish directly between themselves. One of the real worries of good CEOs is that the staff of the bank hates to come and report on unhappy developments because of the fear that "the King will kill the messenger who brings the bad news."

There is a reticence of officers to talk to top management openly about bank problems that results in the type of isolation that can be truly damaging. A bank board member sometimes can serve as the link that bridges this gap.

OMBUDSMAN

In addition, the board member can serve as the communications link between the bank and the community.

Directors are picked because they are leaders in the community and know how and why it functions. They should be able to use this same ability to see where their bank does and does not fit into the community's infrastructure, and where it fails to fill community needs.

In most banks, the board is used as an arm for marketing—looking for business and talking up the bank. But there is not enough use of the board as an information "feeler"—serving as the eyes and ears of the bank so that its role in the community can be more effective.

Sometimes a bank that sees it is lacking in some area in its service or operations finds that by having a task force that includes both directors and officers, or even only directors, can get to the bottom of what is needed much more effectively than when the job is done only by bank officers. Often the latter are too close to day-to-day operations, and too defensive of present practices.

This task force approach gives the bank added talent to do the job. It also makes the board feel that they have an active role in determining policy instead of just reviewing what has already been decided. And it makes board members who do take an active role in the task force feel far closer to management and the bank, and much more willing to work harder in their advisory and marketing roles.

SPECIALIZED EXPERTISE

Board members often have individual skills that can be of tremendous value to the bank.

A bank may be considering a loan for a technical venture. If a board member is an engineer trained in this area, he or she can be of real value in helping determine whether that venture has a chance of being a success or not, something the bank's loan officers could not determine themselves because of less technical training.

Similarly, an individual may be a specialist on the community where an understanding of what ventures may succeed or fail can help the bank avoid difficult.

DRAWBACKS AND PROBLEMS

What are the major drawbacks and problems? There appear to be three in number;

1 Conflicts over power: Bank executives and board members must make sure they are not in conflict over running the bank. The board must recognize that its ideas are advisory and that day-to-day operations of the bank belong with the officers hired for that purpose. This does not mean a rubber-stamp board. But it does mean that the CEO's wings should not be clipped by powerful board members who like to do things their way.

2 Security: A board member must have the security to know that his or her tenure will not be ended if there are any objections to management's decisions or policies. The nominating committee for reelection to the board should be outside-board-member-dominated, so that directors are confident that if they are doing their job to the satisfaction of their colleagues on the board they will not be booted from their posts because of an honest disagreement with management. This gives board members the backbone to do the job they are sworn to do.

3 Be active, not just honorary. Board meetings are not just a nice place to go once a month to break the monotony of retirement. (Some banks make directors retire from the board when they retire from their own businesses.) The board must look upon the responsibility and opportunity as a trust that must be followed with energy or surrendered. With the honor of being a board member comes both liability and also a responsibility that must not be forgotten or allowed to backslide.

But if these three caveats are remembered, the board can be one of the top resources of the bank.

20 Responsibilities of a Bank Director

Responsibilities of bank directors

To a large extent, the responsibilities of being a bank director are individually determined—each director must look at his or her role in the bank from the viewpoint of answering two questions:

> Am I doing all I can to help this bank prosper and serve its community, its employees, and its shareholders?
>
> Is there anything I am doing to take advantage of my responsibilities and opportunities as a bank director so that I am favoring myself personally over the bank's posture in any dealings with the bank?

As shown earlier, there is always a question as to whether the bank director is being favored in a transaction over someone who was not a director, or whether the bank is offering a director preferential rates and terms because of his board membership status.

One answer to this might be to simply decide that bank board members should not do business with that bank, but rather should do their banking elsewhere. This would avoid all possibility of conflict.

Actually, this has happened in a number of institutions. Both the executives and the directors have tried to keep the relationship between the bank and its board completely free of any possible taint by such a radical step.

But this hurts both the bank and its board members. Undoubtedly one basic reason why an individual was wanted on the bank board in the first place was because of the importance of that individual in town, because of his or her business connections and banking business, and because of the stature that comes to the bank from tying these key individuals in the community even closer to the bank by making them board members.

If a bank were to rule that its own board could not do any business with it, then both the bank and the directors would suffer. The bank would lose the opportunity to get the business, or keep the business, from the people in its community that management and the board felt were the top individuals in town. Moreover, by accepting the prestige and responsibility of board membership, the individual candidate for the directorship would also be forcing upon himself the necessity of breaking his bank relationship and developing a new one elsewhere. This would be carrying the fairness doctrine to an extreme.

WHAT DIRECTORS SHOULD DO

What, then, are the rules a bank director should follow to make sure he is being fair to the bank, while at the same time not denying himself or the bank the opportunity of continuing a business relationship?

Charles Van Horn, former Regional Administrator of National Banks for the Second National Bank District, has helped the bank director solve this dilemma. He prepared a listing of the minimum requirements that he and supervisors of banks in general felt directors should meet in fulfilling their obligations as bank board members:

1. Provide for competent, resourceful executive officers, including successor management.
2. Know the strengths and weaknesses of the bank's active management.
3. Formulate clearly defined policies covering personnel, investments, lending, internal controls and other activities of the bank.
4. Effectively supervise implementation of board policies.
5. Attend regular and special board meetings and committee meetings.
6. Keep accurate and complete minutes.
7. Carefully review written reports submitted by various committees of directors.
8. Require and carefully review periodic management reports.
9. Examine the affairs of the bank, or cause the same to be done on your behalf by a competent independent accountant.
10. Carefully review, in detail, reports of examination submitted by supervisory authorities and outside independent accountants.
11. Take prompt, vigorous steps to strengthen weaknesses cited in supervisory reports.
12. Know the banking needs of the bank's service area and render the bank responsive to those needs.
13. Be familiar with banking laws and regulations, asset values, financial statements, capital adequacy, liquidity, and related matters dealing with policy formulation.
14. Maintain an unblemished personal and business reputation.
15. Refrain from self-dealing transactions and police your associates on the board.
16. Keep inviolate all confidential information relating to affairs of those who deal with the bank.

Summing it up, Mr. Van Horn concluded: "Directors must be enlightened and must be attentive to the affairs of the bank."

SELF-ANALYSIS

A director can look at these 16 points and begin to worry. He well knows the potential liability he bears, and that the responsibility of the bank director may bear no direct relationship to what he does himself. It is just as bad to do nothing and let the bank get into trouble as it is to take active steps that harm the bank for one's own personal gain.

The conclusion that screams for attention in Mr. Van Horn's listing is "be active or get out."

This, then, appears to be the toughest moral dilemma of the individual who has accepted a bank directorship or is contemplating the acceptance of a board membership.

It is not the matter of self dealing so much as it is the fear of "what do I do if I see things going wrong and find I am legally required to blow the whistle, no matter the consequences on bank management or the bank itself?"

Look at the various responsibilities listed by Mr. Van Horn. For each of them, the next question is: "Did I as a bank director follow up to make sure corrective action was taken or that matters were run well in the first place?"

This is not an easy question to answer. Reports of supervisory authorities, accountants, and of other board members involve criticism of management. It is top management that generally picked the individual for the board in the first place and gave him or her the opportunity for stature in the community that board membership provides.

"Do I have to be the one who hammers down and makes the CEO change policies he likes or even makes him resign after all he has done for me? Wouldn't it be easier just to sit back and let someone else do the dirty work?"

Unfortunately that is not the way the law is construed. Follow up and investigation, as Mr. Van Horn indicates, are the basis of the board member's responsibilities.

Look at point No. 15—the conflict of interest question. Here the basic conclusion is not just that the board member must keep free of self-dealing with his bank but that he has a responsibility to police other members of the board as well. Is it easy to come to a board meeting and complain that your neighbor who has been on the board with you for years is getting bank credit when his business is weakening and he really does not deserve it? Is it easy if you know that this can make or break your neighbor's enterprise? Is it easy to be man enough to place the impersonal institution ahead of a personal friend and to place pressure on management so that it makes sure the bank's interests are best served, even if the co-director who has worked with you for years is placed in dire circumstances?

However, this is what a bank director's responsibilities involve. And it has been failure to take such distasteful steps that a number of board members have faced legal action and even indictment by law enforcement agencies. Directors must be active watchdogs for the bank rather than passive determiners of policy who simply let management follow through.

Areas of Responsibility

The major areas of directors' responsibilities can be grouped into these categories:

- Directors must take measures to see that the bank is adequately staffed, that salaries are high enough to attract and keep good people, and that age differences between the various levels of officers are not so great as to cause problems of management succession.
- Directors must supervise bank loans to make sure they are sound and meet standards of the regulatory and supervisory authorities.
- Directors must see that periodic and careful audits are carried out so that the soundness of the institution is protected as effectively as possible.
- Directors must insure that the bank has sufficient capital to cushion deposits so that depositors' funds are maintained with as much safety as possible.
- Directors must see that the bank lends and invests its funds in a manner that provides adequate liquidity to meet unexpected deposit outflows and increases in loan demand that cannot be refused.
- Directors must insure that the bank is operated profitably, so that new capital can be generated and attracted, and so that depositors maintain their confidence in the bank.

These are clear-cut responsibilities and they need continual monitoring.

The individual who does not keep these goals in mind, both in his role as a director and in his secondary role as a director doing business with the bank as an individual, is violating his trust.

MAKING A COMMITMENT

These are several simple and clear-cut areas in which a bank director must be willing to make a commitment to his institution:

- An individual must be willing to learn about banking and follow his bank day to day, or he should not be a director.
- An individual should be willing and able to follow through with unpleasant tasks, even up to the point of firing management, if necessary to insure the bank's liquidity, capital adequacy, and continued ability to serve the community.
- An individual should be willing to take the difficult step of blowing the whistle on fellow directors and bank officers if there is a feeling that some other "insider" is taking advantage of his position to the detriment of the bank.
- An individual should realize that being a board member is neither an opportunity to become the local gossip column nor an interesting opportunity to pick up information on competitors. If he uses the material learned as a director to harm or help someone else, he is as guilty of violating trust as if he had tapped the till. And even if the sole motive for telling bank secrets, or secrets of borrowers who have revealed their positions to the bank, is to be popular because of what he knows and can reveal, this too is very wrong.
- Finally, if an individual looks at board membership as an opportunity to have a nice, interesting place to go once or twice a month after retiring from active business elsewhere, he could be violating sworn obligations.

To continue holding a position on the board after one's other business interests have ended is filling a place that could be held by someone else who could be more valuable to the bank. The result might well be that by staying too long, an individual could tarnish the reputation he had developed for loyal and devoted service to the bank built up over many years. This is why some banks have a policy of making directors into "directors emeritus" when their own business activities halt. In fact, many directors voluntarily remove themselves from active board membership, whether required by bank statutes or not, when their other business and financial endeavors slacken off or are terminated.

Bank directors should continually monitor the bank and its people, never taking anything for granted or feeling that yesterday's decision is adequate for today. What could be more typical of a resolve to follow such a policy than for a board member to monitor himself and determine when his value to the bank is beginning to wane?

21 How Directors Can Help Their Banks

In many cases, there is little bank directors can do except to ratify the effective actions by management. One bank chief executive officer (CEO) tells the story of when a director retired from his full-time business and was then removed from the board. (Bank policy was to have only people actively involved in the community serve as directors.) "The next day, the son of this director came in and pleaded with me: 'If you take Pop off the board, he will have nothing to do. He loves the board meetings.' "

In essence, the son wanted the bank to have its board serve as an activities center for a retired person rather than as the vital center of the bank.

These cases are the exception. Most board members do add immeasurably to their bank. They perform an extremely valuable function in giving the bank stature by having their names attached to it, just as the bank's name can give them stature.

To recap, it is not only directors' names that aid the bank, however. If a director is chosen because he is a specialized attorney, has technical expertise the bank could use, or has great political acumen and contacts, this can be extremely useful in helping the bank plan its operations to get the best performance in that community.

In many instances, this board member, because of his background, has a perspective that can save the bank some serious difficulties and embarrassments that could hurt its growth and bottom line.

Additionally, the board member can serve as a link between the CEO and his staff and the community. While many employees are afraid of talking honestly to the CEO, fearful they will be the messengers killed because they bear bad news, a board member can serve as an intermediary. The director can also learn what people in town think of the bank and certain policies and relay this information to the top brass. He can also work the other way, by explaining bank policies to the staff and the community.

In sum, the director can be the eyes and ears of the bank in the community and the eyes and ears of the community in the bank. Additionally, by thinking of the bank as he goes about his day-to-day business, he can make the talents that got him his board membership in the first place truly valuable to the bank and to the community.

GETTING INVOLVED IN PLANNING

Directors should become involved in the long-range planning functions. Here are a few questions board members should ask about planning:

Does the bank have quantified goals for deposit growth, loan expansion, income, expenses, and net earnings?

If the bank does have goals, on what basis were these goals developed.? Did a few officers just sit around and pick numbers that looked reasonable, or were the goals based on economic and market forecasts that could provide a firm foundation for meeting the goals successfully?

Are goals set too low so that everyone would look like a hero when the year was over? Board members should check on how other banks in the community or of similar size are doing, so they can determine whether the bank is really not taxing itself too much in its goals.

Does the bank have real plans, fixing responsibility, with reporting deadlines? If not, today's goal becomes tomorrow's waste paper. Board members also can make sure the bank has a program of incentives and penalties so that things happen after the goal has been set.

Can results be measured periodically and are corrective changes made when results fall short of the mark?

The board's members have the responsibility to provide a perspective as to where the bank is going. Otherwise they will have no choice but to come to the meetings and approve whatever has happened, following the old adage "if you don't know where you're going, any road will take you there."

UNDERTAKING PROJECTS

Board members should make sure the top executives develop task forces of board members to examine problem areas or to explore new opportunities. They cannot just walk into the bank and ask employees what's new. But if a task is assigned, then exploration does become part of the director's responsibility. Frequently, the exploration to prepare the report the task force is developing uncovers other material that might be equally interesting or even more important to the bank than the project originally assigned.

Some banks go a step further and rotate board members on and off the executive committee at periodic intervals, so they can have even more understanding of how the bank is running. This service on the executive committee makes the board members assigned to director task forces more valuable, as it is easier for directors to probe when they have spent time closer to the day-to-day working of the instituion.

If management arbitrarily repulses the proposals of board members, or downgrades the importance of what they are trying to do for the institution, then this could be the first place for investigation—to learn why management is so negative to the idea of an active board.

BRINGING IN BUSINESS

Any discussion of the functions of bank directors must include the role they play in business development. It is no secret that most board members and especially advisory board members are picked for the ability to generate business, and they know this. Undoubtedly, there must be some resentment among many board members who feel that their basic value to the bank is to generate business, and that their ideas of anything else, except how the bank can get more business, are placed on the back burner. But even here, if the bank works effectively and honestly with the board, there are ways in which the board can perform this function more efficiently and more satisfactorily to both parties. Here are some of the steps that should be taken:

Management should spend the time training directors on what services the bank actually has available and how profitable they are before the bank relies on board members to generate business.

How often has the top management of a bank sat in sadness as a leading board member has come in all excited about a new certificate of deposit or some other account he has brought in, when management knows that at that time (or at any time, for that matter) the type of business this director is bringing in is just not profitable to the bank?

Once the confrontation develops, the bank loses either way. If it takes the business, it incurs a possible loss to keep from embarrassing a director who felt he was doing the bank some good. If it turns the business down, it deflates that director, makes him look bad with his friends, and also insures that he will not be anxious to generate new business for the bank at a later date.

The bank can solve this problem by training board and advisory board members early as to what business is profitable and what is not. However, this training should be updated and altered as business conditions change so that board members do not work on out-of-date data in generating new bank business.

On top of this, board members need to be appreciated for what they do when they bring in profitable business. Some banks feel that incentive programs are beneath the dignity of directors, because they are being rewarded specially for what they should be doing in the first place. A vast majority of others, including the authors, feel otherwise. To reward people for what they do is important to all of us. We all appreciate recognition.

Thus, many banks have set up programs with special awards given to the board members who do the most to build the bank, who do the most in public service to help the bank's image, and who otherwise make truly valuable contributions to bank growth and prosperity. Special clubs for achieving directors and special trips for those who generate business (with more points by far awarded for highly profitable business than for marginal business, and no points awarded for expensive business the bank prefers not to have) have a decided value in encouraging bank directors to think of the bank and work for it.

Annual recognition dinners and placques can play a valuable role also. No matter how high our position in the community, we all like recognition, and especially recognition among our peers.

22 What Directors Should Not Do

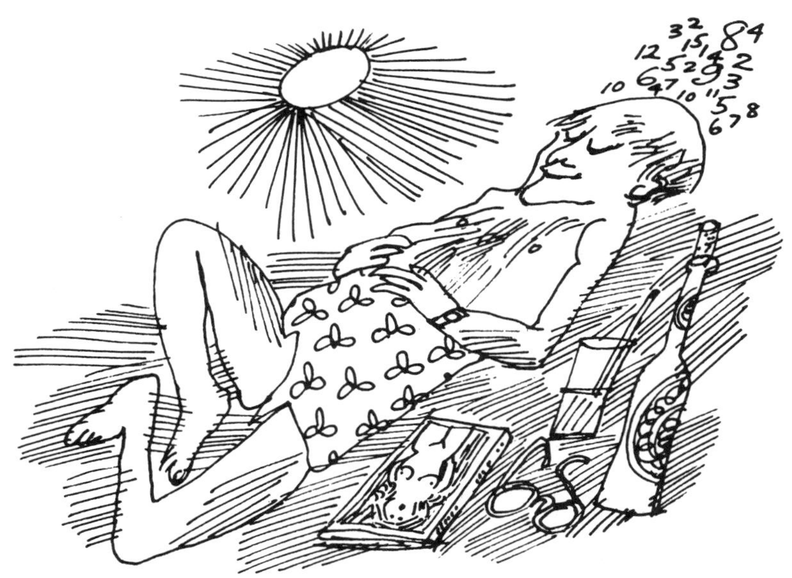

What directors should not do

If a director really wants to become involved in the bank, there is a lot he or she can do to help the institution prosper. Ironically, according to those with considerable experience, directors are sometimes most helpful by avoiding certain actions and attitudes. Here are a few "don'ts" for bank directors:

AVOID POSSIBLE CONFLICTS OF INTEREST

All directors recognize what conflicts of interest involve. As they become directors, they accept the fact they must represent the bank rather than themselves should there be an area of conflict between serving two masters. Even so, many directors let conflicts or potential conflicts of interest develop when they could be avoided.

For example, requests for loans for oneself or friends can easily lead to conflict. Bank officers have a difficult time being as tough or demanding on terms and rates for a director as they normally would be. If at all possible, directors should keep the pressure on management for credit to a minimum—and keep demands for preference out altogether.

Equally difficult is making sure other board members are not granted favors because of the friendship that has developed while serving together on the board. The director must walk a fine line between hurting the bank by not giving it his borrowing business and hurting the bank by seeking favoritism. A good board member must learn how to walk this fine line.

AVOID USING INSIDE INFORMATION

What happens at bank board meetings is not public information. A board member who uses inside information on his competitor's credit needs to further his own business interests is involved in just as much a conflict of interest as a director-borrower demanding preferential terms. Rather than take a risk of this nature, the board member who sees a competitor's loan coming up for review should absent himself from the discussion.

Equally bad is the use of information gleaned from the board meeting as idle gossip or to make interesting party conversation. What happens at directors' meetings should remain there. A blabbermouth can harm his or her bank as much as a poor lending officer.

AVOID DUCKING UNPLEASANT DECISIONS

The most important job a director has is making sure the banks' top management is capable. If the board is unwilling to fire or even criticize the chairman or the president, should circumstances warrant, who else will? The reason board members are so frequently subject to shareholder suits today is because they have the ultimate responsibility for the bank's operation. If directors avoid making decisions because they would be unpleasant or would harm old friends, then they would be violating the oath they took when becoming directors.

AVOID MAKING THE DIRECTORSHIP AN INTERESTING DIVERSION FROM BOREDOM

Far too many people have stayed on bank boards after their real usefulness to the organization had passed. They probably were picked for the board because of some position in the community or because of their stature in business. Once they have retired or otherwise given up their position of prominence, they should consider resigning from the board and letting someone else fill the place.

If a board member looks forward to board meetings as an opportunity to get out of the house or to bridge the gap between work and retirement, then the bank is being used as a recreational vehicle, not as a way to serve the community and the shareholders of the bank.

23 What Directors Should Know About the Balance Sheet

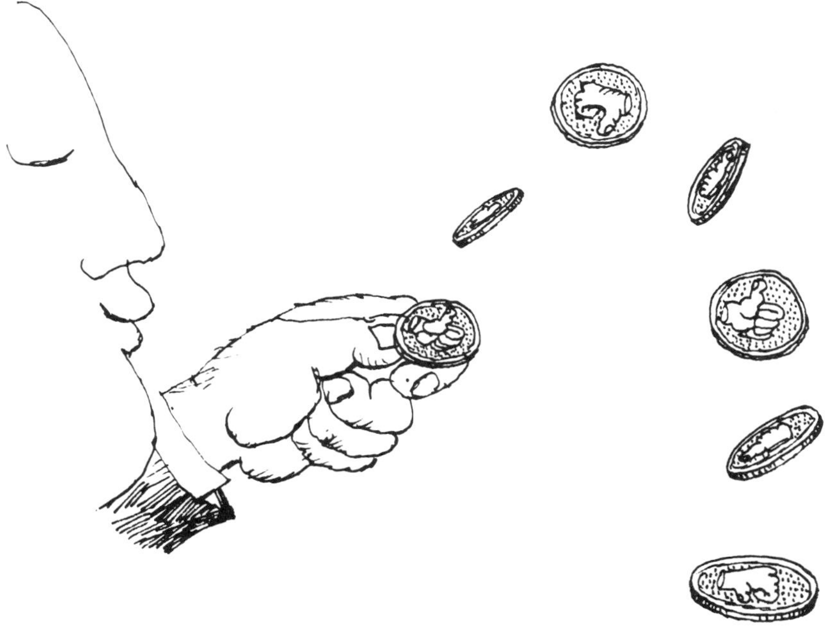

What directors should know about the balance sheet

The more a director knows about his bank, the better he can perform his functions. The problem is that often neither the board nor the bank's top officers know where to start in giving the board a better understanding of what a bank is and how this particular bank is doing.

There must be a starting point that will generate the questions that board members can use to probe into bank policies. And the most obvious starting point available for a deeper understanding of what a bank is and how an individual bank is operating is the bank's own balance sheet. This can tell more about the bank than any other document. A quick examination of what a balance sheet shows should enable any bank director to ask more of the right questions.

What is the balance sheet of a bank? As with any other corporation, a bank actually owns nothing. Every cent it has has been provided by someone. And the balance sheet therefore has a liability side, which shows who provided the money, and an asset side, which shows how each cent has been used. Going down the balance sheet, you can tell a lot about a bank's policies; for what is more critical in analyzing a bank than a picture of where it got its money and how it is using it?

Let's start on the asset side and see what we can learn.

CASH AND DUE FROM BANKS

Cash and due from banks is the picture of the money the bank has either in vault cash or on deposit at other banks.

Vault cash is a simple item. Most banks do not have too much vault cash on hand, as this leads to security problems. And they also try not to have too little, as that could lead to embarrassment when people come in to cash checks; you can't ask the customer to wait while you send a teller across the street to the A & P for some cash.

Far more significant in this category is the money in other banks. This is demand deposit money as a general rule, and it earns nothing for the bank.

Naturally the bank has to keep reserves at other banks and this is a large part of the due from banks item. If the bank is a member of the Federal Resesrve System, this deposit will be at the Federal Reserve Bank of the region. If not, it will be in some other commercial bank. But in either case, the bank earns no return on this money and therefore the deposit should be kept close to the legal minimum.

In a number of states, non-member banks may invest part of their required reserves in government securities that pay interest. If your bank is a nonmember in one of these states, such a policy should be undertaken, as deposits left in other banks earn nothing.

On top of required reserves, banks leave money in other banks as correspondent balances to compensate the other banks for services provided.

Here is a point for deeper analysis by board members. If the bank has an inordinately high cash and due from banks position, higher than the percentage of assets represented in this category in the average bank, then it is keeping more at correspondents than other banks do. This does not mean this is necessarily a waste of bank opportunity for profit. But it is a red flag. If the bank has a very high cash and due from banks total, board members should question whether the bank is getting its money's worth from correspondents. For if high balances at correspondents are a result of tradition rather than the result of services provided to the bank, the board should demand a reexamination of the entire correspondent balance question.

What should a board member do? He can ask what required reserves are. Then he subtracts these from total deposits at other banks. And if the remaining total is pretty high, he should question why the bank keeps so much money in other banks. The answer is likely to be a satisfactory one in most instances. But that should not keep board members from asking the question.

SECONDARY RESERVES

Reserves at the Fed or in correspondent banks and vault cash are not liquid funds available to meet deposit outflows and increases in loan demand. If a deposit is withdrawn, the bank still has to keep reserves to back the remaining deposits.

A secondary reserve of liquidity is not located anywhere in the balance sheet specifically, since it may consist of short-term loans, short-term investments, or both, and the balance sheet only breaks down assets by type rather than maturity. But a board member should ask his management team if the bank has adequate liquidity to meet deposit outflows that can normally be expected and if it has enough liquidity to meet loan demands as they develop.

Both of these are vital questions. The bank that is not liquid enough to meet normal withdrawals of funds is in serious trouble. The Federal Reserve will help it out temporarily if it is a member. But if a bank must turn to emergency fund sources like the Federal Reserve for a considerable amount of money or period of time, the regulators will impose restraints on the bank and may even press for basic changes in policy.

As for the bank that does not have enough liquid funds to meet loan demands, this is equally serious. For, as will be shown directly below, the bank that has to turn down good customers when they want loans will not be likely to keep those customers for long.

LOANS

A bank is in business to make loans. If a customer wants a loan and the bank offers instead a safe deposit vault or a checkbook with a picture of a bagel on each check, the customer will leave in disgust and take his trade elsewhere. Customers maintain bank relationships because they want to know that when they need credit accommodation, this bank will provide it. If the bank is not liquid enough to meet its customers' loan demands, the bank will quickly lose those customers, and through word of mouth, it may also lose other good customers who feel the bank will let them down, too.

One sign of a good bank is one that is making loans to its customers.

This can be carried a step further. The bank that is not making loans and instead is squirreling away funds in investments of cash is also harming its community and thus is hurting the community's potential for growth (and the potential for growth in bank deposits too).

One of the main functions of a board of directors is to be the contact between the bank and the community. Board members try to generate local business for the bank. But a good board member should also look at the linkage the other way and consider that one of his responsibilities is to make sure the bank is thinking of the community's best interests too.

The loan-to-deposit ratio can serve as a good starting point for a board member's inquiry as to whether the bank is doing the job it was chartered for. If the ratio is low, board members should be prepared to find out if management's reasons for the low ratio are good ones.

INVESTMENTS

Since a bank is in business to make loans, the investment portfolio, other than the part that comprises secondary reserves, is a residual use of funds.

As a residual receiver of funds, the investment department receives its money when loan demands are weak, interest rates are low, and bond prices are high. It also must sell bonds and give the money back to the lending officers when loan demands rise, even though this is the time when interest rates are rising and bond prices are falling.

A board member should not be surprised to see his bank lose money in its investment portfolio. But the board member should also be prepared to inquire as to the bank's policies on investments in the expectation that the bank will keep its bond losses to a minimum.

Thus, an inquisitive board member should question whether the bank actually coordinates its expected loan demand trends with its investments, so it does not have to take big losses by selling illiquid long-term bonds to meet loan demands that were not planned for.

Also a good board member should understand the workings of tax laws that allow banks to take bond losses as deductions from normal income for tax purposes. Since the federal government is willing to absorb half the loss on bonds that are sold at a loss, there is no reason why a bank should not take advantage of it. This means that banks with bond losses should sell these bonds and save the taxes instead of just sitting with the depreciated bonds waiting for them to recover and not having the government take a share of the loss.

There are reasons why some banks cannot take tax losses at certain times, but the board member should inquire as to why if his bank is not taking them and he should be sure that management's reason for not doing tax loss planning is a satisfactory one.

BUILDING AND EQUIPMENT

Finally on the asset side (aside from minor items) the bank has its building and equipment. Again while there is not much a board member can say about this, there a few exceptions.

First, does the bank have too much invested in buildings? If it does, and if the result is that the bank has too much of its money in illiquid assets (since buildings are the least liquid asset a bank has) then the board member should ask about a sale-leaseback of the building as a means of replacing an illiquid asset—the building—with a more liquid asset—first the cash proceeds of the sale of the building and then the loans and investments that can be made with the proceeds of the sale. This can reduce the bank's need for expensive capital.

A board member should also be sure that the bank is not placing too much of its funds into a new building, with the goal being a monument to the present CEO when in reality the bank could get along with a smaller new building or no new building at all. This is especially true now that more people are banking by mail and through the use of new electronic remote tellers. Again the balance sheet and a comparison of how the use of funds in building and equipment in this bank differs from that in other banks can serve as a first step to the development of some pointed questions on the effectiveness of bank management and policies.

DEMAND DEPOSITS

Analysis of the liability side of the balance sheet can also determine whether the bank is doing its job. Demand deposits used to be the lifeblood of the bank. Now more people place their funds into time and savings deposits to gain the yield. But if demand deposit growth is slower than in other banks and the percentage of demand deposits to total deposits is lower than in other banks, the board member can ask why.

It may be that the bank has too high a level of service charges. Or else, the bank may be sloppy or a poor marketer. Or it may be a sign of strength, that the bank is so strong a competitor for time and savings deposits that proportionately it has a lower level of demand deposits than other banks do.

But again, the rate of growth from year to year and the percentage composition of demand deposits, when compared with the figures on those categories in other banks, can give the board member a place to start his inquiry.

TIME AND SAVINGS DEPOSITS

Again, what is the relative posture compared with other banks? Some banks, for example, are not aggressive competitors for time and savings deposits because they want to attract the demand deposits of savings banks and savings and loans associations. If this is the case, the percentage of time and savings deposits to total deposits will be below that for other banks and with good reason. If, however, the percentage is below that of other banks and there is no good reason, then it is time for the board member to probe further.

CAPITAL AND SURPLUS

Here a bank faces a tug of war. If it has a low level of capital to deposits, it has good leverage and this should aid profits. For the bank has more deposit funds at work per dollar of shareholders' investment and each shareholder should far better. On the other hand, the lower the capital-to-deposit ratio, the less protection for the bank's deposits.

Thus, the board should question extremes. If the capital-to-deposit ratio is higher than in other banks in the area, the board can question why the bank is so unaggressive and whether it can do something to improve leverage and augment shareholder earnings.

Conversely, if the ratio is low, the board must question whether the bank is providing enough cushion for deposits.

The second question is tougher to deal with than the first. If a bank is overcapitalized, the board should be in concert with management to improve deposit levels, maybe increase dividends, and in some way improve leverage.

If, however, the bank is undercapitalized, this can be sticky. For naturally, the lower the capital, the higher the return per share. But if the bank uses this leverage as the basis of its profitability instead of stressing a good return on each dollar of assets used, then it is leaving itself open to a sharp decline in profitability if the regulators then tell the bank that it must raise more capital and the favorable leverage position is wiped out.

In other words, if a bank is a good earner, but the balance sheet indicates it is leverage that causes it rather than the profitable use of funds on hand, then the bank is an accident going some place to happen. Regulators can force banks to reduce aggressive leverage of capital to deposits, which can end this source of profitability quickly.

Finally, with regard to capital, the board should question management if it does not utilize debt capital as a source of capital funds. The use of subordinated debentures and notes gives the bank the opportunity to have its cake and eat it too. It serves as new capital, but since it is borrowed, it is not equity and does not dilute the shareholders' ownership position.

Again, management may have a good reason for not using debt capital—such as an inability to sell it at the time. But if the bank just doesn't use it without having a good reason why, the board member has another place for serious probing of bank policies.

A FIRST STEP

The balance sheet is like the pretty face. For it can attract attention to questions and policies in the bank, and it can lead to deeper probing of the management's policies and the actual operations of the bank.

Of course there are many times when the questions brought up by superficial balance sheet analysis will be poor ones, or will be quickly answered by management to everyone's satisfaction. But balance sheet analysis remains a first step for the board member who really wants to know what is happening in the bank. It is far better than just sitting at board meetings and hoping that management is telling the truth to the people who have the ultimate responsibililty for the bank's survival, safety and prosperity.

24 Facing Sensitive Issues

Bank directors generally find that their responsibilities can be handled as they handle other business responsibilities.

Yet, every once in a while, the members of a board find they are forced to face extremely difficult questions. These problems frequently involve basic disagreement between a board member or members and top management of the bank. At such times, board members must choose between disagreeing openly with the very people who most likely nominated them for the board, or keeping quiet and letting something they feel is wrong go through because they don't want a rift with management.

More than a few bank boards come into conflict with management. Consequently, directors of other banks must wonder at times how they would handle a similar conflict were it ever to arise in their bank. Some of the questions board members worry about include:

Can we disagree with management and still be renominated?

As bank directors look at difficult issues that must be decided at their meetings, they cannot help but remember that most likely it was top management that suggested them for board membership in the first place. Thus, the board member worries about what will happen if he or she disagrees with what management wants to do.

Yet the board member knows that if he disagrees openly with management policy recommendations too often, he is likely to see his name removed from the slate for renomination, and his days as a board member will be numbered. He wonders just how independent he can be without jeopardizing his opportunity to remain on the board and to continue to enjoy the honor and excitement that board membership can bring.

Can the independent board members get together privately?

All too often outside directors find it difficult or impossible to meet privately just among themselves. A private meeting of outside board members could air topics that might be too embarrassing to bring up in the presence of top management. But it is difficult for an outside director to organize a rump session of the board without the news getting back to management and therefore without his being considered disloyal to the organization.

Efforts of independent board members to get the outside directors together without management present have often split a board and caused disharmonies that can never be healed. The result frequently is a showdown, after which either top management is forced to resign or else the board members who wanted to introduce management criticism are forced to leave.

How can a fellow board member be refused loan requests?

Potential director criticism is not always aimed solely against management. A board member or members may find good reason to take issue openly with the requests of a fellow director for excessive amounts of credit, or for credit on terms too favorable to that director and too unfavorable to the bank.

If a board member's loans get into difficulty, the proxy may inform the entire shareholder list and the community just how much of the bank's money has been loaned out to insiders, and just how favorable the terms have been on the loans he has received.

Other board members who see such loans come up at their meetings may desperately want to deny them. But again they are stopped by the old boy network of privilege that generally involves other board members accepting the requests of a fellow director desiring credit, if top management agrees. In such instances, a board member is forced to approve loans that in his heart he knows should not be placed on the bank's books.

How can a fellow director be dropped if he is ineffective, wrongly motivated, or disruptive?

Board members may look at one of their fellow directors and wish he or she could be removed from the board. Sometimes the reason is because the individual has become senile and uses the board as a social club and a place to reminisce about his career of days gone by. In other cases board members feel that the director in question is merely using the bank's board as a means of gaining inside information on the community, or on his competitors, that he then can use in his own business. Or the person may just be negative and disrupt proceedings with his attitude of "never do something the first time."

How can top management replacement be initiated?

Finally, and most difficult of all, is the question of what a board member should do if he or she ever really feels that top management needs to be replaced? There is nowhere to turn other than the board if the bank is doing poorly, and Truman's "the buck stops here" certainly applies to the dilemma a board faces if management is not up to standard.

It is extremely difficult for individual board members to bring up the topic of replacement of top management or to start gathering other board members into a group interested in the president's or chairman's ouster.

These are some of the tough questions a bank director might face. If he does face them, it is not enough to turn the other way and say: "This is none of my concern, all I do is ratify what top management decides." When trouble strikes, the board is the bank. And the courts have placed responsibililty for problems directly on the board since they have had the ultimate power to handle the difficulties as they arose.

WHAT CAN BE DONE

There are few good solutions to the potential problems outlined above. Understandably, most directors hope and pray they will never be in the spot of having to decide on any really messy internal issues. Indeed, they probably won't. But there are some standard procedures a bank can put in place to help insure that if a director does develop serious misgivings about the way things are being run, he will have the opportunity to express them to other board members without the embarrassment of defying top management face to face at an open board meeting, creating a rift that is almost impossible to heal.

Some policy suggestions board members have found effective are:

Nominate one outside director as the spokesman for all independents.

If the board picks a truly independent director and designates him spokesman for the outside directors, this does not give him the opportunity and the responsibility to call up individual directors or call meetings to discuss issues too touchy for general board meetings.

Establish a policy of secret ballots on sensitive topics.

If the bank board must decide on loans to other directors, or if it must approve or disapprove a top management policy that is controversial, the board can put it to a secret ballot. This would allow independent board members to vote as their consciences dictate without having the embarrassment of disagreeing with management or voting against a fellow director openly. In certain cases, board members might be surprised to find how many other directors agree with them on touchy issues but who are also afraid to vote openly against friends and against a management that might drop them from the board.

Appoint a majority of outside directors to the nominating committee.

This protects the director openly opposed to various management policies, assuming of course that other board members like his suggestions and feel his comments involve constructive criticism.

Talk privately with regulators.

A board should have a policy of open discussion with the regulators if certain members feel bank policy is incorrect, but have been outvoted or if the issues have not been brought to a vote. If no open discussion is possible, the director should talk privately with fellow members. This may seem like being a tattletale, but the point is that if the bank does get into great difficulty, all the board members are held responsible and they can lose both financial wealth and their stature in the community.

25 How Is the Bank Doing?

It may come as a shock to some bank directors, but the basic goal of a bank is profit!

Were any other industry to be analyzed, this statement would not need to be made. Most industries are exceedingly profit-conscious. Banking, however, all too often has been less clear in its goal.

One cannot blame bank executives for a lack of fixation on the profit motive. After all, banking does have other publics in addition to its shareholders to consider.

If a nonfinancial company goes out of business, few are hurt except the employees and owners of the company. If a bank goes out of business, all depositors are hurt, as is the community that depended on it for credit accommodation.

Thus, bankers generally see their role as serving three publics: the community, the employees, and the shareholders. And a bank director generally feels that he, too, has these three publics to consider as he makes his judgments on bank policy issues.

Unfortunately far too often bankers have not placed profit high enough on the list of goals of the institution. Size has been the test of banking, and profit has taken a back seat—far, far behind.

Still, profit must be the prime concern of a bank. Sure, bankers like the ego satisfaction of being the largest or the fastest growing institution in town. But it is for profit that the bank was established. And the bank that does not earn a profit does not have the ability to grow. Retained earnings provide the basic source of capital to back bank deposit growth. In addition, the bank that is not a good earning institution finds it difficult to raise new capital from the outside. An unprofitable bank is an unhealthy bank, no matter what it says about achieving other aims. This should be recognized by every member of the board of directors and should be the basic motivation behind every action he or she initiates or approves.

MEASURING PROFITS

How can a board member determine if his or her bank really is profitable—or is profitable enough?

Most banks earn an operating profit every year, which is unlike virtually all other industries in which there are bound to be companies that may lose money from time to time.

The reason banks generally earn money, except at times of heavy defalcation, or unusual loan losses, is that the regulatory authorities want it that way. The number of banks allowed in any community is limited, even when state law permits unlimited branching, so that established banks do not face ruinous competition. The regulatory authorities keep constantly in mind the fact that if a bank does fail, the community is badly hurt. It is not only the bank's employees and shareholders who suffer.

However, the fact that most banks show a profit every year makes it hard for board members to determine whether their bank is doing as well as it should. It is more difficult to determine whether a bank is earning as much as it could be than it is to determine whether operations are satisfactory in non-financial companies where earnings are more volatile.

This determination is made even more difficult by the fact that bank earnings per share generally rise year after year after year. And to an outsider, the fact that earnings per share are rising generally serves as one indicator of a well performing bank. Yet here is the first place where bank directors should be on their guard. For earnings per share can be the great American tranquilizer that hides the true state of a bank's performance.

EARNINGS PER SHARE

The basic problem with the earnings per share concept is that every year a share represents a different amount of bank capital than the year before. For example, if a bank has shares of stock that represent exactly $10 of capital each, and the bank earns $1 per share after taxes in a year. The bank has earned 10% on capital, or $1 per share.

If the dividend is 50¢ a share, the next year each share of stock represents $10.50 of capital. If the bank has a worse year and only earns 9.8% on capital, the earnings per share rise to just under $1.03 a share, for each share represents more capital than the year before due to earnings retention.

Thus the director who looks only at earnings per share relaxes confidently with the knowledge that EPS rose. But really his bank is earning less on capital than it did the year before.

Does this mean that earnings on invested capital are the basic test of a bank's profitability? Here the answer has to be the typical economist's response: yes and no.

The answer is "yes" for this reason: earnings on invested capital (that is, on equity capital) are the basic test of how well an organization of any kind—bank or non-bank—is doing with its investor's money.

The shareholder invested to earn a return. And earnings on his capital tell how well the individual corporation is doing in using the shareholders' funds.

In banking, for example, the average bank earns around 9 or 10% on invested capital after taxes, and well-performing banks earn upward of 14 or 15% on capital after taxes.

Again, a director would deceive himself to take earnings on invested capital as the only measure of bank performance. This is because one of the most significant factors in determining the return on invested capital a bank earns is the amount of leverage the bank has.

If, for example, one bank has $5 of capital for every $100 of deposits, it is far easier for the former bank to gain a good reteurn on invested capital than it is for the latter. The bank with the 5% ratio of equity to deposits has $20 of deposit funds working to earn a return for each dollar of equity, while the bank with the 10% ratio only has $10 working for it. If each bank earned equally well on total assets available, the bank with the greater leverage would obviously earn almost twice as much on its invested capital as would the bank with a greater capital base, but the same earnings on assets.

Well, then, why doesn't return on invested capital serve as the sole test even if it does reflect different leverage postures? After all, if one bank is able to generate leverage while another does not, shouldn't this be considered as much a sign of good performance of the leveraged bank as would be a better return on assets?

The answer here is that there is a question as to whether the bank will be able to remain highly leveraged. If a bank becomes sloppy in its return on assets because it is highly leveraged and is able to boost its return on invested capital through this leverage, it may well be riding for a fall. If the regulators come in and tell the bank it is undercapitalized and needs more capital, then the bank will quickly find that its earnings plummet. The high earnings of the past had not reflected a good performance in utilizing funds, in keeping costs down, and in developing spread management; rather, the good returns of the past will have reflected the leverage and the leverage alone. Once the high leverage is removed by the infusion of more capital, the bank's earnings will decline sharply.

Therefore, a director should look both at earnings on assets and at earnings on capital.

If earnings on bank assets are about 1 per cent per year after taxes, it reflects a fairly good earnings position. If earnings on invested capital are about 14 or 15 % per year or more after taxes, this also reflects good earnings.

What does it mean if the bank earns well on capital but poorly on assets? It obviously means the good return on capital is the result of high leverage, and that the bank is susceptible to a sharp decline in earnings if the regulators demand a capital infusion. This is a sign of danger.

What if the bank earns well on assets and poorly on capital? This is a sign of a well-run bank that is overcapitalized. The emphasis of the directors should thus be on utilizing the excess capital to generate new business in order to take full advantage of the bank's strong ability to earn a return on assets employed.

Naturally if the bank earns poorly on both assets and capital relative to the standards, then a deep overhaul of both asset and liability management and capital management appears necessary.

SOME WORDS OF CAUTION

If would be dangerous for a director to look at these numbers as an automatic goal without moderating them by the individual circumstances of his bank and its community.

First, it will be noticed that return on capital was defined as return on equity capital. Debt capital is part of bank leverage; and to the shareholders, all they are interested in is how effective the bank is in utilizing the funds they placed into the institution. If a bank has debt capital, so much the better. It is a sign of effective capital management that improves leverage without causing the regulators to worry about the bank's ability to back deposits with capital.

But as far as shareholders are concerned, they are interested in how well the bank is using their funds. So return on equity is the true test to the shareholder.

Second, bank directors can compare their own banks with other banks in their region by looking at the Federal Reserve Board's Functional Cost Analysis reports. These give the averages of the various banks of similar size in a region with regard to costs, returns on assets, and net earnings.

Again, caution is advised. These functional cost analysis studies are merely a starting point; they are not a be all and end all.

An average is only an average of figures for the various banks of the community or state. It does not, by itself, indicate that the average bank is good in its performance. It may well be that the average bank is rather poor. And the bank director who rests on his laurels because his bank is above average may be missing a real opportunity to prod his institution into far better earnings.

These studies do serve as a decent starting point to determine whether there are special circumstances in the community or region that should make all banks in the territory either better or worse earners than the national averages.

Finally, earnings of various banks can be distorted by the decisions the bank makes on investment portfolio switches and tax swaps.

A bank that is truly aggressive in its approach to earnings may well have a lower net income level in one year than does a bank that is phlegmatic about earnings. The aggressive bank will realize its losses on depreciated bonds, take the tax savings available because the loss can be deducted from normal operating income in determining tax liabilities, and then realize higher earnings over the years ahead by reinvesting the proceeds and the tax savings in new, higher yielding securities.

What the tax swap impact on earnings implies is the same warning that applies to all ratios and numbers: they are merely starting points for deeper investigation. But at least they *do* lead to deeper investigation. And the bank director who does not start with some bench marks and then work from there to see if his bank is really performing well is missing a major opportunity.

It may be a bank will underperform against the guidelines or the average bank—but with good reason. At least the director can understand why this is so.

Or it may be a bank is average when there is every reason to feel it should be above average. The guidelines can serve as a taking-off place for examination of this possibility.

No bank can be run to meet a hypothetical return on assets, on capital, or on anything else. But these guidelines can be a starting point for the conscientious director seeking to determine how well his bank is really doing.

PART 8 Looking Ahead

Just a generation ago, based on what had gone on before, it would have been relatively easy to predict what might happen in banking 10, 20, even 100 years in the future. Yet, unquestionably, a good many of those predictions would have been way off the mark.

Look at what has actually happened to banking in recent years. For example, two of the the most important developments in banking and finance—the NOW account, which has given us interest on checking accounts, and the Automatic Teller Machine (ATM), which provides us with geographic mobility—would have been difficult to determine back in the 1960s.

Both of these advances were developed by individuals who found ways around restrictive laws. The NOW account was the way in which R. W. Haselton of the Consumer Savings Bank in Worcester, Massachusetts, found it possible to offer checking accounts to his depositors when state law said that they were illegal for savings banks. And John Dean of First Federal Savings & Loan Association of Lincoln, Nebraska, found that he could provide new convenience to his customers by having the clerks in the Hinky Dinky Supermarket chain provide the same banking service in that company's many stores that his tellers could provide in his association's lobby—thereby inaugurating the whole structure of remote banking that has so swiftly led to today's nationwide ATM networks.

The objective here, however, is to look ahead, not backwards. Perhaps the only thing that can be stated with any degree of certainty is that there will be change—tomorrow, next year, and 100 years from now. To put it more forcefully, change will be a constant in the banking and financial services industry.

But generalities such as that are of little value. More specific predictions are called for. And these views and predictions could be woefully wrong. Which brings up a story told by Marcus Nadler. It seems there was the chief of an African nation who was to make a major address about his country's economic resources the following day. So he asked his administrative aide:

"How many elephants do we have in our country?"

"It would take 10 years to find and count them all," replied the aide.

The next day, the chief stood up at the meeting and stated:

"One of our greatest resources is the 4,500 elephants we have in our country."

"How did you find out so fast?" the aide asked in amazement after the talk was over.

"You said it would take 10 years to find the correct number," he replied, "so it will take them 10 years to disprove my figure. And on 10 years I'll take my chances."

It is in this spirit that we move along and attempt to give some indication of what banking will look like in the year 2001 and beyond.

THE STRUCTURE OF BANKING

The difficult, challenging, exciting years ahead are likely to witness the development of two disparate directions in banking structure: the creation of nationwide giant institutions, and the thriving of small, independent banks that serve a particular market.

Both of these structures appear to have a decided need in our nation.

The interstate giants are developing, either directly or indirectly, through linkages and purchase of nonbank organizations by banks and purchase of banks by nonbank institutions. And they are serving the nationwide companies that need nationwide banking.

It is crazy that major companies need to work through so many banks to handle cash management and other financial activities that could be concentrated in one institution. As nationwide financial institutions are developing they are beginning to provide the geographically broad banking service that large companies want and need.

Conversely, the individual American still wants a bank in which the officer on the platform faces the arriving customer, knows him or her by name and announces: "The answer is 'yes' now what do you want?"

Both types of institutions should be able to operate and thrive side by side. All the talk of the giant banks eating up the little ones and leaving the nation with a handful of humongous institutions will slowly disappear as community banks continue to prosper.

Structure will change in one major regard, however: all banks will have to provide more services. And most of the financial institutions that are not banks today will become just like banks, or become actual banks, as time passes.

The public is becoming less willing to continue to have to go to one type of institution for one financial service and to another for a different financial service. Little by little banks, thrifts, credit unions, brokerage firms, and the like will all be allowed to take on each other's coloration until the public will find little or no difference between financial institutions in form or function. It will be pricing, the service provided, and the convenience and willingness to help that will differentiate institutions in the eyes of the general public.

FINANCIAL SERVICES

What type of service will the financial institution of the next 100 years provide? The answer is simple: more than today.

The basic account likely to be perfected is the equivalent of today's cash management account that provides banking, brokerage, real estate purchase and sale finance, and every other financial need under one umbrella account. People should not have to spend so much time juggling money between accounts to cover their various financial needs, and the account of the future will eliminate this mess.

Will the community bank be able to provide this same type of full service account that the giants do? The answer is an unqualified yes.

Between facilities managers, correspondent banks, service bureaus, and the microcomputers that have made electronic financial service so readily available, all institutions will be ready, willing, and able to provide a full menu of financial service to customers. This will allow people to reduce the amount of time they spend handling financial affairs.

In this regard, the true paperless society will develop—something that has been talked about for decades, but that has been extremely slow in coming.

With the ever-falling cost of handling data electronically and the soaring cost of paper handling and processing, financial institutions will price their services so as to induce the public finally to accept the end of the paper trail on many of their financial transactions.

Bill paying, something which takes up so much time and provides so much of the cross-flow of first class mail in the nation, should slowly slip into the history books as electronic and automatic means of moving funds from account to account are utilized. And the public's preoccupation with banking will be reduced to such a point that banking will truly be looked upon as a utility like the electric company, whose services are mandatory and dependable. As a result, banking will receive little conscious thought from the public on a day-to-day basis unless something happens to interrupt the delivery system.

THE ROLE OF GOVERNMENT

With financial institutions becoming almost automatic in their handling of varied financial affairs, there will be fear that government will encroach to tell the banks what to do even to a greater degree than at present. The prevention of this intensified intervention by government is a job that all bankers will have to give major attention to as the concentration of banking powers develops.

It is up to bankers to make sure that they do not abuse the power that comes to them through the control over the data of an indivdual's full financial life. It is up to banks to insure that the data they have is used only for the customer and not used to monitor his life or give marketing organizations an insight into the individual's habits and activities that the individuals do not want them to have. If banking fails in this regard, then the Big Brother concept illustrated in George Orwell's 1948 novel, *1984*, will begin to come true, and banking will be the loser. If government does encroach to a greater degree on people's habits and private data, it will undoubtedly be largely achieved through far more control over the data that flows through our financial institutions.

Otherwise, regulation of financial institutions in the twenty-first century should witness a trend away from governmental control and to more reliance on free market decision-making of the type we have generally called deregulation.

Most parts of society operate far more efficiently when the private sector must compete in the marketplace than when government tells them what to do. In banking, as in trucking, airlines, and many other areas, there will be more reliance on marketplace decisions, as interest rate ceilings disappear, as institutions are allowed to compete with one another to a much larger degree, and as institutions that are not managed properly are allowed to fail to a greater extent than in the past.

The good news of deregulation is that there will be a more efficient financial structure. The bad news is that there will be far more risk in owning and operating a bank than has been the case up to now.

If bankers agree with this forecast of lessened governmental regulation, and feel that banks will be more on their own, then they should look at all the ways in which government intervention affects operations today in order to be prepared to operate profitably without such restraints tomorrow. In every area—from relaxed capital requirements to no interest rate ceilings—reduction of government interference means that an institution must earn its business through good service, acute pricing, solid reputation, and returning to the basics of prudent banking and business operations.

BANKERS THEMSELVES

Finally, what kinds of people will banking require in the year 2001? Here, too, change is a factor. The days when bankers were a breed apart are already over. Banking used to be an industry in which background, stature in the community, and knowledge of the right way to do things were keys to success. Now, banking has entered the business jungle with all other industries. Bankers must be as sharp and well-versed in the ways of the jungle as other business people must be.

Bankers will switch in and out of the industry far more than in the past; for banking will involve technical skills similar to those of other industries. Many of the banks that have done well in today's environment have been ones that have looked at a bank as similar to any other industrial operation—but paper rather than a hard product.

The key factor for success, though, will remain people and knowing what the customer wants. But the banker who considers himself or herself a breed apart, who is guaranteed success simply because he or she works for a bank, is an individual of the past and the kind of person one who will be around far less in the coming years.

Our nation is changing. We had a noble experiment with trying to do everything for everybody. But we have found that this does not work. Nor does it work in banking. Basic competition and survival of the most efficient will be the key to successful banking, as it is and will continue to be in virtually every other industry.

Gone are the days when banking was a "license to steal" and the big event of the day was the luncheon appointment. Every phone call can change a banker's life, and his institution's structure and viability.

To people who happen to be in this industry at the present time, it makes the profession of banking far more exciting than it has been at any time in the past.

Certainly some of the above statements will be proven wrong—and may well be proven wrong in far less time than the 10 years allowed for the counting of the elephants. They are, however, the trends that can be predicted by looking at what is happening to banking and to the public's need for banking service today.

One forecast can be made with certainty: Banking will continue and will continue to change. The industry will be in a perpetual state of flux that will challenge all banks, and all those trying to take away banking's business, far more in the years ahead than was ever the case in the past.

It really has become a banking jungle. But with the right tools and the right attitudes, it is still possible to get through relatively unscathed.

Appendix I. Organization and Structure

ISSUES IN BANKING

A CONVERSATION WITH C. C. HOPE

This interview with Mr. Hope, former vice chairman of First Union Bank, Charlotte, North Carolina, took place about a year after he had served as President of the American Bankers Association.

MR. MILLER: You have been on the road quite a bit for the American Bankers Association. You must have a fairly good idea about what is troubling people in the banking community.

MR. HOPE: This past year, about 95% of my time has been involved with the ABA. I've been in all the states, the District of Columbia and Puerto Rico; and I've spoken at 50 state association conventions. And that doesn't include all of the meetings I've had with bankers and with other groups.

I had one trip in Ohio where I started in Columbus. I went to a midwinter meeting of the Ohio bankers there. I rented a car and, from Wednesday through Friday, I traveled 700 miles by car in Ohio visiting with bankers in different towns. I went to Lima, Ohio, met at the bank there, went out through the community to see some of the people in the town—business people that the bankers suggested I visit. Then I went from Lima down to Hamilton and did the same thing—lunched with some of the bankers there, talked with some of them and their directors; and then from there to Finley, and then to Fostoria, and then to Fremont, meeting in each town with bankers at either luncheons, dinners, or breakfast meetings. And then we went to Youngstown and did the same thing. I did the same thing in Indiana; went down to Seymour, Indiana, up to Anderson, to Bluffton, in addition to Indianapolis. This involved going around and meeting the bank officers and saying, "What's troubling you in this state? What are you concerned with?"

MR. MILLER: One of the criticisms of ABA has been that they represent the big banks. Your actions tried to counter that.

MR. HOPE: Whenever I had an opportunity to be with bankers, I wanted them to know that there was a voice for all segments of banking, and this voice could only express itself if it understood what their problems were. I was at a meeting in Ohio, in Columbus, at one time, with a number of bankers in the room, and they said, "Why do you think you could represent us as president of the ABA? You're with a holding company that has 185 branches, about $3.5 billion in resources." I replied, "Well let me tell you where I come from, and then you'll have to decide whether I can understand your problems and represent banking. My story is that I started in a bank that was $35 million in size in 1947, and that bank at that time had no branches. It operated only within the city of Charlotte, and it had been in business since 1908. Since that time, I've had the opportunity to help that bank grow and to grow with that bank."

MR. MILLER: Back in 1947, that $35 million bank was not a small bank.

MR. HOPE: It still was not a large bank, you know, and even though we are a large bank now, we are really a series of a lot of small banks. In our complex of banking, in our bank, we have banks ranging from $10 million in size in the communities that we represent.

What I was attempting to do was to get out into places like Centre, Alabama, spend the night there and talk with the people, go into the bank and sit down with the president of the bank, see the customers coming in and see a few of the directors, meet the employees and go out in the community, sit down in the local cafe and have lunch, and just get the shirtsleeve feel of what went on in Centre, Alabama.

MR. MILLER: What does go on in Centre, Alabama?

MR. HOPE: Well, the people there have direct contact with the president of their bank. They can walk into the office of the president of the bank and apply for the smallest to the largest loan. They share their hopes for their farm or their business, small business or large business. It began as a small thing, but it's growing into sort of a crescendo: Banking has changed so much, almost within the last 36 months, moving from a business where these people in these small and medium-sized towns had so much direct contact and with customers, gave almost full time to their customers' desires and needs. Now, just a few years later, these same executives in these small banks are finding that they're being smothered with paper work and regulations, and it's removing them from the firing line of the bank; they're having to place this direct contact in the hands of other people so that the management of the bank can spend more time answering the call for all this detailed administration.

MR. MILLER: What new laws have come along that you feel are causing this?

MR. HOPE: ERISA, CRA, FIRA, Truth-in-Lending, of course. All this has changed the relationship between the banker and the customer, not just in large institutions but perhaps even more in the small institutions, where the bankers are required, instead, to sit down with you as a customer from across the desk and say, "Sure, you're applying for this $1,000 loan, and so forth, and sign here." Now it involves more documentation, more maintaining of files to prove that everything was done on a basis that didn't discriminate in any way, and that everything was done in a way that completely meets all the requirements of the new regulations for disclosure.

MR. MILLER: Weren't there problems? Weren't customers sometimes being discriminated against before the laws came along? Were customers getting all the information they should have?

MR. HOPE: I have never, in all the research that we have done, seen the documentation that showed that this was a major problem in banking. As in any industry, you can dig out an example of a problem here and there, but that doesn't mean that the industry was riddled with those problems. But, as a result of a complaint here and there, Congress jumped into the situation, and the regulators implemented these new restrictions that add, really, not only to the burden but to the cost of banking for the people of this country. Untold millions of dollars have been added to the cost burden. Now, I believe it takes some 31 steps to make a mortgage loan—67 pages of documents. Consider all the requirements for maintaining a proper relationship between members of the board and the banks—it's discouraging a lot of people, particularly in the small banks. On board membership, it's causing them to give serious consideration to how much they want to continue to put up with. Everywhere I've gone, banking people have said, "Go to Washington and tell them to cut federal expenditures." This didn't just start with Reagan, you know. It's been going on out in the grass roots of this country at Chamber of Commerce meetings and at town hall type meetings in high school auditoriums and civic centers for several years, and it's been getting louder and louder.

When I speak anywhere in the country and begin to talk about doing something about the regulatory burden, I'm interrupted more with applause for statements of that kind than on any other topic. It seems that the whole country has become aware of the burden of overregulation and, in sort of a frustrated way, really doesn't know how to do anything about it except to express themselves in a forum and try to get somebody to carry their voice back to Washington.

The biggest problem is that once a law is on the books, and once the regulators are required to implement that law, how do you get Congress to turn it back? How can you get something repealed or removed or amended? That's a major burden.

MR. MILLER: But isn't it more than that? For example, the Fed is looking over all its regulations, throwing out some that don't mean anything any more except extra paper work. So it is looking at what it is doing as required by law, but it's looking at what it's doing and simplifying things. Couldn't the other regulators do that, too?

MR. HOPE: Well, they do that to the extent they possibly can. The Comptroller has been doing that kind of thing. And I believe the FDIC has stated that it is trying to do the same. But in a number of areas there are major things that cannot be changed without a change in legislation. It is particularly in those areas dealing with reporting and disclosure where it is difficult to get things changed. Congress might say, "We need this to protect the consumer," and in many cases consumer groups support the regulation. We do not, as an industry, want to be obstructionist to something if it is really needed. So we must walk a tightrope to make certain that some of the reforms that are being called for aren't really needed.

MR. MILLER: All right, let's take Truth-in-Lending, which has been around for a few years. Apparently, there was some sort of a need for a truth-in-lending law, because people were not given, in all cases, precise information on their loans. Then along came Truth-in-Lending, which is probably one of the most complex laws ever written, with all sorts of regulations involved. That's been simplified to an extent; perhaps it ought to be simplified more, but Congress is working on that; it has moved in the right direction on that.

MR. HOPE: Yes, and I think you have used a good example of where we didn't give up and continued to focus the spotlight on the abuses of that law. I think that all we've done to simplify that has gone quite a long way. You know, all of this goes back to a couple of meetings that made a major impact on my thinking. One was the International Monetary Conference. I was President-elect of ABA at the time, and I went to the IMC. There were 150 bankers from the 150 largest banks in the free world. And those top international bankers talked for three days about the same three subjects—inflation, energy, and overregulation.

MR. MILLER: The United States isn't the only place concerned about these problems.

MR. HOPE: We sure aren't. I said that meeting made quite an impact on me. Then about two months later I attended another meeting called the meeting of Felaban, which is the federation of Latin American banks, outside of Saõ Paulo, Brazil. There were 200 Latin American bankers at that meeting, from Mexico and Argentina, Brazil and Ecuador, Chile, Peru, and other countries. These bankers, believe it or not, talked about the same three subjects—inflation, energy, and overregulation.

I came back and I continued my travels around the country, and this commonality was beginning to emerge. Bankers were concerned with energy, but not so much as an industry problem. They were concerned with inflation as a national problem that also affected the industry in which we work. And they were very much concerned with overregulation. As I began to move into the job of President of ABA, and had meetings with the senior ABA staff and with the Board, I asked, "Why don't we take on these national issues as the ABA? Why don't we try to do something about these issues that we see emerging around the world and in our own country? To the credit of the bankers and the ABA staff, they agreed with the suggestion. We, as an industry, as an organization, did take on the battle of inflation and deregulation. We formed the two task forces. We found that there was a charged-up desire to have some impact on these national issues of inflation and deregulation. As I look back at where I've been for the last several years, I can't help but think that our industry has moved itself a long way in a very responsible manner to take on these battles.

MR. MILLER: Let's talk about high interest. What is banking doing to try to keep control of interest rates?

MR. HOPE: The high cost of money, or the interest rate structure, is a result of inflation, not the cause of it. It has to do with supply and demand. If we continue to have a massive vehicle like the federal government spending billions upon billions of dollars more than it's taking in, utilizing the credit markets of this country to a greater and greater extent to finance this deficit, it's going to continue to drive up the cost of money. That's why we must have this change in the attitude of Congress about spending.

MR. MILLER: Aren't some of the banks, some of the smaller banks, also concerned about such things as interest-free checking; and either being gobbled up or put out of business by the larger banks? Aren't those major concerns?

MR. HOPE: Let me put into perspective what their concerns are. The predominant concern of the smaller banks has to do with the competitive climate in which they see themselves beginning to operate today, and it's a new climate.

MR. MILLER: If we're going in the direction of competition, of allowing banks to meet the competition and so forth, we're also talking about getting rid of or modifying the McFadden Act and/or the Douglas Amendment?

MR. HOPE: There is much talk about this, pro and con.

MR. MILLER: And that's going to bother the small banks.

MR. HOPE: You asked if that was the issue today, and I wanted to put it in perspective, and I was talking to the competition first. On the matter of the McFadden Act, I don't foresee any change any time soon. That's the branch banking act. But on the Douglas Amendment, I think that we're going to see some change, and I think that, most probably, instead of seeing it come out of Congress, the change will be made by various states staying within their own boundaries: They probably will make it a reciprocal deal for anyone who wants to come into a state with bank holding company branches. That's the way I look for this to begin to open up.

There are no defined ways that we're going to go on this issue. However, there are many bankers who feel that we ought to at least begin to discuss it, and who believe that valid and intelligent judgments can be made if we gather in all the facts and all the resource data and look at it and then decide how we want to go as an industry. I have confidence that when that is done, we will make the right judgment, I don't believe that the Congress is going to do anything on this McFadden-Douglas business unless there is a strong industry-wide desire to do something. With 14,700 banks, to get a consensus that something in this field ought to be done will take a lot of analysis and thought.

MR. MILLER: But while this analysis is taking place, you might find some of the banks in the states working through their own state legislatures, doing just what you're saying.

MR. HOPE: As you know, Maine is one state that has passed a law that they will do this on a reciprocal basis. Other states, including Delaware and the Dakotas, have taken steps to open their borders. And I think that you're going to see the same in some other states around the country—in fact, we know that other states are already trying to get their legislatures to consider passing reciprocal legislation. And I think that, in all probability, that will be the way it will go rather than with some national thrust.

MR. MILLER: However, the end result will be somewhat the same, even though there is no consensus, even though Congress doesn't do anything.

MR. HOPE: If Congress doesn't do anything, there will still be some states that will pass reciprocal legislation, and if it begins to break down in a fragmented way, it could well be the least controversial way to go.

Appendix II. The Human Side of Banking

INSIGHTS—KEEPING BANKING UNION-FREE

A CONVERSATION WITH JAMES B. CLARK

Mr. Clark is counselor at law with the firm of Yauch, Peterpaul, and Clark, in Springfield, New Jersey.

DR. NADLER: Is unionization a real fear in the banking industry today?

MR. CLARK: Yes, I think it has to be a real fear in banking because of the change in the atmosphere in the United States. We have changed from a society that produces goods to a society producing services. As a result, blue-collar employees have been reduced in numbers and the unions have lost membership as a proportion of the total working population in the United States. Unions are looking for new areas to organize. In New Jersey, for example, we have had organizational efforts among white-collar employees in the banking field by the Office and Professional Employees International Union, Local 153; by the United Food and Commercial Workers Union; by District 65, the Distributive Workers of America now associated with the United Automobile Workers; and also by Working Women, a nationwide organization that has attempted here and there to try to organize. Other unions, including the UAW itself, have indicated that they will try to organize white-collar employees.

Now, if you look for concentrations of white-collar employees that are not organized, the one group that you will find that stands out like a sore thumb is the banking industry. When you turn on a light, you draw bugs; a lot of these banks are very progressive, they are moving ahead, they are in the forefront, they are in the limelight, unions look at them and feel they are an excellent target to organize.

DR. NADLER: Why has banking remained nonunion for so long? After all, someone working in a grocery store earns double what a teller does, and yet the banks haven't unionized.

MR. CLARK: I think there are several reasons. First, the banks are so diverse insofar as the location of their personnel is concerned. The bank might have ten to fifty branches, along with several separate departments. As a result of these various locations, with small numbers of people, it becomes a little difficult for the unions to go out and try to organize one branch, another branch, and another branch. They need a lot of organizational personnel to cover all of those branches. There often is not one big concentration of employees. Second, banks have a great number of female employees, with many of older age, who really are not interested in a union. They are interested in having a job close to home that they can leave at 3:30, 4 P.M., go home and take care of their children. Quite frequently, it's a second job in the family. Such people are not that interested in unionization.

DR. NADLER: With the changes in banking, using the computer and the automated teller machine for the routine operations in the branches, and concentrating talent at headquarters offices, means that the industry is going to be even more susceptible to unionization.

MR. CLARK: If there are greater concentrations of personnel in one location, I would agree. But with ATMs, there are fewer personnel in the branches, maybe more in the computer operation, but I'm not sure that increased unionization will flow from the greater computerization of the banks.

DR. NADLER: Do you recommend to the banks that you work with that they avoid having too great a concentration of people in one spot?

MR. CLARK: Yes, I do. I prefer that they have it as diverse as possible and as widespread as possible, but all under interlocking supervision with an interchange of personnel. Now I might point out that a union can only organize an appropriate bargaining unit. An appropriate bargaining unit is a grouping of employees that has a community of interest, one with another.

There have been some cases before the National Labor Relations Board, for example the Wyandotte Savings Bank in Michigan, where the NLRB held that an individual branch of a bank was an appropriate bargaining unit. That bank had about fourteen or so branches, and there were nine separate NLRB elections. In other words, in nine separate branches, they had elections and the vote was 4 to 1, 3 to 1, 7 to 3, etc. That case presents a problem, even though the court reversed it. I do recommend that the bank become diverse in its personnel so that it doesn't have too big a concentration in one area. You still want to have a community of interest among the various branches so that no branch is standing out by itself and can be picked off by the union. To avoid that, there are certain legal considerations that the bank must look into to protect itself.

DR. NADLER: Could you go into that briefly?

MR. CLARK: A community of interest is a grouping of similarities in terms and conditions of work among employees. For example, all of the employees have the same basic salary structure, they have the same grievance procedure, the same pension, welfare, holidays, vacation, life insurance, profit-sharing, etc. They are all subject to the same general supervision. They interchange jobs; they are interrelated in their jobs; they are interdependent; no one stands out there by himself and does his own thing. Now, the more of these similarities in terms and conditions of work that you can develop, the greater becomes the bond between the employees and the various branches of the bank. And the greater the bond, the larger is the appropriate bargaining unit. In the Wyandotte case, where the NLRB determined that an individual branch is an appropriate bargaining unit, the board looked to a few items. One was, in a word, the autonomy of the branch manager. So in order to overcome an individual branch being an appropriate bargaining unit, we have to be sure that the branch manager does not have autonomy. And looking at the autonomy of the branch manager, we want to be sure that the branch manager does not do his own thing when it comes to resolving grievances. He doesn't receive a grievance, resolve it, and go from there. He ties himself in with the rest of the bank, talking to the personnel department and the operations department about the resolution of the grievance before taking action. Another thing with regard to autonomy is you do not want to have a branch manager in a situation where he determines what type of discipline to give in a particular situation. The discipline for specific situations should be similar throughout the bank. So he ties himself in and he gives up a little bit of autonomy with regard to discipline.

The third area that the Wyandotte Bank case looked at was the evaluation of employees. If the branch manager is solely responsible for evaluating his employees, and then based on that evaluation they receive a wage increase, the Board says he is autonomous insofar as that particular aspect is concerned. To avoid that, the branch manager again should try to draw in personnel and operations when he makes up an evaluation of an employee because that eventually is going to trigger the employee's wage.

There's one other aspect that's important and that is the interchange of personnel. If there are fifteen branches, personnel in the various branches should have the opportunity to move to other branches or to the main office. This may be done by posting jobs and giving promotion opportunities; or there may be a group of float tellers that fill in for vacation, sickness, etc., floating out of the main office into the various branches. These two areas of the movement of personnel, the promotion and the float tellers, bring all of the branches together into one big bargaining unit. It is important that the bank have as big a unit as possible. The bigger the unit, the better the chances for the bank to win. The smaller the unit, the easier it is to be picked off as far as the union's concerned.

DR. NADLER: Who determines what the bargaining unit is? The National Labor Relations Board?

MR. CLARK: Yes. What generally happens is the union will try to organize a particular area of the bank. They may take a branch, a department, a division, or the whole bank. They then go to the NLRB and file a petition for an election. That petition must be supported by 30 percent of the employees that the union contends are in the appropriate bargaining unit. The petition is then sent to the bank, and the Board phones the bank, asking the bank to come to an informal conference at the Board's offices. At that informal conference, the NLRB talks with the bank and the union to determine what is the appropriate bargaining unit. It will try to cajole the parties into agreeing on the appropriate bargaining unit. If the parties do not agree, the Board then holds a formal hearing to determine the appropriate bargaining unit.

Generally speaking, an appropriate bargaining unit in a bank would be called "office and clerical employees." Office and clerical employees are a broad-brush approach to including such jobs as: chief clerks, head tellers, tellers, vault attendants, secretarial types, and file clerks. It might even include messengers, although messengers would have to be specifically mentioned to be included. It would also be necessary to specifically include some groups of personnel in the computer center. Excluded from that bargaining unit of office and clerical employees are maintenance and service personnel, executives, professional employees, supervisors, watchmen, and guards. "Supervisors" is an interesting category in this whole problem because there is a definition of supervisors under the National Labor Relations Act that says that a supervisor is anyone who in the interest of the bank has the authority to hire, fire, promote, lay off, recall, settle grievances or effectively recommend any of those things, or a person who in the interest of management has the authority to assign work. While who are and who aren't supervisors is generally no problem, there are always some people in a gray area. For example, the third person in line in the branch administration might be a platform person or a platform officer. We may think they are supervisory, but they may not fall in the category of supervisors as defined. There are some cases where those persons are included in an appropriate bargaining unit as office and clerical because they are not supervisory.

DR. NADLER: Let's say a union comes in and wins an election with a small group like one branch or one group of clerical people. Will that be the one rotten apple that spoils the barrel? Will the whole bank then have to be run differently if there's a union in part of it?

MR. CLARK: Yes, it will have to be run differently. If the bank has a union in one branch of the bank, the concern is that unionization will spread to the rest of the bank, and the bank tends to isolate that union by giving greater benefits and greater attention to the other branches of the branch. You have to match and try to beat the union contract negotiated in that one branch in order to keep it isolated in that branch. Interestingly, at the Wyandotte Bank it lost three branch elections; the bank took a hard-line position during negotiations. As a result, the union had to call a strike to flex its muscle; and the bank took the strike. Obviously, the union wasn't likely to walk away very quickly. So what it did was picket—not only the three branches that were organized by the union, but it hired college youngsters to picket the main office of the bank and various other branches to bring pressure to bear on the bank. The bank withstood all that and the negotiations did not result in a contract. In essence, if a bank loses to the union in one branch, the union does not have tremendous strength because it has only one out of maybe fifteen branches. It is possible to negotiate the union out of the branch by taking a hard-line position in negotiations; and be willing to undergo the possibility of a strike. However, you have to believe that if a union is going to be so embarrassed by a bank, the AFL-CIO, the building trades, and every other union in the area is going to run to its assistance.

DR. NADLER: So once you've got a union in you've got troubles. Is that it?

MR. CLARK: That's right. There's only a couple of ways of getting a union out. There can be only one election before the National Labor Relations Board each year. That means, if you had an election today and the union won, there could not be another election for a year. During that one-year period, the union has the opportunity to negotiate a contract. It has a license to negotiate a contract. If the union is successful, the contract will then bar an election by the National Labor Relations Board for a period not to exceed three years. So with a three-year contract, there can be no election for three years. Now I don't intend to mislead anyone into believing that it's easy to throw the union out. Generally speaking, to get a union out, there has to be a spontaneous effort by the employees themselves to have an NLRB election; under the law, management cannot be behind it, they cannot push it. Another way to get the union out is to negotiate and take a hard-line position the way the Wyandotte Bank did and force it to a strike or conceivably force the union to walk away because it's not economically feasible for it to continue.

DR. NADLER: What does that mean? That they would not recognize the union?

MR. CLARK: No, because of the certification by the National Labor Relations Board after an election, the union must be recognized. But when the union sits down to negotiate, it will ask for several things. The first item on the shopping list will be what is called a union shop. A union shop is a provision in the labor contract that says all employees must join the union after 30 days of employment. Now, if some employees voted against the union, the bank doesn't want to force everybody into the union. But that is the bread-and-butter issue for the union. Forcing everybody to join means everybody pays dues. So the union probably will strike for that.

DR. NADLER: How can a bank win a strike like that?

MR. CLARK: It's not too difficult to win a strike in a small group because when employees go out on strike, there are certain rights that management has. In the state of New Jersey, for example, an employee doesn't get unemployment benefits when he is out on strike. In New York, he doesn't get any unemployment for the first six weeks. Also, when a person goes out on strike, the bank will immediately cease paying the employee. The bank will also discontinue the employee's Blue Cross, Blue Shield, major-medical, life insurance, dental coverage, prescriptions, eyeglasses, etc. In addition, when the employee is out on strike, the bank has the right to replace that employee. In other words, the bank can hire somebody to fill his job. When the unemployment rate is high, people want a job, even if it means crossing a picket line.

But let's assume the strike goes on for two months, and let's assume that there are ten people in that particular branch that the union organized and eight went out on strike. Two employees did not strike and eight replacements were hired. When the strike is over, these strikers come back and say they made a mistake and they are ready to return to work. The bank tells the employees there are no jobs for them; replacements were hired. The bank says all it can do is to put the strikers on a preferential recall list. When an employee goes out on strike to support his demands, he is called an economic striker, and the bank can replace that person permanently. He is only then recalled if another jobs opens up at a later date. However, there is another kind of a strike called an unfair labor practice strike. If the bank has violated the law and if the union takes the employees out on strike because of that violation, there's an unfair labor practice strike and those people are protected. When the strike is over, those unfair labor practice strikers have the right to get their jobs back, and any replacements hired by the bank must be dismissed unless the bank can keep everybody on.

DR. NADLER: The question of course is, what are these unfair practices?

MR. CLARK: You must bargain in good faith with the union. Sections 8D and 8A5 of the National Labor Relations Act tell us we must bargain in good faith with the union and they tell us what bargaining is. Bargaining is the obligation of the bank to sit down with the union and discuss wages, hours, and terms and conditions of work; to sign a written agreement if agreement can be reached and the union requests it. It also means meeting at a reasonable time and place to discuss those issues. Let's assume that the bank goes to the bargaining table and refuses to discuss a union shop; it just says it's not negotiable, and won't talk about it. Let's assume that the bank refuses to meet except on Monday afternoons on the second Monday of each month. Assume the bank reaches an agreement with the union and refuses to sign a contract. Assume that during the course of negotiations the bank unilaterally takes away some benefit that the employees currently have. And assume that the bank takes one of the negotiators for the union and trumps up a reason to fire him. Any and all of those things are unfair labor practices. If the union challenges those unfair labor practices by picketing, and then fields an unfair labor practice with the National Labor Relations Board, the bank will find that it will have to take those pickets back and remove the people that they hired to replace them. It's a touchy area of the law, and a bank should get the best advice possible at such a time.

DR. NADLER: In other words, you've got to bargain. You may give them nothing, but you've got to be willing to bargain.

MR. CLARK: Absolutely. Section 8D of the law goes on to say that neither side must agree to a proposal of the other side or make a concession. You do not have to agree to anything; however, there are cases that say that the overall approach of management to negotiations by taking a hard-nosed position on everything can indicate a general desire to defeat the union in the negotiation process. Because of its overall approach to negotiations, a bank could be guilty of an unfair labor practice.

DR. NADLER: It's almost like a method acting course where you have to act as if you really care and you are willing to work with them because they won the election, but at the same time you are going to be so tough in what you are willing to accept.

MR. CLARK: I think you put it very well: a method acting course—and actors we are when we sit down to negotiate a contract. We want to demonstrate we are acting in good faith and we want to take a decent shot at it.

DR. NADLER: Have there been many cases when the NLRB election was won by the union and then the bargaining went on so long that nothing happened?

Then the bank took a strike, and the striking employees were replaced so the bank was able to override the NLRB decision?

MR. CLARK: In the banking field you do not have that many banks that are organized—perhaps 30 to 50 banks nationwide are unionized. There have been many more elections, and so the banks have won quite a few. The best case is the Wyandotte Bank. In New Jersey, a couple of years ago there was a bank in Sussex County that lost an election. The bank negotiated a contract satisfactorily with the United Food and Commercial Workers Union. About three years ago, there was an election at a small savings and loan in Kearney that the union won. There was an unfair labor practice and negotiations dragged on until finally a one-year contract was negotiated. At the end of the one-year contract, the employees decided they did not want a union, went to the National Labor Relations Board, petitioned for another election, and the union was thrown out. Oddly enough, the International Brotherhood of Electrical Workers was involved.

DR. NADLER: I heard you say at a meeting of the New Jersey Bankers Association that the bank has to follow a "TIPS" rule. What is that?

MR. CLARK: The TIPS rule is something I have come up with and each letter of the rule stands for something. The rule is really a quick way for an employer, a supervisor, a bank to remember what the prohibitions are under the National Labor Relations Act in the early stages of a union organizational effort. In those early stages, the bank is inclined to step out of line, to take chances without realizing what chances it is taking. Section 8A1 of the National Labor Relations Act says the bank cannot coerce, restrain, or interfere with the rights of employees. Now what does that mean? The word "TIPS" will give you an interpretation of Section 8A1 of the National Labor Relations Act. T stands for "Threats," I is for Interrogation," P is for "Promises," and S is for "Spying."

Threats. The bank cannot threaten any employees in any way based upon their union activity. It cannot say that overtime will be cut, or that employees will be transferred to an outlying branch, or that it will discontinue the coffee, or that a holiday will be taken away. There can be no threats of any kind tied in with the union activity.

Interrogation. Interrogation comes from the word interfere in Section 8A1 of the National Labor Relations Act. It is improper for the bank, its officers, supervisors, or representatives to interrogate any of its employees regarding their union activity. For example, a bank finds out that a particular employee is talking union. So the supervisor sits down over coffee and starts asking questions: how many people signed the union card, what union is it? Who brought the union here, did they meet at your home, what did they promise you, how many people are interested?

Things of that nature. Interrogation of employees is a per se violation of the law. Frequently, before the bank ever gets any advice, it violates the TIPS rule by interrogating employees.

Promises. The bank cannot promise any type of benefit to the employees in order to swing them away from the union. "Get rid of the union, I'll make you a head teller." "Vote against the union and we are going to improve the branch." "Get rid of the union and there will be a wage increase and we'll introduce a personal holiday." No promises of any type are allowed to swing the people away from the union.

Spying. The bank cannot spy on its employees in any way if they are involved in a union activity. For example, a bank finds out that the employees in a particular branch are interested in a union, and a supervisor stands by the lunchroom door as they are talking about the union, out of eyeshot but within earshot—that's spying on the union. If the union is having a meeting at the American Legion hall down the street from the bank, and an official positions himself across the street on top of a roof and takes notes on everybody that's going in, that's spying on the union, and it cannot be done.

The TIPS rule can save a bank a lot of headaches in the early stages of a union organizational effort.

DR. NADLER: What happens if you violate it?

MR. CLARK: A violation of the TIPS rule will cause the bank to be hit with an unfair labor practice. But it is, in essence, a slap on the wrist. It says that you should not have violated the law; don't do it anymore. That's for a mild violation of the law. By the same token, if you take a violation of the TIPS rule and tie it together with some more severe violations of the law, there can be real trouble. For example, the law also provides that an employer cannot discriminate against employees because of union activity. That means a bank cannot fire somebody because they are handing out union cards. Let's assume that a bank has interrogated someone, some threats were made, some promises made, and there was a little spying. Then the bank fires a head teller because he's involved with the union. When you put all of those things together, and the union files an unfair labor practice charge against the bank, it is conceivable that the National Labor Relations Board could find the bank guilty of an unfair labor practice and rule it has been so bad in what it has done that the bank is not entitled to an election and must recognize the union and bargain with the union as though it had won the election.

Sometimes, there's a tendency on behalf of management to poll employees as soon as they find out there is union activity. Don't poll the employees. Even if it is done by secret ballot, you are liable to find out the employees want the union and then you've had your own election and you will have to recognize the union.

Also, sometimes a union official, when he has the majority of the employees signed up, will walk into the office of a branch manager, and say, "I represent a majority of the employees here in this branch, and I want to set up a date to start negotiations next Monday." The branch manager is all flustered; he doesn't know what to do. And he says, "how do I know you represent a majority of the people"? So the union rep gives him the cards; the branch manager looks at them. Now he has seen the proof that the union represents a majority of the people, and he has compromised his position. His position must always be: "I have good faith doubt that the union represents a majority of our people." Therefore, no bank official should look at union authorization cards if anybody offers to show them.

Do not poll the employees. Do not discriminate by discharge or discipline of an employee, and *never* commit a violation of the TIPS rule. And don't look at the cards.

DR. NADLER: During your talk to the New Jersey Bankers, you gave five beautiful rules a bank should follow to keep a union out. Will you go through them please?

MR. CLARK: Sure. Over the years, I have determined that there are five areas that give the union the greatest potential for success in organizing the employees at any bank. There is no order or preference because they are all important. If a bank is weak in any two or more of these areas, it is a potential target for a successful union organizational effort. If it is weak in one, the bank probably can win. But a bank should try to be strong in all.

The five areas are:

Job security
Grievance procedure
Supervision
Communications
Wages

Job security. There are several components to job security. First, when is the last time that the branch manager or department head has gone over to an employee and thanked him for doing a good job? This might sound cornball to some people. But thanking an employee, saying to a teller that "when the machine broke down and you did all of the work by hand the way we used to do it and it got over to the computer—we looked good; the branch looked good, you did a fine job" or "you stayed overtime and I appreciated it, thank you very much," makes the employee feel a lot more comfortable in his job; he feels as though his job efforts have been appreciated by management. It's an important component of job security.

The next part of job security is posting and filling jobs from the inside. This permits employees to gain a promotion, to see that they have a future in the bank. Part of that is training employees so that they can move up through the ranks. It's an important part of job security for an employee to know that there is a future with the bank.

Discipline is another aspect of job security. So often we come across a bank officer who has let an employee be late fifteen or twenty times and all of a sudden fires him. Where was the verbal counseling? Where was the verbal or written warning? Where was the probation or the suspension and then the discharge? Corrective, progressive discipline is essential. By the time the bank hires someone, and gets him on stream, it probably has $2,000 invested in that person. There is no reason just to get rid of such a person. There should be an effort at rehabilitation. The employees recognize that, and they feel comfortable in their job if they know they are going to get a fair shot in a disciplinary situation. Of course, embezzlement or some similar major offense is another thing. But in the ordinary situation, bank officers are well advised to give serious consideration as to how their disciplinary program should be handled.

Another very important aspect of job security is letting people know what their job is and who their supervisors are. Here's an example: There's a teller in a particular bank who has been employed there for about thirty years. He has arthritis now, and can't handle the cash and the coin at the window. So he is put downstairs in the vault, where he's quite happy. His pay had not been cut when he took over the job in the vault. Then the day before the Fourth of July, there is a rush of business before the weekend. One of the tellers is out, so the branch manager goes downstairs to the vault and asks this fellow to please come up and help out as a teller. The man goes upstairs and starts to open up the window, when the assistant branch manager says they are almost our of quarters. He tells him to close the window, go down to the main office, don't tell anybody what he's doing, and come back with a load of quarters. The man returns a half hour later. When he comes back, the branch manger meets him at the door and says,

"Where the hell have you been? I told you to open a window, we got a line going out of the front door, it's the day before the Fourth of July and you are driving around in your car." The poor fellow says, "Wait a second, the assistant branch manager told me to go and get coins." And the branch manager says to him, "Who's boss around here? Me or him?" The man did not know who his boss was because he got directions from two people; he feels uncomfortable. He did not know what his job was because he was a vault attendant, a teller, and a messenger all within a space of an hour. This is not good. Studies on employees and what job security means to them indicate this is one of the biggest components.

Grievance procedure. A disgruntled employee is the conduit by which a union gets into a bank. The way to avoid disgruntled employees is to have a grievance procedure where employees can get their complaints filed and answered. That doesn't mean that because an employee files a grievance, it's right. If he's wrong, he should be told so, but there has to be a procedure; and it must be uniformly administered at all locations. Any grievance that is not handled festers; it goes from employee to employee; and one way to get relief is to run outside to a union. A grievance procedure is very important. Supervisors should be urged to use it, employees should be urged to use it. Grievances must be resolved.

DR. NADLER: How about communications?

MR. CLARK: Communications is extremely important. The employee has to feel as though he's part of the bank. He has to understand what's going on in the bank; he has to feel a certain loyalty for the bank. How is this accomplished? How does a bank look if the first time the president of the bank ever communicates with the employees is when he sends a letter urging them to vote against the union or to reject the union?

Communication covers a lot of things. When is the last time bank officials have had a gripe session with their employees? As soon as the union is around, the bank will want to have a gripe session with the employees to find out what the problems are and to resolve them. It's too late to have that meeting once the union is knocking on the door. Have the meeting now! Find out what the problems are, get the people together, let them have some input, let them sound off.

Does the bank have a personnel policy booklet? I can't think of a bank that has an up-to-date personnel policy booklet. The personnel department is always working on it; it never gets done. The personnel policy booklet is the alter ego for the union contract. It's the thing that the employee can put in his hands and see what his benefits are and understand them. When was the last time a bank had a benefit meeting with its employees to explain pension, Blue Cross, Blue Shield, major-medical, and dental plans? Does the bank conduct exit interviews to find out what are problems of the employees who quit? Does the bank orient employees when they come on board? Do employees understand how they fit in with the rest of the bank? Do the supervisors make the rounds? Does the president of the bank make the rounds so that the various branches and the people know who he is? Does the president of the bank, for example, ever have breakfast with groups of employees? How about a house organ? It doesn't have to be a fancy sort of thing; it can be a newsletter that goes out quarterly or a one-sheet piece of paper that will tell the employees what's going on in the bank. Those types of things in communications are extremely important insofar as employees are concerned.

DR. NADLER: How about supervision?

MR. CLARK: In large part, it's the relationship supervisors have with their employees for six months before the election that is going to determine whether the bank wins or loses an election. If the supervisors show favoritism or discriminate against employees, there is a problem. If supervisors have gone through supervisory training and know how to handle people, if they are sensitive to people, the bank will win. Supervisors have to be trained, they have to know how to handle people.

Consider this example: It's the end of the day, a Friday, the branch manager can get home at 6 o'clock and have dinner with his family. But Lulu, one of his tellers who's been with him for 15 years, was in an automobile accident and she's in the hospital. Wouldn't it be nice if that supervisor stopped by the hospital on the way home to say hello to a valued employee? So what if he gets home a half hour late. The employee will remember that. The supervisor is the alter ego for the shop steward.

DR. NADLER: And finally, what about wages?

MR. CLARK. We complain about take-home pay, yet the only place some bank employees can afford to take their pay is home. Pay scales in banking are generally low compared with other industries. Banks have come a long way in improving wages, but there's a long way to go. It is important to look at the particular area in which the bank is located and what other banks are paying, what other businesses are paying. Employees should know what their salaries are, when their next increase will be, and how much it will be. Employees should know the salary formulas and the ranges for their jobs. A bank cannot afford to be in the low 50% in its particular area.

DR. NADLER: One last question. Do you feel that, by following the type of rules you've given us, banking will remain basically nonunion in the years ahead?

MR. CLARK: There's no doubt about it. If the bank can follow the five areas I've outlined, it will never become unionized.

Appendix III. The Financial Side of Banking

INSIGHTS—BANKING WITHOUT PAPER

A CONVERSATION WITH GEORGE C. WHITE, JR.

At the time of this interview, Mr. White was a vice president of Chase Manhattan Bank. He is now a consultant and publisher of "White Papers."

DR. NADLER: There has been a tremendous amount of talk about the checkless society. Yet, every year, it seems to be pushed further and further away. Why is it that banking isn't getting away from paper?

MR. WHITE: I think we are, at least, beginning to do just that. If you look at the experience of our own bank, while we continue to process that ever-growing number of checks, we are processing credit union check-like share drafts electronically. We stop those share drafts or "truncate" them here at our bank, and then simply transmit the data back to the individual credit union.

The automated clearinghouse is probably the best example of an alternative to checks. (The value is increasing dramatically) primarily because, finally, after many, many years, corporate treasurers and officers are realizing that there are advantages to handling items electronically.

DR. NADLER: What are these advantages? I understand that a corporate treasurer may say, "You're going to rob me of my float and at the same time you're going to charge me to pay my bills this way, pay my salaries this way?"

MR. WHITE: Often, the corporate treasurer is against doing things differently because, within the corporate structure, he is measured on the available funds under his control, and on the float he has created. But now we're seeing several major corporations in this country that are interested in doing things electronically because it makes good business sense. We've had a major insurance company whose business manager wants to pay their annuities electronically because it is economically feasible in spite of the treasurer of that corporation who is not responsible for annuity payments. In other words, the corporate treasurer, who used to be a deterrent sometimes, is not playing the role he used to.

DR. NADLER: What has brought about this change? What made the corporate treasurer stop looking just at float? Was it mail service? Was it recognizing the cost of doing business?

MR. WHITE: I think mail service is one of the reasons. It's inflation, the whole clerical cost of processing. Just as we consumers are faced with rising costs, every corporation has rising costs. I think the undependability of the mail, the fact that you can mail a transaction on one day and have it take two days for delivery in one case and four days in another, is causing many organizations to look for a more dependable way of making payments. Just recently, I received correspondence from one of the largest oil companies in the country that it is considering paying its stockholders through direct deposit because of the undependability of the mail service.

DR. NADLER: Why would a big oil company like, say, Schmidlap Oil come to Chase and say, "Let's automatically deposit our employee paychecks," and what happens if they give you one tape and then you send the payments to banks all around the country?

MR. WHITE: That happens when they have finally had their employees, or stockholders, or pensioneers, or whatever, specify the account where funds are to go. Then they give us the magnetic tape. We pull off those items being handled in accounts here at our own bank for their people, and then we pass the tape on to the automated clearinghouse here in New York. All of those items for local distribution in the Second Federal Reserve district stop there and then a tape is sent through the Federal Reserve System for financial institutions elsewhere in the country. The Social Security Agency, through the Department of Treasury, has some 10 million recipients in this country receiving Social Security payments on a direct deposit basis. That's 31% of the elderly recipients now receiving Social Security payments. Yet so often we hear bankers saying, "Well, old people simply won't change." But they are the biggest users of electronic funds transfer. It should really be our inspiration to get off the dime and start doing something about it.

DR. NADLER: Let's say I'm president of the Schmidlap National bank in Schmidlap, Iowa. I hear that Chase has made a deal with a big oil company on direct deposit of dividends. What can I do about the automated clearinghouse? Should I be a member? What do I get out of it? What are the ways I should look at it?

MR. WHITE: Okay, I'd say you look at it as a major opportunity to serve your customers. If you're with a smaller institution, you probably don't have the capability of getting a major corporation, such as we're thinking about from our New York base, to initiate the transactions. But your individual consumers have pension checks, payroll checks, dividends that are coming in throughout the month. Rather than sit back and wait for someone else to get these items transferred to electronics, all you have to do is ask that individual, through some promotion, to sign up for say, a dividend order that specifies your bank, the transit/routing number, and his or her account number to which funds should be transferred.

DR. NADLER: Wait a minute. Let's say that Max Gridley is a depositor at my Schmidlap National Bank, and Max gets a dividend check once a quarter from IBM. Can the bank go to him and say, "Why don't you have IBM send that dividend check directly to the bank?" Is that what you mean?

MR. WHITE: Yes. Every dividend agent in this country does that. But in many cases the corporations only have a couple of percentage points of their total stockholder base doing this because they don't publicize it. They don't tell them that they can sign a standard dividend order specifying that those funds are to come into their bank by direct deposit. Yet it's very simple to do.

DR. NADLER: What would IBM do? Would IBM send a check to the bank, or would it send a tape, or would it send a memo?

MR. WHITE: If you as a customer did what I'm suggesting, the first thing that IBM would do, on the payable date of the IBM dividend, would be to mail a dividend check to your bank for the deposit into your account. That's still not ACH at this point; that's simply getting a deposit, and some banks are already doing this and have done it for a number of years. From my conversations with large transfer agents, including agents responsible at IBM, those organizations are making plans to take the transactions now going directly to a bank and transfer them over to go through ACH. Then the cost advantages start becoming very attractive if, of course, you're a member of the local ACH.

DR. NADLER: Do I have to join the ACH, then, if I have these deposits?

MR. WHITE: That's still an undecided question. The Federal Reserve pricing program does not necessarily force you to join a local automated clearinghouse association. They're trying to encourage you to be a participant, but some of the local ACH organizations are charging relatively high fees for members that, in many cases, relate to their marketing expenses and are not really true operating expenses. So, there's some question in the industry whether you have to join that local association for benefits that may not be that valuable to the individual institution.

DR. NADLER: Let's look at it this way. I run Schmidlap National Bank. Up to now, all my customers have their IBM stock; they get their IBM checks; they put their IBM checks in the bank. Now I say to them, "You have those IBM checks sent directly to me and I'll put them in your account for you." What's in it for me?

MR. WHITE: Initially, when you're simply getting the transfer to have them mailed directly to you versus the customer coming in, it's not very attractive. The cost is almost the same. But the Federal Reserve Systems is charging each depositing institution for all checks put into the banking system. Since most of those checks for these large companies will be drawn on a bank in the New York area, local institutions are paying up to a nickel apiece for each check deposited. We have many corporations, particularly the national ones, converting their payrolls over to electronic processing through the automated clearinghouse. Their problem is getting their employees signed up. But you've got to start somewhere. In a marketing sense, unless you ask that customer to start making direct deposits someone else may ask, and, before you know it, you have lost that customer.

DR. NADLER: So, if you were president of a community bank, you'd want your customers to sign up. It will be cheaper for the customers—our service charges will be lower to you; and it will be cheaper for us. Is that it?

MR. WHITE: Yes. I would start making it more attractive for them. If I were president of that bank, I would go to the person in my bank who's responsible for marketing and ask, "What are we doing with this opportunity with the automated clearinghouse?" And I'd tell them, "Don't tell me all the reasons why it's not going to work. Tell me all the reasons you're going to make this work for our bank." As the chief executive, I'd get my own people to realize that there's an opportunity out there that we should take advantage of.

DR. NADLER: What are the opportunities? Let's say you are running a community bank, a $100 million bank, and there's an automated clearinghouse fifty miles away in a major city. What would be the advantage of your bank joining it?

MR. WHITE: One advantage is that you would be able to serve your customers at a lower cost than by the physical handling of checks. Now, we have been talking simply about the depositing function of those Social Security payments, annuities, payrolls, dividends. On the other side, I think as we go further into the 1980s, we're going to see the involvement of home computing, payment through telephones, that will require this capability. And if a bank is not within this kind of network, it will have greater difficulties offering such services to its customers. Depending on the size of the institution, many of the services we're talking about can be offered through a correspondent. But, the point is to offer them to your customer. Your customer doesn't care if you're doing it yourself, if your local service bureau is doing it on a joint basis with other financial institutions, or if you're doing it with a correspondent. The idea is to use the resources available to better serve customers. Any way you look at the physical movement of document and the increasing cost of clerical handling of any kind of transaction, it is obvious that it's going to be cheaper to do it electronically.

DR. NADLER: But, how about the other way of looking at it? Say I have customers in my bank. Is there any reason I should try to talk them into having their electric bills paid automatically, their phone bills paid automatically, their department store bills paid automatically?

MR. WHITE: In most cases it has to be the corporation that's initiating repetitive payments done on a fixed period of time. I would look to see if these telphone bill payment services—some done through service bureaus—would not be attractive as another alternative for handling transactions. As we move further into the 1980s, we'll have a variety of ways different customers can handle transactions. As you know, telephone payment programs have not been all that successful. It's partially inertia on the part of the customers; they have to sign up, they have to do something. Yet it's another way that a bank can serve customers.

DR. NADLER: What about the horrendous costs of telephone bill paying programs?

MR. WHITE: If you're going to design a system from scratch, the cost is horrendous. Our bank has spent a great deal of money developing a system that I think we might have developed more cheaply if we had gone to one of the existing services and made arrangements to pay them on a fixed-fee basis for the transactions. Just like anything, there are many ways that you can do it. I would encourage people to look at some of the telephone bill paying services that are available today from other organizations or purchase a low-cost computer "package."

DR. NADLER: Is it cheaper for a bank to have its customers pay bills by telephone than to use regular check procedures?

MR. WHITE: In today's checking environment, the consumer writes a check, inserts that into an envelope, and then puts 18 cents postage on it—and the consumer is standing the burden of the postage. With rising costs, consumers may well want a different way of paying—maybe by the telephone. The cost on the bank side is not cheaper to handle an item electronically than the present low-cost way of handling just the check by itself. But the total cost to the customer would not include the postage and can be more attractive if you look at it in that total payment sense.

DR. NADLER: What type of pricing mechanism would you use to achieve that? How would you inspire the customer to go to these more modern approaches?

MR. WHITE: That's an extremely difficult question. You've got to be creative in the sense of offering something that will provide sufficient return for your cost. I've seen some successful uses of combined accounts that try to give a lower cost for the service if the customer uses it. The idea is to set prices in a way that will encourage the customer to use the other systems.

DR. NADLER: Have there been banks that have tried the market just by saying, "Look, we're going to charge you 20 cents for each electronic item, but you save the time writing a check, you're saving the cost of a check, you're saving the postage"?

MR. WHITE: Much of our promotion is based upon just that philosophy. We say right now that if you write ten checks per month at 18 cents postage, you spend $1.82, forgetting about the other expenses or costs of the check, but our service is no more than $1.50 per month. Therefore, you save right there if you write nine or more checks per month. And we start advertising that type of approach, trying to show the economics of it to the consumer. Now, what we have not overcome is that there are start-up efforts for the consumer. The consumer has to list all the bills to be paid, and all of us postpone doing something this week until next week, so there's been a lot of inertia to overcome. But the volume keeps going up every month, so that there's constant conversion, although not as fast as we'd like to see.

DR. NADLER: Look at it from the viewpoint of the Chase. You're charging $1.50 a month to do all of this work. As the customers pay these bills, unless the person receiving the money is a Chase depositor, you're talking your customers into folding their deposits down more quickly. You're hurting your own float.

MR. WHITE: Ah, but we draw out from the customer's account on the day they tell us, either the day they telephone us or if they say pay it in the future, we pull it out at that date. Then we simply send the money to the corporation being paid, because most of the corporations, practically all of them in this country, are not now receiving these items electronically. We do have float from those transactions, so the actual payment to the corporation is some days after the money has come out of the account of the consumer.

DR. NADLER: Isn't that a tremendous expense, taking all these individual requests, tying them up, and then issuing the checks on it?

MR. WHITE: No. I am not proposing that what we're doing is the right way, but there are two alternatives for initiating the payments. One is with the Touch-Tone telephone. If you look at the initiation with the Touch-Tone telephone, in which you key in a code that says, "This is XYZ Utility, and I want to pay them so many dollars," you have no human intervention.

Very low cost. We do have, unfortunately, a lot of organizations and individuals that do not have Touch-Tone telephones, and they call in and talk to an operator. I would have preferred that we priced our service so that if you had a Touch-Tone telephone, you would in turn get a lower cost. If it's $1.50 for one, it's $1 for the other. But the feeling was in pricing this out that there were too many homes that did not presently have Touch-Tone telephones. So the strategy was taken that we'll offer the same price and hope that more of these will convert to electronics.

DR. NADLER: Will you take only certain people who will receive money, or will you let somebody send a check to anybody who's authorized?

MR. WHITE: We will let a person send a check to anyone authorized, provided that that particular company has said they will receive it. Some corporations, some insurance companies, for example, have refused to accept such payments for fear that they may come in late after a death claim and there will be legal suits.

DR. NADLER: If I were a Chase depositor and accepted your telephonic transfer, you would give me a list of authorized people that I could pay bills to. I couldn't pay just anybody; I couldn't send a check to Aunt Minnie every month.

MR. WHITE: Yes, you could send a check to Aunt Minnie. You can send a check to anyone you want, provided you give us the address of that organization or person you want to pay.

DR. NADLER: Then that goes into your computer file and becomes automatic.

MR. WHITE: That's right. Now, there are a few organizations—we have a savings bank here in New York that offers a telephone bill payment service but excludes doctors and dentists. I think that's a decision they made that makes their service less attractive. I think it's far more attractive if you could pay everyone you want to.

DR. NADLER: And there's no extra cost to you or to the customer of putting Aunt Minnie down for a monthly payment?

MR. WHITE: No, because even though there might be only one person paying Aunt Minnie, we can do it very inexpensively. When Aunt Minnie accepts that payment coming to her account by an automated clearinghouse transaction, then we're talking even greater savings that makes it even more attractive.

DR. NADLER: Let's talk about Federal Reserve pricing. The Fed is trying to inspire the public to change its banking habits by the way it's charging for its services under. What do you think of it? What does all this mean for the community bank?

MR. WHITE: First of all, the Federal Reserve pricing is really not an initiative of the Federal Reserve but is a result of the Depository Institutions Deregulation and Monetary Control Act of 1980. That forces the Federal Reserve to quit what we have called their "implicit pricing" that was based on the reserves of the members and, in turn, start charging the true cost of transactions. I see this as a very good thing; it's going to get us away from subsidizing checks, which has kept us in the checking environment.

I would take one exception to one thing you just said about the Federal Reserve, that it's trying to move us in a better way. I sense that the Federal Reserve is really not pricing to make us move to an electronic environment. That's what my big argument on pricing has been. The Federal Reserve's pricing today is going to charge the depositing party for the cost of checks. The only one who can do something differently is the one initiating the transaction. So I'm suggesting that the Fed should really be charging both parties, the initiator and the depositor, so that there is some financial motive to do it cheaper, such as through an automated clearinghouse. However, even though I have that problem with the Federal Reserve pricing, I think it at least is waking up corporations to the fact that now, with their being dependent on checks, it's finally going to start costing them the true value of moving those checks. And that's going to get them to look more aggressively at how they might pay in an electronic environment.

One of the big issues we've had here at Chase and at the other New York Clearing House Association banks is that the Federal Reserve is basically subsidizing the check-processing system by continuing to allow Fed float. If you look at 1979, the cost of Fed float was twice the value of moving checks, so it is a form of subsidy; it encourages corporations to pay from remote locations, to draw a check from a West Coast organization to pay a customer on the East Coast. What we've said here in New York is that we should move those availability schedules back. If it takes more than one day to get a check to Texas, let's make it two days so that you simply don't have Fed float being generated because the Fed could not move the check quickly. "Eliminate it tomorrow. Make every point from moving checks two and three days in the entire country, and you can get rid of the Fed float."

DR. NADLER: If you made it two days, though, wouldn't the bank simply send distant items through the Fed and everything else they do direct payment?

MR. WHITE: Could be.

DR. NADLER: Wouldn't that result in a lot of float?

MR. WHITE: Not necessarily. If you're using direct sends for payments, you don't have float in that case.

DR. NADLER: But what I'm saying is that the Fed would get only the garbage items; that it would take longer than two days.

MR. WHITE: Let the private sector do it. I think what you said is fine. Let that happen. The Fed does not want to give it up. I've heard people from the Fed say they want to maintain their market share of 40% of the checks. The Monetary Control Act legislates that they must address the issue of Fed float. Even though it may be delayed a year or so in the implementation, it's going to be charged for. That's why it behooves all of us to look at ways we can capitalize on the newer systems with Fed float out of the system.

DR. NADLER: Let's see what this means to the community bank. You say the corporate treasurer is going to have to pay for what it costs to send a check. If I am a corporate treasurer who uses a medium-sized bank, I'm going to have to pay for float if I write a check in Schmidlap, Iowa, and send it to Klamath Falls, Oregon. I'm going to have to pay a float premium, an extra fee to use the Federal Reserve wire network. What do you think the bank is going to charge me for each item that clears?

MR. WHITE: Our figure in the cost to the Federal Reserve is in the area of 10 to 15 cents if you put the value in there for the Fed float. Obviously, a large check is costly in the system and a small check is not as far as the Fed float is concerned. The Fed is talking about some complex means such as fractional availability and electronic check presentment to try to solve this problem. I would say it's going to be solved and you should look for the float disappearing. In talking to corporate treasurers about this issue, those who have been playing the game of writing checks from different points, doing what we call remote disbursing, simply say that if it is not attractive, they'll quit using that mechanism and look at lower-cost alternatives. But we're also seeing those corporations on the receiving side of large funds beginning to think in terms of specifying the value date, when they need those payments in hand. Rather than say that the terms of the transaction are 2%/10 days, and assuming that it's the tenth of the month, or postmarked the tenth of the month, they're starting to consider specifying that they be in good funds on the particular day they demand and then charge interest if late. I don't see many doing this, but they're starting to move that way, particularly with the high cost of funds. It's the game playing of drawing checks and capitalizing on the float that is hurting a lot of corporations. Some are benefiting unjustly and others are not. I think that's what will be terminated by recognizing the issue of Fed float.

DR. NADLER: In other words, the banks are going to have to charge enough so that the corporate treasurers don't play games by moving the checks all over.

MR. WHITE: That's right. It's already happening.

DR. NADLER: But won't a bank cut its nose to spite its face? If I go to my corporate treasurer and I say, "Look, I don't want any more of your writing checks on me to pay Schmidlap and Company. We'll have float for four days." I mean, the bank loses the use of those funds, doesn't it?

MR. WHITE: Yes, except that the float has not been out of the bank; the benefit has gone to the corporation without hurting or helping us. However, now those funds that have been free from the Federal System will be taken away.

DR. NADLER: Let me ask a stupid question. Let's say 1984. What do you think a bank will be charging a corporation or individual for each check written? Do you think it will be in the 40-or-50-cent range?

MR. WHITE: I think it will be more likely in the 10-to-15-cent range, but I think we'll be doing it in a variety of ways. We'll charge one fee for those checks that are returned to the customer. If that customer allows those checks not to be returned but stopped or "truncated" as its own financial institution, much as the credit unions are doing now, we'll have a different charge for them. If a customer lets checks be stopped or truncated at the first processing point, then they'll simply stop there and there will be a lesser charge. That will simply be an ACH transaction with a lower charge. So in answer to your question, there is going to be a range of options for a customer to select.

Some of the big corporations we're talking to are looking at the Fed pricing as it's now proposed that includes charging for every check they receive. Let's take the oil company that you were talking about earlier. Say that all the checks for payment to them in this country are mailed to a single processing point. They deposit those checks with their local bank for collecting throughout the country. Now, under the present Fed schedule, they'll be paying approximately 5 cents apiece for each of those checks. It starts making it attractive to that company to forget what the banking industry is doing, saying, "Why don't we ask our customers to let us not return their checks. When they pay, we'll simply send back to them through the ACH for any of those who have agreed to this service the data including the name of the company, their account number with that company, the dollar amount, and when the funds were taken out of their account. No check comes back to them." You start thinking of it that way, and you don't need that check. When we talk to companies like Consolidated Edison here in New York City with their 3 million customers or New York Telephone with their 6 million customers, these are attractive ways that they could substantially reduce their costs by starting to use the electronic mechanism.

DR. NADLER: This year saw the beginning of nationwide NOW accounts. A great many people thought that banks should use this as a time to truncate checks. Why didn't banking go to truncation?

MR. WHITE: I would like to know the answer to your question. From what I have read, only one or two major financial institutions are even considering truncation as an option. I think that's another case of a missed opportunity. Here in New York City, the savings banks have had the right to offer checks for a few years. Many of us in commercial banking proposed to them when they gained this privilege, "Why not use this as a time to offer a new low-cost service of not returning checks?" And their answer was, "We want to look just like the commercial bank." I would think that now they wish they had gone the other way.

DR. NADLER: Chase handles more share drafts for credit unions than any other bank in the country. Are they, or are most of them, nonreturnable checks?

MR. WHITE: All of them are. It's required that they not be returned.

DR. NADLER: What do you do with those vouchers?

MR. WHITE: Roughly half of all the share drafts in the entire country come in to our bank, and the number is growing each month. First, we microfilm every one of them. If there is a reject because of insufficient funds, we physically send that item back the next day through the check collection system. We destroy the other drafts after two months. Then, if a customer requests a copy, we obtain it from a microfilm record. The procedure is working beautifully. It's cheaper. And it would be even cheaper if we stopped those checks at the first processing points, rather than let them go through the entire check-processing system.

DR. NADLER: Do you feel, then, when we talk of the "Checkless Society," that it finally is under way, that we're finally getting to a point where we're getting away from the use of paper?

MR. WHITE: I would like to say it's moving faster. But if you look at our own bank, Chase Manhattan, and realize that we, as one single bank, have 25%

of the national private-sector volume in the ACH—more even than any single ACH except New York—it indicates that most of the banks in this country don't think it's very important. There is one major bank in New York City that's often thought of as the EFT bank, yet it is one of the smallest initiators of transactions into that network, with less than one percent of the transactions initiated in our local area. Banks like Lincoln First up in Rochester, Marine Midland, most of the major New York banks are ahead of that other bank, simply because they've never set a priority on these types of transactions.

DR. NADLER: Have you found that more and more of the customers of companies are going along with them when they talk about preauthorization?

MR. WHITE: Yes, in many of these cases. We've had the case with preauthorized payments for the insurance companies that account for a lot of the volume that we've generated through the clearinghouse. Those customers have already agreed to have their accounts debited on a monthly basis; therefore dealing electronically has not caused much change in a customer's pattern. These companies have also found that they have fewer cancellations. Consider preauthorized payments. Every bank in this country has installment loans. In many cases, when a customer is making an installment loan, we as an industry generally don't tell them that payments will be automatically debited to their account. We give the consumer the option of coupon books. As far as I know, the only bank here in New York that has really aggressively gone after repetitive-type payments just to pay installment loans has been the Manufacturer's Hanover Bank. They give a one-quarter percent discount if, at the time of signing for the loan, the customers authorize debiting against their accounts. The idea is to make that the attractive option that leads them into automatic electronic payment.

DR. NADLER: Let's take a case where you're doing automatic payroll deposit. You're sending out one check to the employee's bank?

MR. WHITE: We're sending it through the ACH.

DR. NADLER: If the bank is a member.

MR. WHITE: That's right.

DR. NADLER: Is this more expensive to bank than a check as a general rule?

MR. WHITE: Most of them find the cost is similar. let's take the case of a nonautomated bank that gets a listing of these transactions. Even though they came into the local ACH's electronic items, if the financial institution cannot receive a magnetic tape, it is possible that it will cost a little more because it will have a listing which it will have to key into their own internal system. But I find that most of the banks have some form of automation, either through a service bureau or a correspondent, or they're doing it themselves. And most of these are already receiving Social Security payments in some automated way, although these are usually smaller numbers of transactions.

DR. NADLER: And they're getting the money earlier because it's automated and there's no float.

MR. WHITE: On the fixed time, that's right. Without the person necessarily coming into the branch, with the cost of cashing a check and all those expenses. It's going directly to the customer's account. We're finding that the customers like this service. I encourage anyone looking at direct depositing to look at the experience of the Treasury Department for Social Security payments. Over 50% of the recipients of Social Security payments in Florida and Arizona are now getting direct deposit on the third of each month.

DR. NADLER: The bank, of course, has to be willing to have the money withdrawn from the account at a certain date whether it has come in or not, right? The bank has to be dependable or the customer won't buy it.

MR. WHITE: That's right. Usually we find that the first time customers sign up for this service, they usually come in to check on the payment. In some banks they've had problems making sure the credit is there on that exact date, but we find that after the first or the second month, the customers realize, "Well, it's there." They don't have to do anything.

DR. NADLER: What happens if there's a mistake, if one month there's a slip-up and you don't have the tape and the money transferred automatically to the community bank. They then have the cost of covering the checks, right?

MR. WHITE: There would be the cost of inquiry to find out where the check is, what happened. But the accuracy is high. Once you have the account data for receiving deposits, it goes smoothly and there's no problem. I would say that on the debiting or preauthorized payment side, there are cases where you have insufficient funds and the transaction is rejected—about 2 to 3% of the transactions are rejected for insufficient funds.

DR. NADLER: For instance, somebody's paying his insurance bill automatically . . .

MR. WHITE: That's right, and he forgot the transaction was coming in and didn't have sufficient funds in his account.

DR. NADLER: If you were going to give some advice to bankers looking at the ACH, and trying to determine the benefits, where could they learn more about it? What can they do if they see that there is value to their bank to get the public to accept this?

MR. WHITE: I suggest that a banker ask others who have had experience in using these services what they have done. A bank like ours is constantly talking with other bankers. They call on the telephone, they come in to visit, or they meet us at conferences. They ask us what our experience has been, and we share with them the kinds of things covered here.

DR. NADLER: From the viewpoint of a large bank, and also from the viewpoint of a community bank, do you feel that this whole ACH approach to banking without paper can improve the profitability of the banking industry? Are the costs that much lower than traditional costs so that it really can be of value to the institution?

MR. WHITE: In the long term it has to be of value. The problem we constantly run into, with less than one percent of the check volume now being handled through the ACHs, is that too little volume sometimes is more costly to handle. But those banks not taking advantage of ACH will never get there. They'll find that their customers will be served by others that are making these plans to handle ACH transactions. We have cases right now where some remittors of payrolls are asking their employees to change certain deposit accounts and move to other banks that can better handle the transaction. So behind the scenes, a lot of pressure is building that may not be obvious to the bank that is not fully serving those customers.

DR. NADLER: Can we sum up by saying that banking without paper is feasible, that if the volume gets up there it can truly be a cost-saver for banks of all sizes, and the key to getting public acceptance is knowledge and incentive pricing?

MR. WHITE: Yes. But it is the banks which also must accept the premise. Sometimes we are our worst enemy in not looking at the opportunities that we have ahead. I am concerned that competitors are getting ahead of us because we in banking are not looking sufficiently at the opportunity that we have.

Appendix IV. The Business of Banking

INSIGHTS—TECHNOLOGY VERSUS TRADITION

A CONVERSATION WITH DONALD G. LONG

Mr. Long is a consultant with IBM.

DR. NADLER: How would you characterize the situation in banking today?

MR. LONG: The industry has some major potential problems in the future related to their profitability and growth. They obviously have major competitors, new competitors from outside the banking industry, and I think the industry needs to make some very basic changes in the way services are delivered, the kind of services delivered, the way that those services are priced, and perhaps most importantly, the structure within which the services are provided to their customers.

DR. NADLER: What about changes in the basic services: What services do you think banks should be offering that they are not? What are they offering that they shouldn't be offering?

MR. LONG: By my best estimate the banking industry currently provides at least 155 separate and distinct services to consumers. What really would help is to develop a relationship with the consumer which will virtually eliminate the need for all of those separate services—and substitute for that a relationship that will give one service offering with an infinite number of varieties. That is to say, each individual will be provided with those services that he requires, based on his resources, his sophistication, and his ability to pay, rather than services being provided at the convenience of the institution. Services today are, in my opinion, structured more to make it easier for the institution to provide the services than they are structured to provide the specific service that an individual may require.

DR. NADLER: Does that mean that the bank will become sort of like a Merrill Lynch "cash management account," where it handles all of your activities under one umbrella?

MR. LONG: I think the cash management account is probably the best example that we have today of what I mean by a relationship. However, I would carry the CMA a step further and extend its asset base beyond the securities that we normally associate with the CMA into other readily valued assets that the consumer has, including his home. Consider, for example, the value of collectibles and antiques and such items; things that can be valued by appraisal. They are assets which I might like to have access to the value of in a more ready manner than I do today.

DR. NADLER: How are we going to get the talent for this in banking? Is this going to mean that only a few banks are going to survive that have super experts, or a variety of staff?

MR. LONG: The people who sell these services to the average consumer are not going to have to be MBAs, because the average consumer doesn't require the level of service that, let's say, the upper 5 or 10% do. The average consumer requires better service than he can obtain today, more tailored to his needs, but his position doesn't change that rapidly. His relationship will not be as dynamic as the selected few that we view as upscale customers. For those upscale customers, we may very well have to apply more talent in working with those relationships than is in place today. Those relationships, in fact, will look very much like the bank's corporate customers do today, and probably have to have a similar kind of attention paid to them.

DR. NADLER: Well, let's start talking about the technology of this. Will the banks have to have different types of equipment on hand to provide this full financial service to the people? Are the vendors broad enough to offer the banks the hardware and software required?

MR. LONG: These systems will evolve; the relationship won't be created overnight. There may be half a dozen different delivery mechanisms, and the primary emphasis of those mechanisms will be on self-service. Self-service is a fairly broad term, of course. It can include a corporation doing its payroll through the automated clearinghouse and the individual paying bills by pushing buttons of his telephone—a remote banking mechanisms around what we know as the automated teller machine today. The automated clearinghouse mechanism will be further developed, including a corporate transfer mechanism, for business-to-business payments.

DR. NADLER: What will that do to the capital commitment that a bank will have to make? Let's say a bank has a small computer and normal peripherals. Will it have to spend a fortune on equipment to be a full-service provider?

MR. LONG: In the home-banking delivery mechanism, the devices—the capital-intensive equipment—will probably belong to the consumer rather than to the bank. It will have been purchased by the consumer as a home-services mechanism, not as a home-banking device, because there will be a lot of other services that will be delivered to the home over that mechanism. The bank will probably not participate to any great extent in any capital investment in that device. The automated clearinghouse is virtually in place today. The devices that corporate treasurers may use to accommodate business-to-business payments will probably be devices attached to systems within the corporation that also have other applications in which the financial officers of those corporations are involved.

DR. NADLER: And do you think that the typical community bank has the expertise to handle these outside forces—these appliances?

MR. LONG: I don't think most banks will need significant technological grounding in how to evaluate the specifics of particular devices, because I think that a lot of these mechanisms will be put in place by third parties, large financial entrepreneurs, or by consortiums of depository institutions. The community bank will, therefore, have the ability to access those mechanisms without having had to install the mechanisms themselves.

DR. NADLER: You are talking about all these things that are going to come down the pike, and all of them involve using more equipment. But haven't we seen some significant failures? Hasn't John Fisher of BankOne in Columbus indicated that the point-of-sale terminal was a flop? Haven't some people said that banking in the home is a gimmick that people will just talk about to sell newspaper and magazine articles?

MR. LONG: The major problem with many point-of-sale installations has been a lack of understanding on the part of the banker as to what the retailer's problem is. After all, when you deal with a point-of-sale system, the customer for that system is the merchant, not the consumer. That's a very important distinction. If you want to sell a product to somebody, you must understand in some depth the problem that you're trying to solve for that party. I don't think that the banking industry understands enough about the retailer's problem, and therefore has been unsuccessful in communicating to the retailer what the advantage is of an electronic payment system in a merchant point-of-sale.

DR. NADLER: I gather that BankOne found that its point-of-sale simply was not profitable. Glendale Federal found that its system didn't generate enough business. What do you feel was wrong with those point-of-sale programs?

MR. LONG: Let me start by saying what I think was *not* wrong. It was not technological problems that made those systems failures. In the case of Glendale Federal, the institution attempted to develop a proprietary system with one major supermarket chain. The problem there was one of critical mass—there were not enough customers of that supermarket who were also customers of Glendale to provide any particular incentive for the supermarket to have any great deal of interest in pushing the application. Nor did it turn out to be of great benefit to the savings and loan, because its market was much broader than just that which could be served by that supermarket. In the case of the system in Columbus, one of the errors that I believe was made there was the check-guarantee application. There has to be a question in the minds of a lot of bankers! "Is check guarantee something I really want to do?" There are a couple of reasons for this. One is that it's not clear that the application can be priced in such a way that it will be profitable to the banking industry. Second, many believe that we ought to get rid of the check over time, so why guarantee it? So the problem has not been one of technology in the system in Columbus, but one of commitment on the part of the banking institution.

DR. NADLER: Getting back to Glendale, I would have to infer from what you have said that point-of-sale services should be on a cooperative basis—that all the banks have to get together with all the supermarkets.

MR. LONG: You will find that both point-of-sale and home-delivery systems will tend to be a shared environment because the environment in which you are delivering the service does not belong to, nor is it controlled by, the depository institution. As a consequence, the advantage has to be to the owner and holder of the environment, either the consumer or the merchant in these cases.

DR. NADLER: Let's go a step further. Do you feel that automated teller machines have to be a shared environment also?

MR. LONG: No, I don't. The automated teller machine has a couple of connotations to it. One is efficiency on the part of the banking industry in delivering transactions electronically. Another is that of delivering service conveniently. There are a lot of studies that indicate that convenience generally manifests itself in location. And location is the primary reason why most consumers do business with a given depository institution. The automated teller machine has locational convenience potentially, either through its installation in existing facilities which, presumably, were located because of convenience to the customers, or through their installation in apartment houses, plants, office buildings, and so forth, where you can literally take the banking business to the customer. The major competitive value of the ATM, I think, indicates a need for cautions when considering sharing because sharing, at some point, is the antithesis of competition.

DR. NADLER: You have indicated that the best place to have an ATM is in the wall of the bank—not standing alone—so it can be a supplement during regular banking hours and a replacement when the bank is closed.

MR. LONG: My feeling is that the primary advantage of ATMs is through all-hours access. Now that may imply an installation in a vestibule in a downtown environment where it is accessible twenty-four hours a day. It may also imply installation in an apartment complex where access is both day and night. Or it may imply kiosks in the parking lot of a shopping center, or installation through the wall of an existing bank branch. The key is to make the device accessible 24 hours a day, seven days a week, to maximize the convenience and to allow the customer to do his banking when he wants to do it. This will tend to level out the transaction volumes, rather than causing the kinds of peaks that we're faced with today because of constrained hours.

DR. NADLER: What are your thoughts on banking in the home? Is it a gimmick that makes newspaper stories, or do you really see it coming down the pike?

MR. LONG: Oh, it is coming down the pike, Paul, but it is not a banking application that, in our opinion at least, can be justified on its own. It will not be installed in the home as a stand-alone application to any level beyond the telephone bill payment stage. If we're going to deliver financial services through the television set, which is probably what we conjure up when we think about home banking, the cost of the network and the cost of the hardware involved does not appear to be justified on the basis of banking alone. There have to be other applications—home shopping, security monitoring, energy management, news, the ability to play games, make reservations for airplanes or dinner, or whatever it might be.

DR. NADLER: You indicated earlier there were 155 services to the customer. Do you think that many of them are unnecessary; that we're going to cut down the number of services?

MR. LONG: I think that ultimately we will cut down the number of services to one, and that service will be the relationship. But how it is provided to you, what it means to you, how it is priced, and how you pay for it will depend on your individual needs and circumstances.

DR. NADLER: Another question—one that comes up continuously—is: Can the small-to-medium-size bank honestly compete in the technology battle against the giants? Does the small-to-medium size bank have the resources available to it, or is it going to be beaten by these guys who can devote fifty people to a project?

MR. LONG: I think the community bank is going to be around for a long time. The community bank has a major advantage—it knows its local environment.

It has the capability to provide unique service in the local community. Now, there are a number of community banks that probably don't fulfill that charter, and probably will cease to exist over a period of time. But the community bank that does provide that unique service in its local environment is certainly going to survive. I simply don't believe, for example, that the large New York banks will populate the world with ATMs and overrun all the small banks. You must have the capability to obtain relationships before you can service them. And the local bank has a special capability to obtain relationships. While the large bank may have the temporary advantage of being able to develop technological solutions and delivery mechanisms, the small bank, either as a serviced institution of a larger entity or through third parties, is going to have the capability to provide those same technological delivery mechanisms.

DR. NADLER: But when the computer first came into banking, in the early 1960s, you had to be of a certain size before you could afford the technology. With this complicated technology today, is there a minimum size below which a bank is at a tremendous disadvantage, considering the changes you see in the relationship environment?

MR. LONG: The difference today, Paul, as compared to those early days, was that then we were talking about the point at which a bank could afford its own batch-oriented computer system. Today, through telecommunications, we have the capability to deliver services to locations through devices that are very low in cost-terminal type devices. There are a great many small banks, like the one that I deal with myself, that have ATMs today. So the problem has changed, and the main reason that it's changed has been the ability to deliver services over a telephone line as compared to having to have your own system in-house.

DR. NADLER: Does that mean then that you see a trend toward the typical bank buying its services instead of providing them itself? Are we less likely to see a bank involved in its own technology, comparable to the fact that a bank doesn't generate its own electricity?

MR. LONG: I think you will see a trend in that direction for a period of time. However, we are also improving the capability for a smaller institution to have its own processing power. Why is this desirable? The primary reason is so that one can design unique services for its own customers. Now, there may be a level at which even today a bank can't afford to do that. The gating factor, if you want to call it that, is our ability to hire programmers and people of that kind. They tend to be fairly expensive, and the very small bank can't afford that kind of investment. But I think smaller and smaller banks will be able to justify that capability. Ultimately, every bank will be able to have its own processing system.

DR. NADLER: What about the other side? Some people talk about distributive processing, that banks like Citibank are trying to break up their data processing into smaller bite-sized units that have no contact with other units, to try to be like a small bank. Do you see that coming?

MR. LONG: Actually, the trend will probably be in the other direction. And the reason will be the overwhelming requirement to develop a customer relationship, as we've talked about earlier. That relationship implies that I don't split pieces of my business apart, but that I have a way of tying all those pieces of business—particularly as it relates to an individual customer. The distributive processing that we will see in the future will primarily be oriented to saving cost rather than functionally splitting up the institution.

DR. NADLER: How about the inroads being made into banking by others: by brokerage firms, by the Sears Roebucks? Do you see any way in which technology will play a role in that, and in defending the position of the community bank or leading to its demise?

MR. LONG: I guess if I were a Sears Roebuck or a Merrill Lynch, part of my view of why I might want to emphasize consumer financial services would be that I could see my way clear to (1) delivering those services nationwide, and (2) delivering them in a more efficient manner than the banking industry has delivered them in the past. These services have been delivered with paper, bricks, and mortar and a heavy personnel-intensive environment in the past. The new competitors can deliver a lot of these services in a less costly manner. Therefore, they have an advantage, or a potential advantage, in that regard. The main thing that the banking industry has to combat that advantage—at least at this point in time—is the fact that location and convenience are still the primary reasons why customers do business with particular financial services institutions. When services are delivered to the home, that kind of locational convenience tends to go away—if there is a window through which the banking industry must change its ways and make its delivery mechanisms more efficient. We have a window that we can step through which is probably, let's say, 10 years in length. If the banking industry fails to step through that window and make its delivery mechanisms more efficient, then these new competitors will have their way.

DR. NADLER: That brings up a point that's seldom stressed. As people write about the Merrill Lynch and Shearson Prudential mergers, these nonbanks getting into banking start off with a clean slate. They don't have the trappings of paper to worry about, they can start with an automatic system, What can banking do to catch up? How can banking get rid of the paper tradition?

MR. LONG: The main system—and it's in place today—that will help the banking industry get away from the paper monster that it has created is the automated clearinghouse. By itself, the automated clearinghouse has the capability to displace perhaps a third of the checks that are written today. This means through direct deposit of recurring items and through preauthorized payment of fixed amount recurring items. Probably another 40 to 50% of the paper can be eliminated as a by-product of the automated clearinghouse—through applications such as business-to-business payments, home banking, point of sale, any number of other applications which will use the automated clearinghouse in whole or in part as the transfer mechanism.

DR. NADLER: You've indicated that pricing is a key to success. What type of pricing is needed to get rid of the paper tiger in banking?

MR. LONG: Basically, pricing has been a seat-of-the pants, not very scientific, endeavor in the banking industry. Pricing has had little relationship to the cost or benefit of an application to either the bank or the bank's customer. Pricing can be used to cover costs, but there are a number of other aspects to it, as well. Pricing can be used as an incentive for customers to do things the way the bank wants them to. Probably the best example in the history of pricing is that of the phone company's ability to get people to dial their own calls by charging them less for it. I think the banking industry can do somewhat the same thing through pricing. For example, the bank might charge less for an automated teller machine transaction than for a check that was written and cashed inside one of my branch offices. The bank might provide more benefit to the customer in terms of earning credits or interest paid for deposits that were made electronically than for deposits made in the form of paper. So there are a number of things that it can do to provide incentives to customers. Also, the bank can charge customers on the basis of benefits they perceive. Convenience is a perceived benefit. ATMs are installed all over the United States today, yet in only a few cases are banks charging for the use of the automated teller machine. Well, why not charge? There's a benefit there that the customer may well pay for.

DR. NADLER: How do we reconcile the fact that we have to use pricing to get the customer away from paper, and yet make the customer pay for this technology that we are putting in?

Mr. Long: The technology has to be justified on its own merits. That is, an automated teller machine has to be justified on a cost-versus-benefit basis. And there are a number of costs that it can displace; there are some new revenues that can be derived. It's necessary to evaluate all that, and to evaluate each new application.

Dr. Nadler: A great many people say retail banking is dead; that a bank should concentrate on the corporate side—the middle market. Yet much of what you've said deals with how a relationship can be of value to the retail customer. Will banks continue to rely on retail business in the years ahead or will retail business go to the credit unions, the Sears Roebucks, and others?

Mr. Long: The trend would indicate that the consumer as a customer of depository institutions will continue to increase in importance over this decade. So I find it hard to believe that depository institutions can turn their backs on retail business. The corporate business, as a matter of fact, is a very tough business today, in great part because there are other sources of services for corporate treasurers today—both in terms of where they put their funds to work and where they obtain the funds that they need for their businesses. I don't think the corporate business area is going to get any easier; if anything, it will get tougher. As the big banks find more difficulty in making money on their national accounts, they are going to turn to regional businesses as a way of shoring up their corporate business. Competition in the middle market can be expected to heat up a good deal.

Dr. Nadler: You recently were elected to the board of a $15 million bank. As you go to the board meetings, do you feel a sense of optimism as a new bank gets started?

Mr. Long: Absolutely. If a bank is conceived with the idea in mind that it wants to serve the community and that it wants to grow and prosper in that community, it can do just that. If the only purpose for the creation of a new bank is an opportunity to sell out to somebody else in a short period of time, then you probably don't have that incentive. But that's not the kind of community bank that I'm talking about when I talk about the ones that will prosper and grow in the future. It's the kind that are really committed to serving the community and the people within the community that will succeed.

Dr. Nadler: You've indicated that technology is nothing for the community bank to fear; that the technology will be available either directly or indirectly.

If you were president of the Schmidlap National Bank, a $100 million bank, and you were analyzing your computer expenditures—your DP expenditures—what would your attitude be toward suprises that might be on the horizon; toward reevaluating and seeing if you're doing the right thing now? How would you look at the technology that you are paying for today?

MR. LONG: If your question is related to the direction that we see in technology and the cost of technology, I think that at any point in time one has to carefully evaluate the monies he spends on a solution—whether it's technological or nontechnological. But that's sort of a motherhood statement. The cost of technology will continue to come down over the foreseeable future, probably at a rate that will approximate that which we've seen in the last decade. So I don't look for any wall or any barrier to continued reduction in the cost of technology or to continued improvement in the price performance of technology.

DR. NADLER: Would there be surprises? Some people believe that vendors have sold certain equipment and then made it obsolete. Are there reasons for a bank to keep very fluid in its capital commitments to technology these days? Or do you think we already see the changes that are going to take place in the next decade or so?

MR. LONG: Well, I think we see the application changes that are going to take place. We are now starting to see what may in fact be the ultimate delivery mechanism—that of delivering service to the home. That's starting to come into focus now. Technology continues to change at an accelerating rate, but I think that if an investment in technology is carefully evaluated, that its life can still be significant. A good example of that might be the development over the past decade of automated teller machines. It has truly been an evolutionary development, and will continue to be so. Vendors cannot move a market; vendors can only provide a product and the market will then accept it or not. Obviously, the acceptance of the product is tempered by the availability of capital and resources within the institution.

DR. NADLER: Let's go back to where you are president of Schmidlap National, and someone comes in from IBM or one of its competitors and tries to scare you, talking about all the changes that are taking place and how you must prepare for the changes. Would you, as the buyer, take a more complacent attitude, that it's going to be an evolutionary change, that the changes are going to be in marketing and pricing, and not in technology? Or would you listen and feel you have to get religion?

MR. LONG: Technology, in general, will be there to satisfy the requirements of the industry. That has historically been true and will continue to be true. To the degree that we try to drive the industry based on where the technology is, I think we tend to make mistakes. The right way to do things is to figure out what changes need to take place in the industry and its relationships with its customers—and then develop the technology to satisfy that.

Appendix V. Relationships

INSIGHTS—A REGULATOR'S POINT OF VIEW

A CONVERSATION WITH JOHN G. HEIMANN

Mr. Heimann until recently, was deputy chairman of Becker Paribus Incorporated. At the time of the interview, he was Comptroller of the Currency.

MR. MILLER: How is it being Comptroller under a Republican President?

MR. HEIMANN: The same as being Comptroller under a Democrat.

MR. MILLER: No change?

MR. HEIMANN: No change whatsoever. The Comptroller's Office is considered by all to be primarily an independent agency, and I have noticed no difference in terms of the way the office is viewed by the incoming administration and the outgoing administration. As you know, the office is involved in a series of quasi-judicial actions, and there's been a long tradition that administrations as well as the Congress do not interfere with that process. Congress may hold hearings afterward, but there's very little political—and I use that word with a small "p"—interference with the operation of the Comptroller's office. That's the way Congress designed it, and that's been honored by all parties.

MR. MILLER: I notice that you do considerable traveling, and I think that kind of thing is in your job. But your predecessor, Jim Smith, got a lot of flak for doing a great amount of traveling, didn't he?

MR. HEIMANN: It seems to me that, in a country as big as this, we're responsible for American banks abroad as well as here. Moreover, the financial systems of the world are now so inextricably intertwined. It's really part of our responsibility to get out there and find out what's going on. I think it's absolutely essential. I think one of the great criticisms you can make of the federal government is that its leaders don't get out enough to meet the "people"—and I use the word very broadly—the people whose decisions are affected by the decisions that are made in agencies such as the Comptroller's Office. My own view is that we should meet not just banks but also the community groups and those who are not regulated by us but who are peripherally involved in our world. And certainly the community groups are involved with the problems of urban areas and banking and finance.

MR. MILLER: You certainly have not had the criticisms that came to your last two predecessors, or last three predecessors. You apparently are satisfying both banking and political constituencies.

MR. HEIMANN: I don't think that I'd use the word "satisfy." It's more that we've always tried to get people to focus directly on the merits of the issues, and we base our actions on an evaluation of all the facts. We haven't looked at any one issue as strictly a national bank problem. My view, and I think everyone's view here, is that we have a safe and sound national banking system. But we also have to have a safe and sound commercial banking system. Therefore, in the last few years we have tended to reach out far more to those who are involved in the whole process, even though they don't fall directly under what you might call the supervision of the Comptroller's Office. That may make some difference. I think it's our job to accommodate, or at least to understand, the broadest aspects of a problem, and then make our decisions in terms of our view of what has to happen overall. Not everyone agrees with some of our decisions that have been based on this approach.

MR. MILLER: Let's get into the area of interstate banking. I notice that a lot of banks are trying to purchase pieces of other banks, up to 5%.

MR. HEIMANN: 4.9%.

MR. MILLER: Well, less than 5%.

MR. HEIMANN: Right. A holding company can make a 4.9% investment in anything.

MR. MILLER: What do you think of this situation?

MR. HEIMANN: First of all, those making the investments have not been the largest banks. The regional banks have been tending to do this more than the giant banks. It hasn't been the Citibanks and the BofAs and the Chases. It's been the Provident Nationals, and others.

MR. MILLER: They're really positioning themselves for the advent of interstate banking.

MR. HEIMANN: That's right. What they are saying, it seems to me, is that this world is going to change; that eventually there will be transborder movement by domestic banks; that there are institutions in other areas that are perfect targets for my bank to become associated with, or some other bank from somewhere else will want to become associated with. Therefore, a bank considers this kind of investment to be fundamentally great. It can serve as a future part of some kind of regional network; or if some other bank wants to set up such a network, it will have to pay a price to buy one out, and my bank will get a handsome return on its investment. So this kind of buy makes sense if you're in the position of the regional bank looking to the future as opposed to the money-market bank. That is what I think is going on. I have never seen it expressed that way exactly, but it makes sense.

MR. MILLER: But a lot of banks are doing things to get ready for interstate banking, circumventing the current laws, to some extent or another.

MR. HEIMANN: I wouldn't use the word "circumvent." They're doing things the best they can within the framework of the laws.

MR. MILLER: All right. Apparently some states are relaxing their laws to attract other banks, out-of-state banks. In addition there seems to be movement toward reciprocal banking laws. Doesn't all this make the job of Comptroller harder because you're operating within the framework of a lot of different laws that are changing?

MR. HEIMANN: No, I don't think it makes the job harder. In all dynamic societies, the only constant really is change. The question is whether the pace of change is slow or rapid. Now, the pace is becoming increasingly rapid. It makes the job of all supervisors difficult, because events are outrunning the pace of statutory change.

MR. MILLER: But wouldn't it be better if there were national legislation rather than piecemeal moves?

MR. HEIMANN: To a great extent, yes. If you had one overall plan that accommodated the problem and was phased in over a period of time, it would be easier than having it come at you piecemeal. But our system doesn't seem to work that way, the United States being the kind of country it is. Local interests, local concerns start to change. The pace of change becomes very rapid, and all of that happens before you have a national accommodation to that change. A perfect example is Regulation Q. All of the things that led up to Congress phasing out Reg Q all were happening bit by bit in the market over the previous decade. Yes, that kind of piecemeal change makes the job tougher. But it's also the nature of our system. In the long run, it's probably for the best because it permits the testing of ideas. The perfect thing for supervisors might be a totally controlled system, but that would probably be regressive.

MR. MILLER: Back a few years, the Comptroller's Office said that ATMs were not branches.

MR. HEIMANN: That's right. That was before my time, while Jim Smith was Comptroller. And then that was overturned by the court.

MR. MILLER: Yes. And now we're getting into EFT networks which isn't quite the same thing. But it means that a variety of banks and customers will utilize the same facilities, so we're really going back to what had been decided earlier. Do you think that the concept of ATMs as branches might be overturned?

MR. HEIMANN: I don't think it makes any difference anymore. The concepts on which Jim Smith was working are ones with which I fundamentally agree. The court saw it otherwise, and we don't argue with the courts. But the world has changed so markedly since then that I don't really think it's necessary to revisit the question. One way or another, the demands of the market—the convenience of customers—must be met. Let me put it a different way. You can buy cash in every airport in this country from American Express. Now, those American Express machines are not ATMs; I don't know what you call them, but they're not part of a regulated institution. Meanwhile the commercial banks cannot provide that very same service. There's something irrational about that whole situation.

MR. MILLER: American Express is not governed by the banking laws.

MR. HEIMANN: That's what I'm saying. There is an American Express machine doing what an ATM would do, which is permit you, the customer, to get some cash. I believe that eventually the competitive pressures from unregulated competitors like American Express will break down these antiquated laws. If Congress doesn't want to do it, the marketplace will haphazardly do it.

MR. MILLER: But apparently nothing will happen in Congress this year.

MR. HEIMANN: I don't know. I've been in government now almost six years, and I've come to an Olympian view. And that is, it isn't really important whether it happens in three months or six months or a year—what's important is that it will happen. And the smart folks out there, the entrepreneurs, will adjust for it and adapt to it and make it work for them. But those who do not will slowly but surely be overrun by the process of change. That process is a market-dominated process; it's not government-dominated. There are other examples. The cash-management account of Merrill Lynch, which will soon be copied by four of the other major brokerage firms, you know, puts all of these arguments about ATMs out the window as far as the public is concerned. Some bankers are going to fight until they drop dead over ATMs while the competition is chewing them up.

MR. MILLER: That's right, and you've got to be concerned as a regulator because this whole process can hurt the industry you are regulating.

MR. HEIMANN: I agree. All you can do is go out and fight for more rational change to reflect what's going on in the marketplace. I mean, all you can do is say the obvious and keep saying it until you're blue in the face. But you can't make it happen because it requires congressional action. Our job is not only to administer the laws as they exist and to argue for changes in law, but to respect the law.

MR. MILLER: Don't you feel, however, as we move closer to interstate banking, that the smaller banks are going to be hurt by this kind of thing?

MR. HEIMANN: No. There's no evidence at all to indicate that will happen. If you look at the history of the states that have gone from limited branching to statewide branching, you'll see what I mean. Look at what happened in Ohio and in New York, with which I'm very familiar. Each of those states permitted multibank holding companies but held off on branching for several years. In New York, there was a five-year delay in statewide branching. During those five years, banks that didn't want to compete sold out and made money. Those that did want to compete got into a competitive stance, by the time statewide branching came in. Look what happened. Big New York City banks opened branches all over the state in the first year or two. But in the last two years they've been closing many branches. The profits of the community banks have not been hurt; in fact, they've done very, very well. They've improved their profit margins compared with the big city banks. Those who got squeezed were not small banks because the small banks had knowledge of their market areas that no big bank could duplicate. The problems were with medium-sized institutions. They weren't big enough to compete with the big banks, and not small enough to have true integration with the community and its needs and people.

MR. MILLER: What you are also saying then is that in the future it looks like there's going to be a lot of big banks and a lot of little banks.

MR. HEIMANN: Well, it depends on definitions again; I think that's one of the problems. My view of the future would be a little bit different from that. And I don't want to use the terms "big-little" because they tend to make you think you're talking about the \$10-million bank versus the \$100-billion bank. I think the way it will shake down over time is that the money-market banks will continue to grow but not at the same rate as in the past, because there will also be some very large regional money-center banks. So it's not going to be the old pattern of concentration in New York, Chicago, and San Francisco. I would think twenty years from now, New York will still be important, certainly Chicago, certainly San Francisco, but you'll also see some real big guys in the Southeast—Atlanta and probably Miami. Also, depending on the market area, you'll find medium-sized institutions doing very well. I'm not sure a medium-sized institution can do all that well, say, in New York City, but a medium-sized institution can do very well in upstate New York. I think we have to be careful about predicting numbers because it will be more a market area phenomenon than a size phenomenon. After all, if small banks can't survive competition, how can any independent community bank exist in the State of California? Even though the big banks are good and you've got BofA, with a thousand or so branches, you've still got lots of small community banks all over the state.

MR. MILLER: And more open every day.

MR. HEIMANN: They open every day and make money. If the big guys are so murderous to the small guys, how can that happen? I don't think we'll ever see the demise of the community bank in this country, and I think it would probably be bad if that happened, because they do serve a very important function.

MR. MILLER: But many community banks are scared of the future.

MR. HEIMANN: I understand. Most people are scared of the future. It's a very human trait. But I think community banks are selling themselves short; they're doing themselves a disservice. I guess interstate banking is a frightening prospect for those who have thrived in a protected market. But I'm not frightened for them. They've proven themselves too many times.

MR. MILLER: You feel that there are going to be fewer banks?

MR. HEIMANN: Yes, I do, because part of this natural trend will be some consolidation. But by fewer banks, I don't mean five or six banks.

MR. MILLER: We're not going toward the situation in Canada with only a handful of banks.

MR. HEIMANN: Absolutely not, However, because of economic circumstances, there may be enormous merger and consolidation activity in the thrift industry. That's not government-ordered; that's not the FSLIC or the FDIC making mergers. This consolidation is all taking place not through government intervention at all but through true market judgments on the part of the people who run these thrift institutions.

MR. MILLER: But the S&Ls are being squeezed—and a lot of them are in trouble—primarily because of the high interest rates.

MR. HEIMANN: Right, but the ones who are merging are not in trouble because no one wants to acquire financially troubled institutions. You'll find that the merger partners tend to be institutions which are on the road to doing well. They tend to be those which are well-managed and have good old-fashioned entrepreneurial intelligence. And I think you'll find the same thing in commercial banking, as the competition becomes more intense—not only from the big banks, but from mutual funds, from cash-management accounts and from the thrifts. That's the history of financial markets. And that's the best way for change to happen because it's based on real private decision making, not forced by government.

MR. MILLER: Earlier, you mentioned the fact that you have no regulatory authority over the thrift institutions.

MR. HEIMANN: Well, only directly through the FDIC—I'm on the FDIC Board.

MR. MILLER: You are also on the DIDC, aren't you?

MR. HEIMANN: Yes.

MR. MILLER: Well, that's still another regulatory agency.

MR. HEIMANN: There are seven of us. Congress, in its passion for deregulation, has created two more financial agencies, the FFIEC and the DIDC. The quickest way to deregulate apparently is to create more regulators.

MR. MILLER: What is happening, of course, along with the Monetary Control Act of 1980, is that you're blurring the differences between the various institutions. Do you think this blurring will continue? Or will it come to a halt somewhere along the line?

MR. HEIMANN: That's a difficult question to answer. I think you have to look at it from a number of different vantage points. It seems to me that what's happening is that the thrifts will clearly become more commercial bank-like in the consumer area, although perhaps not in massive business financings and government financings. In that sense there will certainly be a blur. Some banks will choose to compete more and more directly for consumer business, so that blurring will become greater, whereas some banks will choose to go wholesale. Bankers Trust, for example, with their decision to sell off some of the branches in New York, made a statement that they wanted to become a different kind of commercial bank, one that did not cater to consumers. Some commercial banks will start to move away from being retail banks and concentrate on the nonconsumer side of commercial banking. Obviously, the blurring of distinctions will not be as great for those institutions. Simultaneously you have the investment brokers and the brokerage firms coming in and engaging in some traditional commercial bank-type activities, transactions (i.e, the CMA-type account, the money-market account). Their activities will then blur into what the thrifts are doing and what the retail commercial banks are doing. At the same time, the commercial banks will attempt, one way or another, to gain more authority to provide the kind of services that invesment bankers provide in their continuing search for revenue dollars. What this all means is that we won't see an overall blurring of everybody into each other. We will see blurring on a service basis, but the institutions themselves, I think, will begin more and more to select their markets and will select for themselves areas in which they are particularly good.

MR. MILLER: Right. I understand that there may be some legislation forthcoming in the area of failing banks.

MR. HEIMANN: Yes. We introduced an emergency takeover bill last year.

MR. MILLER: Yes, and I would gather that under that bill, a bank from new Jersey could take over a bank in New York, or something like that. The prohibitions against the sort of thing were a problem when Franklin National was in trouble.

MR. HEIMANN: You couldn't arrange an intrastate takeover, because the Justice Department would be concerned with antitrust issues. And you couldn't do it interstate, because of McFadden-Douglas.

MR. MILLER: So you were limited in what you could do in an unfortunate situation. Now, if such legislation does pass, and it may be about the only legislation this year that will pass, what will that do to our laws and to your administration of laws?

MR. HEIMANN: Let's assume for a moment the legislation is passed. Even then, what we can do depends on what the legislation says. For example, the legislation could say that, with a troubled institution that meets certain size requirements, we should first look at like institutions intrastate and then like institutions interstate. And Congress could very well include a regional limitation. In other words, if we were talking about interstate takeovers, commercial bank to commercial bank or thrift to thrift, we wouldn't be able to consider institutions all over the country. We would have to look at institutions in contiguous areas, and that wouldn't necessarily be that big a break. Once you've considered like institutions, you could follow the same procedure for unlike institutions intrastate and unlike institutions interstate. The whole process would depend on the limitations Congress included in the law. Theoretically, any institution we're talking about would have to be a very good size because normally you could handle problems in a smaller institution another way. The whole question is a hard one to answer. My own view is that you would want to do it in a way that would do the least damage to the existing concepts of geographic limitations on banking—until Congress chose to change these limits. Now, I happen to believe there should be such a change, but the law is the law.

MR. MILLER: But do you feel that there ought to be some sort of emergency takeover provision?

MR. HEIMANN: There has to be. There has to be. Let me put on my supervisor's hat and use commercial banks as an example, although the same thing would apply to other institutions. What do you do, hypothetically, in a state where you have two very large commercial banks, both about the same size, and also a bunch of smaller commercial banks. There are a number of states with statewide branchings that are like that. Let's just assume for a moment that one of the two big banks is in serious trouble. What do you do? You're not going to take the one that's in serious trouble and merge it into the good one, so that you then have one giant bank in the state. And you can't break it up, because breaking up a large institution is very tough, if not impossible, to do. So I think it's absolutely necessary to have some safety net for that kind of problem. There is one other thing that could be done—sell the big bank with problems to a foreign institution. But what kind of policy is it where the only solution to the failure of a large depository institution is to find a willing foreigner to buy it? That's why we would like to see a change in the law to be used for just such an emergency.

MR. MILLER: How do you rate the state of the banking community today?

MR. HEIMANN: For all depository institutions, inflation is a very difficult problem. That's a given, because depository institutions operate on the spread, and they don't have assets that appreciate substantially. The quality of earnings depreciates regardless of how good the management is. With that in mind, if you look at the whole range of institutions, those that have been the most restricted on the asset side of their balance sheet are having the most serious problems. And in that case, we are talking about the thrifts, because by statute they have been most restricted. The large bulk of their fixed assets is long-term. Simultaneously, the market and Congress have freed up the liability side of their balance sheet. On the liability side, they're paying floating market rates, and on the asset side, they're stuck with fixed-rate, long-term loans. The thrifts have the greatest problems in the financial system—and so do some of the smaller banks. If you look at the balance sheets of a lot of small banks, they look pretty much like those of the thrifts—5% mortgages, 5% fixed loans, and so forth. The closer you get to a bank which has assets and liabilities that are relatively decently matched, the stronger the bank is. Unfortunately, as a whole, the commercial banking system is unable to do that.

I would say that, considering inflation, the commercial banking system at the present time is quite sound. But I would qualify that statement depending on the kind of recession we have in this country, because a recession means that there are bound to be loan losses.

What I'm trying to point out is that the condition of the banking system depends on the economic cycle. The commercial banks reflect, with unbelievable accuracy, the economic conditions in this country—except they lag when we go through an economic downturn, and we have bankruptcies, whether individual or business bankruptcy, in which downturns show up a year later in loan losses in banks. Loan losses are a lagging indicator, not a leading indicator. From the standpoint of a supervisor, the proof is after the fact, not before the fact.

MR. MILLER: So, right now, the system is fairly strong.

MR. HEIMANN: Oh, yes. Of course, as you know, in a system as big as ours, there can always be a couple of individual banks that had done the wrong thing at the wrong time. But generally, yes, it's a sound system. . . .

In a dynamic system, there probably should be failure—but I don't like to use the word "failure." A better word is "disappearance," meaning institutions going out of business but not disaccommodating the innocent public by causing them to lose money in the bank. And it seems to me that in a dynamic system there probably should be more disappearances.

MR. MILLER: There should be more?

MR. HEIMANN: Probably. Right now we have a very protected banking system. But as competition increases, with the thrifts, investment brokers, and other banks, not all of the managements of all of these banks are going to be able to keep up. We've got 14,600 banks in the United States of America, and they're not all run by geniuses. There are a lot of smart guys out there, but there doesn't seem to be any reason that all should be perpetuated in business merely because they own "a bank." What we don't want to have happen, and I don't think anyone does, are discordant, disruptive, chaotic conditions, which really upset the public so people become frightened about the safety of their money. I don't think that's the issue. But the managed (and I use "the managed" in the true sense of the word) disappearance of a bank, regardless of size, can be handled in our society, and I have no fear of that. I think that is the way a dynamic, capitalistic society should and does work. It's really a question of managing such disappearances rather than just letting them happen and thereby permitting the spread of a lot of panic and fear. That goes for the big banks as well as for the small ones. End of speech.

MR. MILLER: And end of interview. Thank you for meeting with us.

Appendix VI. The Bank Board

INSIGHTS—STRAIGHT TALK ABOUT BANK DIRECTORS

A CONVERSATION WITH CHARLES A. AGEMIAN

At the time of this interview, Mr. Agemian was chairman of Garden State National Bank. He is now retired, but serves as a director of Sterling Bank Corporation in New York City.

DR. NADLER: You have been an outside board member with Garden State National Bank back when it was called the Hackensack Trust Company and now you are chairman and the chief executive officer. Let's talk a little bit about how you choose good people for the board of directors. What qualities do you want?

MR. AGEMIAN: First of all, I think it would be most helpful if in some way this fellow had shown his loyalty to the bank and, of course, was a respected customer of the bank. But that does not qualify him as a board director. I think his standing in the community, his respectability, his integrity, his reception by his neighbors and friends, is most important to us because everywhere he goes, everything he does will reflect on the image of the bank.

When I appoint somebody or suggest somebody for the board, I am giving away one of the best assets I have in the bank—the privilege to serve on the board and to help me in the running of the bank.

DR. NADLER: Are there any other talents you're looking for—legal talents, credit talents?

MR. AGEMIAN: You can have an overabundance of legal talents, in which case you don't get anything done. As a matter of fact, my reaction would be that the fewer lawyers you had on the board, the more flexible, the less burdensome, the CEO's job would be. On the other hand, we know and we realize that on certain transactions legal opinion must be received. But I would rather receive it from someone who is not giving it to me as a director but as a legal professional.

One of the things that I think is most acceptable on the board, outside of citizenship in the community, is that I like to have a couple of accountants on the board—CPAs who are professional men and who will act as alternating chairmen of my examination committee. That's comforting to me. It is also very comforting to me when reviewing loans. They have objectivity. They will suggest the pitfalls in the loans that we may not have seen in our close intimacy with the people to whom we make the loans.

DR. NADLER: Okay, we don't want too many lawyers. We want at least a CPA or two. Any other talents that you would like to have on a bank board?

MR. AGEMIAN: A man who has been extremely successful in his own business and who runs a business with many employees and knows labor relations. I think that this is terribly important.

DR. NADLER: Any age qualifications?

MR. AGEMIAN: We have just put in a mandatory retirement at age 72. We didn't say that if you were 71 or 72 you could stay two years. We cut if off rather sharply. This was done after talking to all such members who would have been let out because of the age limit.

On the other hand, we have another limit which says that if a director is no longer connected in the same capcity with the same company as when he was appointed, the board *may* ask for his resignation or it *may* reappoint him.

DR. NADLER: So your bank does not have a list of board members all of which say "investments" or "retired" as the main occupation?

MR. AGEMIAN: No way. And I'm not much on internal directors.

DR. NADLER: Okay, let's talk internal directors.

MR. AGEMIAN: Let's talk first about the Comptroller of the Currency's attitude toward retirement, which I find fault with.

DR. NADLER: Fine.

MR. AGEMIAN: The Comptroller's office doesn't help you to put in the 72 mandatory, or any other year mandatory, retirement because they claim it would be a way of boxing out an individual who may own a big block of stock. Frankly, I think that this is an unusual reason, because if someone does own a block of bank stock, by this time he must have had a son or some other successor who would vote his shares and be able to treat his beneficial interest, his directorable interest, in the same manner he did. As a matter of fact, I find it rather inadequate—that a man who may have reached the calendar age of 72, but has the mental age of 93, tries to pursue this protective interest when he really is not capable of doing it. So I don't buy that. I think a fellow should retire and if he has a lot of stock then he can divest it. Or he can place it with someone in whom he has confidence.

DR. NADLER: Now let's talk about internal directors.

MR. AGEMIAN: I'm against them because I've seen too many weak CEOs use this as a cushion. In our place, the only internal directors we have are the ones we're required to have by law. The president of the bank must be a director. That's it. We have a vice-chairman of the board—he's a member—and myself, and that's it. We don't believe that any other person should be a director.

DR. NADLER: In other words, you are afraid if somebody works for the bank he will be just a "yes man" to the CEO because his job is at stake?

MR. AGEMIAN: Obviously. In my opinion, that's the reason he would be there in the first place. On the other hand, all our senior officers attend all executive committee meetings. So the contact is there, and I encourage directors to talk directly to the senior officers when they want something.

DR. NADLER: That leads into my next question. Once you've got your board, how do you get the members to know what's going on so they're not completely dependent upon you as the chief executive?

MR. AGEMIAN: My board members probably know every vice-president, senior vice-president, and executive vice-president by their first names. That's because they have had weekly intimate contact with them at the executive committee meeting. Periodically, the controller and the auditor and the executive vice-presidents will make a presentation about their department to the board at a monthly directors' meeting. We insist the auditor do it at least every three months. Even if he has nothing to say, he comes up and he'll say I have nothing to say or nothing to report.

DR. NADLER: Do you ever have the outside board members sit down with officers without you being present?

MR. AGEMIAN: Many, many times.

DR. NADLER: Do you find times when you learn what's going on inside the bank through your directors? Do they find out things from the officers that you did find out directly and the first time you hear about it is from a board member?

MR. AGEMIAN: No question about it. Of course, you have some board members who like to talk to the chairman, and I don't discourage that.

DR. NADLER: A lot of board members complain that they really don't know what is going on in the bank. They say they have the responsibility, but they wish they knew what's happening.

MR. AGEMIAN: Let me tell you something. This is something that really bugs me. I think that some CEOs simply tolerate their board of directors, and that bugs the hell out of me. All of our directors, unless they were physically incapable, have gone to the Directors' Seminar meetings, some two times, at the bank's expense. I have seen CEOs say "Good God, you must be out of your mind! What the hell are you doing, looking for trouble? You want to smarten up your directors?" And that's the damnedest thing I've ever heard. Directors should be treated as successful men who have been successful in their own business, and might well be able to run a bank if they were given the opportunity to learn. If you've got a lot of clinkers on the board, you know, that's something else again. I've lived with board members whom I tolerated but I probably didn't pay much attention to what they had to say. As a matter of fact, if they agreed with me, I figured that I must have been wrong.

DR. NADLER: When you were an outside director, how did you find out what was going on besides talking to officers? Would you sometimes just go in and talk to people in the lobby, talk to the tellers? What did you do?

MR. AGEMIAN: When I had the time, I would come here to the bank and I would talk to the senior officers. I had enough stock at that time to warrant my doing it, you know. I wanted to know what was going on. The officers knew me; I had a good personal relationship. I didn't encourage officers talking behind other officers' backs or their president's back. That isn't necessary. But, on the other hand, I think I probably knew enough about the banking business to ask some damn penetrating questions. I would encourage all bank directors to do this kind of thing.

DR. NADLER: Okay. You have your board, and they can go into the bank and look for information. They are not afraid of the CEO. What do you want them to do? Many people look at the board as solely business development. Do you consider that the prime function of the board, or way down the list?

MR. AGEMIAN: I would hope that 10 or eight members of a board of 20 or so would be new business getters, always talking the bank up. They are people who I know are extremely active socially, who know the best people in town. By the best people I mean financially, and who could talk about the bank, and the community respects their judgment. I know that it will make an impact.

DR. NADLER: What else do you expect from a board member besides new business? When you come to the board meeting, do you frequently find that you have a credit that you liked and the board will veto you—that their judgment will be the opposite of yours?

MR. AGEMIAN: I have had some. There are also some cases where I'm not too sure of the loan—even though the balance sheet looks good, I may have heard around that the borrower is a bit of a rascal, and I happen to know that some of my board members may know him; they're in the same business or they have had contact with him. I will bring that up to them and ask them what they think about the fellow. If a guy is a rascal, I don't give a damn what his balance sheet looks like. Therefore, I expect my board to intimately know an awful lot about what's going on in the community served by the bank.

DR. NADLER: What else do you want from your board?

MR. AGEMIAN: I want them to support me also in credits which I'm pretty certain are all right. I have one board member, when I come up with a loan and maybe it is a little marginal, he will say, "Has Murphy had his drink?" meaning did I make the loan. I say, "Yeah, Murphy had his drink," and then he supports me. But his job should be to see that I don't let too many Murphys have drinks.

DR. NADLER: Well, how about the other side? Do you find many board members who look for favoritism? Who come in and they say, "Look—I'm on the board; grant this loan?"

MR. AGEMIAN: That is something the CEO should straighten out once and for all. Be very firm, take a position that you're not going to do any favors—and we do not. But be careful that you don't throw business out, either. You must have some sort of balance. I have found that since we've shown that we want no conflict of interest in this bank, we don't stand for it ratewise or any other wise. No favored rates.

As a matter of fact, I encourage our directors' borrowing. Why the hell should I throw good business out of the bank? I know they're good people or they would not be on the board. But they are going to pay the going rate. I'm not going to penalize them for being directors, but I think that if you stay close to the prime rate, nobody can criticize you.

DR. NADLER: What happens if a director comes in and says he has a brother-in-law who wants a mortgage loan and you know damn well that it is not a good deal for the bank right now?

MR. AGEMIAN: Creditwise or ratewise?

DR. NADLER: Both. Either one.

MR. AGEMIAN: I had a case the other day. One of our affiliates came in and said that we have this wonderful employee, and he said would you loan him the money? A $60,000 mortgage down in Jackson, New Jersey, which is way out of my territory. I said, "No, your affiliate doesn't even have a balance with me." I said, "I can't afford to do that. You're sticking your hand in my pocket." I said, "If you open up an account that's substantial, I will recognize this mortgage." It was a good mortgage, remember. There was a rate—9%; it was the highest I could go.

DR. NADLER: So what you are saying is that you will go out of your way on rates for board members, but you will never go out of your way on credits. Is that fair?

MR. AGEMIAN: I'm not so sure that I would go out of my way even on rates. Incidentally, this happened to be a $60,000 account and that account will be there. So I don't give them any break in the rate.

DR. NADLER: Okay, Next question. What about bouncing a board member? Have you ever had to bounce one?

MR. AGEMIAN: Oh, yes. Oh, yes. Well, don't call it that. Make me a little kinder than that.

DR. NADLER: Have you ever had to ask a board member not to stand for reelection?

MR. AGEMIAN: Yes, I did. When I first came on as board chairman, there were people whom I asked not to stand for reelection. They were not interested in the bank, and I could use those seats very advantageously for the bank. So I asked them not to stand for reelection. It wasn't easy; I got many calls. I even had the son of one of them call me and ask me what I was doing to his father. I said, "I'm doing this because your father never did anything for us." As simple as that. We let quite a few go at that time.

Last year three left because of mandatory retirement. Sometimes when you do that, you let some people go whom you may want to stay, but you can't pick and choose. The only picking and choosing you do, is if he is no longer president of the company. He is retired then.

DR. NADLER: Do you ever have other reasons for asking a guy to leave? I mean that he has done something that could be harmful to the bank? What you've indicated is that these people are just not helpful to the bank. Did you ever find a case where a man hurts the bank by being a board member? Either by his reputation or by what he does?

MR. AGEMIAN: Let me tell you what would happen in that case. I haven't had such a situation, but if I ever found out that a member was talking badly against the bank because I may have turned down one of his loans or his brother-in-law's loan, that fellow wouldn't last five minutes. He would be off the board. I don't know how the hell I would do it, but I would find a way so he wouldn't come into any board meetings. I wouldn't trust him and I would ask for his resignation.

DR. NADLER: Would you give him a chance to prove his side of the case?

MR. AGEMIAN: No way! No way!

DR. NADLER: In other words, if there is any doubt, there's no doubt.

MR. AGEMIAN: You're damn right! This is a very tender situation on this board and we talk rather plainly about things, and I couldn't afford to be looking at him worrying when he was going to next shoot off his mouth.

Also, if he wants to talk when he goes home, he's in trouble. I feel very strongly about this. This is sanctum sanctorum, and there is nobody on that board who is going to be talking about the business of this bank outside the bank.

DR. NADLER: How about people who use the information they learn about competitors for their own benefit—let's say a builder sees that another builder has come up for a loan?

MR. AGEMIAN: He would be out the next time around. We're not going to have it. I just can't imagine it happening because the tenor of our board—they know what I think is right and what is wrong. I don't think that the thought would pass their mind.

DR. NADLER: What should the role of the board be in mergers and acquisitions? I've heard some people say the less the role the board plays the better, because they sort of mess things up. They stick their hands in, yet others say they're invaluable. What's your view?

MR. AGEMIAN: This goes back to the same situation about the board members keeping their mouths shut. There's nothing that can hurt a merger or acquisition more than the news leaking out because somebody talked too much. In many cases, I have had discussions with people about possible acquisitions or mergers. I may want to avoid my board's possible conversation on the subject, but more often the other people wanted it that way. And my board has given me that freedom to carry on talks without making an ultimate decision or judgment before coming to it. And they understand why we want to do it. I have seen more good acquisitions screwed up because somebody talked too much.

DR. NADLER: How have your attitudes toward the role of the board changed when you switched sides of the table from being the outside board member to being the CEO?

MR. AGEMIAN: Well, I was an outside board member, but had quite a bit of the stock. And I was really sort of a consultant to the bank. The president of the bank would call me and many of the senior officers would call me with full permission of the executive officer. So I was very intimate in the running of a bank. But I found out, however, and this is my fault, that I may have been running the bank a little too much as a director and should not have done that. I don't think that is a good way to develop executive officers. On the other hand, being a director isn't quite like being on the scene when you have to worry about success and management. I guess it was mostly a financial thing on my part. Now it has gotten to be an emotional thing. In other words, nothing bugs me more than if I hear we made an error in something or somebody. But now I'm in there and it's a different kind of a thing. I'm in there and I'm doing it, and some of the errors and mistakes are mine. Now I wonder why people can't be more tolerant.

DR. NADLER: The CEO is going to be far more mellow than an outside board member?

MR. AGEMIAN: This is true.

DR. NADLER: Well, would you want mellow board members?

MR. AGEMIAN: Hell, no. Do you want to know the truth? I wish I had three Charlie Agemians on my board.

DR. NADLER: Even though you would have an ulcer every hour?

MR. AGEMIAN: I probably would. Then I would have the choice of whether I'd have an ulcer or just a hell of a good time competing with the three Agemians.

INDEX